D1583416

EMPOWERING PEOPLE WITH SEVERE MENTAL ILLNESS

EMPOWERING PEOPLE WITH SEVERE MENTAL ILLNESS

A Practical Guide

Donald M. Linhorst

OXFORD
UNIVERSITY PRESS
2006

OXFORD
UNIVERSITY PRESS

Oxford University Press, Inc., publishes works that further
Oxford University's objective of excellence
in research, scholarship, and education.

Oxford   New York
Auckland   Cape Town   Dar es Salaam   Hong Kong   Karachi
Kuala Lumpur   Madrid   Melbourne   Mexico City   Nairobi
New Delhi   Shanghai   Taipei   Toronto

With offices in
Argentina   Austria   Brazil   Chile   Czech Republic   France   Greece
Guatemala   Hungary   Italy   Japan   Poland   Portugal   Singapore
South Korea   Switzerland   Thailand   Turkey   Ukraine   Vietnam

Copyright © 2006 by Oxford University Press, Inc.

Published by Oxford University Press, Inc.
198 Madison Avenue, New York, New York 10016

www.oup.com

Oxford is a registered trademark of Oxford University Press

Library of Congress Cataloging-in-Publication Data
Linhorst, Donald M., 1956–
Empowering people with severe mental illness : a practical guide / Donald M. Linhorst.
    p.   cm.
Summary: "Presents a model of empowerment and then applies it to seven areas that the have
potential to empower people with severe mental illness, including treatment planning, housing,
employment, and others. Provides practitioners, administrators, and policymakers with specific
guidelines and actions to promote empowerment"—Provided by publisher.
Includes bibliographical references and index.
ISBN-13: 978-0-19-517187-7
ISBN:0-19-517187-X
1. Mentally ill—Services for—United States.   2. Social work with people with mental disabilities—
United States.   I. Title.
HV3006.A4L56 2005
362.2'0425—dc22   2004030360

9 8 7 6 5 4 3 2 1

Printed in the United States of America
on acid-free paper

To Ann, my wife and research colleague, for her love, support, and guidance

Preface

The purpose of this book is to examine pragmatically the opportunities for and limitations to empowerment among adults with severe mental illness who, historically, have lacked power and have been the focus of stigma and discrimination. Empowerment is important for at least three reasons. First, people with mental illness should have a right to participate in decisions that affect their lives and to have access to opportunities to improve themselves. Second, people with mental illness who are empowered have an improved quality of life. Third, empowerment of people with mental illness benefits society. Empowered individuals may collaborate with mental health service providers to improve services to all agency clients, vote and participate in the political process, be productive citizens by engaging in volunteer work or employment, or participate in other beneficial activities, as will be discussed throughout this book.

My central premise is that despite significant limitations to empowerment, people with severe mental illness can be empowered when certain conditions are met. Building on the work of Joel F. Handler (1986, 1990, 1992, 1996), I outline nine conditions under which empowerment is likely to occur and to be sustained long term. Some conditions are internal to people with mental illness, such as having psychiatric symptoms managed to the degree required to participate in a particular activity that can be empowering. Other conditions exist in the sociopolitical environment, such as having access to resources needed to be empowered. I then apply those conditions to determine the circumstances under which people with severe mental illness can be empowered through participation in each of seven activities, including treatment planning, housing, organizational decision making, planning and policy making, employment, research, and service provision.

My interest in the topic of empowerment grew out of my work with people with severe mental illness. During the 1980s, I worked for 7 years at Places for People, Inc., Missouri's first supported housing program and psychosocial rehabilitation center for people with severe mental illness. For most of the 1990s, I was employed at St. Louis State Hospital, one of four state psychiatric hospitals operated by the Missouri Department of Mental Health that provides long-term care and treatment. Since 2000, I have been a member of the advisory board of BJC-Behavioral Health (BJC-BH), which provides a range of community-based mental health services. At each of these programs, I observed and, in some instances, was directly involved in the development and implementation of activities that sought to empower people with severe mental illness. Many of these activities were successful. I also saw well-intentioned attempts at empowerment fail. Some efforts never developed beyond vision statements. Others were implemented poorly. Still others faded away when important individuals left the program. These experiences engrained in me both the opportunities for, and the substantial limitations to, empowerment, as well as the fragile nature of empowerment when it occurs.

Two notes are needed regarding language. I use the term severe mental illness to refer to those mental illnesses that can result in significant functional limitations, including bipolar disorder, major depression, and particularly schizophrenia. In the United States, it is estimated that approximately 2 million adults are diagnosed with schizophrenia, 2 million with bipolar disorder, and 10 million with major depression (U.S. Department of Health and Human Services [US DHHS], 1999). There is no universally accepted word or phrase for referring to people with severe mental illness. Different terms have been used including patients, clients, consumers, users, expatients, and survivors. Through most of the book, I use the term people with severe mental illness or people with mental illness, although sometimes I use the term clients or consumers. In chapter 2, when presenting the history of powerlessness among people with mental illness, other terms are used that are considered derogatory today but that were appropriate for, or widely used, during a particular era.

I derived the content of the book primarily from the United States and international professional literature related to empowerment and to people with mental illness. I also incorporated case studies based on findings from two research projects that I conducted. The first study examined empowerment of people with severe mental illness living at St. Louis Psychiatric Rehabilitation Center (SLPRC), formerly St. Louis

State Hospital, a 212-bed, long-term Missouri Department of Mental Health psychiatric hospital. At the time of the study, SLPRC was divided into three treatment programs distributed over four 25-bed hospital wards and four 8-bed cottages on hospital grounds that served as step-down units for the ward programs. A fourth treatment program was for clients residing in ten 8-bed cottages also located on hospital grounds. SLPRC was largely a forensic facility. Criminal courts referred 80% of SLPRC clients; some were found incompetent to stand trial but most were found not guilty by reason of insanity. The remaining 20% of clients were nonforensic and admitted by their legal guardians. The average length of hospitalization was 6 years. The second study examined empowerment among people with severe mental illness living in the community and receiving mental health services from BJC-BH. It contracts with the Missouri Department of Mental Health to provide mental health treatment, rehabilitation, and support services, including psychotropic medications, intensive case management, employment supports, and other services, to approximately 5,000 adults annually. Services are provided out of four offices, located in urban, suburban, and rural areas. Most clients have health and mental health insurance coverage through the government-provided Medicaid or Medicare programs or are without any insurance.

In both the SLPRC and BJC-BH studies, I examined client empowerment in the areas of treatment planning, housing, organizational decision making, and mental health policy making. Although not the focus of the studies, I also gathered a limited amount of information on clients' involvement in employment, evaluation activities, and service provision. The coevaluators and I reviewed written documents and held focus groups with clients and staff of both agencies. Detailed descriptions of the research methods and findings from the two studies were included in unpublished reports (Kryah, Linhorst, & Anderson, 2003; Linhorst, Young, Eckert, & Hamilton, 1999), and findings from the SLPRC study were incorporated into published articles (Linhorst & Eckert, 2002, 2003; Linhorst, Eckert, & Hamilton, 2005; Linhorst, Hamilton, Young, & Eckert, 2002). In addition, I conducted individual interviews with three employees from the Missouri Department of Mental Health central office, with the executive directors of three mental health advocacy organizations that had affiliations with national organizations, and with an individual who was a liaison to a statewide consumer advocacy group in Missouri. I also reviewed written materials that each provided about their respective organizations and topics.

The first four chapters of the book are foundational. Chapter 1 defines the term "empowerment" and explores its components. Chapter 2 provides an historical view of powerlessness among people with severe mental illness in the United States. Chapter 3 examines recent efforts to promote the rights of people with mental illness through state and federal legislation and case law, as well as legal and informal means of coercion that continue to exist in the United States. Chapter 4 presents the conditions for empowerment that are applied in subsequent chapters. In Chapters 5 through 11, I apply the conditions for empowerment to seven activities that have the potential for empowering people with mental illness. At the end of each of these seven chapters, I include case studies that incorporate findings from the two empowerment studies to illustrate the opportunities for, and limitations to, empowerment of people with mental illness residing in long-term psychiatric hospitals and in the community, and I then offer guidelines for promoting empowering. In the final chapter, I review the opportunities for and limitations to empowerment, identify the roles that various parties can play in creating the conditions for empowerment, and describe what it means for people with severe mental illness to live empowered lives.

It is my intention that this book will be useful to those who want to move beyond the rhetoric of empowerment to address limitations to empowerment and create meaningful opportunities for empowering people with severe mental illness. The discussion of the seven empowerment activities increases general understanding of empowerment and provides pragmatic guidance to those who wish to create these empowerment opportunities in their own programs, agencies, or communities. The conditions for empowerment also provide a useful structure for designing different activities that can be empowering and for evaluating empowerment in existing programs. As such, this book should be of interest to people with mental illness who serve in leadership positions in mental health and advocacy organizations, to families of people with mental illness who advocate for improved mental health services and policies, to mental health professionals who provide treatment and rehabilitation services, to researchers, to administrators, to national mental health advocacy organizations and their state and local affiliates, to policy makers, and to people interested in the general topic of empowerment of vulnerable populations. The book also has utility as a primary or secondary textbook in mental health treatment and policy courses in educational programs for those professions that work with people with severe mental illness, including counseling, the ministry, nursing, psychiatry, psychology, rehabilitation, and social work. Finally, it can serve as a textbook for courses that focus on empowerment practice, social justice, human rights, and similar topics, with a range of populations.

Acknowledgments

First and foremost, I would like to thank my wife, Ann Dirks-Linhorst, for her support of my research in general and of this book in particular. She, in fact, was the person who suggested that I write it. She patiently engaged in many discussions about the content of the book and reviewed the entire manuscript. I also would like to recognize three others who have had a lasting influence on my work with people with severe mental illness. Francie Broderick was director of the psychosocial rehabilitation center at Places for People, Inc., in St. Louis, Missouri, when I worked there in the 1980s, and she is now the agency's executive director. She taught me to view people with mental illness first as people, to respect them, and to recognize their strengths. Gary Hamilton was the professor for my most memorable course in my master of social work program at Saint Louis University, which focused on the involvement of vulnerable populations in decision making. I was fortunate that he still was on the faculty when I later joined it in 1997. He assisted with the two empowerment studies and served as a coauthor on several published articles. One of his many contributions to this book was introducing me to the work of Joel Handler. Finally, I had the pleasure of working with Anne Eckert during my years at St. Louis State Hospital and afterward as a research colleague and coauthor. She demonstrated to me how to be a strong advocate for people with mental illness, how to facilitate change in mental health organizations, and how to truly empower people with severe mental illness.

I also would like to recognize those people and organizations that assisted with my two empowerment studies. They included three master of social work students from the School of Social Service at Saint Louis University, Eric Young, Rachel Kryah, and JoyLynn Anderson; staff and clients from St. Louis Psychiatric Rehabilitation Center and BJC Behavioral Health, who so freely shared their thoughts; and Anne Eckert and Terri Gilbert, who served as liaisons from their agencies for the empowerment studies. Two sources provided partial funding for the empowerment studies: the Emmett J. and Mary Martha Doerr Center for Social Justice Education and Research in the School of Social Service at Saint Louis University and the Saint Louis University Beaumont Faculty Fund Award.

Next, I would like to express my immense appreciation to those who reviewed the entire manuscript, including Ann Dirks-Linhorst, Michael Rose, Bruce Vieweg, and two anonymous reviewers selected by Oxford University Press, whose contributions resulted in a much-improved manuscript. In addition, I want to recognize those individuals who participated in individual interviews or reviewed selected chapters; they are Lynn Carter, Anne Eckert, Carol Evans, Terri Gilbert, James House, Anthony Menditto, Marge Parrish, Carolyn Reese, Joseph Rogers, Vicki Fox Smith, Christina Squibb, Marilyn Turner, and Joe Yancey. I want to express my appreciation, as well, to Stephen Wernet, Marla Berg-Weger, and William Brennan, my university colleagues, for their assistance and encouragement. Also, I would like to recognize the publishers of two journals that gave permission to use components of two of my previous works. Parts of chapter 4 were published previously in Linhorst, D. M. & Eckert, A. (2003). Conditions for empowering people with severe mental illness. *Social Service Review, 77*(2), 279–305, © 2003 by The University of Chicago, all rights reserved. Parts of chapter 10 were published previously in Linhorst, D. M., & Eckert, A. (2002). Involving people with mental illness in evaluation and performance improvement. *Evaluation and the Health Professions, 25*(3), 284–301, © 2002 by SAGE Publications, all rights reserved. Finally, I want to give my deepest appreciation for the opportunity and assistance provided by Oxford University Press, particularly Maura Roessner.

Contents

EMPOWERING PEOPLE WITH SEVERE MENTAL ILLNESS

1

Conceptualizing Empowerment

The term empowerment has become part of popular culture in the United States. There are many examples of its use in a variety of settings. There are now empowerment zones in low-income neighborhoods to promote economic recovery (Brazeal & Finkle, 2001). The term is used in advertising to sell many products, including newspapers (Moses, 2003). Music reviewers describe some songs as "empowerment" songs (Walters, 2003, p. 140). A real estate developer was described as practicing "empowerment through homeownership" by helping people who previously were unable to buy homes to do so (McGee, 2002, p. 116). Human service professions, in particular, have incorporated the language of empowerment into their work. The fields of nursing, psychiatry, psychology, rehabilitation, and social work have added the term into their codes of ethics, or individuals within the professions have urged that empowerment be part of practice within that profession (Barker, 2001; Bloch, Chodoff, & Green, 1999; National Association of Social Workers, 1999; Nelson & Walsh-Bowers, 1994; O'Hara & Harrell, 1991). Empowerment is now associated with practice with a wide range of populations. Gutiérrez, Parsons, and Cox (1998), for instance, related empowerment to social work practice with women, poor communities of color, lesbians and gays, people with disabilities, people who are homeless, families, youth, and people with mental illness.

The term empowerment especially has been associated with people with mental illness (Clark & Krupa, 2002). The term has now been incorporated into models of practice with people with mental illness, including psychiatric rehabilitation and the recovery perspective

(Anthony, 1993; Cook & Hoffschmidt, 1993; Jacobson & Greenley, 2001). The term also has been incorporated into mental health advocacy organizations. As an example, a 1992 federal grant helped to create the National Empowerment Center (n.d.), located in Lawrence, Massachusetts, which is operated by people with mental illness, in part, to assist local groups to develop consumer-run programs (Chamberlin, 1996).

Despite widespread use of the term empowerment in the popular culture and in mental health, some argue it lacks substance and specificity. Barnes and Bowl (2001) stated the term "is used to mean very different things and at times appears to lack any real content" (p. 2). Warner (2000) described it as a "buzzword used and abused by those at both ends of the political spectrum" (p. 39). Handler (1996) wrote that power and empowerment "are much used and abused words, sometimes slogans but at other times imbued with important meanings" (p. 9). Adding to the difficulty in defining empowerment is the term's complexity (Chamberlin, 1997; Clark & Krupa, 2002). Before determining what it means to empower people with severe mental illness, it is necessary to clarify concepts related to empowerment. In this chapter, eight empowerment concepts are discussed and then applied to create a working definition of empowerment of people with severe mental illness.

BASIC EMPOWERMENT CONCEPTS

Power, Control, and Influence

Deegan (1997) argued that empowerment involves the meaningful sharing of power; that power is generative and can be created between people. This is contrary to the notion that power is finite and that one tries to have power over another. Similarly, Barnes and Bowl (2001) perceived empowerment as involving a partnership, shared decision making, and negotiation. Likewise, Handler (1996) viewed empowerment as clients not necessarily controlling the agency from which they receive services but having a genuine voice in participating in decision making, with both sides benefiting. Means and Smith (1994) described a continuum of participation in decision making, ranging from most empowering to least empowering. At the most empowering level of participation, people have the authority to make decisions about important areas of their lives. This is followed by people having authority to make some decisions, people having an opportunity to influence decisions, people's views being sought to influence decisions, and decisions being publicized and explained before implementation. Least empowering, and not empowering at all, is people being given information about decisions after others have made them. Zimmerman

(2000), too, argued that having actual control may not be necessary for empowerment to occur. In some situations, it may be empowering to gain experience in the decision-making process even when not making the actual decision. Not everyone, however, views empowerment as existing on a continuum. Swift and Levin (1987), for example, argued that empowerment occurs only when the people in question make the actual decisions.

Even when those holding power seemingly seek participation by others, ulterior motives may prevent meaningful participation, and thus empowerment, from occurring. Croft and Beresford (1992) provided several examples of this. Participation may be sought in order to delay decisions, to co-opt people into arrangements that limit their effectiveness, or to give the appearance of participation when decisions already have been made. Croft and Beresford also cited the importance of people with power being honest about the level of participation that others can expect when working with them. They stated, "The answer may lie not in rejecting participation but first in being clear about its nature and objectives; where control lies and what opportunities it may offer. Then people can make rational decisions about whether to get involved" (p. 38).

Resources and Empowerment

Resources and empowerment are strongly linked. Dubois and Miley (1999) wrote, "Empowerment hinges on having access to resources" (p. 26). Hasenfeld's (1987) definition of empowerment incorporates, and describes, the importance of resources: "Empowerment is a process through which clients obtain resources—personal, organizational, and community—that enable them to gain greater control over their environment and to attain their aspirations" (pp. 478–479).

Empowerment as a Process

Empowerment can refer to a process, as well as to an outcome or an ideology (Clark & Krupa, 2002; Fitzsimons & Fuller, 2002; Zimmerman & Warschausky, 1998). Zimmerman (1995) differentiated empowerment processes from outcomes: "The former refers to how people, organizations, and communities become empowered, whereas the latter refers to the consequences of those processes" (p. 583). Zimmerman and Warschausky (1998) provided a more detailed definition of empowerment processes: "Empowerment processes are the mechanisms through which people, organizations, and communities gain mastery and control over issues that concern them, develop a critical awareness of their environment, and participate in decisions that affect their lives" (p. 5). Any process that prepares people to participate more effectively in an activity that increases their power, control, or influence can be considered empowering (Zimmerman, 2000). As a case in point, participation in employment can be empowering because it provides individuals with resources to exercise a range of life choices.

Empowerment as an Outcome

Empowerment outcomes are the consequences or results of empowerment processes (Zimmerman, 1995). These may include such things as increased confidence, improved social skills, greater knowledge of resources, stabilization of psychiatric symptoms, having decision-making power in a particular situation, or any other outcome that facilitates individuals' ability to exercise power and influence over their lives. Empowerment outcomes can be categorized according to whether or not they reflect an individual's ultimate goal. Long-term outcomes are the ultimate desired condition or state being sought. Alternatively, short-term outcomes are those that facilitate, or are preconditions for, reaching the long-term goal. For example, the long-term outcome sought by an individual may be to obtain and maintain a full-time job. Short-term outcomes may include completing an educational program or initially working part-time. Outcomes are not inherently short-term or long-term; rather they reflect an individual's desired state. While not diminishing the importance of long-term goals, the achievement of short-term outcomes is integral to empowerment. In fact, Kieffer (1984) argued that empowerment is a long-term and continuing developmental process during which people acquire skills and resources, increase confidence, and repeat participatory experiences.

Empowerment outcomes also can be divided into subjective and objective outcomes (Fitzsimons & Fuller, 2002). Subjective outcomes are those that are self-perceived, intrapsychic, or attitudinal. Examples include changes in one's self-perceived sense of control, self-esteem, and being valued. Objective outcomes are those typically expressed behaviorally. Some use the term "actual power" or "products" instead of objective outcomes (e.g., Rappaport, 1987; Staples, 1990). Examples of objective outcomes include greater access to resources, improved social skills, the acquisition of desired employment, and increased decision-making power. Subjective and objective empowerment outcomes are related in at least two ways. First, specific subjective and objective empowerment outcomes may be incongruous. People may perceive themselves as more empowered because they participate in the empowerment process when, objectively, they are not (Kieffer, 1984; Riger, 1993). Also, Rosenfield (1992) believed that objective outcomes can lead to improved subjective outcomes. For instance, as people are successful in their endeavors, it can increase their self-confidence. While both subjective and objective outcomes are important to empowerment, Riger (1993) cautioned against promoting subjective outcomes at the expense of objective or actual outcomes. Her concern was that many empowerment activities, such as increasing self-esteem, seek to increase individuals' subjective power to act without ever increasing their actual power. She stated this creates the illusion of power when, in fact, individuals have not meaningfully increased their participation in decision making.

Empowerment as an Ideology

Empowerment also can exist in the form of an ideology (Clark & Krupa, 2002; Zimmerman & Warschausky, 1998). An empowerment ideology is comprised of the values and beliefs that support empowerment. Given the complexity of the concept of empowerment, a wide range of values and beliefs comprise an empowerment ideology (Clark & Krupa, 2002; Parsons, 2002; Zimmerman, 2000; Zimmerman & Warschausky, 1998). This range includes a focus on strengths and self-efficacy rather than pathology, wellness over illness, and competence over deficiency; the professional roles of collaborator, being a resource, and an advocate, rather than solely being the expert; full participation of individuals in all aspects of change processes; a belief in natural helping systems and peer support; viewing individuals in their environment, integrating a multisystem approach, and targeting empowerment processes at the individual, organizational, community, and policy levels; and values of egalitarianism, belonging, inclusion, trust, and faith in people. The adoption of an empowerment ideology certainly promotes the development of empowerment processes and the achievement of empowerment outcomes. Assuming an empowerment ideology, however, does not guarantee that empowerment will occur in a particular setting. As exemplified throughout the book, many factors can limit empowerment, even when individuals and organizations hold strong empowerment ideologies.

Interconnected Relationship Between Individuals and Their Environment

Empowerment incorporates the ecological perspective that individuals and their environment are interconnected and mutually dependent (Rappaport, 1987; Zimmerman, 1990, 2000). Inherent to the definition of empowerment is that individuals are empowered through their ability to control or influence aspects of their environment. Examples of such influence include individuals directing their own treatment, choosing the community in which they live, or influencing social policy through involvement in an advocacy organization. The relationship between individuals and their environment, however, is reciprocal. Families, groups, organizations, and communities can, to varying extents, support or impede the empowerment of individuals. Among other things, these entities provide individuals with resources and opportunities for empowerment. Because of this interconnectedness, interventions with families, organizations, communities, and public policies are required to promote empowerment (Ackerson & Harrison, 2000). Examples of interventions include encouraging social welfare organizations to adopt participatory management models that incorporate their clients into decision making, working with community leaders to promote more low income housing, and testifying at legislative hearings in support of bills that increase clients' service choices. There is value, of course, in also working directly with individuals to promote empowerment. Hasenfeld (1987) offered examples of individual-level interventions to promote empowerment, some of which include educating clients about agency resources, training clients to assert their rights, referring clients to mutual support groups, and organizing clients to lobby for supportive legislation.

Empowerment Is Situational

Neither empowerment processes nor outcomes are static. Both are time, situation, and contextually specific (Fitzsimons & Fuller, 2002; Handler, 1996; Swift & Levin, 1987; Zimmerman, 2000). Dubois and Miley (1999) explained, in part, why this is the case: "The combinations and permutations of psycho-social-cultural factors, persons, situations, resources, and solutions are countless. Because each circumstance, set of actors, or combination of influencing factors is unique, the process that leads to empowerment is highly individualized and nonreplicable" (p. 27). As one aspect of this, empowerment processes and outcomes would be expected to be different for different activities that have the potential for empowerment. As examples, if the activity is legislative advocacy, empowerment processes may include forums to explain important pieces of legislation and provide information on how to contact legislators, and if the activity is to correct an identified problem in an agency, an empowerment process may be the formation of a work group in which staff and clients participate as equals to resolve it. It also is possible for individuals to be empowered in one area of their lives and not other areas (Zimmerman, 2000). For example, people may be empowered in their employment situations but not in their relationship with the organizations from which they receive mental health services.

As another aspect of the situational nature of empowerment, Handler (1996) emphasized the tenuous nature of empowerment over time. He found that empowerment is highly dependent on the stability of relationships integral to empowerment, on the continued availability of resources, and on the needs of those in power, to name a few examples. Empowerment of vulnerable people is highly fragile and can end quickly as the context in which empowerment is occurring changes. For instance, people may no longer be empowered in their relationship with their mental health treatment teams if those team members who are most inclusive of their participation leave the agency, or empowerment outcomes may decrease if the government greatly reduces needed mental health and support services.

One Cannot Empower Another

Technically speaking, one person cannot empower another (Rappaport, 1985). As Simon (1990) stated, "The one function that ... anyone else *cannot* perform for another person is that of empowerment. Empowerment is a reflexive activity, a process capable of being initiated and sustained only by the agent or subject who seeks power or self-determination" (p. 32). Therefore, while this book focuses on empowering people with severe mental illness, they must empower themselves. Having said that, however, those holding power play a critical role in the empowerment of vulnerable populations. Staples (1999) described this role:

> There is a facilitative role that helpers can play in the empowerment process by establishing relationships, providing access to resources, furnishing opportunities, strengthening capacities and creating options which enable individuals and groups to obtain and exercise greater power to control their own lives.... Often, the ability of [mental health] consumers to empower themselves will be impacted profoundly by how well provider professionals play a facilitative role and the extent to which organizations sanction empowerment opportunities. (p. 119)

Table 1.1 summarizes the concepts that comprise empowerment, which are incorporated throughout the book.

APPLYING EMPOWERMENT CONCEPTS TO PEOPLE WITH SEVERE MENTAL ILLNESS

Empowerment is defined as the meaningful participation of people with severe mental illness in decision making and activities that give them increased power, control, or influence over important areas of their lives. The incorporation of the term "meaningful" in relationship to participation recognizes that people with mental illness may not have final decision-making power in many instances, yet a range of participation has the potential to be empowering. Heeding Riger's (1993) warning not to underestimate the importance of actual power, this book's discussion of whether participation constitutes empowerment is placed within the context of the specific activity under consideration. For instance, it is expected that most people with mental illness would control decisions about the content of their treatment plans. It is unlikely that they would have final decision-making power over agency policies, yet they may have meaningful participation in the organizational decision-making process and thus be empowered through it. Because empowerment is situation specific, this book examines the empowerment of people with

Table 1.1 Basic Concepts of Empowerment

Empowerment involves holding power, control, and influence—Holding final decision-making power is most empowering. However, empowerment exists on a continuum, and it can occur in some instances through a sharing of power.

Resources are critical to empowerment—Obtaining resources helps individuals to gain increased control over their lives.

Empowerment can refer to a process—Any process that prepares people to participate more effectively in an activity that increases their power, control, or influence can be considered empowering. For example, participating with staff to review an agency policy can be an empowering process for clients.

Empowerment can refer to an outcome—Empowerment outcomes are the consequences or results of empowerment processes. The enactment of a revised policy that clients preferred that resulted from a client and staff work group is an example of an empowerment outcome.

Short-term and long-term empowerment outcomes—Outcomes can be short-term, such as completing an educational program, or long-term, such as obtaining a competitive job of one's choice.

Subjective and objective empowerment outcomes—Subjective outcomes are those that are self-perceived or attitudinal, such as one's sense of control or self-esteem. Objective outcomes reflect actual power held and usually are reflected behaviorally.

Empowerment can refer to an ideology—Ideology refers to the values and beliefs that comprise empowerment.

Empowerment involves an interconnection between individuals and their environment—Empowerment is reflected in power over one's environment, but one is dependent on the environment for resources and opportunities that others control.

Empowerment is situational—Empowerment is specific to particular activities at a specific point in time. Individuals can be empowered in one activity but not another, and empowerment can increase or decease as the context or circumstances change.

One cannot empower another—People must empower themselves. However, others play a critical role in providing individuals with supportive relationships, resources, decision-making opportunities, and other things many people need to empower themselves.

---

mental illness in seven different areas that have the potential for empowerment. For each of these areas, the empowerment processes that support people with mental illness are explored, as are the empowerment outcomes, both subjective and objective, that can result from these processes.

The focus on empowerment of people with severe mental illness is important and warranted for both practical and philosophical reasons (Croft & Beresford, 1992). From a practical perspective, the empowerment of people with mental illness through meaningful participation in decision making benefits both them and the organizations that provide services to them. People with mental illness who meaningfully participate in treatment planning, for instance, are more likely to meet their treatment goals and be satisfied with their services (Bassman, 1997; Liberman, Hilty, Drake, & Tsang, 2001; Roth & Crane-Ross, 2002). Similarly, people with mental illness who select their residences and have control over major residential decisions are more satisfied with their housing and function more independently within it (Brown & Wheeler, 1990; McCarthy & Nelson, 1991). Likewise, mental health agencies that promote client participation in organizational decision making are more likely to develop service programs that are responsive to their clients' needs (Kent & Read, 1998; Salzer, 1997). A focus on empowerment also is important because participation can be viewed as a right (Katan & Prager, 1986). Simply put, people should have right to participate in decisions and activities that will affect their lives. It is particularly important to make a conscious effort to involve people with severe mental illness in decision making because of their long history of powerlessness, which is the subject of the next chapter.

2

A History of Powerlessness

Historically, people with severe mental illness have not been empowered. Powerlessness, or the subjugation, by others, of the personal power of people with mental illness to act on their own behalf, has occurred through several means. Some people with mental illness have been subjected to inhumane physical treatment in the community and while hospitalized. Access to mental health services and other resources often has been limited. Many people with mental illness have been the target of stigma. Stigma can be defined as "a cluster of negative attitudes and beliefs that motivate the general public to fear, reject, avoid, and discriminate against people with mental illnesses" (President's New Freedom Commission on Mental Health, 2003, p. 4). Finally, some argue that the mental health system has functioned as a social control mechanism (e.g., Rothman, 2002a, 2002b; Scull, 1989; Szasz, 1974). In the context of people with mental illness, social control can be defined as "social responses to deviant behavior by people defined as mentally ill, and the means used to foster and maintain order and conformity" (Aviram, 1990, p. 82). Journalists, historians, sociologists, psychiatrists, people with mental illness, and others have written about aspects of powerlessness among people with mental illness both in the present and historically. To fully appreciate powerlessness and empowerment today, it is important to take an historical view of powerlessness. This helps to put into context current limitations to empowerment and provides direction for creating opportunities for empowering people with severe mental illness that avoid past mistakes.

As a means of organization, this historical review is divided into four time periods, the latter three being associated with major mental health reform efforts. This chapter draws heavily on the comprehensive histories of people with mental illness in the United States written by Deutsch (1949), Grob (1973, 1983, 1991), and Rothman (2002a, 2002b). As history is reviewed with present-day knowledge about mental illness, it is important to keep in mind that some practices that were considered to be the best treatment at particular times in history would be considered abusive today, while other actions toward people with mental illness would be considered abusive in any era. This synopsis does not attempt to present a balanced view of actions toward people with mental illness. Rather, the intention is to illustrate the ongoing nature of powerlessness experienced by many people with mental illness that continues to the present.

THE COLONIAL ERA (1600s and 1700s)

During the American colonial era, people did not understand mental illness. Some considered mental illness to result from such things as demonic possession, although by the end of the colonial era, others began to argue that mental illness had natural causes, such as disease or stress (Rochefort, 1997). There were few attempts at treatment, however, and little expectation of recovery. Community attitudes toward people with mental illness ranged from shame, if the individual was a family member; to indifference, if nonthreatening; to annoyance, if community life was disrupted and intervention was required; to hostility and distrust, if appearing violent. Community attention typically was shown not out of concern for individuals with mental illness, but to control those who posed a nuisance or danger to the community (Deutsch, 1949; Grob, 1973). People with mental illness who were poor were treated no differently than other poor and dependent populations, such as those who were sick, elderly, or orphaned (Rothman, 2002b).

Local communities were solely responsible for care of people with mental illness during the colonial era. If found harmless, people with mental illness who were without family or ties to a particular community often were allowed to roam the countryside. Many local communities enacted settlement laws that sought to prevent these people and others who were potentially dependent from entering or staying in their communities (Deutsch, 1949). Deutsch (1949) described that when communities identified individuals as posing a risk of dependency, such individuals could be "warned out" of the community, that is, forced to leave. If they returned, they could be subjected to a public whipping or other penalties. To illustrate, one New York community passed a law in 1721 that people who had been warned out but returned were to be subjected to 36 lashes if a man and 25 lashes if a woman. Deutsch continued that it was a common practice for townspeople to transport people with mental illness in the middle of the night to another community to absolve themselves of the responsibility and costs of care.

When people with mental illness had an established community connection and were unable to care for themselves, families often took care of them, either at their own expense or with local government subsidy (Grob, 1973). While one assumes most family care was benevolent, examples abound of inhumane care by family members. If displaying management problems or violent behavior, people with mental illness could be chained or locked in rooms or cellars in the home (Deutsch, 1949). Deutsch (1949) noted that even those who were nonviolent were sometimes locked up for years in the home to avoid the public shame that often was associated with having a relative who had a mental illness. In other instances, small buildings were constructed on family property to house the individual. Deutsch provided the example of residents of a small community in Massachusetts who allocated funds in 1689 to a man to construct a building seven feet long and five feet wide to house his sister who had a mental illness.

When people with mental illness had no family, the community sometimes would pay individuals to care for them in their own home. One can speculate that the quality of care was sometimes poor in these homes, as it was in the homes of relatives. Rochefort (1997) provided an extreme example of abuse. He stated that in 1651, in Rhode Island, the community turned over the care of a woman with mental illness to six men who were given the authority to sell her possessions to help offset the costs of care. One month after living with the men, she died outside during a storm after wandering around alone and naked. Near the end of the colonial period, it became more common to assign people with mental illness to private individuals through public auctions (Deutsch, 1949). Community officials literally put the person on public display, and then awarded the contract for care to the lowest bidder.

If individuals with mental illness were violent and unable to be cared for by family members or in private homes, they commonly were placed in jails to assure public safety. If small communities did not yet have jails, they sometimes allocated funds to construct a small building to house them (Grob, 1973). Rochefort (1997) provided an extreme example of the creation of a special building to house a person with mental illness. He indicated that a Rhode Island community erected a small building on poles with wide spaces between the floorboards. This building housed the same man with mental illness for 20 years with little clothing and without heat. The building was visible from the main highway, it can be assumed, to warn dependent people not to enter the community.

As communities grew in size during the latter part of the colonial era, it became too costly to pay for care for people with mental illness in private homes. In response, they developed a range of institutional options, including workhouses, houses of corrections, and almshouses, to contend with people with mental illness and others who were poor and dependent on the community for support (Deutsch, 1949; Rochefort, 1997). According to Deutsch (1949), workhouses essentially were a combination of a penal institution and a poorhouse for "rogues and vagabonds, idle and vicious" (p. 51), as well as "the mildly insane" (p. 52). Their purposes were to force the able-bodied poor to work and to deter dependency. Deutsch stated that the first workhouse opened in New York in 1736, and that it contained a special dungeon for people with mental illness if they became unmanageable. Houses of corrections were penal institutions. However, they frequently housed people with mental illness who had not committed crimes, but who were dependent. Early examples of such institutions appeared in Rhode Island in 1725 and in Connecticut in 1727. Both explicitly stated the houses of correction included people with mental illness as a target population. A third institutional option was the almshouse, which became widespread in the 1800s and would become the primary institution for people with mental illness throughout much of the 1800s (Deutsch, 1949). Communities placed people with mental illness in almshouses along with other dependent people who were sick, blind, elderly, chronic alcoholics, or poor. Living conditions often were deplorable. Grob (1973) pointed out, though, that conditions typically were no worse for people with mental illness than other residents.

Another institutional option for people with mental illness, hospitalization, was in its infancy during the colonial era. The first general hospital in America opened in Philadelphia in 1756. It included an area for people with mental illness, which was located in the basement. It was damp and unhealthy, and many people with mental illness died of physical illness associated with these conditions (Grob, 1973). People with mental illness were subjected to strict discipline and physical punishment, such as whippings, if they violated rules. It also was not uncommon for them to wear leg irons and to be chained to the walls or floor. One custom that quickly developed at the hospital was the charging of admission fees to the general public to have the opportunity to view the hospitalized people with mental illness. Grob (1973) concluded that conditions at the hospital were no better for people with mental illness than were those at almshouses. The first hospital exclusively for people with mental illness opened in Williamsburg, Virginia in 1773. It was paid for with state funds and developed, in part, because of the disruption that people with mental illness were causing in the local almshouses (Deutsch, 1949). Little is known about its early years, although one historian believed that it most likely resembled care offered to people with mental illness in the Philadelphia hospital (Deutsch, 1949). The Williamsburg hospital was the only hospital exclusively for people with mental illness until a private hospital opened in 1817, and the second state-funded hospital opened in 1825 (Deutsch, 1949).

THE ERA OF MORAL TREATMENT AND THE DEVELOPMENT OF STATE ASYLUMS (1800s)

At the end of the colonial era, there still was little hope of recovery for people with mental illness, and their care remained largely undifferentiated from other dependent populations. This would begin to change with the advent of moral treatment and the development of state asylums. This era extended roughly throughout the 1800s. Versions of moral treatment were introduced by Phillippe Pinel in France and William Turke in England in the late 1700s (Deutsch, 1949; Grob, 1973; Rothman, 2002b). Moral treatment was a loosely defined approach that sought to aid people with mental illness to develop internal controls in order to self-regulate their illnesses. This was to be achieved by living in a small, quiet facility located in the country; by receiving kind and gentle treatment rather than physical punishment; and by adhering to a strict daily routine (Rothman, 2002b). These facilities were to provide asylum from societal stresses. Evenson, Holland, and Johnson (1994) provided an excerpt from the annual report of a public asylum published in 1876 that illustrates how at least one facility conceptualized moral treatment:

> Treatment of insanity, as practiced here, consists of raising the physical health to the highest condition it is capable of obtaining, by plenty of good nutriment, sleep, fresh air, cleanliness, exercise, and suitable medication; in diverting the mind from its hallucinations and absorbing delusions by means of work, books, papers, music, dancing, billiards, croquette, etc.; in encouraging the patient to express his self-control, and in firmly, though gently, impressing upon him the necessity of submitting to a healthy discipline, and of accommodating himself to this environment. (p. 1028)

Some of the first asylums in the United States to employ moral treatment included the Friends' Asylum founded by Quakers in 1817 in Frankfort, Pennsylvania and the Bloomingdale Asylum founded in 1821 in New York, both of which were private facilities (Deutsch, 1949). Other private asylums soon opened. Evidence suggests that these early asylums largely were successful in creating the type of atmosphere conducive to moral treatment (Grob, 1973). These early asylums boasted about high rates of curing the mental illnesses of its patients (Deutsch, 1949). Access to care in these asylums, however, typically was limited to the middle and upper social classes because they could afford to pay privately, although some asylums sponsored by religious organizations offered their services to people with mental illness who were unable to pay for them (Dowdall, 1996; Grob, 1973). By the 1830s, most states still did not have any special facilities for people with mental illness. Those states that had opened hospitals did not include enough beds to accommodate the large number of people with mental illness who could have benefited from their services (Deutsch, 1949).

Deutsch (1949) outlined the care options for people with mental illness who needed assistance and could not access the limited number of beds in hospitals and asylums in the early to mid-1880s. First, many people resided with their families. Some communities continued to provide a subsidy to families. However, aid had to be temporary or less than the cost of other types of care. Second, the practice of putting people with mental illnesses on the auction block and awarding custody to the lowest bidder flourished in this era. Deutsch indicated that farmers often bid on people with mental illness, as well as those with mental retardation, because many were physically healthy and could provide an inexpensive labor source. Third, in the early 1800s, some communities began to contract with a single provider for the care of all dependent people with mental illness within their jurisdiction. Fourth, some people with mental illness continued to be placed in jails and houses of corrections. Finally, many people with mental illness who were poor were placed in public almshouses.

The use of public almshouses as a source of care for people with mental illness, which begin in the colonial era, greatly expanded in the 1800s. New York and Massachusetts provide examples of states in which the number of almshouses increased during this period. Massachusetts had 83 almshouses in 1824, 180 in 1839, and 219 in 1860 (Grob, 1973). The almshouse population in New York more than doubled between 1830 and 1850, increasing from 4,500 in 1830, to 8,200 in 1840, to 10,000 in 1850 (Rothman, 2002b). Conditions in many of these facilities were atrocious. Deutsch (1949) provided one example of such conditions based on a report by a county almshouse director to the New York legislature in 1834. The report indicated that of the 174 residents (called "inmates"), 10 had mental illnesses (were "lunatics") and eight others had mental retardation (were "idiots") (p. 130). The director complained of overcrowding. In one unheated room, for instance, 25 men and boys, including two people with mental illness, slept in 11 beds. In another room, two men with mental illness were regularly chained to the floor. The administrator admitted conditions were poor and vehemently complained that he was required to accept all people who were sent to him, yet he was not given the resources to care for them. Rothman (2002b) reported on conditions in one almshouse in Oswego, New York during this same time period. He said that 75 people, including "young, old, sick, lame, idiotic, and insane paupers" (p. 199), were indiscriminately housed in nine rooms and were supervised by one man with the assistance of two residents. Dowdall (1996) provided another example from the Buffalo, New York area. He reported that by 1850, the majority of poor people with mental illness resided in the local almshouse, not the state asylum. The almshouse had a high mortality rate, fed its residents a near-starvation diet, mixed people with mental illness with other residents, and provided no treatment to people with mental illness. Dowdall also reported that later in the 1850s, a new almshouse was built that included a separate building for people with mental illness. However, people with mental illness continued to be shackled to the floor and tied to furniture. Dowdall described the same almshouse in 1865, which had a population of approximately 500 people, of whom 121 had a mental illness. Because of continued overcrowding, not all people with mental illness had beds. At least 20 regularly slept on straw that was changed every 1–2 weeks. People with mental illness received no treatment and were cared for by other residents of the almshouse.

It was in response to the mistreatment of people with mental illness in almshouse, jails, houses of correction, and private care that reformers advocated for accessible treatment for all people in publicly funded asylums. Private asylums provided hope that people with mental illness could be cured, and they served as a model for public care (Rothman, 2002b). These early asylums proclaimed high cure rates. To illustrate, one asylum superintendent declared a cure rate of 82% in 1834, and another declared in 1842 to have cured the mental illness of all the people he had treated (Rothman, 2002b). Not surprising, these statistics were later found to be inaccurate, although Rothman reports that widespread attacks on these statistics did not begin until 1877. At the time these results were being released, they were accepted by most people and offered hope that mental illness could be cured (Rothman, 2002b).

By the end of the 1820s, most states were beginning to recognize that private asylums were not going to meet public needs and that governmental action would be required (Grob, 1973). The most famous reformer and supporter of public asylums during this era was Dorothea Dix (Brown, 1998; Gollaher, 1995). She began her reform efforts by conducting an extensive assessment of the conditions of the facilities for people with mental illness in Massachusetts. During 1841 and 1842, she visited every private asylum, jail, and almshouse in the state, as well as some private houses caring for people with mental illness, and found deplorable conditions. She compiled her findings into a written report, which she presented to the Massachusetts legislature. One of her biographers presented her testimony before the legislature. "I proceed, Gentlemen, briefly to call your attention to the present state of Insane Persons confined within this Commonwealth, in cages, closets, stalls, pens! Chained, naked, beaten with rods, and lashed into obedience" (Gollaher, 1995, p. 143). Dix then proceeded to list examples of abuse on a region-by-region basis:

> Concord. A woman from the hospital in a cage in the almshouse. In the jail several, decently cared for in general but not properly placed in a prison. Violent, noisy, unmanageable most of the time. Lincoln. A woman in a cage. Medford. One idiotic subject chained, and one in a close stall for 17 years.... Granville. One often closely confined; now losing the use of his limbs from want of exercise. (Gollaher, 1995, pp. 143–144)

Combining these horrific accounts with reports of the generally accepted high cure rates of private asylums, Dix's advocacy helped gain passage of state legislation in Massachusetts and later in other states that funded the building of 30 state hospitals (Grob, 1973). Gollaher (1995) contended that Dix was successful because she was able to humanize people with mental illness. Gollaher wrote:

> In contrast to the keepers, who appear to have forgotten that their charges were human beings, she was compassionate, always sensitive to the personalities of the insane.... She asked her readers to sympathize with them and to acknowledge their dignity. By drawing pictures of real individual men and women with a dramatic intensity usually found in fiction, she transported the insane out of the realm of impersonal phenomena. (pp. 151–152)

Despite her successes at the state level, Dix's ultimate goal of federal support for state asylums was not met. In 1854, President Pierce vetoed a bill that would have transferred federal lands to states to support the development of public asylums (Brown, 1998). The legislature was unable to muster enough votes to override his veto. It would be almost another century before the federal government would become involved in mental health issues.

By 1860, 28 of the 33 states had a least one public asylum (Rothman, 2002b). However, these institutions were unable to meet the needs of all people with mental illness who were poor. For example, an 1855 report to the New York legislature estimated that the state contained 2,000 people with mental illness who were dependent. However, only 300 were being treated in the state asylum (Deutsch, 1949). The report found that most of the remaining individuals continued to live in jails, houses of corrections, and almshouses. The New York legislature had to pass legislation in 1890 to remove people with mental illness from almshouses (Deutsch, 1949). By the latter part of the 1800s, the percentage of people with mental illness receiving care in public asylums had increased. The 1880 U.S. census included a count of people with mental illness. It identified over 90,000 citizens with mental illness, of whom 9,000 were in almshouses, approximately 40,000 were in public asylums, and the remainder were in their own homes (Deutsch, 1949; Grob, 1983). Those who were admitted to public asylums typically displayed extreme behaviors, which could include violence, suicide attempts, or extreme symptoms such as major depression, hallucinations, or delusions (Grob, 1983).

The growth of public asylums could not meet the demand, and they increasingly could not provide treatment to those placed in their care. State legislatures underestimated demand and did not authorize sufficient numbers of facilities or beds (Grob, 1973; Rothman, 2002b). Overcrowding of asylums often occurred soon after they were opened. By the end of the 1800s, many public asylums had 3,000 or more patients (Grob, 1973). At least two factors account for this growth (Grob, 1973; Rothman, 2002b). One was the large influx of immigrants who often were poor and were diagnosed to have high rates of mental illness to the United States during the second half of the 1800s. In New York City, for instance, among the 11,141 admissions to the New York City asylum between 1847 and 1870, 77% were immigrants, of which 61% were Irish and an additional 24% were German (Grob, 1973). A second factor was the transfer of responsibility for care of people with mental illness from local communities to state governments. This transfer was consistent with the trend during the late 1800s for states to assume responsibility for social welfare programs. Recognizing a financial benefit, local communities redefined mental illness to include elderly people who were senile, and sent those who had been in almshouses (care paid for through local communities) to state-funded asylums (Grob, 1983). Rothman (2002b), Scull (1989), and others have offered an alternative explanation for the growth in the public asylum census during the 1800s. They argued that public asylums served a social control function to contend with the instability that occurred as American society experienced dramatic changes in the early 1800s. According to this perspective, treatment was never a prominent goal of asylums for people with mental illness.

Overcrowding and the increased size of public asylums negated efforts to apply moral treatment. Public asylums, which began because of the well-intentioned efforts by reformers to provide care and treatment, soon provided only custodial care (Grob, 1973). Even custodial care was sometimes provided in inhumane fashion. By the 1870s, state legislatures could no longer ignore reports of physical abuse in public asylums. This abuse was associated with overcrowded living conditions, staffing shortages, poorly trained staff, and poor working conditions (Grob, 1983). Also, at least some people considered the frequent use of mechanical restraints in public asylums to be abusive. Grob (1973) argued that the use of mechanical restraints was one of the most controversial issues of the 1800s in the emerging profession of psychiatry. While attempts were made in England to minimize its use during this period, American psychiatrists argued for its acceptance. Deutsch (1949) included accounts provided by some psychiatrists of that era justifying the restraints. "Some forms of forcible restraint would always be necessary to the proper discipline of a mental hospital. The very walls and gates were coercive. Institutionalization of the insane *per se* implied coercion, as it was often effected against the will and wish of the patient" (p. 216). In addition, "To supplant mechanical restraint by attendants would necessitate larger staff and consequently greater expense" (p. 216). Such rationale won out, as restraint use would continue throughout the 1800s and 1900s and remains an issue today.

Personal accounts of the experiences of people with mental illness who had been confined in public asylums illustrate the abuse that sometimes occurred. Geller and Harris (1994) assembled the published stories of women who had been confined in public asylums and hospitals. Their stories are particularly telling. Elizabeth Stone, confined between 1840 and 1842, described her asylum as "... a system worse than slavery, and any crime can be done there and covered up under the garb of derangement, and no one interfere" (p. 39). Phebe B. Davis, confined between 1850 and 1853, wrote, "When I said anything to the Doctors about the wrongs of the house, they would tell me that was my insanity. I told them that a fact was no less a fact because it was told by a crazy person" (p. 51). She continued, "It was not safe for a patient to report one of the attendants to the doctors, for they would listen to hear what the patients said to the doctors, and then they would watch their opportunities for revenge for the patients" (p. 54). Sophia Olsen, confined between 1862 and 1864, wrote:

> In this prison was exacted the most immediate and uncompromising obedience to rules and requirements which a slave holder would have blushed to inflict upon his human chattels. Our own preferences were never consulted. "You must do this because I want ye to," was all the reason given. ... There is absolutely no escape from obedience here, no matter what is required. I have many times, seen even tardy or reluctant obedience punished with fearful severity; I have seen the attendant ... twist their arms and cross them behind the back, tie them in that position, and then beat the victim till the other patients would cry out, begging her to desist. (pp. 72–73)

Tirzah F. Shedd, confined in 1865, wrote:

> I saw Mrs. Comb held by the hair of her head under a streaming faucet, and handfuls of hair were pulled from her head, by their rough handling, simply because she would not eat when she was not hungry. ... The prisoners are not allowed to write to their friends what kind of treatment they are receiving, and an attempt to do so clandestinely, is punished as an offense. (pp. 83–84)

Adeline T. P. Lunt, whose exact confinement dates during the 1800s were unknown, wrote that "... another risk which is not altogether to be lost sight of in their system—the danger of a falling into apathy of the patient, growing out of a too protracted detention" (pp. 121–122).

Geller and Harris' (1994) most famous contributor was Elizabeth Parsons Ware Packard. She was involuntarily confined in an Illinois public asylum between 1860 and 1863 upon an order initiated by her husband and eventually won her release through a writ of habeas corpus. She went on to author five books and become a nationally prominent advocate for the revision of civil commitment laws (Sapinsley, 1991). Ms. Packard wrote "[I] now know it to be too sadly true; for the Statute of Illinois expressly states that a man may put his wife into an Insane Asylum without evidence of insanity" (p. 60). She continued:

> The law and society have so regulated this principle [life, liberty, and pursuit of happiness], that the insane are permitted to be treated and regarded as having no rights that any one is bound to respect. . . . Whoever can leave an insane asylum without a feeling of moral degradation, and a self loathing, debased human feeling of himself, as a human being, must have attained to the highest plane of divine influences. (pp. 62–63)

Gender, as the personal accounts by these women suggest, as well as social class, ethnicity, and race played a role in the care of people with mental illness during the 1800s. Grob (1973) ranked the quality of care received by different groups. He concluded that during this era, native born Americans of the upper social class who could afford to pay received the best care. It was not uncommon to separate people by social class in public asylums, with more intensive care going to the people of the upper classes. Differential care also was found between private asylums, comprised mainly of the upper class, and public asylums, comprised mainly of poor people. Private asylums spent considerably more per patient than public asylums. As a case in point, in 1848, McLean Hospital, a private facility, spent $194 per patient; two public asylums, Worcester State Lunatic Hospital and Utica State Lunatic Asylum, spent $107 and $116 per patient, respectively. In 1868, the same private hospital had increased its per-patient rate to $858; at the same two public hospitals, the per-patient rates were $195 and $245, respectively (Grob, 1973). Grob indicated that as early as the 1850s, people were warning of the dangers of having two systems of care, one for people who were poor and another for people in the upper class.

Second on Grob's (1973) quality-of-care ranking were people with mental illness who were native born and poor, followed by those who were poor and immigrants. Discrimination against immigrants, particularly those from Ireland, was rampant during this period. Immigrants with mental illness tended to be housed in city-operated asylums in the major urban areas. Overall, these city-operated asylums tended to provide much poorer care than those run by the state. Grob's (1983) description of the Cook County Lunatic Asylum in Chicago in the 1880s illustrates the poor care that was provided in at least some city asylums. "Lice abounded; patients died without receiving medical care; and restraints were used indiscriminately and without any controls upon attendants. Whiskey and drugs were freely prescribed, and a serious drug addiction problem existed among patients" (pp. 27–28).

Finally, Grob (1973) argued that African Americans received the poorest quality of care among the major groups in the United States during this era. This was a function of the social attitudes and discriminatory practices that existed in both the North and South during the 1800s. Not only was the quality of care generally poor, but also many public and private asylums in both the North and South refused to treat African Americans during much of this era. As examples, Grob indicated that Ohio state asylums did not accept African Americans until the 1870s, and African Americans with mental illness in Cincinnati were housed in the county jail. When facilities were available, African Americans typically had segregated living quarters. The operation of the St. Louis City Insane Asylum located in Missouri provides another example of practices and attitudes related to African Americans (Evenson et al., 1994). When the asylum opened in 1869, the wards were racially integrated. In the 1887 annual report, the superintendent argued for racially segregated wards, reasoning it was better for African Americans. He wrote:

> The sudden demand [of freedom] upon sluggish and uncultivated brains...competing with the dominant and cultivated Caucasian...[causes] melancholy that comes like a blight with the sense of failure and the hopelessness of contention, it [results in the] generating of diseased brains and disordered minds.... As...social equality between races is impossible, unattainable, and undesirable; so, with an asylum a distinction should be made where a difference exists. The Negro insane should be maintained separate from the white inmates. (p. 1027)

Soon after the turn of the century, wards at this hospital were racially segregated.

While Grob (1973) did not include women as a factor in his ranking of the quality of care, one can assume that the repressive social attitudes toward women during the 1800s were reflected in care and treatment of women. The stories of women who had been hospitalized during this era previously presented by Geller and Harris (1994) illustrate the poor care that at least some women received. In addition, radical treatments for women began to become prominent in the late 1880s, including the removing of ovaries. Grob (1983) reported that this

occurred primarily among middle class females who had vaguely defined symptoms. This practice, however, was never widespread in state
hospitals. Women also may have been disproportionately subjected to
the inappropriate use of the involuntary commitment process, as
Ms. Packard argued when she was hospitalized in 1860 (Sapinsley,
1991). Evenson et al. (1994) offered some additional examples of women who may have been inappropriately hospitalized during this era:

> Minnie K was admitted because of a homosexual relationship. She
> died in the asylum 15 years later. . . . Laura H, a 32-year old feeble-
> minded widow, was cheated out of her money by her appointed
> guardian and sent to the asylum. Tauusa T, aged 54, a widow, was
> giving a "stern lecture" to a crowd of men when she was arrested
> because she was "scantily dressed," that is, not wearing a hat or
> shoes! Annie B, age 31, a housewife, who had moved all the furni-
> ture out of the house into storage after an argument with her hus-
> band, was sent to the asylum. (pp. 1026–1027)

While institutional care was emphasized during this era, Geller
(1989) and Rothman (2002b) indicated that some psychiatrists of this
era supported community treatment for many of their patients. Geller
found, however, that many communities opposed the discharge of
people with mental illness from asylums into their communities. This
was based, in part, on their fear that people with mental illness were
dangerous. While the practice of auctioning off people with mental
illness was discontinued during this era, some hospitals attempted to
board released patients who did not have families into private homes
because of the absence of community placement options. This practice,
however, never became widespread (Grob, 1983).

THE ERA OF MENTAL HYGIENE AND GROWTH
OF STATE HOSPITALS (1900 TO 1950s)

By the end of the 1800s, the optimism of effective treatment of mental
illness through moral treatment in small asylums had long since van-
ished (Rothman, 2002a). Instead, people with mental illness received
care in large, overcrowded state institutions that were more custodial
than treatment oriented. In addition, large numbers of people with
mental illness remained in jails, houses of corrections, and almshouses.
In reality, few people with mental illness benefited from moral treatment
(Deutsch, 1949). However, a new sense of optimism for people with
mental illness that was fueled by the social reforms of the Progressive
Era began to develop at the turn of the century (Rothman, 2002a). Psychiatrists espoused that new, innovative treatment techniques could
prevent or cure most mental illnesses. This movement was labeled
"mental hygiene" by its most influential promoter, Adolf Meyer

(Rothman, 2002a). Like moral treatment, the mental hygiene movement was vaguely defined and meant different things to different people. At its most basic level, it sought to obviate the need for long-term care in state hospitals through the development of preventive programs, community clinics, psychopathic hospitals to treat acute mental illness, and aftercare for people discharged from hospitals (Rochefort, 1997; Rothman, 2002a). Regrettably, most people with severe mental illness did not benefit from the mental hygiene movement, just as most did not benefit from moral treatment. Insufficient numbers of clinics and acute care hospitals were established to make a difference.

Additional attempts at boarding out people with mental illness into nonrelative family homes failed too. In 1939, for instance, 1,300 people were in family care homes, which constituted only 3% of the hospital population (Rothman, 2002a). Rothman (2002a) referenced a report from Massachusetts, the state most involved in this endeavor, about the difficulties persons with mental illness encountered with family homes. First, the report indicated that some patients did not want to leave the hospital because they were uncertain of the care they would receive in their new setting and they would miss the friends they had made at the hospital. Second, many family members resisted placement for fear they, themselves, would be criticized for not taking their relative into their own homes. Third, communities resisted placements into their neighborhoods, even though only people who were nonviolent were placed in those homes. Finally, the report indicated that it was very difficult to find reputable families that would assume care for these discharged patients. Rothman also cited resistance from state hospitals to the discharge of patients into family homes. The type of patient that was appropriate for home care often was the hospital's best worker, so they were concerned with the loss of free labor. Also, state legislatures were unwilling to allocate new funding for family homes, so any funding for them would have come from hospital budgets. This especially was a problem because the monthly rate for family home care was much higher than the monthly rate paid to hospitals.

In the absence of sufficient numbers of family homes, community-based services, and acute inpatient treatment, it is not surprising the number of people in state hospitals continued to rise. Between 1903 and 1940, the number of residents in state hospitals increased from 150,000 to 445,000 (Grob, 1983). The state hospital population reached its peak in 1955 with over 550,000 patients (Geller, 2000; Scull, 1985). Several factors contributed to this increase. First, the U.S. population was increasing. Between 1880 and 1923, for instance, the total population more than doubled from 50 million to 109 million, respectively (Grob, 1983). Second was a decrease in the number of people with mental illness confined to almshouses. To illustrate, in 1880, the total almshouse population was 66,000, of which 24% were people with mental illness. In 1904, the total almshouse population was 82,000, of which 10.3% were people with mental illness. In 1923, the total almshouse population was 78,000, of which 5.6% were people with mental illness (Grob, 1983). Third, state hospitals began admitting people with a greater range of illnesses than they traditionally had admitted. Many of these new illnesses were chronic physical illnesses, rather than mental illnesses that were treatable and had some chance of cure, such as what now are known as schizophrenia, bipolar disorder, and depression. Instead, the growth in state hospitals was associated with increased numbers of elderly who were senile, people with paresis (brain damage caused by syphilis), and those with Huntington's chorea, which progresses to dementia (Grob, 1983).

Public hospitals changed as their work with people with mental illness increasingly became medicalized. First, most remaining asylums were renamed hospitals at the beginning of this era to reflect their new orientation (Rothman, 2002a). These hospitals began to use a number of new and invasive medical treatments for mental illness (Grob, 1983). One was the injection of a foreign agent to produce a fever, which was thought to reduce symptoms for particular mental illnesses. This treatment was most popular in the 1920s and 1930s (Grob, 1983). Another treatment was shock therapy, developed in the 1930s. It had been observed that the symptoms of some people with mental illness who had been in comas improved when they regained consciousness. Hospitals induced shock by the use of insulin, Metrazol, and later electricity. By 1940, Grob (1991) indicated that almost every hospital in the United States was using shock therapy, with electroshock therapy gaining increasing use in the early 1940s. By the late 1940s, electroshock therapy was highly criticized, however, for its use as punishment for ward rule infractions, its indiscriminate use without accompanying needed therapies, its application by poorly trained personnel, and the lack of follow-up of patients who had been given the treatment (Brown, 1985; Grob, 1991).

The most invasive treatment during this period was psychosurgery, also referred to as lobotomies. Lobotomies involved surgically severing the fibers that joined the prefrontal lobe with the rest of the brain (Grob, 1983). This procedure was used typically with people with psychoses who had not responded to shock therapy. Its primary benefit was to calm previously unmanageable behavior (Grob, 1983), which Brown (1985) framed as social control. Its use began in the early 1940s and reached its peak in 1949, when over 5,000 people with mental illness received lobotomies. Although highly criticized by some because the effects of lobotomies were irreversible and the potential existed for abuse, their use diminished only after the introduction of psychotropic medications in the mid-1950s (Grob, 1991). Although its use declined after this, Brown indicated that its social control function was more evident in the use of psychosurgeries that extended into the 1960s and 1970s.

Another medically oriented treatment that began at the end of this era was the introduction of psychotropic medications (Grob, 1991). Thorazine and then Serpasil were introduced in the mid-1950s. These medications and others that soon followed helped to manage the symptoms and control the behavior of large numbers of hospital patients. By the early 1960s, almost half of all state hospital patients were receiving these new medications (Grob, 1991). The use of medication in these early years was not without problems. Some psychiatrists tended to overuse and inappropriately use these medications, particularly among people with mental illness being treated in the community (Brown, 1985; Grob, 1991). In addition, the new drugs produced physical side effects in many patients, the most severe of which was tardive dyskinesia (Brown, 1985). This condition produces noticeable bizarre muscular movements. Its effects are irreversible, even when the medication is removed. Brown (1985) contended that these side effects became known in the 1950s, yet psychiatrists and drug companies did not begin to address them on a widespread basis until the 1970s.

A hospital procedure from past eras, mechanical restraint, remained widespread. In their review of state hospital programs in the late 1940s, the Council of State Governments (1950) concluded that their frequent use was inappropriate, stating "Mechanical restraint is rarely if ever justified. . . . It should be strictly controlled and closely supervised; and full records should be kept" (p. 12).

As another form of social control, the eugenics movement, which targeted people with mental illness along with people with mental retardation, some types of criminals, and selected other groups, began in the late 1800s. This movement sought to improve the hereditary qualities of Americans by promoting reproduction of the "fit" and reducing reproduction of the "unfit" (Grob, 1983, p. 167). This movement grew out of a concern held by some Americans that other countries were trying to dump their outcasts on the United States, and that restrictions in immigration failed to stem the tide of these undesirable populations from entering the country. Eugenics was manifested in at least two ways. One restricted the rights of people with mental illness to marry. Connecticut was the first state to pass such legislation in 1896 (Grob, 1983), and most states subsequently passed similar laws (Deutsch, 1949). A second means was surgical sterilization, which was performed on both males and females. Indiana was the first state to pass a sterilization law, which it did in 1907 (Grob, 1983). By the 1940s, 30 states had passed laws allowing for sterilization (usually involuntary sterilization); most of these laws included people with mental illness. Deutsch (1949) reported that between 1907 and 1946, 45,127 people were surgically sterilized under these laws, of which 47% were people with mental illness, 49% were people with mental retardation, and the remaining 4% were of other types. California had by far the highest rates of sterilization of people with mental illness, accounting for over 50% of the total, followed by Virginia with approximately 13% and Kansas with approximately 9% (Grob, 1983).

The deplorable conditions and abusive treatment within state hospitals identified in the latter part of the 1800s continued, and even worsened, through the 1950s. Further deterioration of conditions was related to increased overcrowding and staffing shortages, both of which were related, in part, to the lack of resources associated with the Great Depression of the 1930s and World War II (Grob, 1991). In 1939, for example, only 12 of 182 state hospitals had 500 or fewer patients, and 27 hospitals had 3,000 or more patients (Grob, 1983). A survey of state officials conducted in 1948 concluded that overcrowding was the most pressing problem faced by state hospitals (Council of State Governments, 1950). Deutsch (1948) provided specific examples of overcrowding and understaffing. The Philadelphia State Hospital had a capacity of 3,400 patients, yet it held 6,100 in 1946. According to recommended standards of the day, the hospital should have had a minimum of 1,100 attendants but had 180; it should have had 200 nurses but had 41; and it should have had 34 physicians but had 14. In 1946, the Cleveland State Hospital had one third the minimum number of physicians, nurses, and attendants needed. Rockland State Hospital had bed capacity for 4,700, yet it housed 6,100 patients. It had one half of the minimum number of doctors and nurses, and one third the minimum number of attendants. Conditions in public hospitals were even worse in the South (Grob, 1983). On average, Southern states spent less money overall on their state hospitals than did Western or Northern states. Moreover, they allocated more resources to patients who were White than to those who were African American. To illustrate, in 1907, two North Carolina hospitals that served only White patients spent $155 and $185 per patient; the state's all–African American hospital spent $111 per patient (Grob, 1983).

Deutsch (1948) provided vivid descriptions of the poor conditions of state hospitals derived from his visits to facilities across the country. The accounts first appeared as magazine articles and later were published as a book in 1948 titled *Shame of the States*. His explanation as to why he conducted the studies, and publicized the results, reflect the lack of advocacy for those hospitalized that existed at that time. He wrote: "The insane have no vote, so calculating politicians, in the absence of public pressures, tend to forget their desperate needs. The personal friends and relatives of the institutionalized insane do vote, but they are generally frightened, confused, and ashamed" (p. 13). The following are descriptions of selected state hospitals during the mid-1940s that Deutsch included in his book. The themes that ran through his case studies were buildings that were in need of repair, overcrowded conditions, understaffing, lack of access to treatment, and the provision of custodial care. His findings were consistent for public hospitals operated by both states and cities.

At Philadelphia State Hospital, also known as Byberry, Deutsch (1948) found deplorable living conditions on one ward and a lack of basic resources at the hospital:

> Three hundred nude men [on the male "incontinent" ward] stood, squatted and sprawled in this bare room, amid shrieks, groans, and unearthly laughter. These represented the most deteriorated patients. Winter or Summer, these creatures never were given any clothing at all. Some lay about on the bare floor in their own excreta. The filth-covered walls and floors were rotting away....Many patients [throughout the hospital]...had to eat their meals with their hands. There weren't nearly enough spoons or other tableware to go around at Byberry. (p. 49)

As part of his report on Cleveland State Hospital, Deutsch (1948) included the findings of a grand jury investigation of the hospital conducted in 1944, which were as follows:

1. Cleveland State Hospital presents a case history of brutality and social criminal neglect. Patients have died shortly after receiving violent attacks from the hands of attendants or other patients, made possible only by the lack of proper supervision. In other cases patients have died under circumstances which are highly suspicious.
2. Frequent active assaults have resulted in broken bones, lacerations, bruises, and a consequent deterioration of the mind. Favorite weapons have been the buckles of extremely heavy straps, the loaded end of heavy key rings, metal-plated shoes, and wet towels which leave no mark after choking.
3. Violent patients have been used for "strong-arm" purposes by attendants who persist in running the hospital as a penal institution. The atmosphere reeks with the false notion that the mentally ill are criminals and subhumans who should be denied all human rights and scientific medical care. (p. 58)

Deutsch (1948) described the decaying physical conditions at the Manhattan State Hospital. "The present institution is in appalling state of deterioration and disrepair as a result of the years of neglect in expectation of abandonment. It is grossly overcrowded and under-manned, like most state hospitals. Some of its wards are crowded double beyond capacity" (p. 66). He then stated the consequences of this overcrowding:

> Staff doctors can't practice good psychiatry when they have to handle hundreds of patients apiece. One had a load of more than

800 patients.... The official state regulations require that each hospital patient has to be interviewed at least twice a year. Yet Manhattan State doctors told me of many cases that had not been interviewed for as long as five years. (pp. 67–68)

He also discussed the requirement that patients work at the hospital:

A considerable number of able-bodied patients are put at institutional labor on a full eight-hours-a-day basis—in the coal yards, laundry, repair shops, etc. But they get no pay for their full-time work. They get only extra rations of tobacco.... I have seen patients even more miserably exploited in other state hospitals. I've seen them, in some places, reduced to slaves and serfs, worked for 12 and 14 hours a day, seven days a week, with no return but candy and tobacco handouts. Sometimes this exploitation operates under the guise of "industrial therapy," when the real motive is not to speed the patient's recovery but to squeeze all possible labor out of him. (p. 69)

As a final example, Deutsch (1948) reported on the excessive use of restraints at Detroit's City Receiving Hospital:

Many patients were strapped to their beds by leather thongs. Others sat rigid in chairs to which they had been bound hand and foot. Still others lay tightly wrapped up on "restraining sheets." Steel handcuffs restrained the movements of a large number of patients. Fully one out of every four patients was under some form of mechanical restraint. Many more were in what is called "chemical restraint," that is, doped up to render them quiet and tractable. (p. 107)

He described other aspects of the poor quality of care at the City Receiving Hospital. "No supervised recreation was afforded the unhappy patients.... They were condemned to deteriorating, day-long idleness in oppressive restraint, weeks, months, and even years on end.... I was told that some had been there for three years—in a place intended for a few days' or a few weeks' maximum stay" (pp. 108–109). Quoting a psychiatrist at the hospital, "Psychiatric treatment? There is none. There isn't time. There aren't enough psychiatrists or nurses or other needed personnel. All we can do is feed them and sleep them while they're with us" (p. 112).

Grob (1983) summarized the state of public psychiatric hospitals by the 1940s:

"There was general agreement that too many patients had become 'institutionalized' and hence were destined to spend the rest of their lives as pitiful guests dependent on public largesse; that brutality and neglect were endemic; that deteriorating physical plants and inadequate care were common; that lethargy, neglect, and overcrowding had reduced mental hospitals to the status of inadequate poorhouses" (p. 199).

Goffman (1961) offered yet another damaging perspective on public hospitals at the end of this era. Based on his case study of a public hospital in the 1950s, Goffman characterized such psychiatric hospitals as total institutions that highly regimented life and treated people, not as individuals, but as a group. He argued that normal adaptation of people with mental illness in such an environment produced attitudes and behaviors that were antithetical to those needed for independent community living. Hospital living reduced self-esteem and fostered apathy, complacency, and dependence. In fact, he argued, institutional living produced the very symptoms that people associated with mental illness.

Personal accounts of the experiences of people with mental illness while they were hospitalized provide a fitting end to the description of this era. The most well-known account was Clifford Beers' (1908) *A Mind that Found Itself: An Autobiography*, published in 1908. This book quickly received international acclaim (Dain, 1980). He wrote of his treatment and perceptions of the system while hospitalized for 3 years, beginning in 1900, in three hospitals, two private and one public. Adding to the power of this book was that he freely admitted that he had a mental illness and needed treatment, but the hospitals had not helped him (Rothman, 2002a).

At one point, Beers (1908) described being choked by attendants on two occasions. "The two attendants threw me off the bed and choked me so severely that I could feel my eyes starting from their sockets" (p. 117). "In each instance an insane man, conscious of his rights, was assaulted by two sane but untrained and unfeeling men whose brutal methods were countenanced by a sane physician" (p. 123). He also discussed the use of physical restraints. "It is the abuse rather than the use of such instruments of restraint against which I inveigh. Yet it is hardly worth while to distinguish between 'use' and 'abuse,' for it is a fact that where the use of mechanical restraint is permitted, abuse is bound to follow" (pp. 125–126).

On several occasions throughout the book, he discussed violence by attendants. "In a word, a 'violent ward' is too often a ward wherein violence is done to helpless patients by ignorant, untrained, and unsympathetic attendants" (pp. 152–153). "Sometimes days will pass without a single outbreak. Then will come a veritable carnival of abuse—due invariably to the attendants' state of mind, not to an unwonted aggressiveness on the part of the patients" (p. 169). Beers continued:

I can recall as especially noteworthy ten instances of atrocious abuse. Five patients were chronic victims, beaten frequently. . . . Three of them . . . suffered with especial regularity, scarcely a day passing without bringing to them its quota of punishment. . . . Day after day

I could hear the blows and kicks as they fell upon his body, and his incoherent cries for mercy were as painful to hear as they were impossible to forget. (p. 170)

He concluded, "The central problem in the care of the insane is the elimination of actual physical abuse" (p. 228). Beers discussed the parties responsible for the abuse. "But can we put all the blame on attendants for assaulting patients when the management shows no aggressive disposition to protect the latter? Such indifference is far more reprehensible than the cowardly conduct of ill-paid men, the majority of whom have had few advantages of education" (p. 229).

In addition to Beers' (1908) personal accounts, Geller and Harris' (1994) reprinted accounts from women who were hospitalized included several from the first half of the 1900s. Margaret Isabel Wilson, hospitalized between 1931 and 1937, wrote:

I can count my many blessings, and can also look back at the things I sorely missed in Blackmoor: (1) liberty; (2) my vote; (3) privacy; (4) normal companionship; (5) personal letters and uncensored answers; (6) useful occupation; (7) play; (8) contacts with intelligent minds; (9) pictures, scenery, books, good conversation; (10) appetizing food. (p. 282)

Lenore McCall, hospitalized between 1934 and 1938, wrote:

There I sat hour after hour, dissolved in bitter tears and racked by sobs. I wept for my lost world, wept in fear and horror, wept because I could see nothing ahead for me but life in this hospital, a downward progress which I was quite sure would end in Foster House, that large building across the grounds which became my bugaboo. (p. 283)

Finally, Frances Farmer, hospitalized between 1943 and 1950, wrote in poetic fashion:

For eight years I was an inmate in a state asylum for the insane. During those years I passed through such unbearable terror that I deteriorated into a wild, frightened creature intent only on survival. And I survived. I was raped by orderlies, gnawed on by rats, and poisoned by tainted food. And I survived. I was chained in padded cells, strapped into straightjackets, and half drowned in ice baths. And I survived. The asylum itself was a steel trap, and I was not released from its jaws alive and victorious. I crawled out mutilated, whimpering and terribly alone. But I did survive. (p. 314)

To conclude the contributions from people with mental illness during this era, Judi Chamberlin (1978) wrote about her experiences while in a psychiatric hospital in the 1960s. Her comments reflected Goffman's (1961) view of psychiatric hospitalization:

> The whole experience of mental hospitalization promotes weakness and dependency. Not only are the lives of patients controlled, but patients are constantly told that such control is for their own good, which they are unable to see because of their mental illness. Patients become unable to trust their own judgment, become indecisive, overly submissive to authority, frightened of the outside world. . . . The experience [of hospitalization] totally demoralized me. I had never thought of myself as a particularly strong person, but after hospitalization, I was convinced of my own worthlessness. I had been told that I could not exist outside of an institution. I was terrified that people would find out that I was an ex-patient and look down on me as much as I looked down on myself. (pp. 6–7)

THE ERA OF DEINSTITUTIONALIZATION (1950s to PRESENT)

A number of circumstances arose from the 1940s through the mid-1970s that resulted in a massive reduction in the number of people in public psychiatric hospitals. Eventually labeled "deinstitutionalization," this movement sought both to reduce the hospital census and to provide treatment to people with mental illness in the community (Bachrach, 1983). The first aspect of deinstitutionalization, the reduction in state hospital census, has occurred. From its high point of approximately 550,000 patients in public psychiatric hospitals in the mid-1950s, the census reached 54,826 by the end of 2000 (Center for Mental Health Services, 2003). The second aspect of deinstitutionalization, community treatment, has yet to be fully realized. As described throughout this book, many people with mental illness do not have access to the range of mental health and support services they need.

Deinstitutionalization had its roots in the early 1900s in the mental hygiene movement, which emphasized prevention of mental illness, community treatment, and short-term hospitalization for acute mental illness (Rochefort, 1997; Rothman, 2002a). Developments beginning in the 1940s helped to revitalize this optimistic approach. World War II had several effects (Rochefort, 1997). It highlighted the high frequency of mental illness among Americans and offered hope that mental illness could be treated without long hospitalizations. Twelve percent of all inductees for military service during World War II were rejected for neurological or psychiatric reasons, which accounted for 40% of all rejections. The incidence of mental illness also was common among soldiers experiencing the war, with 37% of all disability discharges being psychiatric in nature. To contend with mental illness experienced by soldiers, the military developed short-term therapies to treat them, which later were applied and expanded to citizens after the war. The experiences of the federal government with mental illness among soldiers led to the first major piece of federal legislation directed to mental illness, the National Mental Health Act of 1946. This act supported research on diagnosis and treatment of mental illness, established training programs for mental health personnel, funded pilot projects for community clinics and outpatient treatment, and created the National Institute of Mental Health (Grob, 1991).

Another influence on deinstitutionalization was the completion of two governmental studies on mental illness that offered policy directions supporting deinstitutionalizaition. The Council of State Governments (1950) conducted the first study through a 1948 survey of the 48 states. The report included 40 recommendations to improve the mental health system. The council sought improvements in state hospitals, as well as the development of outpatient clinics and other community resources for people with mental illness. It argued for better coordination between hospitals and community mental health services by placing both service types under a single mental health authority. It also sought better cooperation between departments of government to meet the diverse needs of people with mental illness who live in the community. The report recommended that states, not the federal government, be solely responsible for administering and funding psychiatric treatment.

The second study was mandated under the federal Mental Health Study Act of 1955. The Joint Commission on Mental Illness and Health, assembled to implement this act, conducted the most comprehensive national study of mental illness at that time. The final report, published in 1961 (Joint Commission on Mental Illness and Health, 1961), made some recommendations similar to the report offered by the Council of State Governments approximately 10 years before, including the improvement of state hospitals, the expansion of community psychiatric services, and better coordination of mental health and social services. It differed in emphasizing the need for public information on mental illness to curtail the harmful effects of stigma, the recommendation that one community mental health clinic be developed for every 50,000 people, and the suggestion that expenditures for treatment of mental illness should be doubled within 5 years and tripled within 10 years, with the federal government assuming part of the fiscal responsibility.

Deinstitutionalization also was promoted by exposés and studies of the poor conditions in state hospitals, of which Goffman's (1961) *Asylums* was just one (Rochefort, 1997). These were provided by social scientists. Articles also appeared in newspapers and popular magazines. Such publicity cast further doubt on the ability of state hospitals to effectively treat mental illness and directed attention to community-based alternatives.

The introduction of psychotropic medications in the mid-1950s facilitated deinstitutionalization as well. These medications helped to manage the symptoms of many people and offered hope that medication use could prevent some people from experiencing long-term hospitalization (Grob, 1991; Rochefort, 1997). Passage of the Community Mental Health Centers Act of 1963 further contributed to deinstitutionalization (Rochefort, 1997). This act and its 1965 amendment provided federal funds for the construction and staffing of community mental health clinics. These clinics were to provide, among other things, treatment to people leaving state hospitals.

A series of court cases beginning in the 1960s and 1970s also promoted deinstitutionalization by modifying civil commitment processes to better protect the civil rights of people with mental illness and, in doing so, reduced the number of people involuntarily hospitalized (Reisner & Slobogin, 1990). The effects of these rulings on deinstitutionalization were the release of some state hospital patients who no longer met the criteria for commitment and the reduction in new civil involuntary admissions.

A final development, which some argue was the most important influence on deinstitutionalization, was passage of federal social welfare legislation, particularly Medicaid in 1965 and Supplemental Security Income in 1972 (Brown, 1985; Levine, 1981). These two programs provided a financial incentive for states to transfer patients from state hospitals, which states solely funded, to nursing homes and boarding homes, which were paid largely with federal Medicaid and SSI payments. While the decrease in state hospital census began at the time of the introduction of psychotropic medications in the mid-1950s, it proceeded at a pace of less than 2% annually through 1965, at which time it accelerated (Rochefort, 1997). Thus, deinstitutionalization was spurred, in part, by states attempting to decrease their state budgets by transferring some of the costs of care to the federal government.

It is accepted by most people that deinstitutionalization has been a failure (Brown, 1985; Lamb, 1998; Scull, 1985). However, some say the concept is sound, but its implementation has been poor (Lamb, 1984). Deinstitutionalization initially failed, in part, because only approximately half of the projected number of needed community mental health centers was built; many of those that were operational provided minimal, if any, services to people with severe mental illness; and the care provided by state hospitals and community mental health centers was poorly coordinated (Brown, 1985). While subsequent amendments to the Community Mental Health Centers Act of 1963 and other federal actions sought to correct some of these problems, fragmentation of care and lack of access to mental health services remains a significant problem today (President's New Freedom Commission on Mental Health, 2003).

The failure of deinstitutionalization has resulted in serious consequences for people with severe mental illness. First, many people who left state hospitals experienced transinstitutionalization (Brown, 1985). That is, they moved from one institution, state hospitals, to another institution, nursing homes or boarding homes, where the rigid control over people's lives remained. Brown (1985) described many of these latter institutions as "... dangerous, unhealthy, and oppressive environments. They lack rehabilitative and therapeutic services, provide little or no follow-up by hospitals, offer few recreation facilities, are understaffed, rely on heavy drugging, and are filled with health and fire hazards" (p. 104). Other people with mental illness who left state hospitals entered what Levine (1981) described as "psychiatric ghettos" (p. 88). These were low-income communities in which high numbers of former state hospital patients lived. As examples, he stated an uptown Chicago neighborhood housed 13,000 former state hospital patients; as many as 800 lived in old hotels in Long Beach, New York; and hundreds lived along one street in Washington, D.C.

In addition, many consider deinstitutionalization to be responsible for, or to have significantly contributed to, the large number of people with mental illness who are homeless and are incarcerated in jails and prisons (Dowdall, 1996; La Fond & Durham, 1992; Lamb, 1998). While prevalence estimates vary widely, people with mental illness comprise at least one fourth of the homeless population (Rochefort, 1997). In their review of the literature, Lamb and Weinberger (1998) found that between 6% and 15% of city and county jail inmates, and between 10% and 15% of state prison inmates, have a severe mental illness. They also noted that a large percentage of people with mental illness incarcerated in jails were homeless before entering jail.

Deinstitutionalization also promoted a new wave of stigma toward people with mental illness (Brown, 1985). Fear and hostility grew in the general public as people with mental illness became more visible in the community. In particular, public fear of violence among people with mental illness increased (Link, Phelan, Bresnahan, Stueve, & Pescosolido, 1999). Stigma remains a significant problem in the United States today. The Surgeon General's recent report on mental health concluded that stigma decreases the willingness of people with mental illness to seek out services, as well as the willingness of the general public to pay for mental illness services through increased insurance premiums and taxes (U.S. DHHS, 1999). The President's New Freedom Commission on Mental Health (2003) reached similar conclusions and recommended that a national campaign be instituted to reduce stigma.

Furthermore, deinstitutionalization has not eliminated the need for state psychiatric hospitals that provide long-term care. Hunter (1999) argued that social control has become a more clearly defined responsibility of state hospitals in the era of deinstitutionalization. Today's state hospitals treat primarily those people with mental illness who continue to have severe psychiatric symptoms despite treatment in the community; who display behaviors that are unmanageable in community settings including overt sexual, violent, or self-destructive behaviors; and who have a forensic legal status, that is, who were committed to the state hospital by the criminal justice system most typically for an inpatient pretrial psychiatric evaluation, for restoration of competency to stand trial, or for care and custody following an insanity acquittal (Belcher & DeForge, 1997; Hunter, 1999; Linhorst & Turner, 1999; Scalora, 1999).

While conditions within state hospitals have improved immensely following the downsizing of most hospitals during deinstitutionalization, periodic reports of abuse continue to surface. As one example, Dowdall (1996) described allegations of ongoing abuse of patients at a state hospital in New York during the mid-1980s. These allegations included physical and sexual abuse of patients by staff, patient neglect, overcrowding, understaffing, the harassment of staff and patients by security staff, drug and alcohol trafficking on the wards, and treatment plans not being written or followed. Following an extensive investigation, 25% of the 95 allegations were supported, which resulted in loss of the hospital's certification for several years. The inappropriate use of mechanical restraints remains a problem as well. As such, the President's New Freedom Commission on Mental Health (2003) included a statement in its report that the use of restraints is inappropriate for purposes of discipline, coercion, or staff convenience. Furthermore, it stated that the use of restraints was not treatment and should be used only as a last resort as a safety intervention. In recent years, both the Joint Commission on the Accreditation of Healthcare Organizations, which accredits many private and public psychiatric hospitals, and the federal Centers for Medicare and Medicaid Services, formerly the Health Care Financing Administration, which certifies mental health organizations that receive Medicare or Medicaid funding, have instituted new regulations to better oversee and limit the use of restraints (Dougherty, 2001; Joint Commission revises standards for behavioral health care, 2000)

Implicit in the concept of deinstitutionalization was that people leaving state hospitals would be integrated into the communities to which they were discharged. This, too, has been a failure of deinstitutionalization. Bevilacqua (1995) articulated this failure. "The quality of life for persons with serious mental illness continues to be marginal and unsatisfactory. Too many consumers struggle with the demons of inadequate income, lack of meaningful and fulfilling activities, and an illness that isolates them even when they live in the community" (p. 27). Wells (2001) summarized the systemic barriers to community integration that continue to exist. These include the lack of income support and entitlements, affordable housing, and competitive and supported employment. She also found that barriers to accessing appropriate health and mental health services exist, in particular treatment for trauma related to sexual or physical abuse, use of the new antipsychotic medications, and treatment for the co-occurring disorders of mental illness and substance abuse. Accessing community services also was related to difficulty in scheduling and maintaining appointments, a lack of transportation, living in rural areas, cultural and language barriers, and a shortage of qualified mental health professionals. She cited stigma and discrimination directed toward people with severe mental illness as yet another barrier to community integration.

Finally, deinstitutionalization was to eliminate the negative effects of institutionalization. In this area, it has been only partially successful. Estroff (1981) articulated this result when concluding her ethnography of people with severe mental illness residing in the community:

> Deinstitutionalization has, for the most part, been simplistically effected through movement away from the architectural embrace of hospitals. But institutions, of course, are complex, extending beyond walls to the articulation of traditions and values at a society level. In this sense, the institutions of chronic mental illness have been little affected by the escape from institutional buildings. The roles, expectations, stereotypes, and responses that accompany being a backward patient or a long-term community outpatient have changed little. It is as if we thought what was noxious to patients was somehow present in the actual walls of hospitals. That if we got away from the buildings it would help. Clearly the architecture has had little to do with the creation of chronicity. The people who build, inhabit, and administer the buildings, and now the programs that have taken over their functions, need our careful examination. The patient, the family, culture, and treatment beliefs need our scrutiny. The setting we must investigate is not just a physical one. (pp. 253–254)

Judi Chamberlin, a person with a mental illness, also wrote of the failure of community treatment to provide a humane atmosphere. Based on her observations of the operation of a community mental health center, Chamberlin (1978) wrote:

> We also saw patients demeaned and degraded. One woman had to wait in the hall if she arrived late for the day activities program, which caused her to feel like a small child. The one room in the entire center where people could smoke and drink coffee had to be vacated by patients whenever staff wanted to use it. A poster designed by a patient to publicize the patients' rights group was torn down under circumstances indicating that it had been done by a staff member. (p. 102)

Quotes from scholars and people with severe mental illness that reflect the degree of powerlessness currently experienced by people with severe mental illness conclude this history. Among scholars, Jackson (2001) wrote:

Mental illness is widely recognized as disempowering. In fact, as a group, people with mental illness are *disempowered*. . . . For those with mental illness, conditions of daily living have been made worse by poverty, homelessness, and the debilitation of illness itself. They are often unable or feel they are unable to influence or control the social, economic, and political forces that directly affect their lives. (p. 65)

Rapp (1998) believed:

People with severe mental illness continue to be oppressed by the society in which they live and reinforced by the practices of the professionals responsible for helping them. This is rarely done intentionally or with malevolence but, rather, is provoked by compassion and caring. Because the oppression is dressed up in the clothes of compassion, it is difficult to identify, to understand its underlying dynamics, and to develop alternative approaches. (pp. 1–2)

Warner (2000, p. 37) stated: "The mentally ill are some of the least powerful people in society, confronting the restrictions of poverty, unemployment, stigma, discrimination, social exclusion, jail incarceration, hospital admission . . . and even outpatient treatment."

A final quote from Chamberlin (1978), who has a mental illness and has received treatment in hospitals and in the community, helps to link the history of powerlessness of people with severe mental illness to present-day interactions with people with mental illness. She wrote:

Many ex-patients are angry, and our anger stems from the neglect, indifference, dehumanization, and outright brutality we have seen and experienced at the hands of the mental health system. Our distrust of professionals is not irrational hostility, but is the direct result of their treatment of us in the past. We have been belittled, ignored, lied to. We have no reason to trust professionals, and many reasons to fear them. (p. xiv)

3

Individual Rights, Coercion, and Empowerment

Beginning in the 1960s, federal and state case law and statutes sought to protect the rights of people with mental illness, as well as to promote their integration into the community. This occurred, in part, in response to increased recognition of the mistreatment experienced by people with mental illness confined in public psychiatric hospitals. These actions also had their roots in the civil rights movements of the 1960s and 1970s, which sought to increase citizen rights among oppressed populations, particularly racial minorities and women (La Fond & Durham, 1992). Within the past two decades, however, the failure of these governmental actions to fully achieve their intentions increasingly has been recognized (Appelbaum, 1994). Much of the coercion of people with mental illness has continued, and new forms of coercion have emerged (La Fond & Durham, 1992).

This chapter provides an overview of the major case law and statutes that seek to protect the rights of people with severe mental illness and to promote their community integration. It also defines coercion and discusses types of legal and informal coercion of people with mental illness that exist today. It next presents views on coercion held by people with mental illness, their family members, mental health professionals, and the general public, which illustrate the diversity of opinions on coercion. Finally, it discusses the complex relationships between individual rights, coercion, and empowerment, an understanding of which is necessary to identify limitations to empowerment and to create opportunities for empowerment.

RIGHTS OF PEOPLE WITH MENTAL ILLNESS

In the 1960s and 1970s, statutes and case law focused primarily on establishing basic rights concerning civil involuntary commitment and accessing mental health services for people with mental illness. Since the 1980s, the focus of these statutes and case laws has been on securing rights that promote community integration (Petrila & Levin, 1996). These latter rights extend beyond narrow mental health issues to include accessing housing, employment, public and private facilities, and other aspects of community living. Petrila and Levin (1996) summarized the future direction of rights-oriented laws affecting people with mental illness:

> In the future the law will continue to influence the direction and shape of mental health services. Much of the concern will be with the implementation of the ADA [Americans with Disabilities Act] and FHAA [Fair Housing Amendments Act] because these statutes create the framework for gaining access to the social supports and community services that are often inaccessible to people with mental disability. (p. 59)

The following sections present overviews of the major areas in which federal and state statutes and case law have sought to increase the rights of people with mental illness.

Changes to Involuntary Civil Commitments

States historically have involuntarily committed people to psychiatric hospitals under two legal models (Weiner & Wettstein, 1993). One is parens patriae, which allows the state to protect those who cannot care for themselves. Under this model, states can involuntarily hospitalize people with mental illness when they are incapable of taking care of themselves or unwilling or unable to seek needed treatment. States also have committed people under a police power model. This model supports state intervention to protect the general welfare and public safety of its citizens. Under this model, states can involuntarily hospitalize people with mental illness when they are believed to be dangerous. States have used two approaches to reaching commitment decisions (Petrila & Levin, 1996). Under one, commitment is primarily a medical decision; under the other, commitment is primarily a legal decision.

In recent years, the United States has moved from more of a medically oriented parens patriae approach toward a legally oriented police power approach. This is reflected in the adoption of a dangerousness standard for commitment and of a commitment process similar to the legal due process found in criminal courts (Petrila & Levin, 1996; Weiner & Wettstein, 1993). The standard of dangerousness was set by the U.S. Supreme Court in *O'Connor v. Donaldson* (1975). In that decision, the court unanimously ruled that the state cannot involuntarily confine a nondangerous individual. In order to involuntary hospitalize people with mental illness today, the state must demonstrate that the individual has a mental illness and is dangerous as a result of that mental illness. States vary on definitions of dangerousness, but the definitions typically include dangerousness to self or to others. More recently, some states have added the inability to care for oneself, also referred to as grave disability, when that condition, if untreated, can lead to dangerousness.

In *Lessard v. Schmidt* (1972), a federal district court ruled that individuals undergoing civil commitment were entitled to due process procedural rights similar to those found in the criminal justice system because of the deprivation of liberty that results from involuntary hospitalization. Procedural rights now legislated by most states are a hearing before a judge, notice of the time and place of the hearing, presence at the trial, representation by an attorney, examination of witnesses, trial by jury if requested, and an independent psychiatric examination (Petrila & Levin, 1996; Weiner & Wettstein, 1993). At civil commitment hearings, the role of the attorney for the state is to demonstrate by at least clear and convincing evidence, as required in *Addington v. Texas* (1979), that the individual has a mental illness and meets the standard of dangerousness established in state statute. Another important right is periodic review of the commitment status. According to Weiner and Wettstein (1993), all states have provisions for an initial emergency commitment, after which a hearing must be held within a short amount of time. This time frame varies from 24 hours to 20 days, with from 3 to 5 days being the most common. If civilly committed, most states limit the duration of commitment to a specific period of time, typically 6 months, after which the person must be released or a new hearing held to consider if the person meets the criteria for continued commitment. The intent of these changes to involuntary civil commitment was to minimize the risk of arbitrariness, abuse, and inappropriate commitments that previously existed (La Fond & Durham, 1992).

Right to Least Restrictive Environment

It is now widely accepted, and reflected in the statutes of many states, that people with mental illness have the right to be treated in the least restrictive alternative setting (Parry & Gilliam, 2002). This concept was first applied to people with mental illness in *Lake v. Cameron* (1966), in which the court ruled that less restrictive alternatives must be considered before someone could be involuntarily hospitalized. Less restrictive alternatives apply to a range of settings, such as hospitals (e.g., maximum security vs. minimum security hospitals), locations within hospitals (e.g., locked wards vs. open wards), hospitals instead of congregate community settings, and congregate community settings instead of independent living in the community.

Rights of Hospitalized Persons

Until recent years, people with mental illness had few, if any, rights when they entered a psychiatric hospital (Weiner & Wettstein, 1993). *Wyatt v. Stickney* (1971, 1972a, 1972b) changed that, setting minimum standards for hospitals that accept people committed involuntarily. These standards are now reflected in the statutes of all states (Weiner & Wettstein, 1993). Weiner and Wettstein (1993) summarized the common rights that are available in most states. These include sending and receiving mail, receiving visitors, making telephone calls, having access to an attorney, being presumed to be competent to make decisions unless a judge has ruled otherwise, receiving humane care and treatment, accessing reasonable amounts of money, refusing to participate in research, possessing some personal items, being able to vote in public elections, practicing one's religious faith, and having one's case periodically reviewed to determine the appropriateness of transfer to a less restrictive alternative or of discharge to the community.

Also, employment among people hospitalized is now regulated to prevent the exploitation of their labor that historically had occurred. *Souder v. Brennan* (1973) required that the minimum wage and overtime compensation provisions of the Fair Labor Standards Act be applied to those hospitalized. This act still allows people who are hospitalized to work if they receive at least minimum wage. For some jobs, such as those found in sheltered workshops within state hospitals, the act permits hospitalized people to be paid a wage commensurate with their productivity as compared to a nondisabled worker, even if the hourly rate is less than minimum wage. There are minor exceptions to this act, such as allowing residents to maintain their own living space without being financially compensated.

It is important to note that at least some of these rights can be abridged under certain circumstances. For instance, residents' mail may be checked if they send letters that contain threatening content. Some states, such as Missouri, also have eliminated selected rights of people committed to hospitalization by the criminal courts as not guilty by reason of insanity.

Right to Hospital and Community Treatment

The majority of states now recognize that people with mental illness who are hospitalized have a right to treatment (Weiner & Wettstein, 1993). Court cases in the 1960s and 1970s promoted this right initially for those who were involuntarily committed (*Donaldson v. O'Connor*, 1974; *Rouse v. Cameron*, 1966; *Wyatt v. Stickney*, 1971, 1972a, 1972b), largely as a result of the poor conditions that existed in state psychiatric hospitals (La Fond & Durham, 1992). The U.S. Court of Appeals most clearly articulated the rationale in *Donaldson v. O'Connor* (1974). The court ruled that if the state assumed a parens patriae rationale for commitment, then it followed that the state should provide needed treatment. The court also indicated that treatment was a fair exchange for the loss of liberty that occurred with the involuntary commitment (Weiner & Wettstein, 1993).

The right to treatment in the community is much less certain. Far fewer states statutorily indicate that community treatment is a right (Weiner & Wettstein, 1993). In addition, the U.S. Supreme Court has never indicated such a constitutional right exists (Parry & Gilliam, 2002). One move toward the federal statutory right to community treatment was reflected in *Olmstead v. L.C., by Zimring* (1999). The court ruled that people with mental illness residing in a state hospital have a limited right to community services under Title II of the Americans with Disabilities Act, if both the person hospitalized and state mental health professionals supported the community placement, and if the community placement was reasonable given the state's resources when considering the needs of all people it served (Parry & Gilliam, 2002). The federal government has called upon states to develop plans that meet the community service mandate of *Olmstead* (Meinert & de Loyola, 2002; Parry & Gilliam, 2002). To date, no national studies have been published that evaluate outcomes for people with mental illness resulting from *Olmstead*, such as increased access to housing and community mental health services. One recent national study, however, did examine *Olmstead's* implementation 5 years after the decision (Rosenbaum & Teitelbaun, 2004). The study found that *Olmstead* directly led to incremental policy changes at the federal level and in some states. "State and federal policy makers have made efforts to design new programs, new methods of service delivery, and innovative approaches to administering existing programs in order to achieve greater levels of community integration" (p. 16). On the negative side, the authors reported that only 29 states have submitted the required comprehensive plans, and budget problems continue to hamper many states from increasing services. They also found that services essential to achieving *Olmstead*-directed community integration, particularly housing, transportation, education, and employment, remained seriously underdeveloped and underfunded. They concluded, "Without question, a long road lies ahead" (p. 26).

Informed Consent and the Right to Refuse Treatment

Since the beginning of the 1900s, U.S. courts have found that people have a right to give informed consent before receiving medical treatment, including the right to refuse treatment (Petrila & Levin, 1996;

Weiner & Wettstein, 1993). This right has been applied to people with mental illness only since the late 1970s, however, and has been supported by numerous judicial decisions (Weiner & Wettstein, 1993). Informed consent requires that decisions be made voluntarily by a competent person who has knowledge of the risks and benefits of the treatment, the risks associated with refusal, and alternative treatments (Weiner & Wettstein, 1993). It was assumed historically that mental illness automatically rendered people incompetent to make such decisions, particularly among those committed involuntarily to a state hospital. A major change associated with the application of informed consent to people with mental illness was the recognition that they, indeed, were capable of making informed choices about their psychiatric treatment, despite their mental illness, and should be assumed to be competent even if civilly committed (Petrila & Levin, 1996).

A corollary to informed consent is the right to refuse treatment, most typically associated with refusal of psychotropic medications, which is now law throughout the United States (Petrila & Levin, 1996). The right to refuse psychiatric treatment can be denied, however, in at least two instances (Petrila & Levin, 1996; Weiner & Wettstein, 1993). First, persons deemed incompetent can be medicated against their will on an emergency basis if they would be immediately dangerous without the medication, although definitions vary on what constitutes an emergency. Second, the right to refuse medication can be denied to those persons found to be incompetent to make clinical decisions. The rendering of competency decisions and approval of forced medication typically is made by judges. Administrative reviews may be acceptable in selected instances. The power of states to force medication is predicated on the legal models of parens patriae and police power (Kapp, 1996).

Right to Community Integration

The federal government has enacted at least three major pieces of legislation in recent years to facilitate the community integration of people with disabilities, including those with severe mental illness, by prohibiting discrimination against people with mental illness in most areas of community life (Rothman, 2003). The first law, the Rehabilitation Act of 1973, prohibits discrimination based on disability by entities receiving federal funds. Next, the Fair Housing Amendments Act of 1988 prohibits discrimination based on disability in public and private housing. Finally, the Americans with Disabilities Act of 1990 addresses discrimination on the basis of disability in the areas of employment (Title I), access to transportation and public facilities (Title II), access to a wide range of private facilities and services (Title III), and access to telephones and television for people with speech and hearing difficulties (Title IV). Rothman (2003) argued that the Americans with

Disabilities Act is the most comprehensive piece of legislation supporting people with disabilities and is significant for developing enforceable standards and clarifying the role of the federal government in enforcement. Together with the aforementioned rights associated with psychiatric services, these three laws provide a legal basis to support the meaningful participation of people with mental illness in life's everyday activities. Table 3.1 summarizes the major case law and statutes promoting the rights of people with mental illness just discussed.

Table 3.1 Major Case Law and Statutes Promoting the Rights of People With Mental Illness

Lake v. Cameron (1966)—Ruled that less restrictive alternatives must be considered before someone can be involuntarily hospitalized.

Rouse v. Cameron (1966)—Ruled that people with mental illness who are involuntarily hospitalized have a right to treatment.

Wyatt v. Stickney (1971, 1972a, 1972b)—Set minimum standards for hospitals that accept people committed involuntarily and outlined basic rights for people committed to hospitals.

Lessard v. Schmidt (1972)—Ruled that individuals undergoing civil commitment are entitled to due process procedural rights similar to those found in the criminal justice system.

Souder v. Brennan (1973)—Required that the minimum wage and overtime compensation provisions of the Fair Labor Standards Act apply to work performed by people who are hospitalized.

Rehabilitation Act of 1973—Prohibited discrimination based on disability, including mental illness, by entities receiving federal funds.

Donaldson v. O'Connor (1974)—Ruled that people with mental illness who are involuntarily hospitalized have a constitutional right to treatment.

O'Connor v. Donaldson (1975)—Set the standard of dangerousness for civil commitment and found that states no longer can involuntarily confine a nondangerous individual.

Addington v. Texas (1979)—Set the standard of evidence for civil commitment as clear and convincing evidence that the individual has a mental illness and is dangerous.

State statutes, beginning in late 1970s—Stated that people with mental illness have a right to give informed consent before receiving treatment and to refuse treatment.

Fair Housing Amendments Act of 1988—Prohibited discrimination based on disability, including mental illness, in public and private housing.

Americans with Disabilities Act of 1990—Addressed discrimination on the basis of disability, including mental illness, in the areas of employment, access to transportation and public facilities, and access to a wide range of private facilities and services.

Olmstead v. L.C., by Zimring (1999)—Ruled that people with mental illness residing in state hospitals have a limited right to community services under the Americans with Disabilities Act.

Enforcement of Rights

A wide range of mechanisms exist at the federal, state, and local levels to enforce the rights of people with mental illness and others covered by federal, state, and local statutes and case law. For example, offices of civil rights exist within some federal departments, such as the U.S. Department of Education and the U.S. Department of Health and Human Services. Also, when the U.S. Department of Health and Human Services' Centers for Medicare and Medicaid Services certify programs that receive Medicare or Medicaid funding, they evaluate program adherence to selected rights. In addition, important federal legislation, such as the Rehabilitation Act, the Fair Housing Amendments Act, and the Americans with Disabilities Act include enforcement provisions, some of which are enforced by federal agencies. State and local governments, too, have mechanisms for protections of rights established in their statutes.

Enforcement comes from nongovernmental sources as well. One such mechanism is the national system of Protection and Advocacy agencies, which are federally funded, nonprofit agencies operated independently in each state (Meinert & de Loyola, 2002; National Association of Protection and Advocacy Systems, n.d.). Their general purpose is to protect the rights of people with disabilities. Created through the Developmental Disabilities Assistance Bill of Rights of 1975, Protection and Advocacy was expanded to people with mental illness residing in inpatient facilities in 1986, and to those living in the community in 2000 following the *Olmstead* (1999) decision. These agencies are authorized to investigate abuse, neglect, or rights violations; to bring lawsuits on behalf of people with mental illness to protect their rights; and to advocate on their behalf. As independent agencies, their specific focus within this general mandate varies from state to state. Private organizations that accredit services frequently used by people with mental illness also include standards that seek to protect participants' rights. Three of the main accrediting bodies include the Joint Commission on the Accreditation of Healthcare Organizations (n.d.), the Commission on Accreditation of Rehabilitation Facilities (n.d.), and the National Committee for Quality Assurance (n.d.). Finally, individuals who believe their rights have been violated can hire private attorneys to file lawsuits on their behalf. However, legislation often requires that individuals have exhausted all their administrative remedies before filing such suits.

COERCION OF PEOPLE WITH MENTAL ILLNESS

Most people typically associate empowerment with the ability to control one's life, or, stated another way, to be free of coercion. Solomon

(1996) defined coercion as the use of power to get people to do something they ordinarily would not do. She stated that power can involve the use of force or threats of force; manipulation that can involve the use of dishonesty, deception, and misusing the relationship; and persuasion typically in the form of some inducement. Solomon also stated that the use of power is not always coercive. The work of Monahan et al. (1999) on the relationship between pressure and coercion in psychiatric hospital admissions helps to explain Solomon's statement about the relationship between power and coercion. Monahan et al. distinguished between positive and negative pressures. Positive pressures included persuasion and inducements that sought to demonstrate to people with mental illness that they would be better off if they made a particular decision. Negative pressure included threats and force that would result in people with mental illness perceiving that they would be worse off if they would not make a particular decision. Monahan et al. found that when negative pressures only were used to get people with mental illness admitted to psychiatric hospitals, almost all people reported feeling a high level of coercion in the admission decision. In contrast, only a small percentage of people reported feeling a high level of coercion when positive pressures only were used. Thus, not all types of power (or pressure) are experienced as coercion.

One of the recent advances in the study of coercion has been the reexamination of the relationship between legal status and coercion, particularly as it relates to participation in psychiatric treatment. It previously was assumed that coercion was found among people who were involuntary committed for psychiatric treatment but not found among people who entered psychiatric hospitals under a voluntary legal status. There is now considerable evidence, however, that some people who are legally mandated to enter psychiatric hospitals through involuntary civil committed do not feel coerced when they entered the hospital, while some people who enter the hospital under a voluntary legal status feel that their hospitalization was coerced (McKenna, Simpson, & Coverdale, 2003; Monahan et al., 1999). Monahan et al. (1999), for instance, reported that 34% of a sample of people who voluntarily entered a psychiatric hospital did not believe they had a mental illness, 49% indicated someone else had initiated their coming to the hospital, and 10% perceived a high level of coercion in the admission. Among those involuntarily committed, 22% reported it was their idea to seek admission, and 35% did not feel the admission was coerced. Monahan et al. summarized the relationship between legal status and coercion. ''Legal status is only a blunt index of whether a patient experienced coercion in being admitted to a mental hospital. A significant minority of legally 'voluntary' patients experience coercion, and a significant minority of legally 'involuntary' patients believe that they freely chose to be hospitalized" (p. 26). The following sections first describe the major forms of sanctioned legal coercion that can emanate from the civil and criminal justice systems and then examine informal coercion of people with mental illness.

Civil Commitment to Hospitalization

Despite changes to the civil commitment process over the past several decades, civil commitments continue to constitute a sizeable percentage of all admissions for inpatient psychiatric treatment. The number of involuntary commitments in 1986, the most recent year for which national findings could be located, illustrates the extent of its use (Monahan et al., 1999). During that year, 424,450 of the 1.7 million admissions to inpatient psychiatric care were involuntary commitments. Just under half of all involuntary admissions occurred in state and county psychiatric hospitals, and, overall, involuntary commitments constituted 62% of admissions to these public hospitals. Although national data could not be located, the experience from one state suggests that most civil commitments to hospitalization are for a short duration. Missouri statute requires that civil commitment hearings before a probate court judge occur within 96 hours after admission, and that rehearings occur at 21 days, 90 days, and 1 year if the state believes individuals continue to meet civil commitment criteria. According to unpublished data from Missouri, 10,312 civil commitments occurred between July 1, 2001 and June 30, 2002. Of that number, 83.5% occurred at 96 hours, 14.0% at 21 days, 2.2% at 90 days, and 0.3% at 1 year.

Many have criticized the implementation of the revised civil commitment statutes for not being consistent across jurisdictions and failing to adhere to required standards and processes (Appelbaum, 1994; Holstein, 1993; Rubin, Snapp, Panzano, & Taynor, 1996; Winick, 2001). Turkheimer and Parry (1992) summarized findings on the ineffective implementation of civil commitment by attorneys, judges, and clinicians. They found, for example, that attorneys representing people with mental illness often did not fully understand or have experience with the commitment process. They frequently were poorly prepared for court, and their questioning of witnesses often was general and ineffective, if questioning occurred at all. They reported that when attorneys assumed an informed and active role in the process, the number of civil commitments significantly decreased. Turkheimer and Parry also observed that judges faired no better in their implementation efforts. They often discouraged attorneys from actively participating. They often managed the proceeding informally, and in doing so, failed to comply with all procedural safeguards in notifying those people being committed of their rights. They often failed to consider less restrictive alternatives. Moreover, they often uncritically accepted the recommendations from mental health clinicians. Turkheimer and Parry reported that clinicians' opinions carried great weight in the outcome of hearings. However, clinicians did not always interview participants before the hearing and often considered nonlegal factors in their decisions. In their own studies, Turkheimer and Parry found that these failures occurred even more frequently in recommitment hearings. Turkheimer and Parry argued that poor implementation, and what may be the over commitment of people with mental illness, stemmed from perceptions on the part of attorneys, judges, and clinicians that the community mental health system was inadequate, and thus forced hospitalization periodically was required for at least some people with mental illness to access treatment.

Finally, Nicholson (1999) reviewed studies that examined the treatment outcomes associated with involuntary psychiatric hospitalization and concluded that outcomes of people who are involuntarily committed are similar to those people who voluntarily enter treatment. He cautioned, however, that most studies had methodological problems, considered outcomes at the end of the hospitalization or shortly thereafter, and used a limited number of types of outcomes. He found that little evidence on the long-term effects of involuntary commitment exists.

Civil Commitment Into the Community

Civil coercion also can occur in the community. One type is conditional release, in which individuals are discharged from a psychiatric hospital on a provisional basis provided they adhere to selected conditions of release (Elbogen & Tomkins, 2000). They remain under the supervision of the hospital for the duration of the civil commitment, and the hospital has the authority to rehospitalize them should they violate their conditional release or deteriorate psychiatrically. A second type of community commitment applies to those people who meet the criteria for civil involuntary commitment, but the community, not the hospital, is the less restrictive alternative (Petrila, Ridgely, & Borum, 2003). A third type of community commitment applies to those who do not meet requirements for civil involuntary commitment for hospitalization, yet they meet lesser criteria for community commitment (Gerbasi, Bonnie, & Binder, 2000). This latter type exists in the fewest states and is far more controversial than the other types of community commitment and to civil commitment to hospitals (Miller, 1999; Munetz, Galon, & Frese, 2003). Torrey and Kaplan (1995) referred to the second and third types as outpatient civil commitment because in both cases the initial commitment was into the community, in contrast to conditional release where the commitment began in the hospital and the releasing hospital retains jurisdiction under the original civil commitment order. In 1994, Torrey and Kaplan identified 35 states and the District of Columbia that offered outpatient civil commitment, with 3 states having criteria for community commitment that were different from involuntary hospitalization criteria.

Individuals have made passionate arguments for and against outpatient civil commitment (Allen & Smith, 2001; Hoge & Grottole, 2000; Schopp, 2003; Torrey & Zdanowicz, 2001). Hiday (2003) summarized those arguments. The primary argument currently against outpatient commitment is that it unjustifiably and unnecessarily extends the social control function of the mental health system. This is particularly the case when outpatient commitment is used for preventive detention in those few states that have commitment criteria based on standards less stringent than civil commitment to hospitalization. Those supporting outpatient commitment argue that it should be limited to individuals who do not comply with treatment in the community and frequently are hospitalized for brief periods. They assert that commitment of these individuals is humane, is less costly, and is a less restrictive alternative to involuntary hospitalization or incarceration in a jail or prison.

Aside from these largely normative arguments, considerable problems exist in implementing outpatient civil commitment. Torrey and Kaplan's (1995) survey of the 35 states and the District of Columbia that permitted outpatient commitment in 1994 found outpatient commitment use was common or very common in only one third of the states, while 21 states indicated use was rare or very rare. Even among states that used outpatient commitment, it was used inconsistently within regions of those states. Implementation problems identified by states included the lack of enforcement mechanisms, civil liberty concerns among those who potentially could refer individuals, the fiscal costs of service provision and monitoring, commitment criteria being too restrictive, and lack of information within the states about its availability.

Consistent with civil commitment to hospitalization, research generally has found positive outcomes associated with outpatient civil commitment. Hiday (2003) summarized the findings from studies of outpatient commitment and then from the recent Duke Mental Health Study, the most methodologically sound study of outpatient commitment completed to date:

Earlier studies found reduced rehospitalization, improved compliance, higher retention in voluntary outpatient treatment, and better adjustment in the community for persons under outpatient commitment relative to persons ordered to involuntary hospitalization, to persons voluntarily hospitalized, or to themselves prior to the mandatory community treatment. . . . The Duke study found reduced hospitalization, violence, arrests, and victimization relative to persons given equivalent mental health services. However, it must be emphasized that the Duke Mental Health Study found the effects of outpatient commitment manifested themselves only in conjunction with services; a court order by itself did not make the difference. (p. 22)

The final point made in this quote deserves repeating. In the absence of access to a range of needed mental health services, outpatient civil commitment, in and of itself, is unlikely to produce positive outcomes for people with mental illness or society.

Guardianship

A third means of civil coercion occurs when civil courts declare people incompetent to manage some or all aspects of their lives and appoint a substitute decision maker for them. In doing so, the state is exercising its parens patriae powers to protect those unable to care for themselves (Weiner & Wettstein, 1993). Most states use the term guardian for all decisional areas with the exception of the conservator who represents financial interests. Some states, though, use the term conservator in place of guardian for all decision types. The criteria and processes for determining incompetency vary somewhat across states. Generally, however, there must be a physical or mental condition that results in the loss of ability to make decisions or to function (Parry & Gilliam, 2002). Once declared incompetent, people lose their right to manage their finances, to enter into contracts, make personal decisions, make treatment decisions, serve on a jury, appear as a witness, vote, and marry (Weiner & Wettstein, 1993). Once a person is declared incompetent, the civil court typically assigns a guardian to manage the affairs of that individual. Courts may appoint one or more guardians. A guardian may be an individual or an organization. Guardians often are family members or public administrators. Most states allow limited guardianship, in which people still can make decisions in all areas, except for those for which they are declared incompetent. Courts rarely exercise this alternative, however (Weiner & Wettstein, 1993).

Little information on the use of guardianship with people with mental illness or the outcomes that result from its use exists. Most reports are anecdotal or are studies that used weak methodological designs. Among the few published studies, Lamb and Weinberger (1993) reported that conservatorships (i.e., guardianships) are commonly used in California with people with severe mental illness and are useful in facilitating both inpatient and community psychiatric services. Geller et al. (1997) stated that the use of guardianships in Massachusetts to promote community treatment resulted in positive outcomes related to decreased days hospitalized and number of admissions. Finally, Isaac and Armat (1990) described the use of limited guardianships in one Wisconsin county for the sole purpose of managing psychiatric treatment. In that county, in the late 1980s, people with mental illness constituted the largest percentage of guardianships in that court, even more so than people with mental retardation or the elderly, and 25% of the people with mental illness residing in that community were under some type of court-facilitated treatment mandate.

Probation and Parole

Probation and parole is a system of monitoring people in the community who have been convicted of a crime and are under the jurisdiction of the criminal justice system (Draine & Solomon, 2001). In order to live in the community, individuals must agree to adhere to conditions of release set by either the court or a probation or parole board. Typical conditions include reporting to the probation or parole officer, attending some type of structured day activity such as working or going to school, living at a particular address, and abstaining from use of illegal drugs. Additional conditions unique to the individual, such as compliance with mandated psychiatric treatment, can be added. Individuals typically are assigned to probation and parole officers who are responsible for monitoring compliance with those conditions. A number of implementation issues can arise when probationers or parolees are mandated to participate in psychiatric treatment. Draine and Solomon (2001) found that most people on probation or parole did not question the authority of the criminal justice system to incarcerate them if they did not comply with required treatment. They found, however, that some people on probation or parole were uncertain of the nature of the collaboration between parties in the mental health and criminal justice systems, which led to their mistrust of both parties. Implementation issues reported by the Group for the Advancement of Psychiatry (1994) included inappropriate mandates for psychiatric treatment, probation and parole officers having caseloads that were too large to provide proper supervision of compliance with mandated treatment, and mental health professionals not cooperating with probation or parole officers and sometimes even withholding relevant information. There also is some evidence that collaboration between criminal justice and mental health professionals increases the amount of threats of reincarceration made by probation or parole for noncompliance with treatment and the use of incarceration for violations of treatment requirements (Draine & Solomon, 2001; Solomon, Draine, & Marcus, 2002). This occurs because mental health professions often increase the monitoring of those on probation or parole beyond what the probation or parole officer could do. Finally, there is some evidence that participation in psychiatric treatment reduces the risk of reincarcerations for violations of the probation or parole conditions (Solomon et al., 2002).

Criminal Justice Diversion Programs and Mental Health Courts

A second category of criminal justice coercion includes programs that seek to reduce the amount of time people with mental illness are incarcerated in jails and prisons, or to divert people with mental illness from the criminal justice system into the mental health system (Lamb, Weinberger, & Gross, 1999). Diversion programs can target people at the prebooking stage, prearraignment stage, or postarraignment stage of the criminal justice process, or at a combination of these stages (Steadman, Morris, & Dennis, 1995). Diversion programs typically work with people who have been charged with misdemeanors and lower level felonies. One recent program innovation to divert people out of the criminal justice system, or to reduce or eliminate incarceration, are mental health courts, which developed during the late 1990s (Watson, Luchins, Hanrahan, Heyrman, & Lurigio, 2000). A standard definition of mental health courts does not yet exist. Typically, though, they consist of a specific court docket designated for people with mental illness; recommendations for mental health treatment, a supervision plan, and a party responsible for oversight; and court monitoring with possible sanctions for noncompliance, such as reinstating charges or sentences (Steadman, Davidson, & Brown, 2001). People who enter mental health court programs may receive reduced sentences, or have their criminal charges dropped, after successfully completing the mental health court program (Griffin, Steadman, & Petrila, 2002). While courts maintain the authority to incarcerate participants who do not comply, its actual use to date has been rare (Griffin et al., 2002).

A study of four of the first mental health courts identified implementation issues (Goldkamp & Irons-Guynn, 2000). These included distinguishing defendants appropriate for these courts early in the process, determining whether participation should be voluntary, contending with the conflict that sometimes arose between the goals of the criminal justice and mental health systems, and defining what constitutes program success. Silberberg, Vital, and Brakel (2001) identified other issues in implementing community-based mandatory treatment programs for people with mental illness under criminal commitments, including judges' lack of knowledge about recent innovations in the treatment of mental illness, the lack of training among mental health professions on working with those mandated to participate in treatment, the unavailability of mental health services, and poor collaboration between the mental health and criminal justice systems. Early outcome studies of mental health courts have found some support that they can facilitate greater access to mental health services and decrease reincarceration (Boothroyd, Poythress, McGaha, & Petrila, 2003; Trupin & Richards, 2003). Other types of diversion programs also have reported success. Lamb, Weinberger, and Reston-Parham (1996), for instance, found that a mental health consultation program to misdemeanor courts reduced rehospitalizations, rearrests, acts of physical violence, and incidents of homelessness among people with mental illness who participated in the program.

Conditional Release of People Found NGRI

Another scenario under which people with mental illness may experience coercion is the conditional release of people found not guilty by reason of insanity (NGRI). People found NGRI were charged with criminal offenses and subsequently acquitted of those charges by a criminal court because of the presence of a mental illness at the time of the commission of the crime that rendered them not responsible for that crime. Inaccurate public perceptions persist that the insanity defense is misused and overused by defendants to avoid prosecution, and, that once acquitted, they pose a public safety risk if released into the community (Silver, Circincione, & Steadman, 1994). Contrary to public opinion, the insanity defense is rarely used or successful. Defendants plead the insanity defense in less than 1% of felony cases and are successfully acquitted as NGRI in only one fourth of that 1% (Steadman et al., 1993). In addition, in many instances, people found NGRI are likely to be hospitalized as long as, or longer, than they would have been if convicted and incarcerated in jail or prison (Silver, 1995; Linhorst, 1999). In most states, public safety considerations dominate the commitment and release process (La Fond & Durham, 1992). Although states vary in their practices, once found NGRI, these individuals typically are automatically committed to a psychiatric hospital, are subjected to hospital release criteria that are much more stringent than civil commitment criteria, and are committed to the jurisdiction of the mental health and criminal justice systems either indefinitely or until the length of time they would have been incarcerated had they been convicted, unless they meet stringent criteria for unconditional release from supervision (Brakel, 1988; Linhorst, 1999).

Conditional release from hospitalization of people found NGRI is used by many states to attempt to balance the concern for public safety with the treatment needs and rights of people found NGRI (Bloom & Williams, 1994; Morris, 1997). Like conditional release of people who are committed involuntarily to hospitalization, people found NGRI are released if they comply with certain conditions, and they can be rehospitalized if they violate those conditions. While hospital personnel or civil courts typically issue conditional releases of people civilly committed, states vary in the party granting the conditional release for people found NGRI. Release authorities can include civil courts; the original criminal court that granted the insanity acquittal; an independent, nonjudicial board similar to a parole board; or a combination of the three (Griffin, Steadman, & Heilbrun, 1991; Morris, 1997). Like the length of time hospitalized, length of time on conditional release can be limited or indefinite. Most states have provisions to monitor people while on conditional release in the community, and to revoke conditional releases if they violate conditions under criteria that are generally less stringent than revocation of probation or parole (Callahan & Silver, 1998a; Griffin et al., 1991). That is, it is easier to revoke the conditional release of a person found NGRI than to revoke someone on probation or parole. Moreover, states use their authority to revoke conditional releases. While time frames for studies varied, Callahan and Silver (1998b) found that roughly one third of persons conditionally released are eventually revoked. Attributable at least in part to restrictive conditional release criteria, community monitoring, and use of revocation, people found NGRI tend to have low arrest rates while on conditional release. Wiederanders, Bromley, and Choate (1997), for example, found that annualized rearrest rates of people found NGRI on conditional release ranged from 3.4% to 7.8% in the three states studied. As one point of comparison, one national study of almost 300,000 inmates released from state prisons in 1994 found that 44% were rearrested within their first year in the community (Langan & Levin, 2002).

Informal Coercion

Everett (2001) wrote that it is "magical thinking" (p. 10) to assume that coercion of people with mental illness occurs only through formal, legal means. She stated that coercion is much more complex and can occur through both "overt" and "covert" (p. 11) means. In addition to the major legal means of coercion just discussed, Solomon (1996) argued that coercion can occur informally, most typically from residential facilities, treatment providers, and family members. Examples of informal coercion that can result from these and other sources include threatening involuntary hospitalization, denying services, ignoring the expressed desires of a person with mental illness, restricting access to friends or visitors, denying financial resources, and threatening loss of housing, to name a few (Everett, 2001; Miller, 1999; Solomon, 1996). Subsequent chapters discuss the use of informal coercion as it applies to specific topic areas. Table 3.2 lists the major types of formal and informal coercion that people with mental illness may experience.

VIEWPOINTS ON LEGAL COERCION

One's viewpoints on legal coercion are a component of an empowerment (or disempowerment) ideology, which ultimately will affect interactions between those with power and people with mental illness. Differences of opinions on the use of coercion are likely to occur, both between groups of people and within groups, as people seek to balance individual rights with the perceived need for coercion, either for paternalistic reasons under a parens patriae model or to protect public safety under the police power model. The viewpoints of legal coercion are considered among four parties, including people with severe mental

Table 3.2 Types of Coercion

Coercion Through Civil Courts
- Civil commitment to hospitalization
- Outpatient civil commitment
- Guardianship

Coercion Through Criminal Courts
- Probation and parole
- Criminal justice diversion programs
- Mental health courts
- Conditional release of people found not guilty by reason of insanity

Informal Coercion (selected examples)
- Threatening involuntary hospitalization unless the individual complies with a demand
- Denying services unless the individual complies with a demand
- Ignoring the expressed desires of a person with mental illness
- Restricting access to friends or visitors
- Denying financial resources unless the individual complies with a demand
- Threatening loss of housing unless the individual complies with a demand

illness, families of people with mental illness, mental health professionals, and the general public.

Viewpoints Among People With Mental Illness

One of the innovations in research in recent years has been solicitation
of viewpoints of people with mental illness on the use of coercion. In
general, this research has found that a segment of people with mental
illness strongly opposes any form of coerced treatment, while others
assume a more positive view of it. Frese (1997) wrote that he himself
has greatly benefited from forced treatment, although he states he can
understand why some people with mental illness are so adamantly
opposed to any form of mandatory treatment, given the history of
misuse of psychiatric treatments and the potential of some treatments
to have major side effects. Lucksted and Coursey (1995) solicited the
opinions of people with mental illness about their experiences with
coerced treatments. Thirty percent indicated they had been pressured
or forced to take medications in the past year, 26% to attend rehabilitation or therapy in the past year, and 57% to enter a psychiatric
hospital in their lifetime. Lucksted and Coursey also found that approximately 40% of respondents wanted to be pressured or forced into
treatment if they refused, approximately 25% wanted to be pressured
or forced only in certain instances, and approximately 20% said they
never wanted to be pressured or forced into treatments. One study of
outpatient civil commitment found that at one extreme, approximately
30% of participants reported little or no negative pressures, exclusion
from the decision-making process, or perceived coercion to participate

in treatment. At the other extreme, approximately 17% reported a high level of negative pressure, process exclusion, or perceived coercion (Swartz et al., 1999). In a study of people with mental illness placed on parole and mandated to participate in treatment, greater than 75% agreed they needed treatment and that they did not feel coerced into treatment (Farabee, Shen, & Sanchez, 2002). Similarly, Poythress, Petrila, McGaha, and Boothroyd (2002) found a low level of coercion to participate in mental health treatment for participants of a voluntary mental health court program.

Perceptions of coercion may change over time. Gardner et al. (1999) found that just over half of the 64 people included in their study who reported that they did not need treatment when involuntarily hospitalized later reported they actually had needed treatment during follow-up interviews after being discharged. However, feelings of being coerced typically did not change from admission to follow-up, even among those who later admitted they needed treatment. Nicholson (1999) reached similar findings in his review of studies of coerced hospitalization. "Despite generally positive findings observed in such studies [that reported perceived benefit and satisfaction with treatment], a sizeable minority of involuntary patients continue to harbor negative feelings about their hospitalization and treatment after discharge" (pp. 163–164). Even less satisfaction was found among people mandated to treatment under outpatient civil commitment. Swartz, Swanson, and Monahan (2003) found that only 48% of people believed they benefited from the commitment prior to discharge from that commitment; the level of satisfaction was reduced to 28% one year after the commitment ended.

One factor that consistently has been found to at least partially mitigate perceptions of the use of coercion held by people with mental illness is procedural justice (Lidz et al. 1995; McKenna et al., 2003; Poythress et al., 2002). Procedural justice refers to the perceptions of fairness in decision-making processes, particularly those involving the use of legal coercion (Poythress et al., 2002). Procedural justice is enforced when people with mental illness are able to express their views; when their views are given serious consideration by those contemplating the coercive action; when they are treated with dignity and respect; when they are given accurate, relevant, and understandable information; and when people contemplating coercion express genuine concern for their well-being (McKenna et al., 2003). Everett (2001) identified the importance of procedural justice. "Coercion threatens trust.... Procedural justice focuses on preserving trust, insofar as it is possible in power-over circumstances, in order that the client/professional relationship survives, and continues to sustain clients before, during, and after a coercive episode" (p. 17). Winick (2003) provided a detailed discussion of how to incorporate procedural justice in outpatient civil commitment proceedings. Everett (2001) offered a list of questions that mental health professionals should ask themselves to promote procedural justice when considering the initiation of community treatment orders (CTOs), which are Ontario, Canada's version of outpatient civil commitment:

(a) Do clients have full information about CTOs?
(b) Do they understand which of their behaviours, actions, or symptoms can lead to the application of a CTO?
(c) Have all less-restrictive alternatives been exhausted?
(d) Do clients fully understand their rights?
(e) Do they understand under what conditions a CTO can be lifted?
(f) Have they had an opportunity to talk through their feelings and have their views heard? (p. 17)

As mental health professionals attempt to promote procedural justice, it is important to note that people with mental illness, mental health professionals, and family members may have different perceptions on whether a particular interaction reflects procedural justice. Monahan et al. (1999), for instance, found that people with mental illness rated the degree of procedural justice much lower than did both the mental health professionals and family members involved in the same process.

Viewpoints Among Family Members

Families of people with severe mental illness and advocacy organizations with large memberships of family members, such as the National Alliance for the Mentally Ill (NAMI), typically support the use of involuntary treatment in hospitals and in the community (Lefley, 1996, 1997). NAMI (1995), for example, issued a position paper on involuntary and court-ordered treatment that, among other things, supported the existence of such options and called for broadening of the criteria for commitment to include the need for treatment in cases when an individual is likely to substantially deteriorate without it. It often is with great ambivalence, however, that families seek involuntary commitment for their relatives (Lefley, 1996, 1997). As such, the NAMI position paper stated that involuntary treatment should be used only as a last resort. Isaac and Armat (1990) succinctly expressed this feeling of ambivalence and the effects of initiating involuntary commitment that can occur. "When families, desperate to obtain treatment, reluctantly initiate court hearings where they must testify against their children, they often obtain no help; they may even find they have made the situation worse" (p. 252). Similarly, Lefley (1997) stated, "Families would greatly prefer alternatives to involuntary interventions. They are humiliating and painful to all concerned. They not only have an adverse impact on the self-esteem and integrity of the individuals involved but also may generate resentment and alienation against family members faced with impossible choices" (p. 9). When considering the initiation of involuntary treatment, families may be motivated by two factors (Lefley, 1997). One, of course, is concern for their family member with mental illness and the desire to see a return to a level of functioning that is normal for him or her. A second factor is concern for the emotional and physical safety of the family. Lefley (1997) stated, "Families must balance their relative's right to autonomy against their own right to protect themselves from acute personal suffering and possible physical danger" (pp. 8–9).

Viewpoints Among Mental Health Professionals

Many mental health professionals also feel ambivalent about the use of legal coercion with people with mental illness. Davis (2002) related this to dual demands placed on them. There is an emphasis on empowerment of, and self-determination for, people with mental illness supported by the consumer movement and the adoption of the recovery perspective by many mental health systems. He stated there also are demands on mental health professionals to use a paternalistic approach with people with mental illness, which comes from the availability of new forms of commitment such as outpatient civil commitment, pressure from family members, and the use of more aggressive treatment models such as Assertive Community Treatment. Of the major professions that work with people with mental illness, psychiatry is most outspoken in its support for mandatory treatment. As a case in point, the American Psychiatric Association recently published a document supporting the use of mandatory outpatient treatment and a statement about the future of psychiatric services that included strong support for mandatory treatment (Gerbasi et al., 2000; Sharfstein et al., 2003).

Viewpoints Among the General Public

Like people with mental illness, their family members, and mental health professionals, the general public in the United States also reports ambivalence about the use of legal coercion with people with mental illness (Pescosolido, Monahan, Link, Stueve, & Kikuzawa, 1999). Studies of public perceptions have linked attitudes to two factors (Morrissey & Monahan, 1999; Pescosolido et al., 1999). First, people are more likely to support mandatory treatment for people with schizophrenia over those with major depression. Second, when people perceive that those with mental illness are dangerous, they are almost unanimous in their support for mandatory treatment. In addition, La Fond and Durham (1992) argued that public willingness to use coercion with people with mental illness declined in the 1960s and 1970s but reemerged to become firmly established in our culture beginning in the early 1980s. This coincided with a new period of political conservativeness that promoted incarceration of criminals over rehabilitation; with increased fear of people with mental illness following the assassination of President Reagan by John Hinckley and his subsequent acquittal as NGRI, and in response to sensational media coverage of other crimes committed by people with mental illness; and with public concern over increased numbers of people with mental illness who were homeless.

RELATIONSHIPS BETWEEN RIGHTS, COERCION, AND EMPOWERMENT

The relationships that exist between individual rights, coercion, and empowerment are complex. Exploring those relations, though, is critical to furthering an understanding of the opportunities for, and limitations to, empowerment. Each permutation is considered separately.

Rights and Coercion

Ethical dilemmas invariably arise because of the tension that exists between seeking to recognize and preserve the rights of people with mental illness, and yet sometimes perceiving a need to coerce them through legal or informal means in order to promote either their well-being or that of society (Davis, 2002; Munetz et al., 2003). Most people now accept that coercion is necessary for at least a limited number of people with mental illness in limited instances because of the debilitating nature of mental illness (La Fond & Durham, 1992; Gerbasi et al., 2000). Consequently, the question becomes how to balance individual rights with the perceived need for coercion. The balancing of rights and coercion is essentially a normative process. Research can help inform normative decisions such as this (Paris & Reynolds, 1983). Research, for example, on the extent to which mental illness can limit decision-making capacity in particular instances, and on the long-term effects of various types of legal and informal coercion on attitudes, treatment compliance, and functioning of people with mental illness, would be relevant to discussions of balancing rights and coercion. Hiday (2003) emphasized, though, the limited role that research plays in normative decision making in the context of mandatory treatment:

> It is also a debate involving the normative issues of what we as a society believe we ought to do, what we believe to be the right role of the state in exercising its power and in protecting the weak, and what we believe to be the civil rights of the individual in being protected from state infringements on liberty.... Empirical research can clarify assumptions on which normative arguments rest, but

ultimately the debate of moral and political values cannot be settled with data. (p. 26)

Professional codes of ethics should provide some guidance, too, in seeking to balance rights and coercion. The codes of ethics of the nursing, psychiatry, psychology, rehabilitation, and social work professions incorporate individuals' right to self-determination and respect for human dignity (American Nurses Association, 2001; American Psychological Association, 2002; Bloch et al., 1999; National Association of Social Workers, 1999; Scott, 1998). Some of the codes also reference that some people may be limited in their capacity to make decisions and then indicate ways to address these limitations. The code for nurses, for instance, includes the following statement when discussing the right to self-determination. "The nurse recognizes that there are situations in which the right to individual self-determination may be outweighed or limited by the rights, health and welfare of others.... Nonetheless, limitation of individual rights must always be considered a serious deviation from the standard of care" (p. 9).

Similarly, the code of ethics for psychologists states, "Psychologists respect the dignity and worth of all people, and the rights of individuals to privacy, confidentiality, and self-determination. Psychologists are aware that special safeguards may be necessary to protect the rights and welfare of persons or communities whose vulnerabilities impair autonomous decision making" (American Psychological Association, 2002, p. 4). The code of ethics continues by discussing informed consent. "For persons who are legally incapable of giving informed consent, psychologists nevertheless (1) provide an appropriate explanation, (2) seek the individual's assent, [and] (3) consider such persons' preferences and best interests" (p. 7). Similar to other codes of ethics, the social work code states, "Social workers respect and promote the right of clients to self-determination and assist clients in their efforts to identify and clarify their goals. Social workers may limit clients' right to self-determination when, in the social workers' professional judgment, clients' actions or potential actions pose a serious, foreseeable, and imminent risk to themselves or others" (National Association of Social Workers, 1999, p. 7). It continues in its discussion of informed consent by stating that "In instances when clients are receiving services involuntarily, social workers should provide information about the nature and extent of services and about the extent of clients' right to refuse service" (p. 8). Despite attempts to address issues related to rights and coercion, Davis (2002) argued that codes of ethics fail to give clear direction for resolving ethical dilemmas related to rights and coercion because of the complex nature of individual, potentially coercive situations.

Another attempt to contend with issues of rights and coercion is the emergence of therapeutic jurisprudence. Therapeutic jurisprudence focuses on the potential of law to promote therapeutic ends and to minimize its antitherapeutic effects (Wexler, 1990, 1992). This position purports that legal rules and procedures, and the legal actors that enact them, including judges, lawyers, and people from the helping professionals, can produce therapeutic outcomes without violating other legal ends (Wexler, 1996). Although initially developed within the context of mental health law, it has now been expanded to many other areas, including, for example, work with people with HIV, divorce and other aspects of family law, and criminal law (Stolle, Wexler, Winick, 2000). Winick (2001, 2003) provided detailed examples of how to apply therapeutic jurisprudence to civil commitment to hospitalization and to outpatient civil commitment. In reference to the former, Winick (2001), for example, stated that lawyers should learn from the recent research on procedural justice and listen to their clients' concerns, respect their preferences, and fully support their position in civil commitment hearings. They also can discuss the advantages of voluntary admission, should it appear likely that an involuntary commitment will occur. Therapeutic jurisprudence makes a significant contribution by focusing attention on making the legal process more therapeutic. It has limitations, though, in resolving the ethical dilemmas associated with rights and coercion. Proponents are explicit in stating that it does not assign values to different positions internal to the person (e.g., right to refuse treatment vs. need for treatment to improve functioning) or external to the person (e.g., rights of the person vs. community safety) (Winick, 1997; Slobogin, 1995). A second limitation is that it is limited to legal coercion. It does not attempt to address the many types of informal coercion.

Individuals have offered their own suggestions for balancing rights and coercion. Based on their research on coercion, Monahan et al. (1996) stated that if rights are to be infringed upon, positive pressures should always be used first. Negative pressures should be used only as a last resort, and, when used, the principles of procedural justice should be practiced. Davis (2002) concluded that mental health agencies can best balance rights and coercion by setting guidelines on staff actions in particular situations, and by having ongoing forums in which staff can discuss ethical issues.

Coercion and Empowerment

By definition, coercion is disempowering. The very act of coercion reduces individuals' options or roles in decision making. As previously discussed, however, treating people with fairness and respect, showing genuine concern, and considering their opinions can lessen the feeling of coercion. Because empowerment is situational, acts of coercion do not necessarily prevent empowerment from occurring in other areas of people's lives (Rooney, 1992). For instance, people involuntarily committed to hospitalization still can achieve a degree of empowerment through meaningful participation in treatment planning at the hospital to which they were committed. Similarly, it can be empowering for people to work toward ending their coercion.

Rights and Empowerment

Legal rights established through federal and state case law and statutes can promote empowerment of people with severe mental illness through several means. They can limit the legal coercion of people with mental illness, such as was done with civil commitment in the 1970s. They also can give people with mental illness a greater voice in decision making, such as was done with informed-consent and right-to-refuse-treatment case law and statutory changes. In addition, they can facilitate access to mental health services and community integration, as was done with right-to-hospital-treatment case law and the Americans with Disabilities Act.

There are, however, limitations to legal rights promoting empowerment. Manderscheid and Henderson (2001) emphasized that rights cannot make up for insufficient resources. "Rights will mean little unless fundamental needs are also met. Included are such basic needs as communities that protect against violence, adequate housing and appropriate education for all, and productive roles that promote self-esteem and well-being" (p. 1). Also, legal rights do not eliminate all forms of legal coercion, and they cannot address informal coercion, which can substantially limit empowerment. Next, legal rights must be properly implemented, which often does not occur for various reasons. Appelbaum (1994), for example, found that the civil commitment statutory changes, which should have been revolutionary, did little to change the practice of judges and lawyers at hearings. Finally, Handler (1986) argued that the system of rights that arose during the past 40 years has failed to provide justice to the country's most vulnerable populations, including people with severe mental illness. He explained why:

> In order for this system [of rights] to work there has to be a *complaining client*. Our legal system is not proactive. People have to know that they have suffered a harm, they have to blame someone other than themselves, they have to know how to pursue the remedy, they have to have resources to pursue the remedy, and the potential benefits of winning have to outweigh the potential costs. (1990, p. 19)

Many people with mental illness are unable to navigate through these processes to protect their legal rights when they are infringed upon because they are powerless. It was in recognition of the inability of legal rights to empower vulnerable populations that Handler (1986; 1990; 1996) turned to the study of conditions that promote empowerment, which is the subject of the next chapter.

4

Conditions for Empowerment

Given the history of powerlessness among people with severe mental illness and the forms of legal and informal coercion that continue to exist, is it possible for people with severe mental illness to be empowered? Can they meaningfully participate in decision making and activities that allow them to take more control over their lives? The limitations to empowerment, as perceived by people with mental illness themselves, reiterate the sense of hopelessness that one could draw from the historical perspective and the discussion of coercion. Limitations to empowerment reported by many people with mental illness include poverty and a lack basic resources; social isolation; the effects of stigma held by the public at large and mental health professionals; the effects of the psychiatric disability at some times and in some areas; the unintended effects of institutionalization, particularly dependency and compliance; and the inequitable distribution of power and the lack of models to share power (Manning, 1999).

Handler (1992) argued that it is possible to empower vulnerable populations. For him, the greater question is not *if* it is possible, but *under what conditions* empowerment is likely to occur. He wrote, "The task is to discover the conditions that will facilitate the creation and nurturing of empowerment in discretionary dependent relationships..." (p. 291). In his various works, Handler (1986, 1990, 1992, 1996) studied the decision-making processes between parties of unequal power in a range of areas, such as informed consent in medicine, special education, community care for elderly persons who are frail and poor, neighborhood organizations, public housing, nursing homes, and water pollution regulation. From these diverse settings, he developed a general set of conditions for empowerment that can be applied to the analysis of relationships of unequal power. Each condition typically must be met for empowerment to occur. Meeting an individual condition is not sufficient, in and of itself, for empowerment to occur.

Handler (1996) took a realistic view of the potential for creating the conditions for empowerment. He found that empowerment of dependent persons is not the norm in human service agencies, and when it does occur, it is never permanent. The relationships that form the basis of empowerment exist in a particular context, and contexts are always changing. As such, he described the examples of empowerment identified in his cases studies as "special and fragile" (1992, p. 293). Because of changing contexts, he said that empowered clients must continually struggle to preserve their status (1996). To support clients, continual efforts are required to develop and maintain the conditions for empowerment.

Handler developed his conditions for empowerment to apply to participation in decision making among parties of unequal power. He identified four conditions for empowerment in his earlier works (1990, 1992) and later reduced them to three (1996). This book expands upon his conditions in two ways. First, it adds other conditions that can be extrapolated from his work. A total of nine conditions that apply to empowerment of people with severe mental illness are derived. Second, as Handler intended, these conditions are applied to analyses of decision making. These conditions, with some modification, also are applied to empowerment through participation in activities that have the potential for empowerment.

The following is a description of the nine conditions for empowering people with severe mental illness. For each condition, the work of Handler and relevant material from the general empowerment literature are presented first. Then, incorporating the mental health literature, each condition is applied to empowerment of people with severe mental illness. These conditions provide the structure for assessing empowerment in the seven specific activities included in chapters 5 through 11. This chapter does not discuss how to create the conditions for empowerment. That is reserved for subsequent chapters.

MANAGED PSYCHIATRIC SYMPTOMS

Handler (1990) argued that clients must be free of internal constraints to meaningfully participate in decision making. Some potential internal constraints are the symptoms of an individual's severe mental illness. There is substantial evidence that some people are incapable of meaningful participation in decision making and other activities because of symptoms related to their mental illness (Grisso & Appelbaum, 1998;

Hoge & Feucht-Haviar, 1995; Husted, 1999; Rosenfeld & Turkheimer, 1995; Spaulding, Sullivan, & Poland, 2003). The presence of a severe mental illness can, among other things, impede a person's ability to concentrate; to process information; to screen out irrelevant information; and to make logical, constructive decisions. These cognitive abilities can be further limited by the presence of co-occurring disorders, such as a personality disorder, mental retardation or other developmental disabilities, or a substance abuse disorder. The most common co-occurring diagnosis is a substance abuse disorder, which is held by as many as half of people with severe mental illness (Mueser, Noordsy, Drake, & Fox, 2003; US DHHS, 1999). Studies have found that the presence of this co-occurring diagnosis is associated with exacerbated psychiatric symptoms, increased psychiatric hospitalizations, a greater risk of depression and suicide, and other negative outcomes (Mueser et al., 2003; US DHHS, 1999).

Handler (1990) reminded us that decision-making capacity is context specific. Having a mental illness does not by itself negate people from participating in decision making or other activities (Gerhart, 1990; Grisso & Appelbaum, 1998; Torrey 1994). Gerhart (1990) summed it up this way: "Most chronic mentally ill persons suffer from impaired areas of judgment at one time or another, but the person who cannot exercise any judgment in any area at any time is a fairly rare case" (p. 57). Impaired cognitive abilities can change over time in inconsistent patterns and can occur when people are taking medication or are off their medication (Torrey, 1994). As such, these fluctuating abilities require that the participation capacity of people with mental illness be examined in the context of the specific decision or activity in which they seek to engage.

PARTICIPATION SKILLS

A second potential internal constraint is the lack of skills that enable one to meaningfully participate in a particular activity. Handler (1990, 1996) found that powerless populations often lack decision-making skills, and that skill training is required before some people can participate. As one example, Handler (1996) indicated that New York City officials had to provide tenants of city-owned property with extensive skill training in a number of areas to enable them to take over ownership and management of some of those properties.

The inability to acquire and perform skills is one manifestation of severe mental illness, and it is just as much a part of the illness as symptoms such as delusions, mania, or depressed mood (Spaulding et al., 2003). Mental illness can affect the wide spectrum of skills that people with mental illness need for successful community integration. Some of these skills include verbal and nonverbal communication skills, problem-solving skills, personal and health care skills, interpersonal skills, education skills, work skills, household skills, and leisure activity skills (Gerhart, 1990). Spaulding et al. (2003) reminded us that the inability to perform a skill does not by itself indicate abnormality. Rather, it means the person simply does not possess a particular skill, or that something is preventing the use of the skill that a person possesses. The skill needed is context specific. It varies by activity, as well as within a particular activity. Skill levels can range from having no skill in the area to performing the skill perfectly. A wide range of skill within this continuum is often sufficient to complete a particular task (Spaulding et al., 2003). That is, people do not always have to perform a skill perfectly to achieve the task at hand.

People with severe mental illness can learn skills, at times, even when experiencing severe symptoms (Anthony, Cohen, Farkas, & Gagne, 2002; Cook & Hoffschmidt, 1993). Improving psychiatric symptoms through medication or other means does not necessarily result in improved skills and functioning, however. Participation in educational and rehabilitative activities usually is still necessary to learn, or relearn, needed skills. Examples of activities in which skill training was provided to people with mental illness to increase participation include treatment planning (Starkey & Leadholm, 1997), mental health policy advocacy (Hess, Clapper, Hoekstra, & Gibison, 2001), and employment (Henry, Nicholson, Clayfield, Phillips, & Stier, 2002). Part of learning skills is practicing them. Penney (1994) called for the mental health system to provide people with skills and the opportunities to practice those skills in meaningful activities. Similarly, Dillon (1994) argued that the lack of experience in decision making among people with mental illness is the primary obstacle to their participation.

PSYCHOLOGICAL READINESS

A third, and final, potential internal constraint to empowerment is the lack of psychological readiness to meaningfully participate in an activity that has the potential for empowerment. Handler (1990, 1996) noted that people who do not hold power can use various means to avoid the subjective feeling of powerlessness. This can be manifested as fatalism, self-deprecation, and apathy. Such internalized psychological states can prevent people from choosing to participate in potentially empowering activities.

Even when people with mental illness meet the conditions of managed psychiatric symptoms and minimal participation skills, they may not participate in empowering activities because of the lack of psychological readiness. Both Chamberlin (1978) and Manning (1999) talked about hospitalization promoting dependency among people with mental illness, which decreases their willingness and motivation to make decisions or to participate in activities that could promote their return into the community. Pratt, Gill, Barrett, and Roberts (1999) and Rapp (1998) discussed the lack of confidence among some people to participate even in rehabilitation activities. Pratt et al. believed this lack of confidence stemmed from repeated failures associated with "relapses, lack of necessary skills, inadequate environmental supports, ineffective training, poor planning, and from setting goals inappropriate to an individual" (p. 116). Rapp stated that lack of confidence stems from feelings of powerlessness and fatigue. "Powerlessness refers to feelings of anger, frustration, and dependency as efforts to make decisions and engage in behaviors to change circumstances fail to yield desired results. The constant emotional energy that is expended in this process may serve to decrease the level of energy needed to sustain goal-oriented efforts" (p. 100). Nelson, Lord, and Ochocka (2001) described the lack of personal motivation as being associated with self-defeating thinking and a lack of self-esteem, as well as fear of failure, fear of making one's own decisions, and simply fear.

Finally, Flannery, Penk, and Addo (1996) and Spaulding et al. (2003) related lack of psychological readiness to learned helplessness. Flannery et al. (1996) defined learned helplessness as the incorrect generalization of the lack of control in one area of life to most other situations. They found that in people with mental illness, learned helplessness could result from repeated presence of severe psychiatric symptoms, being victims of violence in the community and in mental health settings, and the societal presence of stigma that limits opportunities. Spaulding et al. (2003) referred to it as "the behavioral immobilization that results from protracted frustration and failure to control aversive events—common in the experiences of people with severe mental illness" (p. 199). According to Flannery et al. (1996), learned helplessness can have four outcomes. These include a lack of perceived control; a lack of involvement in tasks related to employment, family, and many other areas; the disruption of daily, planned, and purposeful routines; and social isolation. People with mental illness may experience one or a combination of these outcomes.

MUTUTAL TRUST AND RESPECT

Handler (1990, 1996) believed that mutual trust and respect between clients and agencies are critical to empowerment. He elaborated on this viewpoint:

> In order for the workers to share responsibility with the clients, the workers must believe that the clients understand, agree, and are willing to cooperate; workers must respect the capabilities, autonomy, and responsibility of the clients. The clients, in turn, will not

give this kind of response unless they have confidence in the workers' competence and professionalism, and believe that they share a common belief in the clients' best interests. (1990, p. 136)

Although not listing it as one of his three conditions, at one point Handler (1990) indicated that trust, as a condition for empowerment, was a given.

Themes of mutual trust and respect are found throughout the empowerment literature related to people with severe mental illness. At the individual-treatment level, for example, Rapp (1998) wrote, "The relationship needs to be based on a high degree of trust" (p. 63). At the organizational and policy levels, Fitzsimons and Fuller (2002) wrote that participatory decision-making structures are most effective when they emphasize mutual respect, while Staples (1999) stressed the importance of trust in such structures. Procedural justice, introduced in the previous chapter, can facilitate mutual trust and respect, even in potentially coercive decision-making scenarios (Lidz et al. 1995; McKenna et al., 2003; Poythress et al., 2002). Those in power demonstrate trust and respect when they genuinely listen to the preferences of people with mental illness and act on them whenever possible, show concern for them in the proceedings, and give them accurate information about decision-making processes. As research on procedural justice has found, these actions promote a sense of fairness on the part of some people with mental illness even when their preferences are not enacted. Dillon (1994) discussed one outcome of mutual trust and respect. "Sincere people can differ, and . . . through mutual respect and compromise, more effective alternatives, never before considered, may be found" (p. 125).

RECIPROCAL CONCRETE INCENTIVES

Handler (1990) held that the decision-making process is augmented by both clients and staff having concrete incentives for meaningfully participating together in decision making. This was one of his three conditions for empowerment. In later work, he referred to this condition as an exchange of material resources (1996). In order to engage in an activity, he said that clients must believe they will get something concrete or material out of the relationship that is worth the effort it takes to engage in that activity. Likewise, staff must believe they, too, have something material to gain from meaningful client involvement. In reference to material benefits for staff, Handler wrote (1990), "Reciprocal concrete incentives . . . increase the client's value to the worker and thus change the power relationship. With these incentives, if the client fails, the worker fails. The worker, thus, has a concrete professional stake in client empowerment" (p. 152). Stated another way, staff are less likely to involve clients in decision making when staff have nothing to gain from that participation. He believed that trust alone was not sufficient to sustain participation. Rather, both parties, especially the party in power, need to receive something material in return. Going back to the housing example, Handler cited that tenants benefited through their participation by improving their living conditions, and in some cases becoming property owners. New York City officials benefited because the city was relieved of some financial burdens and negative publicity surrounding the city's ownership of substandard housing. As another example, a home health agency providing services to the frail elderly found that it could not remain fiscally solvent under its publicly funded contract without assistance from the informal caregiver in completing part of the work. As a result, the agency benefited by meaningfully involving the elderly and their informal caregivers, usually family, in the development of the care plans. Without such involvement, it is unlikely that the caregivers would have been willing to provide the needed assistance. Improved client and program performance also can be a material benefit to staff for client involvement, assuming that improvement is important to staff. Handler (1996) indicated that improved student performance was a material benefit to teachers for involving children in special education. In addition, he stated that improved program performance as a result of client feedback on the quality of services was a material benefit for involving clients in organizational decision making (1990).

Barnes and Bowl (2001), Neese-Todd and Pavick (2000), and Rapp (1998) are some of the few individuals who emphasize the importance of mutual benefits to the creation of partnerships between people with mental illness and those holding power. Barnes and Bowl, for instance, argued that recognizing the capacity for both parties to benefit from participation is a much more effective starting point for increasing the meaningful participation of people with mental illness in activities than an appeal to consumer choice. Neese-Todd and Pavick stated that organizations planning to emphasize empowerment in their relationships with people with mental illness must ask the question, "What are the professional rewards for fostering empowerment?" (p. 106). As examples of staff rewards, they cited that an organization that adopts an empowerment approach with clients also adopts (or should adopt) an empowerment approach with its relationships with staff, and that improved client outcomes are likely to result from client empowerment. Rapp stated that the purpose of strengths-based case management is to help clients develop interrelationships that are mutually satisfying to both parties (e.g., clients and landlords, clients and employers, and clients and friends).

Others, too, have identified the mutual benefits of shared participation in activities. Both Gerhart (1990) and Salzer (1997), for instance, pointed out that involving people with mental illness in organizational decision-making benefits the agency by enriching existing services and creating new services directed to unmet client needs, while clients benefit by having improved services and increased self-esteem and hopefulness. As another example, people with mental illness are more likely to meet their treatment goals when they meaningfully participate in treatment planning because they have a greater investment in the process (Bassman, 1997). Thus, if staff base their professional success on the outcomes of their clients, they have the incentive to involve clients in treatment planning. Likewise, behaviors of hospitalized clients improve when they participate in setting ward rules and establishing daily routines (Holland, Knoich, Buffum, Smith, & Petchers, 1981). Therefore, staff responsible for ward management have an incentive to involve clients in decision making because ward clients are less likely to engage in negative behaviors when participating this way. In order to meet Handler's condition of reciprocal concrete incentives, both people with mental illness and those with whom they are working must have an awareness of the benefits each will receive for having clients participate in the activity. Such benefits are not always obvious and may have to be pointed out to various parties, sometimes repeatedly, to increase and improve participation.

AVAILABILITY OF CHOICES

Handler (1990) noted the importance of having choices. He also cited Hasenfeld's (1987) statement that the ability to choose among alternatives is at the core of power and empowerment. He believed that even choices that are considered wrong by others still can be empowering for powerless individuals. Handler (1996) added that for choices to be informed ones, clients must have information about those choices they can understand and then utilize that information in decision making.

Many people argue that having a range of choices and information about those choices is integral to empowerment of people with severe mental illness (Carling, 1995; Gutiérrez, DeLois, & GlenMaye, 1995; President's New Freedom Commission on Mental Health, 2003; Rapp, 1998). Chamberlin (1997), for example, included the availability of a range of options and information about those options as components of her definition of empowerment of people with mental illness. Dubois and Miley (1999) stated that "Presuming that people will be able to experience empowerment without having options simply makes a mockery of empowerment.... This means that people know about their choices and have opportunities to select their courses of actions from among options" (p. 26). Client choice also is emphasized in psychosocial and psychiatric rehabilitation (Cook & Hoffschmidt, 1993;

Pratt et al., 1999) and in the recovery perspective (Fisher, 1994a; Jacobson & Greenley, 2001; Young & Ensing, 1999). For choices to be empowering, they should be meaningful and desirable to clients (Ferleger, 1994; Hagner & Marrone, 1995; Harp, 1994; Sundram, 1994). Gilson (1998) identifies the consequences of not offering meaningful choices. "To offer scaled-back options, limited opportunities, or inadequate support is not choice; it is a continuation of practices of domination and paternalism" (p. 11).

Carling (1995) and Grisso and Appelbaum (1998) identified requirements that make choices meaningful. Carling cited having real options and knowing about them, knowing one's own preferences, having the ability to make tradeoffs, and having access to supports. Similarly, Grisso and Appelbaum included having the ability to express a choice, to understand relevant information, to appreciate the significance of the information to the individual's own situation, and to logically process the weighing of options. Others, too, have emphasized the importance of having access to information when making decisions (Fisher, 1994a; Hagner & Marrone, 1995; Means & Smith, 1994; Sundram, 1994). Means and Smith (1994) recognized that information "must be presented clearly, attractively and in good time" (p. 95). Note that neither Carling nor Grisso and Appelbaum included the magnitude of the choices in their requirements for choices to be meaningful. For some individuals who have unmanaged psychiatric symptoms or poor decision-making skills, or who lack decision-making experience, making even small choices can be empowering (Carling, 1995; Dillon, 1994; Hagner & Marrone, 1995; Penney, 1994). Carling summed up this position. "Changing consumers' sense of themselves as incompetent, and helping them to learn or relearn what is personally important, can be a major undertaking. This process is greatly facilitated by continually encouraging choices, no matter how small, and then supporting successively more important life choices" (p. 288). The making of small choices, however, should be the exception. Choices typically should be ones that are important to individuals' quality of life.

Consistent with Handler's (1990) position, some believe that people with mental illness should be allowed to make the "wrong" choice. Their rationale is that people cannot improve their ability to make choices without going through the process of making poor choices and learning from them (Carling, 1995; Gilson, 1998). As one person with mental illness stated:

> If you shut people away for years and don't give them the choice, naturally when they get the choice, they're going to be confused and they're going to take risks that might be stupid and dumb. I'll tell you, I've done that. Since I moved out of the institution, I've made some mistakes; I fell flat on my face, but you know what? I learned

from that. And hopefully the person will not make the same mistake twice. But the service system has to allow us to make those mistakes. . . . I think before you can do a good job, you have to have the people involved in making decisions for themselves. (Kennedy, 1994, pp. 25–26)

Ferleger (1994), however, warns of the consequences that can occur when people with mental illness are allowed to participate in activities for which they are unprepared. He wrote, "Excessive respect for the abstract notion of 'choice' can lead to the perpetuation of neglect or to an increase in the risk of neglect and other harms. . . . Choice must be kept in context, and other values (sometimes competing and sometimes complementary) must be weighed in the balance" (p. 75). Slobogin (1995) took a different view on choice, stating that people with mental illness should have the choice not to choose. He argued that giving some people a wide range of options in selected decisional areas can be stressful, and that people with mental illness should be able to choose to defer some decisions to alternative decision makers to decrease stress. He emphasized that someone should be able to defer on one decision at one point in time and still retain decision-making autonomy in all other areas.

PARTICIPATION STRUCTURES AND PROCESSES

Handler (1990) identified having arenas of, or technologies for, conversation between the professional and the client as one of his three conditions for empowerment. Bringing powerless people together with decision makers is not enough, however. Handler emphasized that structures and processes for conversation must bring people together in such a way that clients are participants with something to offer rather than merely subjects. He found that decision-making arenas are most likely to meaningfully involve powerless people using consensus or participatory models. As one example of a structure for the involvement of nursing home residents in organizational decision making and policy making, Handler (1996) cited LIFE, an advocacy organization comprised of activists and nursing homes residents. Handler found that even residents who were quite disabled were able to participate in some of LIFE's activities.

There are a variety of mechanisms through which people with mental illness can participate in activities. Established advocacy groups, for instance, can provide a forum through which people with mental illness can participate in policy making (Havel, 1992). Membership in, or participation with, users' councils, agency advisory boards, boards of directors, task forces, study groups, and committees are options for involving people in organizational decision making

(Carling 1995; Linhorst, Eckert, & Hamilton, 2005; Lord, Ochocka, Czarny, & MacGillivary, 1998). Models for involving clients in treatment planning also are available (e.g., Anthony et al., 2002; Rapp, 1998). A range of mechanisms exist, too, for participation by people with mental illness in evaluation and research, including focus groups, work groups to develop evaluation topics, and forums in which findings are disseminated (Linhorst, 2002a; Linhorst & Eckert, 2002; Rapp, Shera, & Kisthardt, 1993). In many instances, mental health providers will have to develop new structures and processes, or significantly modify existing ones, to meaningfully involve people with mental illness in decision making (Manning, 1999; Means & Smith, 1994). In addition, some people with mental illness, and some individuals with whom they are participating, will require training to work together in these new participation mechanisms (Hess et al., 2001; Smith & Ford, 1986). Decision-making processes should incorporate procedural justice, as discussed in the prior chapter (Lidz et al. 1995; McKenna et al., 2003; Poythress et al., 2002). Even when their preferences are not adopted, people with mental illness still can experience a sense of fairness in the process if that process adhered to the elements of procedural justice. Mediation is yet other process that can facilitate empowerment among people with mental illness (Flower, 1999; Kurtz, Stone, & Holbrook, 2002; Olley & Ogloff, 1995). Kurtz et al. (2002) found that in many instances, peer mediation is both possible and useful; that is, people with mental illness with special training can serve as mediators when disputes arise between them and those in power.

ACCESS TO RESOURCES

Handler (1996) argued that powerless individuals cannot become empowered and stay empowered without obtaining resources. Given the nature of powerlessness, powerless people are unlikely to develop sufficient resources on their own to be empowered and maintain long-term empowerment. Rather than creating resources, Handler saw the primary role of powerless individuals as seeking out and taking advantage of resources that are available to them. Handler identified that resources can come from two sources, including the body within which the individual is interacting in the potentially empowering situation (e.g., family, social service agency, or employer) or from the larger community.

Handler (1990) identified several major categories of resources that clients may need in order to meaningfully participate in empowering activities. These include what Handler termed social movement groups. These groups provide emotional support to clients, as well as a forum to identify common issues and to generate alternatives. An outside person might be necessary in some cases to facilitate such a group. Some clients also may need an advocate to facilitate communication with staff or others assuming powerful positions. One school, for example, provided parents of children in special education with an advocate, who usually was a parent familiar with the system. The advocate's role was not adversarial; rather, it was to facilitate communication between parents and school personnel (1996). Handler included training as yet another major resource. Many clients can benefit from training related to improving skills, knowledge, and behaviors. Logistical resources are another type of resource. Handler (1990) provided an example of a state department of education making available small stipends, day care, and meals to parents to facilitate their participation in training. In another example, Handler (1996) stated that city officials provided support staff, training, technical assistance, and office space to each neighborhood group to facilitate their participation in city government. While Handler (1990, 1996) discussed primarily client resources, he also identified the importance of staff resources. As with client resources, there can be many types of staff resources. Two particularly important types he discussed are staff having the time needed to meaningfully engage clients in an activity and having access to staff development and training.

Each type of resource identified by Handler (1990, 1996) was noted in the mental health literature. First, relative to social movement groups, Nelson et al. (2001) discussed the importance of the availability of natural supports, such a family members or friends, as well as peer support and self-help groups, to promote participation by people with mental illness. Second, advocates for people with mental illness residing both in hospitals and in the community are important (Beeforth, Conlan, Field, Hoser, & Sayce, 1990; Hess et al., 2001; Ishiyama, 1970; Olley & Ogloff, 1995). Advocates may be family members or friends of the person with mental illness, they may be part of special programs created by the agency, or they may be part of independent agencies. Another type of advocate may be needed when people with mental illness enter the criminal justice system. Steadman (1992) discussed the need for "boundary spanners," the term he used to describe staff in designated positions within a mental health organization whose role is to maintain relationships with criminal justice programs. These boundary spanners can serve many advocacy roles, such as ensuring that criminal justice programs are knowledgeable about people's mental illness and their mental health treatment and social service needs.

At least three national organizations fall under the category of independent advocacy agencies. One is the national system of Protection and Advocacy agencies (Meinert & de Loyola, 2002; National Association of Protection and Advocacy Systems, n.d.). These federally funded, independently operated statewide agencies are authorized to investigate abuse, neglect, or rights violations; to bring lawsuits on behalf of people with mental illness to protect their rights; and to advocate on their behalf. As independent agencies, their specific focus within these three broad areas varies from state to state. Two other national advocacy organizations include the National Mental Health Association (NMHA) and the National Alliance for the Mentally Ill (NAMI) (Foulks, 2000). The organization that would later become NMHA originated in 1909 through the efforts of a person with mental illness, Clifford Beers (NMHA, n.d.-b). In addition to the national organization, NMHA (n.d.-a) now has over 340 affiliate organizations nationwide. NAMI was created in 1979 by two mothers of adult children with mental illness. NAMI includes the national organization, state organizations, and over 1,200 affiliate organizations (NAMI, n.d.-b). While these two organizations vary in their structure, activities, and focus, both engage in a wide range of activities to promote the well-being of people with mental illness, including advocacy, education, and research.

As a third resource type, many people with mental illness can benefit from training to facilitate participation in interpersonal relationships (Gingerich, 2002), organizational decision making (Barnes & Bowl, 2001), employment (Ford, 1995), advocacy (Hess et al., 2001), evaluation and research (Morrell-Bellai & Boydell, 1994), and many other areas. Fourth, many people with mental illness will require logistical resources to participate in activities, such as transportation and meals (Lord et al., 1998). Finally, the provision of resources to staff, too, can promote empowerment of people with mental illness. In particular, staff need time within their work day to engage clients in activities, which takes longer than staff making unilateral decisions (Gutiérrez, GlenMaye, & DeLois, 1995; Starkey & Leadholm, 1997). For clinical staff in particular in some settings, the amount of time staff spend with clients will be shaped largely by the value placed on this interaction by payers as indicated by what they will reimburse. That is, staff will be more likely to spend the time needed to involve clients if they can bill for that time. Finally, staff need development and training, especially related to identifying opportunities for empowerment and the benefits of this empowerment to them and their clients, and to learning how to work with clients in situations that have the potential for empowerment (Fisher, 1994a; Gutiérrez, GlenMaye et al., 1995; Spaulding et al., 2003).

SUPPORTIVE CULTURE

Culture may be defined as values, beliefs, and norms (behavioral expectations) that are shared by a particular social system (Glisson, 2000). The culture strongly shapes the interactions within that system. Culture exists at various levels including families, professions, organizations, communities, states, and countries. With a focus on human service agencies, Handler (1990, 1996) was most concerned with one aspect of culture, that being professional norms. He stated that professionals cannot be expected to violate their own professional norms (1990). Consequently, if these norms do not support shared decision making, professionals are unlikely to do so. Handler (1996) stated that for empowerment to occur, "There has to be a change in professional norms on the part of the power holders, that is, they have to come to believe that the dependent clients are part of the *solution* to their professional task" (p. 218). Handler included this as one of his three conditions for empowerment.

The development of an organizational culture supportive of shared decision making is critical to empowering people with severe mental illness (Gutiérrez, GlenMaye et al., 1995; Vandergang, 1996). Organizations with such a culture typically view client participation as a right (Katan & Prager, 1986). By contrast, many mental health organizations hold philosophies and have cultures that do not support shared decision making (Gutiérrez, GlenMaye et al., 1995); thus, organizations must be willing to change themselves in order to create opportunities for participation (Constantino & Nelson, 1995). The success of these change efforts ultimately depends on the extent to which those in power value client input and are willing to share power and provide the resources to support shared decision making (Carling, 1995). Since this book is more diverse than Handler's (1990, 1996) focus on organizations, culture is expanded beyond that of professional norms. The following sections outline various aspects of supportive cultures as they apply to people with severe mental illness.

Stigma Toward People With Mental Illness

The concept of stigma was introduced earlier as part of the discussion of powerlessness of people with mental illness. As previously indicated, stigma is negative attitudes and beliefs about people with mental illness that are erroneous (President's New Freedom Commission on Mental Health, 2003). Stigma typically includes fear that people with mental illness are violent and that they are irresponsible and therefore need someone to make decisions and care for them (Corrigan & Penn, 1999). Perlin (1992) referred to stigma as sanism, to emphasize its similarity to other "isms" including racism and sexism. He believed that sanism is more detrimental because the underlying negative beliefs about people with mental illness, though false, are largely accepted by society. He identified 10 myths that comprise sanism. These include that people with mental illness are less than human, as reflected in beliefs that "They are erratic, deviant, morally weak, sexually uncontrollable, emotionally unstable, superstitious, lazy, ignorant and demonstrate a primitive morality" (p. 393); that they are dangerous; that they are incompetent to make basic life decisions; that mental illness is consistent with popular media portrayals; that pejorative labels are acceptable to describe people with mental illness; that people with mental illness arrested for criminal acts frequently use their mental illness as an excuse to avoid criminal prosecution; and that people with mental illness "simply don't try hard enough" (p. 396) to improve themselves and their situations.

Perlin's (1992) concept of sanism and other negative beliefs are an imbedded part of the culture of many social systems, ranging from individuals, to organizations that provide services to people with mental illness, to communities, to societies (Carling, 1995). As an effect of stigma, Carling (1995) found that mental health professionals may become overprotective and paternalistic in their interactions with people with mental illness and have little hope that they can improve, that communities may engage in practices to exclude people with mental illness, and that the public has an excuse to inadequately fund mental health services. Stigma also can be internalized by people with mental illness; that is, they believe the stigma themselves. By accepting the erroneous beliefs that comprise stigma, people with mental illness may believe they are incompetent, may have low self-esteem, and may fail to seek opportunities that could be empowering (Corrigan & Watson, 2002). Given these manifestations of stigma, the Surgeon General called stigma "the most formidable obstacle to the future progress in the arena of mental illness and mental health" (U.S. DHHS, 1999, p. 3). While some progress has been made in decreasing overt acts associated with stigma, the more subtle and, in many ways, more debilitating attitudes and beliefs associated with stigma continue to be prevalent. Values and beliefs that are antithetical to stigma and that support empowerment are not yet widespread or consistently applied to offset the negative effects of stigma.

Models of Engagement

Numerous models and perspectives shape professional practice and public policy concerning people with mental illness. Four prominent ones are addressed. It is important to note that not all are mutually exclusive, as several share common traits. Models of practice are included in the discussion of a supportive culture because they reflect the values, beliefs, and norms that shape interactions with people with mental illness.

Medical Model

Spaulding et al. (2003) described the medical model, as applied to people with mental illness, as encompassing two aspects. The first is that mental illness is comparable to medical diseases. Second, and following from that assumption, medical treatment for symptoms is considered primary, usually consisting of medication, and the ultimate responsibility and decision-making authority for treatment rests with the physician. Holmes and Saleebey (1993) argued that the medical model is antithetical to empowerment and described the negative consequences when applying the medical model. "Besides reserving the greatest power to the helper, the medical model of care and management gives the professional considerable social control over the client or patient. This sanctioned control, in turn, creates barriers to the very empowerment professional helpers hope to facilitate" (pp. 62–63). They continued by adding, "The unspoken assumption of the medical model is that clienthood and autonomous selfhood are mutually exclusive concepts.... The professional comes to 'own' the client, giving or withholding services according to how well the client plays the role of client in terms of dependence and acquiescence" (p. 64). Guadagnoli and Ward (1998) believed that physicians working within the medical model can, and should, meaningfully incorporate patients into decision making. They wrote:

> We believe that patient participation in decision-making is justified on humane grounds alone and is in line with a patient's right to self-determination. We accept that some patients are not ready to participate in their medical decisions, but this should not mean that physicians adopt a paternalistic stance with these patients. Physicians should endeavor to engage all patients in decision making albeit at varying degrees. (p. 337)

It is important to note that while the medical model is often associated with practice by physicians, other mental health professionals sometimes adopt the medical model in their nonmedical interventions by viewing themselves as experts and clients as lacking the capacity to make meaningful contributions to decision making (Kumar, 2000).

Recovery Perspective

The recovery perspective has no single definition and can refer to a process, a vision, or a guiding principle (U.S. DHHS, 1999). Its essential message is that people with severe mental illness can regain a meaningful life despite their illness (Anthony, 1993; U.S. DHHS, 1999). In contrast to the medical model that focuses on reduction of symptoms, the recovery perspective focuses on increased self-esteem and regaining important life roles (U.S. DHHS, 1999). The use of the term recovery originated in the writings of people with mental illness in the 1980s and was fueled by recent research that found that over the course of two or more decades, a majority of people with severe mental illness regain the levels of functioning they had prior to the onset of their illness (Kruger, 2000; U.S. DHHS, 1999). Jacobson and Curtis (2000) noted that recovery is a manifestation of empowerment.

People with mental illness have offered their own perspective on recovery. In one study, people with mental illness identified recovery as having four dimensions, including recognizing the problem, that is, accepting one has a mental illness; transforming the self, that is, taking action to deal with the condition; reconciling the system, that is, using system resources to improve oneself; and reaching out to others, that is, making connections with others on an ongoing basis (Jacobson, 2001). In another study, people with mental illness identified recovery as having three components, including an initial phase of overcoming "stuckness" (p. 224), that is, acknowledging and accepting the mental illness, having the motivation to change, and finding a source of inspiration; a middle phase of regaining what was lost and moving forward, that is, returning to basic functions, fostering self-empowerment, and learning new things; and a later phase of improving the quality of life, that is, striving to attain an overall sense of well-being and reaching new potentials of higher functioning (Young & Ensing, 1999). Not everyone supports use of the term recovery. Lamb (2001), for instance, believed that recovery implied cure, which could lead some people to deny their illness and reject treatment. He offered alternative terms, such as in remission or recovering, but not recovered because of what he described as the chronic nature of severe mental illness.

Psychiatric Rehabilitation

As with the term recovery, one specific definition of, or approach to, psychiatric rehabilitation does not exist. This is exemplified by the use of different terms, with some referring to it as psychiatric rehabilitation (e.g., Anthony et al., 2002), while others use the term psychosocial rehabilitation (e.g., Hughes & Weinstein, 2000). Essentially, psychiatric rehabilitation is a comprehensive approach that seeks "to restore each person's ability for independent living, socialization, and life management" (Weinstein & Hughes, 2000, p. 35). Cook and Hoffschmidt (1993) and Weinstein and Hughes (2000) described important principles and components of psychiatric rehabilitation. Some of the principles include empowerment, client choice, a biopsychosocial approach, an emphasis on wellness and strengths, family involvement, the provision of ongoing services, and the evaluation of client and program outcomes. Service components include social skills and recreation, crisis services and outreach, case management, residential and housing services, educational supports, physical health services, vocational rehabilitation, and family support. Given the spectrum of service components, psychiatric rehabilitation utilizes individuals from all the major mental health professions. Competencies for individuals from any profession that work within the psychiatric rehabilitation model have been offered (Coursey et al., 2000a; 2000b). One of many competencies is fostering empowerment, which includes encouraging independent thinking, supporting consumers' freedom to make their own choices, supporting choice and risk-taking as leading to growth, avoiding controlling behaviors, and using a strengths-based model (Coursey et al., 2002b). While psychiatric rehabilitation promotes empowerment and independent functioning, Hendrickson-Gracie, Staley, and Neufeld-Morton (1996) observed that paternalism still exists in many agencies that practice this model and is found among all types of professionals working within them.

Strengths Perspective

The strengths perspective is an approach to working with vulnerable populations that promotes change by identifying and building upon the strengths of individuals, groups, and communities rather than focusing on, and treating, their dysfunctions, and by forming helping relationships based on partnership and mutuality rather than exercising power over another (Saleebey, 2002). Empowerment and the strengths perspective are mutually supportive (Congress & Sealy, 2001; Robbins, Chatterjee, & Canda, 1998). Rapp (1998, 2002), most notably, has applied this perspective to the development of a strengths-based model of case management with people with severe mental illness. He stated that the purpose of such an approach is "to assist consumers in identifying, securing, and sustaining the range of resources—both environmental and personal—needed to live, plan, and work in a normally interdependent way in the community" (1998, p. 44). Some of the principles of his approach include a focus on the individual's strengths rather than pathology; the community as an oasis of resources; interventions based on client self-determination; and people with mental illness continuing to learn, grow, and change. Rapp (1998) explained the relationship between his strengths model and empowerment. "In the strengths model, empowerment is used as a state that people aspire to and that clients and professionals collaborate in achieving. The strengths model, itself, is a set of methods and perspectives that embodies the process" (p. 22). A range of methods that can be organized across the following categories are used within this model: the establishment of a partnership between people with mental illness and their case managers, the assessment of strengths, personal planning, resources acquisition, and supportive case management (Rapp, 1998, 2002).

Professional Norms

Professional norms are part of culture, as they embody values and beliefs of the profession and give direction to standards of behavior in working with vulnerable populations. To reiterate Handler's (1990) point, professionals are unlikely to meaningfully engage clients in decision making if it violates their professional norms. The professional norms of the five professions that work most frequently with severe mental illness are considered through an examination of their professional codes of ethics.

Social Work

Among all the major professions that work with people with mental illness, social work aligns itself most explicitly with empowerment. The preamble to its professional code of ethics reads: "The primary mission of the social work profession is to enhance human well-being and help meet the basic human needs of all people, with particular attention to the needs and empowerment of people who are vulnerable, oppressed, and living in poverty" (National Association of Social Workers, 1999, p. 1). Social work principles and values reinforce the commitment to empowerment (Congress & Sealy, 2001; Dubois & Miley, 1999). Simon (1994) documented the long history of empowerment in the social work profession. A number of studies has found, however, that social workers have not always practiced the values and principles held by the profession. In fact, they have been coercive at times in their relationships with vulnerable populations (Handler, 1973; Margolin, 1997). Wilk (1994), for example, examined social work practice in psychiatric hospitals and found that a sizeable minority of social workers either disagreed with, or were indifferent to, patients' rights, and a smaller group even objected to rights that support patients making even small choices, such as the right to choose their clothing. In addition, Specht and Courtney (1994) argued that the profession has abandoned its mission of working with vulnerable populations.

Psychiatry

Professional codes of ethics for psychiatrists are inconsistent in their inclusion of empowerment. Bloch et al. (1999) noted that few codes of ethics exist specifically for psychiatrists. They presented two that pertained to psychiatrists practicing in the United States. The code that was written by the American Medical Association for psychiatrists in the United States, "Principles of Medical Ethics with Annotations Applicable to Psychiatry," contained no reference to empowerment or empowerment related concepts. The second code, "The Declaration of Madrid," was developed by the World Psychiatric Association and contained direct and indirect references to empowerment in its third ethical standard:

> The patient should be accepted as partner by right in the therapeutic process. The therapist-patient relationship must be based on mutual trust and respect, to allow the patient to make free and informed decisions. It is the duty of psychiatrists to provide the patient with relevant information so as to empower the patient to come to

a rational decision according to his or her personal values and preferences. (p. 518)

Psychiatrists, who are physicians with advanced training, are closely aligned with the medical model, which, as discussed before, does not incorporate empowerment as a component. Breakey, Flynn, and Van Tosh (1996) called upon psychiatrists to develop new skills and attitudes to work more constructively with people with mental illness, their family, advocates, and others.

Psychology

The "Ethical Principles of Psychologists and Code of Conduct," developed by the American Psychological Association (2002), does not specifically reference empowerment. It does, however, contain aspects of empowerment. The Preamble, for instance, states that psychologists "strive to help the public in developing informed judgments and choices concerning human behavior" (p. 3). Also, Principle E, Respect for People's Rights and Dignity, states, "Psychologists respect the dignity and worth of all people, and the rights of individuals to privacy, confidentiality, and self-determination. Psychologists are aware that special safeguards may be necessary to protect the rights and welfare of persons or communities whose vulnerabilities impair autonomous decision making" (p. 4). Nelson and Walsh-Bowers (1994), two psychologists, argued that the profession does not incorporate empowerment but should do so. They believed that psychologists need to better "understand the oppressive nature of psychiatric survivors' daily living conditions and experiences and to collaborate with survivors in developing empowering interventions to overcome that oppression" (p. 895).

Nursing

Like psychology, the code of ethics of the nursing profession does not include empowerment, but it does include related concepts (American Nurses Association, 2001). Most directly, these include Provision 1.1, Respect for Human Dignity, and Provision 1.4, The Right to Self-Determination. Part of Provision 1.4 reads:

> Patients have the moral and legal right to determine what will be done with their own person; to be given accurate, complete, and understandable information in a manner that facilitates an informed judgment; to be assisted with weighing the benefits, burdens, and available options in their treatment, including the choice of no treatment; to accept, refuse, or terminate treatment without deceit, undue influence, duress, coercion, or penalty; and to be given necessary support through the decision-making and treatment process. (p. 8)

Vander Henst (1997) noted that the field of nursing has started to promote client empowerment, but Barker (2001) and Sines (1994) argued it needs to be more fully incorporated by nurses working with people with mental illness.

Rehabilitation Professions

The codes of ethics of rehabilitation professions do not include the term empowerment, although, like the other professions, they do include aspects of empowerment (Scott, 1998). For example, the code of ethics of occupational therapists, which is the rehabilitation professional most likely to work with people with severe mental illness who do not also have a medical condition, includes two relevant principles. Principle 3 states that occupational therapists "shall respect the recipient and/or their surrogates(s) as well as the recipient's rights" (American Occupational Therapy Association, 2000, pp. 1–2). Subsection A states that they "shall collaborate with service recipients or their surrogate(s) in determining goals and priorities through the intervention process" (p. 2), Subsections B and C relate to informed consent, and Subsection D relates to the individual's right to refuse services. Although rehabilitation professions do not include the term empowerment in their code of ethics, Emener (1991) argued that empowerment should guide the rehabilitation profession, but that it did not, at least in 1991 when he made that statement. O'Hara and Harrell (1991) provided an example of how to apply an empowerment approach in rehabilitation of people with brain injuries. Even when rehabilitation professionals intend to empower people with mental illness, Townsend (1998) noted from her study of occupational therapists providing mental health services that it was difficult to implement empowerment-based services.

Staff Empowerment

The empowerment of staff is included in the discussion of culture because staff are more likely to adopt values, beliefs, and behaviors supportive of empowerment when they, themselves, are empowered within organizations (Bartle, Couchonnal, Canda, & Staker, 2002). Carling (1995), too, argued that fostering empowerment of people with mental illness requires that staff from the organizations from which they receive services also are empowered. As well as serving as a means to client empowerment, Staples (1999) noted that staff empowerment should be an end in itself because of the benefits to the organization that result from staff involvement in decision making.

Funding of Treatment, Rehabilitation, and Support Services

A supportive culture adequately funds, and provides access to, a range of mental health treatment, rehabilitation, and support services. As previously noted, however, the mental health system in the United

States is poorly funded, and many people do not have access to the services they need (Bianco & Wells, 2001; Mazade, Glover, & Hutchings, 2000; Mechanic, 2001; US DHHS, 1999). The discussion in chapters 5 through 11 of the seven activities that have the potential for empowerment includes the identification of areas that could benefit from increased funding to further support the empowerment of people with mental illness.

SUMMARY OF THE CONDITIONS FOR EMPOWERMENT

Restating this discussion in the form of conditions, table 4.1 lists the nine conditions for empowerment as they apply to people with severe mental illness. The first three conditions are internal to the person with

Table 4.1 Conditions for Empowering People With Severe Mental Illness

Conditions Internal to the Person With Mental Illness

Managed psychiatric symptoms—The person's psychiatric symptoms are managed to the degree necessary to meaningfully participate in a specific activity.

Participation skills—The person possesses the skills required to meaningfully participate in a particular activity.

Psychological readiness—The person has the psychological readiness, that is, confidence, motivation, and willingness to meaningfully participate in a particular activity.

Conditions Involving the Person's Environment

Mutual trust and respect—The person with mental illness and the persons with whom he or she is interacting have the necessary level of mutual trust and respect to meaningfully participate together in a particular activity.

Reciprocal concrete incentives—Concrete incentives exist for both the person with mental illness and persons with whom he or she is interacting to meaningfully participate together in a particular activity.

Availability of choices—The person has choices that he or she values and sufficient information about those choices to make informed decisions about a particular activity.

Participation structures and processes—The person has structures and processes through which to meaningfully participate in a particular activity.

Access to resources—The person has access to the resources needed to meaningfully participate in a particular activity, which may include social support, the availability of advocates, training, and logistical resources; and individuals with whom the person interacts also has access to resources, particularly adequate time to meaningfully participate and training on the benefits of working together and the skills to do so.

Supportive culture—The culture in which the person is interacting in a particular activity is supportive of shared participation. That culture typically includes absence of stigma against people with mental illness, mental health practice models that support empowerment, professional norms that support empowerment, and staff empowerment.

mental illness, while the remaining six exist in the person's interactions with his or her environment.

APPLYING THE CONDITIONS FOR EMPOWERMENT

The conditions for empowering people with severe mental illness have at least three applications. One is to guide the development of new programs or activities that have the potential to be empowering to ensure their design maximizes that possibility that the conditions for empowerment will be present in that program or activity. Programs will want to make certain, for example, that adequate resources are devoted to training clients and staff, that sufficient time to allow meaningful participation to occur is allocated, and that clients and staff have concrete incentives to meaningfully participate together. A second application is to provide a structure for conducting process evaluations of programs or activities that claim to be empowering or would like to be more empowering. Each of the nine conditions essentially becomes an evaluation question. For example, do consumers have the required skills levels to meaningfully participate? Is the culture supportive of shared decision making? A third application is to use the conditions for empowerment as an analytic tool to better understand how, and under what circumstances, specific activities can be empowering. The following seven chapters reflect this third application. The conditions for empowering people with mental illness are applied to seven activities to understand how, and under what circumstances, each one activity can be empowering. The potential of empowering people with severe mental illness through participation in treatment planning is considered first.

5

Empowerment Through
Treatment Planning

Treatment planning is the process by which the needs, strengths, and problems of people with severe mental illness are assessed, treatment goals are established, and treatment and rehabilitation activities are identified to facilitate goal achievement. The plan itself is structured by accrediting bodies such the Joint Commission on the Accreditation of Healthcare Organizations, the Commission on Accreditation of Rehabilitation Facilities, and the Centers for Medicare and Medicaid Services (Spaulding et al., 2003). Typical components of a treatment plan include a list of strengths, problems or obstacles, long-term and short-term goals, and treatment and rehabilitation interventions to help the person meet each goal (Kennedy, 1992; Spaulding et al., 2003). Spaulding et al. (2003) described the function of treatment plans as "a procedural map or blueprint that guides provision of specific services and other aspects of rehabilitation and recovery, toward achievement of the rehabilitation goals" (p. 46). An initial treatment plan, sometimes referred to as a master plan, is usually done when a person enters a mental health program; reviews of that plan take place periodically, such as every 90 days. Treatment plans also may include discharge plans when people are leaving programs to facilitate their continuation of treatment and rehabilitation in a new environment.

Historically, people with mental illness have had little voice in treatment planning (Spaulding et al., 2003). In recent years, however, the importance of their meaningful participation increasingly has been recognized (Pratt et al., 1999; Rapp, 1998; Spaulding et al., 2003; Vandiver & Corcoran, 2002). To illustrate, accrediting bodies now require the participation of people with mental illness in treatment planning (Spaulding et al., 2003). Also, a panel consisting of researchers, clinicians, people with mental illness, family members, and service providers recommended that the ability to engage people with mental illness in treatment planning be a required competency for those who work with people with mental illness (Coursey et al., 2000b). This emphasis exists, in part, because the meaningful involvement of people with mental illness in treatment planning can have positive outcomes. People with mental illness who participate in planning their treatment are more likely to meet their goals (Bassman, 1997; Liberman et al., 2001), are more likely to participate in aftercare when discharged from hospitalization (Kopelowicz, Wallace, & Zarate, 1998), and are more likely to perceive that their needs are being met (Peck, Gulliver, & Towel, 2002; Roth & Crane-Ross, 2002).

Meaningful participation in treatment planning can be empowering for people with mental illness in at least two ways. First, it gives them control over, or at least a significant voice in, a process that can help them to identify, prioritize, and reach some of their life goals (Kilian et al., 2003). Second, it can help people with mental illness secure needed resources. Access to resources, as mentioned before, is a critical component of empowerment. Participation in treatment planning can be particularly empowering for individuals coerced into treatment, because it gives them back some independence and control, even if the coercion results in a limitation of some of the treatment goals and interventions (Rooney, 1992; 2002).

For treatment planning to be empowering, however, people with mental illness must meaningfully participate in the process. There is considerable evidence that this does not always occur, despite general recognition of its importance (Gerhart, 1990; Kilian et al., 2003). Some descriptions of treatment planning still do not incorporate participation by people with mental illness (e.g., Vess, 2001). Also, some programs are more concerned about the treatment-planning document meeting accreditation standards than with the meaningful involvement of people with mental illness in creating the document (Kennedy, 1992). In addition, variation in the adequacy of treatment planning can occur across units within programs (Baer, Goebel, & Flexer, 1993). Next, while there may be widespread agreement that people with mental illness should participate, agreement on the specific role that they should play and under what circumstances their participation might be limited does not exist (Spaulding et al., 2003). It is against this backdrop of the empowerment potential of treatment planning and the inconsistency of meaningful participation that the conditions for empowerment are applied to treatment planning by people with severe mental illness. Table 5.1 summarizes the conditions for empowerment as they apply to treatment planning, each of which will be discussed in turn.

Table 5.1 Conditions for Empowering People With Severe Mental Illness Through Treatment Planning

---

Managed psychiatric symptoms—The person has psychiatric symptoms managed to the degree required to meaningfully participate in treatment planning.

Participation skills—The person possesses the interpersonal and problem-solving skills required to meaningfully participate in treatment planning.

Psychological readiness—The person has the confidence, motivation, and willingness to meaningfully participate in treatment planning.

Mutual trust and respect—The person with mental illness and the clinicians involved in treatment planning have the necessary level of mutual trust and respect to meaningfully participate together in treatment planning.

Reciprocal concrete incentives—Concrete incentives to meaningfully participate together in treatment planning exist for both the person with mental illness and clinicians.

Availability of choices—The person has choices of treatment goals and interventions to reach those goals that are valued by him or her.

Participation structures and processes—The person has structures and processes through which to meaningfully participate in treatment planning.

Access to resources—The person has access to the resources needed to meaningfully participate in treatment planning.

Supportive culture—A culture exists that supports the meaningful participation of the person in treatment planning.

MANAGED PSYCHIATRIC SYMPTOMS

One condition for empowering a person with severe mental illness through treatment planning is that the psychiatric symptoms of the person with mental illness are managed to the degree required to meaningfully participate. As noted in the history of powerlessness, until recent years, people were considered incompetent to participate in treatment planning once diagnosed with a severe mental illness. This assumption is no longer valid, although stigma continues to promote it (Grisso & Appelbaum, 1998). The symptoms of mental illness still can prevent some people, generally recognized as competent, from meaningfully participating in treatment planning at particular times. Symptoms can limit insight into their mental illness and their ability to focus on the topic, to process information, to consider options, to make informed choices, and to understand the consequences of their actions (Grisso & Appelbaum, 1998; Hoge & Feucht-Haviar, 1995; Husted, 1999).

It can be difficult to determine when psychiatric symptoms are managed enough for people to participate in treatment planning. For example, Grisso and Appelbaum (1995) used three methods to determine the level of impaired decision making among people admitted to a psychiatric hospital that would have prevented their meaningful participation in planning their treatment. Across the three methods, the frequency of impairment ranged from approximately 25% to 50% of people diagnosed with schizophrenia, and from 10% to 25% of people diagnosed with depression. Further adding to the uncertainty, some people in the study initially deemed incompetent to participate were able to meet minimal levels of competency when information was provided to them in smaller increments. Consequently, depending on the methods clinicians use to assess ability to participate in treatment planning and to provide people with information, some individuals will be deemed competent to participate while others with the same symptoms will not be. Even when decision making is severely impaired, clinicians still should encourage people with mental illness to participate in aspects of treatment planning that do not include decisions that put them or others at risk. As stated before, it is rare that psychiatric symptoms are so severe that people cannot make any decisions for themselves. Then, as people respond to treatment and the severity of psychiatric symptoms subsides, they can assume greater roles in treatment planning.

PARTICIPATION SKILLS

A second condition for empowerment is that the person with mental illness possesses the interpersonal and problem-solving skills required to meaningfully participate in treatment planning. These skills include being able to identify and express their needs and goals, to weigh options, to cognitively link services and interventions with problem resolution or goal achievement, and to resolve conflicts with staff if they arise during treatment planning. As stated before, many people with mental illness do not possess these skills (Gerhart, 1990; Spaulding et al., 2003). Consequently, it may be necessary to teach people the skills needed for treatment planning. Starkey and Leadholm (1997) presented the experiences of one hospital in promoting skill development for participation in treatment planning. Staff at this hospital offered clients a range of opportunities to improve skills that could be applied to treatment planning, as well as established treatment-planning groups to discuss the importance of treatment planning and to assist clients to identify their personal goals and obstacles to reaching those goals.

PSYCHOLOGICAL READINESS

A third condition for empowerment is that the person with mental illness has the confidence, motivation, and willingness to meaningfully participate in treatment planning. One model of psychiatric rehabilitation refers to this state as rehabilitation readiness (Pratt et al., 1999). Pratt et al. (1999) defined the term and stated its importance. "Psychiatric rehabilitation readiness refers to an individual's desire and motivation to pursue some aspect of psychiatric rehabilitation. Without desire or motivation, an individual will not act to achieve a goal. Some degree of readiness is, therefore, a necessary element for rehabilitation success" (p. 116). The lack of psychological readiness to engage in treatment planning can have many roots for people with mental illness, including past failed attempts to improve themselves, fear of change, a lack of knowledge of themselves and the possibilities that exist for them, feelings of powerlessness, and fatigue, to name a few (Pratt et al., 1999; Rapp, 1998).

Given the diversity of causes of the lack of psychological readiness, multiple approaches may be required to promote the active participation of people with mental illness in treatment planning. Flannery et al. (1996) suggested that some aspects of nonparticipation may be caused by clinical depression. Therefore, treatment of the depression through medication or therapy may first be needed before meaningful participation in treatment planning can occur. Rapp (1998) found that supportive relationships between people with mental illness and their case managers can foster psychological readiness. He explained, "The relationship is best seen as a medium to achievement. For many clients, the relationship with the case manager becomes a primary mechanism for increasing confidence, identifying goals and risking dreaming, and recognizing talents and strengths" (p. 62). Spaulding et al. (2003) sought to reverse the sense of failure associated with the lack of psychological readiness by creating opportunities for success. They wrote, "Ultimately, the best antidote for failure is success. . . . Much of the task of rehabilitation planning is to anticipate . . . success opportunities and exploit them" (p. 185). Finally, a promising approach for increasing psychological readiness is motivational interviewing. Motivational interviewing is used to help individuals identify goals on their own and to develop a commitment to reaching them by identifying the costs and benefits of action and nonaction (Miller & Rollnick, 2002). This approach uses active listening and expressing empathy, avoids argumentation, and supports self-efficacy. Mental health professionals have used motivational interviewing extensively in the treatment of people with substance abuse disorders and, more recently, have applied it to treatment of people with mental illness (Corrigan, McCracken, & Holmes, 2001; Graeber, Moyers, Griffin, Guajardo, & Tonigan, 2003; Kemp, David, & Hayward, 1996; Mueser et al., 2003).

MUTUAL TRUST AND RESPECT

A fourth condition for empowerment is that mutual trust and respect exist between the person with mental illness and the clinicians involved in treatment planning. Clinicians are unlikely to relinquish paternalistic approaches to treatment planning, unless they respect the right of people with mental illness to make treatment decisions and trust that clients can make good care decisions for themselves when provided with choices and understandable information about those choices. People with mental illness are unlikely to want to participate in treatment planning unless they believe clinicians respect their right and ability to participate and have their best interests in mind. Manning and Gual's (1997) statement about informed consent applies to trust in treatment planning. "The spirit of informed consent calls for a partnership between provider and client. Partnerships are based on egalitarian relationships that respect and appreciate the different strengths each bring to the decision process" (p. 111). Hendrickson-Gracie et al. (1996) wrote about the importance of trust and respect in treatment planning from the perspective of people with mental illness. "All of the clients indicated that they did want their workers to directly express any concerns regarding their goals. . . . They valued their workers' experience and input, especially if they felt that the worker really cared about their success" (p. 28).

People with mental illness typically complete treatment plans with clinicians with whom they already have an established relationship. Exceptions include completion of initial treatment plans when people with mental illness first enter mental health programs, or when clients are assigned new clinicians when their previous workers have been reassigned or have left the organization. Because most treatment planning is done between parties that know each other, the relationships that form outside of formal treatment-planning sessions will affect treatment planning. Rapp (1998) and Repper, Ford, and Cooke (1994) offered suggestions for forming relationships based on mutual trust and respect. Although both described client–case manager relationships, their suggestions have applicability to other types of relationships between people with mental illness and mental health professionals. Rapp emphasized the importance of "empathy, genuineness, and unconditional positive regard" (p. 64). He also recommended that case managers self-disclose information as a way to build the relationship and model emotions and actions; reinforce and celebrate accomplishments; schedule meetings at times and places convenient to the client; engage in informal conversations, over a cup of coffee for example, to get to know each other better; and clarify expectations each has for the other. Through interviews with people with mental illness and their case managers, Repper et al. identified factors that facilitate mutual trust. Some included setting realistic expectations with clients, breaking down goals into small steps and recognizing seemingly small yet important accomplishments, demonstrating positive and empathetic understanding of clients, being flexible in meeting clients at times when clients needed them instead of just during scheduled appointments, and having a long-term relationship during which each can get to know the other. Repper et al. summarized their most important finding. "Both the client interviews and the case manager interviews gave a strong impression of the clients as independent people who were worthy of respect, and who valued the respect accorded them by the case managers" (p. 1103).

The development of mutual trust and respect can be more difficult when people with mental illness are coerced into treatment. When planning treatment with people coerced into treatment, it is important that mental health professionals clarify their relationship with the coercive body and apply principles of procedural justice, as introduced in chapter 3. Draine and Solomon (2001) alluded to this in their study of people with mental illness on probation or parole. "Making the extent of collaboration explicit to clients—including the conditions under which incarceration may become an option—may help both systems gain credence with clients. Maintenance of trust depends, however, on both probation/parole officers and mental health workers following due process and accepted guidelines for ethical practice" (pp. 266–267). Mental health professionals can promote trust and respect in people with mental illness coerced into treatment by not judging them, by maximizing opportunities for them to make as many treatment decisions as possible within the limitations placed upon them by the coercive body, and by using the treatment plan when possible to provide a roadmap for them to end the coercion.

The development of mutual trust and respect also can be more difficult with people with mentally illness who are from cultural, racial, or ethnic backgrounds that are different from those of the clinicians with whom they are working. For mutual trust and respect to occur, both parties must be able to understand each other and accept differences, which are more difficult to do when cultural, racial, and ethnic differences exist (U.S. DHHS, 2001). In response, mental health organizations and professions have been called upon to provide culturally competent services, which refers to "the delivery of services responsive to the cultural concerns of racial and ethnic minority groups, including their languages, histories, traditions, beliefs, and values" (U.S. DHHS, 2001, p. 36). This requires that clinicians be given additional training, more time to engage in treatment planning to ensure that they understand their clients' attitudes and needs in order to match them with the best available options, and, in some cases, resources to hire interpreters. Coursey et al. (2000b) stated that conducting treatment in a culturally competent manner is a basic competency that all mental health professionals should possess because of its effect on treatment planning and other aspects of work with diverse populations.

RECIPROCAL CONCRETE INCENTIVES

A fifth condition for empowerment is that both the person with mental illness and the clinician have concrete incentives to meaningfully participate together in treatment planning. At least four incentives exist for people with mental illness to meaningfully participate in developing their treatment plans. First, participation can result in the subjective feeling of empowerment for them (Kilian et al., 2003). Second, they are more likely to have meaningful goals and interventions included in the treatment plan if they share information about themselves and express their preferences. Third, they need clinicians' expertise to assist them to identify the interventions that are most likely to help them meet their goals (Corrigan, 2002). Fourth, if the person is coerced into treatment, the treatment plan can provide a roadmap for ending the coercion. The primary incentive for clinicians to meaningfully involve people with mental illness in treatment planning is that this involvement increases the likelihood that their clients will have favorable outcomes (Liberman et al., 2001). People with mental illness possess information about their illness, their strengths, and their goals that clinicians need in order to develop an individualized treatment plan that is most appropriate for their clients, and that their clients are likely to follow (Corrigan, 2002).

AVAILABILITY OF CHOICES

A sixth condition for empowerment is that the person with mental illness has a selection of treatment goals and interventions to reach those goals that are valued by him or her. The President's New Freedom Commission on Mental Health (2003) summarized the importance of choices. "Without choice and availability of acceptable treatment options, people with mental illnesses are unlikely to engage in treatment or to participate in appropriate and timely interventions. Thus, giving consumers access to a range of effective, community-based treatment options is critical to achieving their full community participation" (p. 29). People with mental illness should have choices across a range of service types (e.g., medication, housing, and employment) and choices within each service type (e.g., choices of types and locations of housing).

The Surgeon General's report on mental health identified the types of treatment, rehabilitation, and support services needed by most people with severe mental illness (U.S. DHHS, 1999). The report stated that an effective delivery system should include medication; case management; assertive community treatment; psychiatric rehabilitation activities; inpatient hospitalization and community alternatives for crisis care; services for people with the dual diagnoses of mental illness and substance abuse disorders; consumer self-help; consumer-operated programs; advocacy services; family self-help and advocacy; housing; income, educational, and employment supports; and health coverage.

One factor seriously limiting choice is the fact that many people do not have access to the services they need. As described in the history of powerlessness, the U.S. system of mental health care for people with severe mental illness is poorly funded, is fragmented across service systems and levels of government, and emphasizes the use of medication at the expense of other types of treatment, rehabilitation, and support services (Wells, 2001; Mechanic, 2001; President's New Freedom Commission on Mental Health, 2003; Spaulding et al., 2003; U.S. DHHS, 1999). Access to services is particularly limited for racial and ethnic minorities and for people living in rural areas (President's New Freedom Commission, 2003; U.S. DHHS, 2001).

Compounding the lack of access to services, and thus the availability of choices, private insurance does not pay for many of the services needed by people with severe mental illness. It also places financial limits on those services it does pay for through the use of deductibles, copayments, and expenditure restrictions that are higher in most cases than insurance for physical health (Mechanic, 2001). Efforts to create parity in insurance coverage between mental health and physical health services have had a minimal effect to date (U.S. DHHS, 1999). The federal Mental Health Parity Act of 1996 eliminated disparities only in lifetime and annual limits. It did not apply to companies with 50 or fewer employees, or require that health insurance plans include coverage for mental health services. Insurance plans can continue to limit visits and require higher deductibles and copayments. Individual states are beginning to pass parity laws of their own. However, coverage varies widely across those states. Also, federal law prohibits states from mandating parity for companies with self-insured health coverage.

Many people who do not have any insurance, have inadequate insurance coverage, or have used all their insurance benefits often resort to state-funded mental health services. These services, too, are lacking. State governments never have funded services to the degree needed. States have further reduced their already inadequate spending for mental health and other social services in recent years because of the downturn in the economy (Mazade, Glover, & Hutchings, 2000). In addition, the growth in Medicaid funding for mental health services has forced states to allocate a high percentage of their resources toward their share of the state-federal funding match. This has left states with few dollars to spend on people who are employed, have low-to-moderate incomes, and cannot afford to pay privately; who do not qualify for Medicaid; and who do not have access to mental health services through private insurance (Frank, Goldman, & Hogan, 2003). As a result, the safety net for mental health services has been reduced significantly. For example, there is anecdotal evidence that some community mental health centers in Missouri and other states are no longer serving prospective clients who do not qualify for Medicaid and cannot afford to pay for services through the private sector, but whom they would have served prior to the recent budget cuts.

The increased use of managed care also can affect choices of mental health services. At this point, however, it is uncertain whether managed care will increase or decrease service options. Managed care is a label applied to an array of methods to administer and finance health and mental health care with the purpose of controlling costs and providing quality services (Wernet, 1999). Reviews of the use of managed care to provide mental health services to people with severe mental illness have found mixed results to date. Shera (2001) determined that managed care placed unrealistic limits on the amount of services and relied too frequently on the use of medication while underutilizing community outreach services and psychiatric rehabilitation. The National Alliance for the Mentally Ill, a mental health advocacy group, sponsored an evaluation of nine major mental health managed care plans that had contracts with state mental health authorities (Koyanagi & Belivacqua, 2001). Its report was highly critical of the plans for not paying for newer, more effective medications, psychiatric rehabilitation, active community treatment, and housing supports. Not all the evidence about managed care, however, is negative. Case studies from Illinois and Iowa, for instance, reported positive applications of managed care to services for people with severe mental illness (Christian-Michaels, Noll, & Wernet, 1999; Ellison et al., 2002). While acknowledging problems with managed care, Mechanic (1999, 2001) and Spaulding et al. (2003) argued that policy makers and mental health advocates should accept its existence, take advantage of its strengths, and work to improve its deficiencies.

Although previous discussion focused on the availability of service choices (or lack thereof) offered through the mental health system, treatment plan choices also can be limited by legal or informal sources that are coercing treatment. With minimal input, if any, from the person with mental illness, criminal justice authorities, for example, may require that probationers with mental illness receive treatment for a substance abuse disorder from a particular provider. As another example, a civil court judge may require that a person found NGRI must agree to take medication and attend a day program in order to be granted a conditional release to live in the community under supervision. As a third example, a legal guardian may refuse to allow a person under his or her authority to move from a group home into a supervised apartment. Finally, as an example of informal coercion, a wife who is separated from her husband may insist that he agree to take medication in order for them to reunite.

PARTICIPATION STRUCTURES AND PROCESSES

A seventh condition for empowerment is that structures and processes that enable the person with mental illness to meaningfully participate in treatment planning are in place. Two basic structures for treatment planning exist: treatment teams and case managers with support from others. Members of the treatment team may include the person with mental illness for whom the plan is being written; mental health professionals including a psychiatrist, a psychologist, a social worker, a nurse, and a rehabilitation professional; other service providers involved with the person; individuals from the person's support network such as family members or close friends; a legal guardian if the person has been found incompetent; interpreters if the person is hearing impaired or does not speak the same language as other team members; and advocates chosen by or for the person (Baer et al., 1993; Liberman et al., 2001; Spaulding et al., 2003). Criminal or civil court judges typically are not considered part of the treatment team, although they may influence treatment plan content or even grant final approval of plans (Spaulding et al., 2003). Psychiatrists traditionally have served as team leaders, directing the treatment plan and all aspects of treatment, although, as Spaulding et al. (2003) noted, laws and accreditation standards do not require this. An alternative to the treatment team structure is for a case manager and the person with mental illness to develop the plan together. Other parties may be brought into the process for aspects of the plan, and accreditation standards typically require that the treatment plan be signed by a supervising psychiatrist and possibly other mental health professionals.

A special note about the role of family members in treatment planning is warranted because, historically, they largely have been excluded from that process. Regardless of the treatment-planning structure, there is widespread agreement that family members should be involved in treatment planning when they have a genuine, constructive interest in their relative, and when the person with mental illness agrees to it (Davis, 2002; Gerhart, 1990; Marshall & Solomon, 2000). Engaging family members in treatment planning is now considered a basic competency for mental health professionals (Coursey et al., 2000b).

Regardless of the treatment-planning structure, the process of treatment planning involves individualizing treatment goals and activities, adapting decision making to the abilities of people with mental illness, resolving any differences of opinions, and modifying processes when the person with mental illness is incompetent or coerced into treatment. For treatment plans to be individualized, people with mental illness need to be present when the plan is written. While this seems obvious, it certainly does not always happen (e.g., Crosby, Carter, & Barry, 1995; Longo, Marsh-Williams, & Tate, 2002). Once present, they must be allowed to express their preferences for treatment goals and interventions. Two barriers to individualized treatment planning are the use of predetermined lists of goals and the use of computerized treatment-planning systems that generate goals based largely on the results of standardized assessment instruments (Rapp, 1998; Vess, 2001).

It often will be necessary for clinicians to adapt the treatment-planning process to the abilities of the people with mental illness. For instance, they may need to break goals down into smaller, more concrete goals or reframe general discussion into goal statements (Rapp, 1998). When treatment planning takes place through a team, it may be less threatening and anxiety-producing for some people with mental illness to meet with one team member to explore possible goals and interventions prior to the formal treatment-planning session with the entire treatment team (Baer et al., 1993). Particularly when people with mental illness are new to programs, case managers or treatment teams may need to spend additional time on treatment planning to ensure that the people with mental illness with whom they are working understand the process and express their opinions. Others may need additional assistance from an advocate to meaningfully participate (Baer et al., 1993). This advocate may be someone from outside the organization, such as a representative from Protection and Advocacy, or a member of the organization (Atkinson & MacPherson, 2001; Robbins & Van Rybrock, 1995; Rosenman, Korten, & Newman, 2000).

Conflicts over the selection of goals and interventions invariably will arise during the treatment-planning process between the person with mental illness and other team members, or between other team members themselves. Some conflicts may be resolved through good faith negotiation (Gerhart, 1990). Others may require mediators to facilitate resolution (Flower, 1999). Regardless of the method of resolution, Spaulding et al. (2003) stressed the importance of having clinical and administrative procedures in place to contend with disagreements. Ideally, these procedures should give priority to the preferences of people with mental illness and include components of procedural justice.

The treatment-planning process will need to be modified when people with mental illness are incompetent or coerced into treatment. If clinical competency is questionable, clinicians may be able to provide people with low-risk choices. If a person has been declared legally incompetent, the courts will have appointed a legal guardian who has decision-making authority in treatment planning. Clinicians and guardians still can ask people for their preferences regarding treatment-planning goals and interventions and support those preferences whenever possible. In addition, some people with mental illness who currently are clinically incompetent may have completed a psychiatric advanced directive that expressed their treatment preferences (Stavis, 1999; Swanson, Tepper, Backlar, & Swartz, 2000). Preferences expressed in these directives should be honored if possible. Few states have enacted special legislation authorizing them, however, and studies have found significant problems with their implementation

(Parry & Gilliam, 2002). In working with people coerced into treatment, it is important that clinicians engaged in treatment planning clearly specify areas in which people with mental illness cannot make decisions and then proceed to maximize choices in all other areas. Spaulding et al. (2003) stressed that other than clients not having veto power over parts of the treatment plan, the treatment-planning process should be no different for those who are coerced into treatment.

ACCESS TO RESOURCES

An eighth condition for empowerment is that the person with mental illness has the resources needed to participate in treatment planning. In the discussion of the previous condition, two resources, advocates and mediators, were identified to support people with mental illness in treatment planning. Rosenman et al. (2000) described an advocacy program in an acute psychiatric hospital in which the advocate had a major role in treatment planning. The advocate participated in treatment-planning sessions and informal meetings with staff, both with and without the person with mental illness present. The advocate expressed clients' preferences and previous experiences with treatment, and, when difference arose, she attempted to negotiate alternatives that would be satisfactory to both staff and the clients. While many staff members initially were hostile to the advocate, over time they developed a positive attitude toward her work. Robbins and Van Rybrock (1995) noted, too, that tension can arise between advocates and staff, which they identified in their discussion of advocates from Protection and Advocacy organizations. Mediation programs can be another resource for people with mental illness. Flower (1999) stated that they are most successful when they are able to facilitate communication without appearing to favor one side over the other. People with mental illness especially must feel a sense of fairness. She argued that mediators should be mental health professionals in order to be able to understand the treatment process, treatment needs, and options, as well as the thoughts, symptoms, and behaviors of people with mental illness. She also believed that attorneys should not be present during mediation sessions because it makes the process more adversarial. Another resource type people with mental illness may need is logistical resources, usually in the form of transportation and day care, that can enable them to attend treatment-planning sessions in clinicians' office if clinicians are unable to meet them in their own homes. Also, some people will need the resource of adequate time for treatment planning, which can be limited if they are working; participating in educational, vocational, or rehabilitation activities; or attending to other responsibilities, such as providing child care or assisting aging parents.

Clinicians, too, need resources. Fisher (1994a) emphasized the importance of staff training focused on staff realizing the potential of people with mental illness to direct their own treatment and thus becoming less paternalistic in treatment planning. Others also have noted the need for staff training, especially about clients' perspectives on treatment planning, including reasons that some clients may not readily participate and ways for staff and clients to work collaboratively in treatment planning (Chinman et al., 1999). Staff also need the time to meaningfully engage people with mental illness in treatment planning. It takes considerably longer for treatment plans to be written when people with mental illness are present and actively participating. Both Chinman et al. (1999) and Starkey and Leadholm (1997) identified that shortage of staff time was a barrier to the involvement of the people with mental illness in treatment planning.

SUPPORTIVE CULTURE

The final condition for empowering people with severe mental illness through treatment planning is that a culture exists that supports their meaningful participation. A supportive culture means, in part, that stigma is minimized within the mental health organization, particularly the beliefs that people with mental illness are incapable of making meaningful decisions and caring for themselves. If either staff or people with mental illness hold these attitudes, empowerment through treatment planning in unlikely to occur. Starkey and Leadholm (1997) provided examples of beliefs that staff of a hospital held prior to the introduction of a new system to increase client participation in treatment planning at the hospital. "It was not uncommon to hear that 'our patients are not able to contribute to a treatment plan.' . . . A basic assumption was that patients needed to be 'taken care of' rather than challenged or allowed to become more independent" (p. 504).

One of the first steps in developing a supportive culture is to adopt models that support people with mental illness directing their own treatment. Models that purport this include the recovery perspective, psychiatric rehabilitation, and the strengths perspective, which were described in chapter 4. Organizations must then operationalize the principles of these models. Rapp (1998) and Spaulding et al. (2003) suggested other ways to create a supportive culture. These included, for example, leaders creating mission and vision statements that incorporate recovery and strengths perspectives; administrators modeling these principles for direct service staff in their interactions with people with mental illness; staff receiving extensive training, technical assistance, and opportunities to discuss engagement issues; administrators developing systems to evaluate client participation and staff competencies related to treatment planning; and administrators establishing caseload sizes at reasonable levels so that staff have time to meaningfully engage their clients in treatment planning.

CASE STUDIES

To increase understanding of the opportunities for, and limitations to, the empowerment of people with mental illness through treatment planning, empowerment is examined through two cases studies, one among people with mental illness residing in a public psychiatric hospital that provides long-term care and treatment (Linhorst et al., 2002; Linhorst et al, 1999), and the other among those residing in the community and receiving services from a publicly funded community mental health agency (Kryah et al., 2003).

Empowerment Among Clients in a Psychiatric Hospital (SLPRC)

Degree of Empowerment

Clients residing in the SLPRC cottage program and ward programs experienced different degrees of empowerment. Cottage clients experienced a moderate amount of empowerment, as most clients meaningfully participated in treatment planning. The primary factors limiting empowerment of cottage program clients were a lack of choice of treatment activities, and the failure of the case manager of one cottage to involve her clients in treatment planning, despite the expectation that she do so. Clients from the hospital ward programs were not empowered through treatment planning. Few ward clients meaningfully participated in treatment planning. When it occurred, it was an exception to practice.

Application of Conditions for Empowerment

SLPRC clients and staff indicated that some clients were unable to participate in treatment planning because of unmanaged psychiatric symptoms and low functioning levels. There was, however, wide variation in the severity of symptoms. Psychiatric symptoms and impaired cognitive ability interfered with treatment planning to a much greater extent among clients residing in the ward programs than in the cottage program. This is expected because one of the criteria for residing in the cottage program at the time of the study was that clients have their psychiatric symptoms managed to the level needed to participate, at least minimally, in treatment planning. Because clients varied in their treatment-planning skills, all cottage clients were required to complete a module on developing treatment plans when they entered the program in order to give them the minimal skills for participation. Clients, and more frequently staff, indicated that some clients did not meaningfully participate in treatment for a variety of reasons that could be classified as lack of psychological readiness. These included apathy, feelings of helplessness, lack of motivation, resistance to change, fear of setting new goals, and refusal to participate. This, however, was identified as a limitation to participation with much less frequency than most other limitations.

Some clients and staff raised issues associated with mutual trust and respect, or the lack thereof. Some clients, and particularly staff, indicated that a limited number of staff maintained paternalistic approaches to treatment planning and did not respect, or have confidence in, clients' ability to meaningfully participate in treatment planning. Some clients reiterated this point by stating that some staff listened to clients in treatment planning better than others. Also, clients in one focus group stated they did not trust staff and feared being labeled oppositional if they disagreed with staff during treatment planning. The biggest limitation to choice in treatment planning, particularly in the ward programs, was highly structured treatment programs that offered clients little choice of activities. The cottage program had many required treatment activities but allowed greater flexibility as clients progressed through the program, particularly as discharge neared. The greatest area of choice of activities for clients in both the ward and cottage programs was leisure and recreational activities. Choices also were limited by insufficient numbers of staff to escort clients who posed security risks to treatment activities, and by activities being discontinued because of staffing reductions associated with recent budget cuts. In addition, some clients had their choices limited because criminal court commitments or their legal guardians required them to participate in particular treatment activities. Finally, because of staffing limitations and statutory restrictions placed on forensic clients, few clients had the choice of participating in community-based activities. There were notable exceptions in which a small number of NGRI clients obtained court orders to be able to attend educational or vocational programs in the community while still residing in the hospital.

Differences in treatment-planning participation structures and processes in cottage and ward programs also affected empowerment. Ward programs used traditional treatment teams led by psychiatrists to develop treatment plans. Clients usually were not present when plans were written. Instead, teams explained the completed plans to clients and discussed any concerns that clients may have with the plan contents. Most staff indicated that they negotiated differences when clients disagreed with components of it, although most clients stated they felt there was no room for negotiation. The cottage program used a case manager structure for treatment planning. The case manager and client usually met to discuss the treatment goals and activities before the formal planning meeting. A formal meeting was then held to finalize the treatment plan, with participants including the client, the case manager, the treating psychiatrist, and selected other individuals involved in the client's treatment. With the exception of one cottage, most clients and staff indicated that there was good faith negotiation of any differences that arose during treatment planning. In the one cottage that was the exception, clients reported the case manager did not respect their choices and would not negotiate differences of opinion. Client advocates rarely participated in treatment planning in either the ward or cottage programs. When they did, they typically were from Missouri Protection and Advocacy. Their involvement in the process often became adversarial and did not appear to increase the meaningful participation of the client in treatment planning. A formal mediation program did not exist for resolving differences experienced in treatment planning. Staff from the ward programs cited that lack of time allocated to treatment planning was a significant limitation to involving clients in treatment planning. In contrast, cottage program staff indicated that treatment planning was considered a significant part of their job duties and sufficient time was allocated to it.

SLPRC attempted to create a culture that would promote the participation of people with mental illness in treatment planning. The vision and value statements of the Missouri Department of Mental Health and the hospital addressed aspects of involvement in treatment planning. One Missouri Department of Mental Health value statement, for example, read, "All people design their own services and supports to enhance their lives and achieve their personal visions." Also, the hospital vision statement was "Rehabilitation through choices: People with mental illness will make meaningful choices about how they socialize, live, learn, and work." To support these and other values, the hospital adopted psychiatric rehabilitation to complement its medical model of practice. The cottage program adopted one particular model of psychiatric rehabilitation that strongly promoted participation in treatment planning. The initial cohort of cottage program staff hired after the adoption of that model received intensive training from a national psychiatric rehabilitation training center that included content on how to meaningfully engage clients in treatment planning, among other topics. In contrast, staff from the ward programs did not receive any training in involving clients in treatment planning or in psychiatric rehabilitation, other than the brief orientation that all hospital employees received at the time of the creation of the new mission, vision, and value statements that incorporated client choice and other principles of psychiatric rehabilitation.

Empowerment Among Clients of a Community Agency (BJC-BH)

Degree of Empowerment

With few exceptions, BJC-BH clients were empowered to a large degree through meaningful participation in treatment planning. There was considerable evidence that most clients identified their goals and selected interventions from the range of available options. Empowerment was limited, however, by the lack of availability of choices in some areas, especially housing, transportation, and quality medical, dental, and optical services. It also was limited by some clients having legal guardians who sometimes did not involve those clients in treatment planning under their authority. Empowerment was further limited by a very small number of case managers who did not believe in client participation or who were "burned out," a phrase some clients used.

Application of Conditions for Empowerment

Clients and staff indicated that a limited number of clients were unable to participate in treatment planning because of unmanaged psychiatric symptoms. When psychiatric symptoms periodically increased among clients, BJC-BH staff indicated they often delayed scheduling treatment-planning sessions. Staff stated that both clients and staff recognized the need to delay scheduled sessions and were comfortable in doing so in order for the client to be able to meaningfully participate later. Staff also spoke of tailoring treatment planning to the skill level of the individual client. For instance, staff helped some clients to reframe goals that were vague or seemingly grandiose into smaller, more workable goals that still captured clients' desires. Most clients were psychologically ready to participate in treatment planning, although some incidents of apathy, lack of motivation, fear of setting new goals, or refusal to participate were noted.

Issues associated with mutual trust and respect were raised in two areas. One staff member believed that during the development of initial treatment plans, new clients often would say what they thought the staff wanted to hear rather than indicating their own preferences. The staff member attributed this, in part, to the absence of client trust in the organization, which had not yet had time to develop. Also, some clients and staff indicated that staff turnover affected the ability of clients and case managers to develop trusting relationships, which affected openness of communication in treatment planning. Some clients humorously talked about the time it took to "break in" new case managers and to develop a trusting relationships with them. Likewise, some clients stated that it sometimes took 6 months or more before they became comfortable fully opening up to new case managers in treatment planning and for the case manager to trust and have confidence in them.

Related to reciprocal concrete incentives, some staff indicated that some clients did not see the value in doing treatment planning, especially long-term clients of the organizations who had been meeting their personal goals for a long while, as well as clients who were receiving only psychotropic medication from the organization and did not have a need for any other treatment or rehabilitation services. In addition, one staff member said that some clients did not want to participate in treatment planning because they desired to be "normal" and treatment planning reminded them they were "sick." Some staff also stated that a very small number of staff did not see the value of treatment planning for either themselves or their clients and, consequently, did not hold treatment-planning sessions that meaningfully involved clients.

Service choices varied considerably. Clients and staff indicated, in general, that most clients had good access to psychotropic medication, case management services, and psychiatric rehabilitation centers. The most frequent unmet service needs were transportation; access to medical, dental, and optical services that provided quality care; psychotherapy services; safe and affordable housing; treatment for substance abuse that was appropriate for people with mental illness; and opportunities for socialization and meaningful activities for clients who chose not to attend psychiatric rehabilitation centers. Clients and staff noted that treatment service choices were also affected by the fact that some treatment plan components were required for clients under criminal court supervision. Similarly, some staff indicated that the legal guardians of some clients did not seek the client's input, although many did. In their experience, those legal guardians who did not consult with the clients tended to be family members. In addition, clients and staff stated that both parties sometimes lacked knowledge of community resources, which further limited choice. Finally, clients and staff stated that many of the clients had very low incomes, which greatly restricted their access to a range of choices.

BJC-BH used a case manager structure to develop treatment plans. These treatment plans had to be signed by the client, the case manager, a master's level social worker if the case manager did not hold that degree, and the client's psychiatrist. Clients and staff indicated that most treatment plans were written with clients present and actively participating. In the few instances when clients were not present, usually because of time pressures, case managers would present the completed plan to clients, discuss clients' concerns, and revise the draft plan as appropriate. Clients and staff stated they typically negotiated any differences when they arose. This negotiation sometimes involved breaking goals down into smaller, more concrete components on which both parties could agree. When this did not resolve differences, the client's goal would sometimes be listed on the plan, and the case manager would make a note of the disagreement in the plan's comment section, or the reverse sometimes occurred, with the case manager–generated goal appearing on the plan and the client's objection appearing in the comment section. Clients stated that they also could involve the case manager's supervisor to settle differences. Finally, a formal mediation program did not exist for resolving differences, and advocates seldom participated, although given the high degree of clients' involvement in treatment planning, few, if any, clients needed these resources.

BJC-BH sought to create a culture that was supportive of clients' meaningful participation in treatment planning, which they did in a variety of ways. One of its value statements was "We value people's freedom and ability to direct their lives and make meaningful choices." The organization adopted both psychiatric rehabilitation and the recovery perspective. Client involvement in treatment planning was strongly incorporated into the training that clinicians received, and it was reinforced in organizational policies. BJC-BH used a case manager structure, and caseloads were low enough to allow staff the time to meaningfully engage their clients in treatment planning.

GUIDELINES FOR PROMOTING EMPOWERMENT THROUGH TREATMENT PLANNING

The degree of empowerment through treatment planning can vary widely, from no empowerment as exemplified in the SLPRC hospital ward programs, to high levels of empowerment among BJC-BH clients. The following guidelines are offered to promote the empowerment potential of participation in treatment planning:

1. *Recognize the important contribution that people with mental illness make to treatment planning.* People with mental illness possess information about their illness, their strengths, and their goals that clinicians need in order to develop an individualized treatment plan that their clients are likely to follow.
2. *Treat the psychiatric symptoms of the mental illness.* Unmanaged symptoms may prevent some people from fully participating in treatment planning. As people with mental illness respond to treatment and their symptoms become managed, their role in treatment planning should expand.
3. *Promote participation even when symptoms are present.* Even with severe symptoms, some people can meaningfully participate in treatment planning when provided with information in small increments. They, at least, should make those treatment-planning decisions that do not put them or others at risk.
4. *Teach participation skills.* Some people with mental illness will need skill training to be able to identify and express their needs and goals, to weigh options, to cognitively link services and interventions with problem resolution or goal achievement, and to resolve conflicts with staff if they arise during treatment planning.

5. *Increase readiness to participate in treatment planning.* A variety of approaches, including mental health professionals treating depression as a primary or secondary symptom, developing supportive relationships with people with mental illness, creating small opportunities for success and building upon them, and employing motivational interviewing techniques may be needed.

6. *Develop trusting and respectful relationships to promote meaningful participation.* Clinicians can facilitate this by demonstrating empathy and genuineness; by self-disclosing information; by reinforcing and celebrating successes, even small ones; by being flexible with meeting times and locations; and by clarifying expectations that each party has for the other.

7. *Adapt the treatment-planning process for clients from diverse backgrounds.* To engage people with cultural, racial, or ethnic differences in treatment planning, some clinicians may need additional cultural competence training, more time will be required to ensure that clinicians understand their clients' attitudes and needs in order to match them with the best available treatment options, and an interpreter may be needed to ensure effective communication.

8. *Increase mental health service choices.* This will require mental health parity in all private and public insurance plans, regulation of managed behavioral health care to ensure that services needed by people with severe mental illnesses are available, and substantial increases in publicly funded mental health services for those people who cannot pay for services through other means.

9. *Include family members in treatment planning.* Family members should be involved in treatment planning when they have a genuine, constructive interest in their relative, and when the person with mental illness agrees to it.

10. *Resolve conflicts that invariably arise during treatment planning.* Clinical and administrative procedures, including the use of mediators, should be in place to contend with disagreements. These procedures should give priority to the preferences of people with mental illness and include components of procedural justice.

11. *Promote participation by people with mental illness adjudicated incompetent.* Even when the person with mental illness is adjudicated incompetent, clinicians and legal guardians still should ask people for their preferred treatment-planning goals and interventions and support those preferences whenever possible, as well as honor the preferences expressed in mental health advanced directives, if possible.

12. *Make special efforts to engage people coerced into treatment.* Techniques include applying principles of procedural justice; being nonjudgmental; clearly specifying areas in which people with mental illness cannot make decisions, and then proceeding to maximize choices in all other areas; and using the treatment plan, when possible, to provide a roadmap to end the coercion.

13. *Include advocates in treatment planning when needed.* Some people with mental illness may need assistance from an advocate to meaningfully participate in treatment planning. This advocate may be another client, a staff member of the organization, or someone from an outside advocacy group.

14. *Provide adequate time for treatment planning.* Clinicians and clients need sufficient amounts of time to meaningfully engage in treatment planning. It takes considerably longer for treatment plans to be written when people with mental illness are present and actively participating.

15. *Provide mental health professionals with training.* Some clinicians and administrators may need training to realize the potential of people with mental illness to direct their own treatment and the benefits of client participation; to understand clients' perspectives on treatment planning, including why some clients may not readily participate; and to learn ways for staff and clients to work collaboratively in treatment planning.

16. *Develop an organizational culture that supports meaningful participation in treatment planning.* Means to do this include adopting the recovery respective, psychiatric rehabilitation, and the strengths perspective; providing staff extensive training on the benefits of client participation and the techniques to involve them; developing systems to evaluate client participation and staff competencies related to treatment planning; and establishing caseload sizes at reasonable levels so that staff have time to meaningfully engage clients in treatment planning.

6

Empowerment Through Housing

Safe, affordable housing is critical to the quality of life for all people, but particularly for people with severe mental illness. Denton and Bianco (2001) considered housing to be the first line of treatment for people with mental illness. Mueser et al. (2003) stated that housing should take priority over all other goals for people with mental illness and co-occurring substance abuse disorders. Quality housing and support services are associated with increased self-esteem, vocational functioning, social skills, social networks, and quality of life, and with fewer psychiatric symptoms and days hospitalized (Parkinson, Nelson, & Horgan, 1999). Gerhart (1990) summarized the importance of housing to people with severe mental illness. "Good housing can mark the difference between health and illness, autonomy and dependency, and it has an effect on their self-image" (p. 222).

State psychiatric hospitals historically have played a significant role in housing people with severe mental illness (Bachrach, 1994). As noted in the history of powerlessness in chapter 2, people with mental illness also have lived in poorhouses, in jails, with family, in boarding homes, in nursing homes, and on the streets. In addition, many people with mental illness have lived, and continue to live, independently in their own residences. Since deinstitutionalization, two models of housing to increase independent living for people with mental illness have emerged. In the continuum of care model, the first model to appear, people move from hospitalization to various types of congregate settings in the community that offer increasing amounts of independence and skill development. According to this model, only after they have demonstrated skill improvement and the ability to handle increased amounts of independence are they considered for placement in apartments, typically with an initially high level of supervision. Housing advocates recently have offered supported housing as an alternative to the continuum of care model (Carling, 1995; Ridgway & Zipple, 1990). In this model, people with mental illness choose regular housing in the community and receive flexible supports to stay in that housing (Carling, 1995). This model contends that progressing through a continuum of residential settings is unnecessary, and that most people with mental illness can live in regular community housing when adequate supports are provided. Although many people still hold on to notions associated with the continuum of care model, supported housing appears to be the trend in housing for people with mental illness (Carling, 1995). The National Association of State Mental Health Program Directors (1996) reflected this stance in their position statement on housing and supports for people with mental illness. An excerpt from this statement read, "Housing options should not require time limits for moving to another housing option. People should not be required to change living situations or lose their place of residence if they are hospitalized. People should choose their housing arrangements from among those living environments available to the general public."

People with mental illness are empowered through housing when they select their own residence from a range of options that are meaningful to them, when they are able to maintain that residence, and when they control their lives within that residence. Residential control includes choosing when to leave and enter the residence each day, deciding when to go to sleep at night and when to awaken in the morning, eating the food one wants when one wants it, and having guests, to name a few examples. Empowerment can occur through housing because being able to control where one lives and how one lives in that home are normal and important life decisions. Empowerment exists on a continuum, and even when people are unable to choose their own housing, they still can be empowered, albeit at a lesser level, if they have some control in decision making related to the operation of the residence. People with mental illness are not empowered through housing if they have no choice in where they live and little or no control over decisions related to their life in that residence.

Despite the empowerment potential of housing, many people with mental illness are not realizing it. The President's New Freedom Commission on Mental Health (2003) found that millions of people with severe mental illness lack housing to meet their needs. Especially during the initial period of deinstitutionalization, substantial numbers of people with severe mental illness experienced transinstitutionalization rather than deinstitutionalization. They moved from hospitals to custodial care institutions, such as nursing homes and boarding homes, which often were as restrictive as the state hospitals that Goffman (1961) described as total institutions (Brown, 1985; Ferleger, 1994; Gerhart, 1990). Residential treatment facilities, such as psychiatric group homes and supervised apartments, also have the potential to be coercive (Allen, 2003; Korman, Engster, & Milstein, 1996). These facilities often make housing contingent on participation in treatment, have rigid rules and requirements, and scrutinize details of daily life from a clinical perspective. Korman et al. (1996) summarized their coercive nature. "Anything but total acquiescence to program and staff mandates can result in involuntary commitment, in summary discharge, or in homelessness" (p. 96). Community residence is further restricted by landlords and communities who have accepted stigmatized views of people with mental illness and resist including them, despite mandates from state and federal housing laws that make housing discrimination illegal. Conditions for empowering people with severe mental illness through housing thus must address a range of limitations associated with the mental health system, communities, and public policies, as well as the limitations of people with mental illness themselves. Table 6.1 provides the conditions for empowerment as they related to housing.

Table 6.1 Conditions for Empowering People With Severe Mental Illness Through Housing

Managed psychiatric symptoms—The person has psychiatric symptoms managed to the degree necessary to obtain a residence of his or her choice, to maintain it, and to control life in it.

Participation skills—The person has the skills needed to make meaningful housing choices from a range of options, to maintain that housing, and to control life in the residence.

Psychological readiness—The person has the confidence, motivation, and willingness to access housing, to maintain it, and to control life in the residence.

Mutual trust and respect—Trust and respect exist between the person with mental illness and individuals who can affect his or her choice, maintenance, and control of the residence.

Reciprocal concrete incentives—The person with mental illness and those associated with his or her housing have concrete incentives to work together.

Availability of choices—The person has a range of housing options from which to choose.

Participation structures and processes—The person has structures and processes to access and maintain housing and to control residential life within it.

Access to resources—The person with mental illness, and those with whom he or she interacts, have access to resources needed to obtain and maintain housing and to control residential life.

Supportive culture—The culture is supportive of the person with mental illness obtaining housing of his or her choice, maintaining that housing, and controlling life within the residence.

MANAGED PSYCHIATRIC SYMPTOMS

One condition for empowering an individual with severe mental illness through housing is that the person's psychiatric symptoms are managed to the degree necessary to obtain a residence of his or her choice, to maintain it, and to control life in it. If symptoms are severe and ongoing, people may be coerced through involuntary civil commitment, by a legal guardian, or by a criminal court judge to reside in a long-term psychiatric hospital. If people continue to display psychiatric symptoms but can be treated in the community, they may be pressured to live in congregate housing by mental health systems that have adopted the continuum of care model. They also may be pressured to reside in congregate housing by informal or legally coercive bodies that have adopted stigmatized beliefs that people with mental illness cannot live in independent housing, even with supports, particularly when experiencing symptoms. In addition, even if people with symptoms seek independent living, behavioral symptoms of mental illness, such as poor hygiene, talking to oneself, and poor social skills, may discourage many landlords from renting to them (Mueser et al., 2003).

Once people with mental illness obtain housing, they may have difficulty maintaining the housing because of unmanaged symptoms. Symptoms may reemerge soon after entering a new residence, which is not uncommon for people who recently were hospitalized, or who move into housing that is inappropriate to their needs or abilities or is of poor quality (Davidson, Hoge, Merrill, Rakfeldt, & Griffin, 1995; Fakhoury, Murray, Shephard, & Priebe, 2002). If these symptoms persist, people may lose their residence if they are unable to complete activities required to maintain independent housing or if periodically rehospitalized. The same behavioral symptoms that can prevent some people from obtaining housing also may result in the loss of housing if too many neighbors complain. Contrary to the continuum of care model, some evidence exists that there is little difference in the level of psychiatric symptoms between people with mental illness living in independent housing and those living in boarding homes (Browne & Courtney, 2004). In addition, people who display behavioral symptoms may be more successful living in apartments than in congregate settings where more people are likely to complain (Gulcur, Stefancic, Shinn, Tsemberis, & Fischer, 2003).

The presence of psychiatric symptoms also can limit the ability of people to control or participate in residential activities. To illustrate, if living in a congregate setting, symptoms may prevent them from participating in a residents' meeting to discuss house rules or to plan a group outing. If living in an apartment, symptoms may prevent them from planning and preparing their meals, securing their residence at night, taking their medication, or enjoying the company of neighbors.

A range of interventions can be applied to mitigate the negative effects of psychiatric symptoms on housing. First and foremost is finding ways to manage symptoms. When symptoms periodically worsen despite treatment, it especially is important for mental health organizations or informal entities to have the capacity to provide additional assistance. This allows people to maintain their housing until they can manage their symptoms and resume their previous level of responsibility for the housing. In addition, some people with mental illness may need training to not display symptoms such as talking to oneself or pacing to landlords or tenants, which may jeopardize their ability to obtain and retain housing. Finally, people with mental illness themselves, mental health organizations, or informal supports may be able to educate landlords or neighbors about the nature of psychiatric symptoms to allay some of their stigmatized concerns.

PARTICIPATION SKILLS

A second condition for empowerment is that the person with mental illness has the skills needed to make meaningful housing choices from a range of options, to maintain that housing, and to control life in the residence. To address the first component, people with mental illness need skills to assess housing alternatives, to make their final selections, and to express their housing preferences. To maintain and control housing, people also need a range of skills. Willer, Guastaferro, Zankiw, and Duran (1992) divided these skills into eight categories including nutritional management, money management, home management, medical management, time management, community use, problem solving, and safety management. It is widely accepted that many people with mental illness lack some of these skills (Pratt et al., 1999). They especially may lack the experience and skills to work with landlords and to maintain their residences (Kloos, Zimmerman, Schrimenti, & Crusto, 2002). Consequently, without active rehabilitation, many people with mental illness will not be empowered through housing (Carling, 1995).

While agreement that some people with mental illness need skills training to obtain and maintain housing exists, opinions on the settings for this training differ. The continuum of care housing model supports placing people with illness in housing that reflects their current level of functioning and then providing in that setting the treatment and skills training necessary to function in more independent housing. For example, someone leaving a hospital may first be placed in a boarding home, then a psychiatric group home, then a highly supervised apartment with 24-hour staff in a unit of the apartment complex, and finally in an independent apartment (Corrigan, 2001). If functioning deteriorates or skills are not learned at a particular level, the individual can remain at that level indefinitely or go back to the previous level that had more intensive treatment and supervision. An alternative model is supported housing, which holds that most people with mental illness are capable of living in normal housing in the community while receiving flexible supports to stay in that housing (Carling, 1995). The supported housing model purports that many of the skills people learn in congregate settings do not transfer to independent settings, and that most people with mental illness can learn skills in an independent setting, such as an apartment, without needing to move through the continuum (Carling, 1995; Ridgway & Zipple, 1990). People with lower skill levels initially need more support to develop their skills (Ogilvie, 1997). Also, it is clear that many people with mental illness who live in nursing homes and boarding homes will not receive skill training because of the custodial and institutional nature of many of these facilities (Brown, 1985; Gerhart, 1990; Weinstein, 2000). Lefley (1996) noted, too, that people with mental illness who live with their family members are unlikely to gain the skills needed for independent living.

PSYCHOLOGICAL READINESS

A third condition for empowerment is that the person with mental illness has the psychological readiness to access housing, to maintain it, and to control life in the residence. Surveys of the housing preferences of people with severe mental illness have found that most want to live in their own homes or apartments (Tanzman, 1993). There are, however, a small number of people with severe mental illness who are reluctant to leave hospitalization and other congregate settings. As Gerhart (1990) stated, "Many patients feel ambivalent about leaving the hospital. On one hand, they are eager to get away from institutional routines and demands. On the other, they are afraid to leave an environment that provides structure, amenities, and respite from the pressures of the outside world" (p. 194). One assumes these same misgivings apply to some people in nursing homes and boarding homes for the same reasons. There is some rationality to this reluctance. There is substantial evidence that many people with mental illness have a poor quality of life living in the community (Davidson & Hoge, 1996).

To promote psychological readiness for more independent living, some hospitals and boarding homes have developed special programs. Bellus, Kost, and Vergo (2000), for example, described a program in a long-term state hospital that sought to provide their clients with the hope, confidence, and knowledge to move into the community. To accomplish this, clients spent half the day in vocational or educational activities in the community, staff took clients on tours of the available residential options, and staff arranged ongoing meetings between clients and the staff of the community mental health programs that would be working with these clients upon discharge. In addition, Pulier and Hubbard (2001) reported on the redesign of a boarding home that sought to increase independence by maximizing client choice and opportunities to participate in community activities.

MUTUAL TRUST AND RESPECT

A fourth condition for empowerment is that trust and respect exist between the person with mental illness and individuals who can affect their choice, maintenance, and control of the residence. In most cases, these individuals include cases managers from the community agency from which people with mental illness receive mental health services; people who make decisions about how long-term psychiatric hospital residential units are operated, including program directors, psychiatrists, charge nurses, or others; operators of congregate community residences, such as nursing homes, boarding homes, and group homes; and landlords, if people with mental illness plan to rent housing in the community.

In the first set of relationships, people with mental illness must trust that their case managers will listen to their housing preferences; have knowledge of housing resources; believe that they can succeed in the housing of choice, particularly independent living; and put forth the effort to help them find their housing of choice. Conversely, case managers must respect the right and ability of people with mental illness to make housing choices and to live in independent housing with supports, if that is their choice. In other words, case managers must overcome stigmatized views that people with mental illness are incapable of making good housing choices, need intensive supervision, and are incapable of living on their own even with supports, beliefs that many mental health professions continue to hold (Denton & Bianco, 2001; Rapp, 1998).

For empowerment to occur in long-term psychiatric hospital wards and community-based congregate living settings, the relationships between people with mental illness and managers of hospital wards and residential facilities revolve around two issues. First is the degree of involvement of people with mental illness will have in the operation of the residential unit. People with mental illness must believe that managers value their ability to contribute to operations, and that managers will not engage in retribution toward them if they disagree with residential policies and work to promote change. Second is the degree to which the facility promotes moving to independent living. People with mental illness must trust that managers believe in their ability to succeed in living that is more independent and will provide them with the treatment and rehabilitation activities to enable them to do so. As with case managers, staff of hospital wards and congregate residential units must overcome stigma in order to develop respect for, and confidence in, their residents' ability to succeed in the housing of their choice.

In a third set of relationships, people with mental illness must trust that prospective landlords will not discriminate against them, and that they will treat them fairly on an ongoing basis in the resident-landlord relationship. Landlords must have confidence that people with mental illness can live independently and be responsible residents. Carling (1995) noted that the resident-landlord relationship can be facilitated when both parties are knowledgeable about their rights and responsibilities. If case managers are involved in the housing, they can increase landlords' confidence in the ability of their prospective residents to live safely in a housing unit by sharing success stories of other people with mental illness who have succeeded in independent housing and by discussing the level of support they can provide to their clients (Rapp, 1998). As with case managers and congregate housing managers, landlords must overcome stigma for trust and respect to develop.

RECIPROCAL CONCRETE INCENTIVES

A fifth condition for empowerment is that the person with mental illness and those associated with his or her housing have concrete incentives to work together in the location, maintenance, and control of the housing. People with mental illness have substantial incentives to participate, beginning with living in the housing of their choice. Participation in the location, maintenance, and control of the housing, itself, can lead to subjective feelings of accomplishment and control. Participation also can result in empowerment outcomes, that is, improvements in aspects of their residential life. Davidson et al. (1995) summarized the benefits of living in the community rather than the hospital as perceived by a sample of people with mental illness. Benefits included having their freedom, feeling safer, having more privacy, living closer to family members, and living in the community in which they grew up. Generally, the benefits of community living are greater for those living in settings that are more independent. Browne and Courtney (2004), for example, compared a sample of people diagnosed with schizophrenia living in independent housing and in boarding homes. Although psychiatric symptoms did not vary between the two groups, boarding home residents had fewer social supports, constructive activities, and employment opportunities than did people living independently. It is important to recall, however, that at least a limited number of people with mental illness do not consider independent living to be beneficial, preferring instead the security of hospitals or other congregate settings.

Those who work with people with mental illness also have concrete incentives and disincentives to involve their clients in obtaining, maintaining, or controlling their housing. The primary incentive for case managers to involve people with mental illness in choosing and maintaining their housing is that they are more likely to function better in that housing if they choose it and thus are more likely to fulfill that rehabilitation goal (Brown & Wheeler, 1990). The primary disincentive for case managers to fully involve them is that it takes considerable effort to locate and furnish independent housing and to provide the support clients need, particularly during the early periods of independent living (Rapp, 1998). It is much easier on case managers to show their clients a limited number of boarding homes or residential treatment facilities and place them in the first available bed, after which they will need to provide only minimal amounts of support. This is especially likely to happen when mental health systems promote the continuum of care model, when case managers have large numbers of clients on their caseloads, and when the type of housing that clients prefer is not readily available in the community.

Managers of hospital living units, too, have incentives and disincentives to involve their clients in decision making related to the residential unit. Involving clients in the operation of the residential unit should be considered part of treatment and rehabilitation. Some evidence exists that clients who are more actively involved in daily activities of the ward and in setting ward rules have better community outcomes upon discharge (Holland et al., 1981). Therefore, staff helps clients to meet their treatment goals by including them in this activity. Some staff, however, may not consider this involvement to be therapeutic or recognize that involvement can improve community outcomes. In addition, it often is much easier for staff to set rules and make decisions about the appearance of the residential unit, food selections, and many other areas than to help their clients make those decisions themselves.

Few, if any, incentives exist for boarding home operators to involve their residents in the operation of the residential unit despite the empowerment potential of such involvement. It is much more efficient for them to run their homes as custodial care facilities than to involve their residents in decision making and promote skill development. Promoting skill development may actually lead to a loss of residents because residents may choose to move after they believe they are prepared for living that is more independent. It may be necessary for an external body to work with boarding homes to promote empowerment though housing. This may be accomplished through a variety of activities. State mental health authorities can educate operators about the roles they play in empowering their residents and promoting independence. Boarding home operators are more likely to change their perception if, in addition to education, they receive financial rewards for assisting residents to move to more independent living, and if they receive additional referrals to maintain their occupancy rates. Pulier and Hubbard (2001) provided an example of a mental health organization that worked cooperatively with a boarding home operator to provide a range of on-site rehabilitation activities that included residents' involvement in many decisions. It is unclear from their report, however, why the boarding home operators allowed the mental health organization to work with their residents. It is possible, for example, that mental health organization promised increased referrals to the home or, conversely, threatened to remove existing residents referred from the mental health organization if they did not comply with the request. An alternative to service provision within boarding homes is to engage boarding home residents in off-site rehabilitation services, such as psychiatric rehabilitation centers, that can help clients to identify residential options, to increase skills, and to move to more independent housing. This, of course, does not address the missed opportunity for empowerment while living in boarding homes.

Finally, incentives and disincentives exist for landlords to rent to people with mental illness. Landlords may believe there are considerable disincentives if they hold stigmatized views that people with mental illness are incapable of living independently or are irresponsible. Newman, Harkness, Gaister, and Raschovsky (2001) identified another potential disincentive. They studied 153 privately owned apartment complexes and found that apartment maintenance costs were higher for people with mental illness than residents without mental illness, particularly when there were few other residents with mental illness living in the building and when they lived in more expensive housing units with greater amenities. Landlords also may fear that behavioral symptoms of mental illness exhibited by some people may scare off existing or potential residents, reducing occupancy rates. There are, however, potential benefits for landlords to rent to people with mental illness. Carling (1995) argued that some landlords are motivated to rent to people with mental illness based on a desire to help others. In addition, Carling and Kloos et al. (2002) believed that people with mental illness can provide stability to housing, particularly in low-income areas. In fact, Carling stated that people with mental illness can be the most desirable residents when case managers provide support to people with mental illness and their landlords. Carling identified supports for landlords including consultation about the symptoms of mental illness, mediation between residents and landlords, special funds to pay rents if residents are hospitalized or do not pay rent in a timely manner, and public recognition for landlords who have become most involved in working with people with mental illness.

AVAILABILITY OF CHOICES

A sixth condition for empowerment is that the person with mental illness has a range of housing options from which to choose. No single type of housing can meet the clinical needs and housing preferences of all people with mental illness (Bachrach, 1994). Most people with mental illness prefer living independently in their own apartments or homes. In a review of studies examining the housing preferences of people with severe mental illness, Tanzman (1993) found at least 59% of people preferred independent living in 24 of 26 studies reviewed, and at least 70% in 20 of 26 studies. Although a minority, some people with mental illness prefer to live with family members or in congregate living situations, at least during parts of their lives. Carling (1993) listed the many temporary and permanent residential alternatives used by people with mental illness. These included homeless shelters, group crisis residences, crisis apartments, short-term hospitalization, consumer-operated safe houses, quarterway houses and other hospital-based housing units, transitional and long-term group homes and half-way houses, family foster care, living with family, boarding homes, nursing homes, transitional apartments, supervised apartments, and supported apartments. Below is a discussion of the seven most common types of housing people with mental illness use on a long-term basis. This is followed by a discussion of the empowerment potential of these types of housing and the limitations people face in accessing independent housing.

Types of Housing

Living With Family Members

Historically, many people with mental illness have lived with family members, and this continues to the present. This residential option is most appropriate in cultures where both family members and the person with mental illness expect it and want it; when continuity of residence is assured as parents or other family caretakers age; or when other housing options may not be readily available, such as in rural areas (Lefley, 1996). Many family members can find it rewarding for their relative with mental illness to live with them (Schwartz & Gidron, 2002). Lefley (1996) summarized the ideal family arrangement. "Family caregiving is valuable when it has therapeutic benefits, when a loving, supportive family ambience helps the person with mental illness adjust to the disorder and ensures a decent quality of life" (p. 218). Given the potential benefits, including cost savings, some countries offer financial stipends or tax credits to family members who house their relatives with mental illness (Warner, 2000).

There may be disadvantages to this housing arrangement, however, for both people with mental illness and their family members. Lefley

(1996) identified and addressed these limitations when providing guidelines on when it is most appropriate for adults with mental illness to live with family members. She first stated that independent living should be the goal for most people with mental illness, and as previously indicated, it is the goal for most people with mental illness. Residing with family often does not help people with mental illness to reach that goal. They usually do not learn the independent skills they need when living with family. It also may not be in the best interest of family members if their relative with mental illness threatens the stability of the household because of unmanaged psychiatric symptoms or disruptive behaviors.

Single-Room Occupancy (SRO) Units

Single-Room Occupancy (SRO) units are another residential options used by some people with mental illness, although these units are one of their least preferred options (Tanzman, 1993). SROs typically are older hotels located in urban areas that offer people a single room, usually without a kitchen or a private bathroom (Gerhart, 1990). They traditionally have served as a low-cost housing option for people who are poor, including those with mental illness. The number of SRO units has drastically been reduced in recent years because of urban renewal, which has led some communities to attempt to preserve at least some units (Linhorst, 1991). The quality of SROs varies widely, as many are located in high-crime areas, are managed poorly, and are socially isolating. There is evidence, however, that when properly managed, they can be a center for social-service and mental health–service provision, can provide people with privacy, and can offer a sense of community (Linhorst, 1991; Shephard, 1997).

Boarding Homes

Boarding homes became one of the primary housing resources for people with severe mental illness during the initial period of deinstitutionalization, and they continue to house substantial numbers of people with mental illness (Carling, 1993; Weinstein, 2000). Boarding homes typically are for-profit residences that provide room, board, and 24-hour supervision and house anywhere from 5 to 300 people, with most facilities housing approximately 50 people (Gerhart, 1990). They have been highly criticized for offering poor care and being just as institutional as hospitals (Brown, 1985; Gerhart, 1990). Despite their substantial shortcomings, many people support them as a necessary low-cost housing option, and state mental health authorities continue pay for people with mental illness to reside in them (Blaustein & Viek, 1987; Pulier & Hubbard, 2001). Pulier and Hubbard (2001) provided one example that boarding homes can be modified to promote independent living and empower residents, although it took substantial mental health resources to accomplish. In addition, some people with mental illness prefer them to psychiatric group homes because boarding homes place less demands on them (Owen et al., 1996; Tanzman, 1993).

Psychiatric Group Homes

Psychiatric group homes are another residential option for people with mental illness (Carling, 1993; Weinstein, 2000). They typically are operated by mental health organizations, house a small number of people, provide 24-hour supervision or on-call staff at night, and offer a range of rehabilitation activities in which residents are required to participate. Some group homes limit the length of residence, such as to 1 year, serving primarily as a transition from hospitalization to apartment living, while others provide people with permanent housing. In her review of housing preference studies, Tanzman (1993) found that group homes were the second choice among 7% to 28% of people in 4 of 26 studies, but was one of the least favorite options in 21 of 26 studies. As stated before, some people do not prefer group homes because they often are highly structured and require participation in treatment and rehabilitation activities.

Supervised Apartments

Yet another residential option is supervised apartments, also sometimes referred to as supportive or cooperative apartments (Gerhart, 1990; Parkinson et al., 1999; Weinstein, 2000). These apartments are owned or leased by a mental health organization and may include an entire apartment building, a portion of a building, apartment units scattered throughout the community, or a combination of arrangements. People with mental illness then lease or sublease the units from the mental health organization, agreeing to participate in mental health services and accept support services from that organization. In larger apartment buildings, staff may have an office or live in the one of the units. Some people will use supervised apartments as their permanent housing, while others will transition to more independent living.

Supported Housing

A sixth major housing type is supported housing (Carling, 1995; Fakhoury et al., 2002; Ogilvie, 1997; Weinstein, 2000). In this model, people with mental illness own or lease the housing units in their own names. Case managers provide support services to help maintain them in their residences, but housing is not contingent on acceptance of services. Services are flexible to meet changing needs and are determined jointly by residents and case managers. More than any other housing type, Allen (1996) argued that supported housing meets the spirit of the intent of the Americans with Disabilities Act to promote community integration.

Independent Housing With No Formal Supports

As a final residential option, people with mental illness may live independently in their own apartment or home without any supports from the mental health system. Despite having a severe mental illness, many people are able to live on their own in housing of their choice.

Empowerment Potential of Housing Types

The type of residence influences empowerment to a large degree. Parkinson et al. (1999) categorized housing for people with severe mental illness into three broad types and examined the empowerment potential of each. They found that custodial institutions, such as nursing homes and boarding homes, typically are not empowering because residents often have little input in being "placed" there, usually have roommates they did not choose, and have little input into residential activities; in addition, the homes have restrictive rules and the staff maintains a high degree of control. It is an exceptional case when nursing homes or boarding homes empower their residents. Parkinson et al. found that small group homes and clusters of apartments owned or leased and serviced by a mental health organization are more empowering than custodial institutions. People tend to have some choice in where they live, with whom they live, and their activities; there are fewer rules than in other congregate settings; and residents and staff share control over the residential unit. The investigators concluded that supported housing is the most empowering of the three types because choice of residence, roommates, and activities are much greater; there are few, if any, rules other those imposed on anyone renting or owning a residence; and residents control decisions about the residential unit. Nelson, Hall, and Walsh-Bowers (1999) reached similar conclusions in their comparison of the same types of housing.

Table 6.2 summarizes the seven types of housing, as well as the empowerment potential of each and the level of preference people with mental illness have for that housing type. These are generalizations, though, and individual settings may vary widely. One psychiatric group home may be very controlling of its residents, while another may heavily involve them in decision making and promote residents' moving to more independent living; some people may like the independence, affordability, and location of a particular SRO, while other SROs may be unsafe and isolating. The categorizations, however, do help to focus attention on the variable nature of the empowerment potential and housing preferences of people with mental illness.

Limitations to Accessing Independent Housing

There are many limitations to people with mental illness accessing the most empowering type of housing, whether that is supported

Table 6.2 **Empowerment Potential and Consumer Preference for Types of Housing**

Type of Housing	Consumer Preference	Level of Empowerment
Living with family members	Low to moderate	Low
Single room occupancy (SRO) units	Low	Moderate
Boarding homes	Low	Low
Psychiatric group homes	Moderate	Moderate
Supervised apartments	Moderate	Moderate
Supported housing	High	High
Independent housing without formal supports	High	High

housing or housing without supports. One major limitation is financial. Many people with mental illness have very low incomes and are unable to afford rental housing in today's market without financial support (Denton & Bianco, 2001). In the United States, there is a critical shortage of low-cost rental units that are of good physical quality and are in safe neighborhoods. Daskal (1998) reported that in 1995, the need for 10.5 million low-cost rental units existed, but only 6.1 million were available. She attributed this 4 million-dollar disparity to a decline in the number of unsubsidized low-cost rental units and an increase in the number of households in need of low-cost housing. It is important to note that not all of the 6.1 million available units were decent and safe housing. Daskal found, for example, that in 1995, 14% of housing occupied by low-income households had moderate-to-severe physical problems. Her report did not address the extent to which low-cost rental housing was found in neighborhoods with high crime rates, although it is reasonable to speculate that at least some was. O'Hara and Cooper (2003) reported that the average rent in the United States is $628 per month for a one bedroom apartment and $531 per month for an efficiency apartment. Many people with mental illness, especially those who receive disability income, are unable to pay these open-market rents. To put these rent figures into perspective, nationally, the average monthly disability payment in 2002 through Supplemental Security Income, the sole income source for many people with mental illness, was $595 (O'Hara & Cooper, 2003).

Because of housing shortages and the importance of housing to the quality of life of people with mental illness, it is critical that state mental health authorities involve themselves in activities to promote housing for people with low incomes, including those with mental illness. The National Association of State Mental Health Program Directors (1996) stressed this involvement in its position statement on housing and supports for people with mental illness:

> State mental health authorities have the obligation to exercise leadership in the housing area, addressing housing and support needs and expanding the available housing stock. This is a responsibility shared with consumers and one that requires coordination and negotiation of mutual roles of mental health authorities, public assistance and housing authorities, and the private sector. (p. 1)

Carling (1995) provided three examples of state and local mental health organizations that took leadership roles to bring people together from the mental health and housing arenas, resulting in increased independent housing in the community. The extent to which these three examples are reflective of efforts across the United States is uncertain, although anecdotally, many state mental health authorities have not dedicated significant resources to housing development, particularly during the current era of state budget deficits and service reductions.

Another limitation to choice of housing is that many landlords discriminate against people with mental illness, even though this practice violates federal housing laws. As previously indicated, some landlords, of course, do rent to people with mental illness. However, they are less likely to do so when vacancy rates are low (Kloos et al., 2002). Renting apartments is particularly difficult for people with mental illness who also have substance abuse problems, criminal histories, or poor tenant histories (Mueser et al., 2003; President's New Freedom Commission on Mental Health, 2003).

The lack of availability of low-cost housing and the unwillingness of landlords to rent to people with mental illness are not the only factors limiting choice of independent living situations. A variety of sources may coerce people with mental illness into more restrictive living situations than they need or want. Mental health professionals who accept the continuum of care model may insist that their clients proceed through a series of living situations, such as boarding homes, group homes, and transitional apartments, before they are willing to approve their moving to supported housing. Also, judges or other responsible parties may require that people with mental illness who are on probation or parole, who participate in mental health courts or jail diversion programs, or who were found NGRI first enter congregate housing when leaving prison, jail, or a psychiatric hospital and later enter supported apartments, if they ever are allowed to do so during the period of oversight. Legal guardians, too, may not believe in the ability of the people for whom they are responsible to live in supported housing, instead requiring that they live in congregate settings either temporarily or permanently. Finally, family or friends of people with mental illness may apply informal coercion to get them to live in congregate housing. A family member, for instance, may agree to contribute to the cost of an apartment, but only after the individual has lived in a group home for a year.

PARTICIPATION STRUCTURES AND PROCESSES

A seventh condition for empowerment is that the person with mental illness has structures and processes to access and maintain housing and to control residential life within it. Structures and processes are addressed in two areas. First are structures and processes to access independent community housing and to maintain people in it. The focus is on independent housing because it is more difficult to access and maintain than congregate housing. Most congregate housing targets people with mental illness, other disabilities, or the elderly, and provides in-house supervision, usually 24 hours daily. Second are structures and processes whereby people with mental illness living in congregate housing and supervised apartment buildings can participate in the control or operation of their residential units. The focus is on the control of congregate and supervised apartment housing because residential life is likely to be much more structured in them than in supported apartments (Parkinson et al., 1999).

Accessing and Maintaining Independent Housing

Mental health organizations can increase the likelihood that the people with mental illness with whom they work can access independent housing by establishing two structures and processes. The first structure and process is to assess clients' resources; determine eligibility for subsidized housing from federal, state, or local resources; and assist clients to apply for subsidized housing if they are eligible. This requires that all case managers, or designated individuals within the organization who specialize in housing resources, are knowledgeable about available programs and their requirements. Ideally, they will have developed working relationships with potential funding sources to expedite the application process. The second structure and process is to assist people with mental illness to locate housing in the community. This may involve compiling a list of landlords with whom the mental health organization previously has worked, or devising an approach to working with landlords that maximizes their willingness to rent to people with mental illness. Rapp (1998) developed a list of strategies for securing community resources that can apply to working with landlords to secure housing. The first strategy is to emphasize the rewards. As previously stated, the primary reward for landlords to rent to people with mental illness is that it can provide stability to housing, particularly in low-income areas and when residents receive a range of support services from a mental health organization, including covering the rent if clients are hospitalized. A second strategy is to cite proven results. This can include sharing stories of other clients who were successful in community housing. It also can include discussing the large number of programs existing locally and nationwide that provide supported housing services to people with mental illness who rent from private landlords. In addition, it can include citing research on the success of supported housing. Rapp cautioned that these latter two conversations must be stated in language landlords can understand. Another strategy is to allow for trial periods. Relative to housing, this could include, for example, the case manager negotiating an initial short-term lease of 6 months, or landlords first renting to one person with mental illness who is associated with the mental health organization and then accepting other housing referrals from that organization if the initial placement is successful to everyone's satisfaction. An additional strategy is to link the message to influential others. In the case of housing, it could include referring perspective landlords to those landlords with whom the mental health organization already has an established relationship in the placement and support of people with mental illness. Finally, Rapp believed that one should avoid high-pressure tactics and minimize threats to security, status, or esteem. Regardless of whether a mental health organization adopts this strategy in all or part or develops another, it is critical that mental health organizations have a process for approaching prospective landlords, and that clients and staff are trained in that process in order to maximize the likelihood that they can find housing in the community that best meets clients' desired housing and needs.

Once housing is secured, some people with mental illness may need structures and process to help maintain their housing. Many people can live independently without support services from mental health organizations. For some people, however, receiving support services will be critical to long-term success in their residences. While individuals' needs will vary widely, many people will need support and skill training in the areas of nutritional management, money management, home management, medical management, time management, community use, problem solving, and safety management (Willer et al., 1992). Brown and Wheeler (1990) described the primary categories of services provided in one supported housing program. These included money management, assistance with structuring time and developing leisure activities, medication management, crisis support, and limit setting. It is imperative that these supports be individualized and flexible to meet the individual's changing needs; that those with less skills receive a greater amount of support; and that supports be available 24 hours per day, 7 days per week (Ogilvie, 1997; Tanzman, 1993).

Many supported housing programs use interdisciplinary teams in order to be able to provide a range of support services. The structure of support provision also can include friends and relatives of the person with mental illness. Their contribution to the process of providing support services can be critical to maintaining people in their own residences (Järbrink, Hallam, & Knapp, 2001). Landlords, too, can be incorporated into the structure of service provision. Many have a genuine willingness to assist in the process of helping residents to maintain their housing (Kloos et al., 2002). Landlords can be a referral source for neighborhood resources and provide positive social interaction with residents with mental illness. Kloos et al. (2002) described a program that formalized the interactions between mental health professionals, residents, and landlords through a number of methods, including training sessions for mental health professionals and landlords; forums in which mental health professionals, landlords, and residents with mental illness could discuss common problems; and the development of brochures discussing the rights and responsibilities of the three major parties. The process of maintaining people with mental illness in their residences also needs to include dispute resolution that ensures due process, particularly when eviction is imminent (Allen, 1996; Carling, 1995; Kloos et al., 2002; Korman et al., 1996). Mental health professionals often assume a critical role in mediating disputes, ensuring that people with mental illness meet their responsibilities and making certain that their rights are protected.

Control Within Congregate Housing and Supervised Apartments

Structures and processes also can be developed to facilitate empowerment through participation in the control of life in supervised apartments with on-site staff and other congregate settings, such as long-term psychiatric hospitals, nursing homes, boarding homes, and group homes. One study of group homes and supervised apartments found that residents preferred a model of decision making in which staff and residents shared control as opposed to substantial staff control or substantial resident control (McCarthy & Nelson, 1991). Decision-making structures typically include some sort of organization of residents that represents their interests in meetings with staff. Such organizations have included patient government (Gerhart, 1990) and patient advisory committees (Starkey & Leadholm, 1997) in long-term psychiatric hospitals, resident councils in nursing homes (Mok & Mui, 1996), tenant groups in group homes (Ware, 1999), and tenant associations in supervised apartments (Ridgway, Simpson, Wittman, & Wheeler, 1998).

Pulier and Hubbard's (2001) description of residents' involvement in the control of their residence in a boarding home illustrates the wide range of activities in which residents can be involved. Some of the activities included residents interviewing prospective residents and staff and making recommendations, selecting menu items, identifying and prioritizing areas of the residence in need of repair, monitoring the status of repair completion, voting on colors when walls needed painting, selecting and caring for house plants and a garden, and maintaining their own immediate residential spaces, to name a few. Ridgway et al. (1998) argued that people with mental illness residing in supervised apartments should be able to set house rules, to participate in the acceptance and eviction of residents, and to take part in the hiring and evaluation of staff, among other things. Group homes described by Ware (1999), which sought to increase resident control to the degree that on-site staff was not required, illustrate the difficulty in developing effective participation. She found that there were frequent disputes between residents, many residents did not feel comfortable in sharing concerns, and it required extensive staff time to assist residents to form decision-making structures and then use those structures to make decisions. In addition, resident decision-making abilities varied widely. Some resident groups dealt effectively with major issues almost immediately, while others needed to make incrementally larger decisions over an extended period of time.

ACCESS TO RESOURCES

An eighth condition for empowerment is that the person with mental illness, and those with whom he or she interacts, have access to resources needed to obtain and maintain housing and to control residential life. People who prefer to live in the community in independent housing especially will need a range of resources. Several categories of resources exist and are described.

Access to Affordable Housing

For many people, a critical resource will be access to affordable housing. Federal, state, and local governments within the United States have acted to address the shortage of affordable housing for low-income people, including those with severe mental illness. However, the majority of low-income people receives no governmental housing assistance. Daskal (1998) reported, for example, that in 1995, only 36% of people who were poor and renting apartments or houses received housing assistance from any level of government. To more effectively and fairly allocate limited housing dollars, the federal government now requires that local communities develop plans to meet housing needs that include substantial input from citizens (Denton & Bianco, 2001). Denton and Bianco (2001) described three major plans. The primary local plan required by the federal government is the Consolidated Plan, which includes a 5-year strategic plan and a 1-year action plan. Two other local plans include the Public Housing Agency Plan and the Continuum of Care Plan, the latter of which specifically addresses homelessness. While these plans affect a broad population, people with mental illness potentially can benefit from housing developed through them. Information on the extent to which state mental health authorities and local mental health agencies have actively participated in the development of these plans, particularly the Consolidated Plan and the Public Housing Agency Plan, is not available. There is anecdotal information, at least in Missouri, that mental health organizations have not actively participated in the development of these plans, potentially missing an opportunity to create new housing resources for people with mental illness.

Several major types of housing assistance are provided by the federal government, some of which is allocated through the three plans. One type is Section 8 housing vouchers, through which people with low income, including those with mental illness, rent low- or modestly priced housing through the private market and pay approximately 30% of their income in rent, with the federal government paying the balance (Denton & Bianco, 2001; Daskal, 1998). Approximately 1.5 million housing units were rented in 2000 with Section 8 vouchers (Denton & Bianco, 2001). Approximately 23% were designated for nonelderly people with disabilities and 17% for the elderly, although it is uncertain how many people with mental illness were included (Denton & Bianco, 2001). This amount did not meet the need, however, as many communities have long waiting lists to obtain Section 8 vouchers. Even if people obtain them, they may not be able to use them because rents may exceed Section 8 guidelines, the available units may not meet federal health and safety guidelines, or landlords may refuse to accept them (President's New Freedom Commission on Mental Health, 2003). In addition, new federal guidelines make it difficult for people with poor rent histories, substance abuse problems, and criminal histories to obtain subsidized housing. Unfortunately, one or more requirements eliminate some people with mental illness from eligibility (President's New Freedom Commission on Mental Health, 2003).

Another type of housing assistance is public housing, where units are owned and operated by a public or quasi-public body (Daskal, 1998). In 2000, there were approximately 1.1 million of these units (Denton & Bianco, 2001). Approximately 18% were designated for nonelderly people with disabilities and 32% for the elderly, although, again, data were not available on the number accessed by people with mental illness. As with Section 8, renters pay approximately 30% of their income toward rent and must meet the same federal guidelines. Also as with Section 8 housing, most communities have a waiting list for public housing.

Two federal housing assistance programs, the Section 811 Supportive Housing for People with Disabilities program and the Shelter Plus Care program, fall under the Continuum of Care Plan (Denton &

Bianco, 2001). The Supportive Housing program funds transitional and permanent housing for people who are homeless, including those with mental illness, and support services to help people maintain their housing. The Shelter Plus Care program provides housing assistance to people with disabilities who are homeless, including primarily those with severe mental illness, AIDS, or chronic substance abuse problems (Denton & Bianco, 2001). State or local governments must match the federal housing assistance with services to support these people in the housing. In 1999, half of the federal dollars awarded through the Supportive Housing program were allocated to assist people with mental illness (Denton & Bianco, 2001). While these programs undoubtedly have provided housing and support services to many people with mental illness, Korman et al. (1996) were highly critical of both programs for two reasons. First, they believed they represented a departure from previous federal housing policy to integrate people with mental illness into general housing. Second, they considered the programs to be coercive because they required recipients to access services in order to receive housing. In addition to these federal programs, state and local governments and private organizations may offer resources for people to access housing. State mental health authorities, for instance, may provide housing subsidies to increase access to congregate and independent housing.

Protection of Housing Access Under Federal and State Law

Even if people with mental illness can afford housing on their own or through subsidies, landlords may refuse to rent to them even though housing discrimination is illegal under the Fair Housing Amendments Act of 1988 and other federal and state laws. Consequently, another resource for people with mental illness and people who advocate with them is to use the protections of these laws to access housing. Under the Fair Housing Amendments Act, for example, people who believe they have been discriminated against can file a civil suit directly in federal court. However, these laws apparently have failed to lessen discrimination. Denton and Bianco (2001) argued that people with mental illness are more likely than other groups to face housing discrimination. This failure is attributable to at least three factors. First, federal enforcement efforts under the U.S. Department of Housing and Urban Development actually diminished between 1989, the year after passage of the Fair Housing Amendments Act, and 2000, despite growing numbers of complaints (President's New Freedom Commission on Mental Health, 2003). Second, landlords may subvert housing laws by refusing to rent to people with mental illness on the basis of low resources, poor credit, or a lack of housing references, when, in fact, the primary reason for not renting to them is that they have a mental illness (Denton & Bianco, 2001). Third, people with mental illness and their advocates may not know about or understand housing laws and how to seek redress under them (Denton & Bianco, 2001).

Support Services

Another resource that many people with mental illness need in order to live in supported housing, supervised apartments, or SROs is a range of support services. Medicaid provides substantial funds for case management and other mental health services needed by people with mental illness. State mental health authorities often fund support services for people who are not Medicaid eligible, or who have inadequate or no private insurance and cannot afford to pay privately. However, fiscal problems in recent years have forced most states to reduce funding for support services for people who are not Medicaid eligible. Consequently, increased numbers of people with mental illness will not receive the support services they need to live in independent housing. As indicated previously, support resources may be provided informally by friends, relatives, or landlords, as well as formally by mental health organizations. With cuts in governmental programs, it is more important than ever to systematically encourage informal supports, although, unfortunately, many people will not have access to them. Yet another resource many people with mental illness who live in independent living settings will need is material support for food, utility payments, transportation, and other daily living expenses (Tanzman, 1993).

Resources to Facilitate Participation in Congregate Settings

To participate in the control of their residences in congregate and supervised apartment settings, people with mental illness may need another set of resources. Some will require training on how to work in groups, run meetings, and interact with staff. Other people may need an outside party to advocate with them or to mediate disputes. Pulier and Hubbard (2001) reported the strongest example of support of this type when mental health professionals worked closely with a boarding home operator to maximize the number of opportunities residents had to participate in decision making.

Resources for Mental Health Professionals

Mental health professionals need resources, too (Brown & Wheeler, 1990). In particular, they need sufficient amounts of time to provide the supports their clients need to remain in the community. High caseloads, staff vacancies, and billing restrictions can prevent that from occurring. Staff also needs flexible work hours to provide services to its clients at times when they need them, rather than working straight day shifts on Monday through Friday. Many staff members also need training on how to provide support services in a way that empowers their clients rather than in a paternalistic manner, training on the potential of many people with mental illness to live in the community with supports, and training on how to work effectively with landlords (Carling, 1995; Parkinson et al., 1999).

SUPPORTIVE CULTURE

A final condition for empowering people with severe mental illness through housing is that a culture exists that is supportive of the person with mental illness obtaining housing of his or her choice, maintaining that housing, and controlling life within the residence. A supportive culture must dispel the stigmatized belief that people with mental illness need 24-hour supervision, are not responsible enough or are incapable of living independently in the community even with supports, or present a danger to the community. Many mental health professionals, mental health organizations, and neighborhoods often hold such beliefs. Unfortunately, federal and state policies also reflect similar biases. While support from mental health professionals can assist people with mental illness to overcome some housing stigma, it also is helpful, perhaps essential in the long run, when a supportive culture exists within the geographic community in which they wish to live. This typically is not the case, as many communities adopt NIMBYism (not in my back yard–ism) and work to prevent people with mental illness from moving into their neighborhoods (Allen, 1996).

A supportive culture at the organizational level is one that also rejects stigma, and instead believes in the ability of most people with mental illness to live independently in the community, sometimes with supports. The creation of a supportive organizational culture often requires that organizations adopt new mission and vision statements that reflect this (Ridgway & Zipple, 1990). A supportive organizational culture also is promoted by adoption of the recovery perspective, psychiatric rehabilitation, or the strengths perspective, all of which support people choosing their own housing and receiving supports to maintain it (Jacobson & Curtis, 2000; Rapp, 1998; Weinstein, 2000). Fakhoury et al. (2002) noted that in agencies that have adopted the supported housing model, organizational culture is largely dependent on the skills and attitudes of staff to minimize the number of unnecessary rules and restrictions in housing. Therefore, staff may need training to move from models of custodial care or a continuum of care to one that promotes independent living. Some argue that the ability to identify and develop housing, assess housing needs, and support people in housing is an expected competency of case managers and other mental health professionals who work with people with severe mental illness (Weinstein, 2000). Finally, intense educational and lobbying efforts are needed first to help public officials overcome stigmatized views of housing for people with mental illness, and then to allocate the resources needed for people to access housing of their choice, to maintain that housing, and to control their lives within it.

CASE STUDIES

To increase understanding of the opportunities for, and limitations to, the empowerment of people with mental illness through housing, empowerment once again is examined through two cases studies, one among people with mental illness residing in a public psychiatric hospital that provides long-term care and treatment (Linhorst et al., 1999), and the other among those residing in the community who are receiving services from a publicly funded community mental health agency (Kryah et al., 2003).

Empowerment Among Clients in a Psychiatric Hospital (SLPRC)

Degree of Empowerment

Focus group discussion addressed two aspects of empowerment related to housing at SLPRC: choice of where clients lived within the hospital and the degree of control they had over their residential units. Based on this discussion and review of documents, clients were not empowered through selection of where they lived. Clients and staff agreed that clients had little or no choice about where they lived within the hospital. This included their initial placement upon entering the hospital, as well as subsequent transfers to different residential units. Some clients were empowered to a moderate degree through decision making associated with their residential units. In both wards and cottages, however, the level of client participation varied considerably across residential units. As one example, clients residing in the hospital wards, who ate all meals in the cafeteria, indicated that they chose from a variety of food items. They said that the dietary department frequently surveyed them about food options and attempted to meet their preferences. Clients in the cottage program ate the majority of their meals in the cottages. Clients in at least half of the cottages said that staff, not clients, ordered and prepared the food that they ate in the cottage, although they expressed interest in doing more of this themselves. Considerable variation existed, too, in the degree of clients' involvement in resolving differences that arose between clients, or between clients and staff. All wards and cottages had at least weekly meetings attended by all clients and some staff. Some units used these meetings as a forum to discuss differences, while in other units, staff used these meetings solely to provide information to clients. As an alternative, some clients worked with treatment teams in the hospital programs, and with case managers in the cottage program, to resolve disputes, although this, too, was highly variable.

Application of Conditions for Empowerment

Empowerment through selection of housing did not exist primarily because several factors greatly limited the availability of choices of where clients lived within the facility. Since the treatment programs are residentially based, clients' clinical symptoms and treatment needs determined their treatment program, and consequently the range of residential units in which they could live. Some clients had severe psychiatric symptoms that did not permit their moving to the cottage program. Also, the hospital typically was at or near maximum census, so new clients were assigned to any available beds within the appropriate program. In addition, the Missouri Department of Mental Health's (MDMH) risk management policies determined when clients were eligible to move to a less restrictive residential unit. Clients' requests for transfer to another ward or cottage within the same program were seldom granted.

Also, reciprocal concrete incentives for clients to move from the hospital ward programs to the cottage program sometimes did not exist. Some clients looked forward to moving to the cottage program because of the additional independence it could give them, and thus had a concrete incentive for wishing to move. Other clients, however, had a disincentive to move to the cottage program. Some feared that cottage staff would take additional time to get to know them before supporting their discharge, which could delay it. Some clients throughout the hospital and some staff from the ward programs certainly held this position. Staff, too, had a concrete disincentive for transferring clients from ward programs to the cottage program and from one cottage to another within the cottage program. Staff from both the old and new residential units had to complete a considerable amount of paperwork when clients moved.

The variation in client input into residential functions and resolution of differences was due in large part to a lack of participation structures and processes. Hospital and program policies did not identify those areas of residential life in which clients should participate or describe how decisions should be made, so each residential unit developed its own guidelines, structures, and processes. It appeared that when clients did not participate in aspects of residential life, staff made decisions for their own convenience, or from an authoritarian standpoint. Other staff, however, perceived participation as a form of treatment and as a method of skill building, and thus had an incentive to involve clients because it helped them meet their goals. Clients also lacked information about options for completing residential functions and for resolving disputes. They often were unaware that practices varied across residential units. Consequently, they did not pursue alternate ways of doing things. In general, though, empowerment through housing failed to occur because the hospital culture did not fully support it. When empowerment did occur, it resulted from the efforts of individual staff members who believed that participation had therapeutic value. The hospital vision and value statements and the adoption of psychiatric rehabilitation supported client choice and participation, at least in the abstract. However, such participation was not operationalized in hospital or program policies and procedures, participation structures or processes, staff training, or other means that could have promoted empowerment through housing. In reality, it is likely that most people with mental illness will not be empowered through selection of housing within hospitals. However, the potential exists for people with mental illness to experience some degree of empowerment by participating in the control of residential units within psychiatric hospitals that provide long-term care and treatment.

Empowerment Among Clients of a Community Agency (BJC-BH)

Degree of Empowerment

The focus group discussion centered on access to, and maintenance of, housing for BJC-BH clients. Wide variation in the degree to which BJC-BH clients were empowered through housing existed. Some clients were able to access housing of their choice and maintain it. Other clients who would have preferred to live in apartments resided in congregate settings. In addition, a limited number of clients were periodically homeless. In total, clients and staff indicated the clients lived in the following types of housing at the time of the interviews: independent apartments, boarding homes, nursing homes, SROs, on the streets (homeless), in shelters when beds were available (homeless), substance abuse treatment centers, jails, rented rooms in private homes, with family members, and temporarily with friends or family while searching for permanent housing.

Application of Conditions for Empowerment

Variability in empowerment was associated with not meeting the conditions of available of choices, access to resources, concrete reciprocal incentives, and a supportive culture. Clients and staff indicated that the biggest obstacle to obtaining housing of choice was the lack of affordable housing. Some clients and staff also indicated that apartment housing was particularly difficult to get for clients with substance abuse problems, with poor credit histories, with criminal histories, with prior housing evictions, who were married, or who had children. In addition, some landlords discriminated against people with mental illness. These landlords either would not rent to clients, or if they did rent to them, the landlords sometimes would not properly maintain the rental units because they assumed that clients had no other housing options and would not move out. Staff and clients emphatically noted, however, that some landlords were very fair in their housing practices and served as a support to maintaining clients in their homes.

Clients used at least three types of resources to maximize opportunities for independent housing, although these were not sufficient to meet all needs. Some clients were able to access public housing and Section 8 vouchers, although they often had to wait for years to be accepted. Unfortunately, some clients who had Section 8 vouchers were unable to use them because they could not locate housing that met rent guidelines or find landlords who would accept them. Since federal housing programs did not nearly meet clients' housing needs, MDMH subsidized rents with a program that was similar to Section 8 vouchers. In August 2003, for instance, 264 clients from the St. Louis BJC-BH offices and 600 total clients living in the St. Louis area who received mental health services from a variety of state-funded mental health organizations received these state-funded apartment subsidies. Even these additional subsidies did not meet the housing needs of all clients.

A second resource that some clients used was the BJC-BH housing specialist, a position specifically created to facilitate clients' access to housing. That staff member had expertise in housing assistance programs, developed lists of landlords who would consider renting to BJC-BH clients, and sought funds for rent and utility deposits. The housing specialist performed general housing development, as well as work with individual clients. Clients could contact the housing specialist themselves, or case managers could refer them. Because of the immense need for housing and other community resources, BJC-BH recently renamed the position Resource Specialist, expanded the duties to include location of housing and other resources that some clients needed to remain in the community, and increased the number of positions from one to three to better meet client needs.

One resource clients used to maintain housing was the support services they received from BJC-BH case managers. Clients and staff overwhelmingly stated that support services largely met their needs. Staff offered one caveat, however. They indicated that they were unable to provide the extensive supports needed by some boarding home clients who preferred to live in independent housing. They did not have the staffing, for example, to spend the night with clients the first few days they were placed in apartments. Although it could not be determined from the focus group interviews whether or not such clients actually needed these extensive supports at least initially, some case managers were unwilling to assist their clients to move from boarding homes into apartments in the absence of the extensive supports that they were unable to provide.

Some decision-making parties did not have concrete incentives to promote clients living in supported housing. Criminal justice agencies, judges controlling the residential status of people found NGRI, and legal guardians believed that the needs of many clients or public safety considerations could be better met by clients living in congregate housing, such as boarding homes, nursing homes, or group homes. Also, consistent with previously discussed staff disincentives to involve clients in supported housing, one Missouri mental health advocate believed that community providers across the state often looked first to congregate housing for many clients because it took much less time to locate and maintain clients in congregate housing than in supported housing in apartments. There was no evidence from the focus groups comprised of BJC-BH staff and clients, however, that this occurred at BJC-BH.

Finally, the culture of the state and local community, as well as the BJC-BH organizational culture, did not fully support people with mental illness living independently in the community with supports. Some neighborhoods and landlords were not accepting of people with mental illness. The resources necessary for independent living were insufficient, particularly rental subsidizes and adequate support services for people who may initially have needed high levels of supports. The continuum of care model continued to influence housing practices within the state. For example, MDMH continued to support placement of people with mental illness in nursing homes and boarding homes. In August 2003, for instance, it provided housing subsidies to 1,346 adults living in the St. Louis area. The majority of the housing subsidies went to people living in congregate housing, including 39% to those living in residential care facilities, that is, boarding homes, and 17% to those living in nursing homes. Less than half of the housing subsidies (44%) went to people living in apartments.

Reflecting on the conditions for the empowerment of BJC-BH clients through housing, it is noteworthy that neither clients nor staff identified any of the conditions internal to clients, including unmanaged psychiatric symptoms, poor skill levels, or lack of psychological readiness to move into more independent housing, as impeding access to housing of their choice. Rather, factors external to BJC-BH clients prevented greater access to housing of their choice. Further empowerment of BJC-BH clients primarily required that they have greater access to housing, increased support services, and a culture that would provide greater support in order to realize their potential to live in housing of their choice.

GUIDELINES FOR PROMOTING EMPOWERMENT THROUGH HOUSING

The following guidelines, derived from the above discussion of the conditions for empowerment, are offered to further promote empowerment of people with severe mental illness through housing.

1. *Support an array of housing options.* No single type of housing can meet the clinical needs and housing preferences of all people with mental illness.
2. *Adopt the supported housing model.* Most people with mental illness can live independently in the community with supports, without having to progress through a series of time-limited congregate residential settings of increasing independence.
3. *Provide housing supports when people need it.* Supports should be individualized and be flexible to meet changing needs, with those people with less skills or more unmanaged symptoms receiving greater amounts of supports, and supports being available 24 hours per day, 7 days per week.
4. *Use multiple sources of support.* For many people, combinations of mental health programs, friends and relatives of the person with mental illness, and landlords can provide support.
5. *Provide skill training in the setting in which people choose to live.* Most people with mental illness can learn skills in independent residential settings, such as an apartment, without needing to move through a continuum of congregate settings.
6. *Educate landlords and neighbors about psychiatric symptoms.* In some instances, it may be appropriate for people with mental illness themselves, mental health organizations, or informal support persons to educate landlords or neighbors about the nature of psychiatric symptoms to allay any stigmatized concerns they may hold.
7. *Develop programs for people in long-term hospitals and other congregate settings.* Some people may need special programs to build confidence in their abilities to live independently in the community, even with supports.
8. *Work with landlords to develop trust and respect.* Resident-landlord relationships can be facilitated when both parties are knowledgeable about their rights and responsibilities. Case managers, if involved, can discuss the level of support they can provide and share success stories of other people with mental illness who have succeeded in independent housing.
9. *Provide boarding home operators with incentives to promote resident independence.* If states support boarding homes, their operators are more likely to promote independence if they receive financial rewards for assisting residents to move to more independent living, and if they receive additional referrals to maintain their occupancy rates.
10. *Involve residents of congregate facilities in psychiatric rehabilitation activities.* Instead of, or in addition to, boarding home operators promoting independence, participation in off-site rehabilitation services, such as psychosocial rehabilitation

centers, can help these residents to identify residential options, to increase skills, and to consider moving to more independent housing.

11. *Provide landlords with supports.* These may include consultation about the symptoms of mental illness, mediation between residents and landlords, special funds to pay rents if residents are hospitalized or do not pay rent in a timely manner, and public recognition for landlords who have become most involved in working with people with mental illness.

12. *Develop processes to help people access independent community housing.* This should included processes to assess clients' resources, to assist eligible clients to apply for subsidized housing, and to locate housing in the community.

13. *Develop dispute resolution processes.* This includes a clear articulation of the rights and responsibilities of mental health programs, residents, and landlords and a mechanism for dispute resolution that ensures due process, particularly when eviction is imminent.

14. *Develop participation structures in congregate settings.* Structures such as residence councils and tenant associations can be developed to give residents some control of their lives within in supervised apartments with on-site staff and other congregate settings, such as long-term psychiatric hospitals, boarding homes, and group homes.

15. *Increase the number of units of affordable housing.* Many people with mental illness do not have access to affording housing that is of good physical quality and is in safe neighborhoods. State mental health authorities should take an active role in promoting the development of affordable housing.

16. *Provide mental health professionals with training and time to provide support services.* Some staff members will need training on how to provide support services in a way that empowers their clients rather than in a paternalistic manner, training on the potential of many people with mental illness to live in the community with supports, and training on how to work effectively with landlords. They also need sufficient amounts of time to provide the supports their clients need to remain in the community, including evenings and weekends.

17. *Promote an organizational culture that supports independent living.* This often requires the creation of new mission and vision statements; adoption of the recovery perspective, psychiatric rehabilitation, or the strengths perspective; and the provision of training to move staff from models of custodial care or continuum of care to one that promotes independent living.

7

Empowerment Through Organizational Decision Making

The focus for organizational decision making is the involvement of people with severe mental illness in decision making within one or more of the organizations from which they receive mental health treatment, rehabilitation, or support services. This involvement extends beyond an individual's treatment plan, hospital ward, or apartment to include those decisions that potentially affect all persons receiving services from that organization, such as the development of services and pragmatic aspects of program operation. For example, Moxley, Jacobs, and Wilson (1992) described the involvement of people with mental illness in the expansion of an agency to include a psychosocial rehabilitation club-house. Clients from that agency worked in conjunction with family members, mental health professionals, governmental officials, and others on five committees to guide its development and initial implementation. Pyke and Lowe (1996) stated that people with mental illness were involved with agency leaders in planning the transformation of their congregate housing to supported housing. On a smaller scale, Pilgrim and Waldron (1998) indicated that suggestions made by people with mental illness led to an expansion of the hours of operation of their day program, to the creation of an advocate position within the agency, and to the publication of a booklet for clients and other interested parties about agency services.

Katan and Prager (1986) offered four reasons to involve consumers of mental health and social services in organizational decision making. First and foremost, they argued that clients have a right to participate because of the immense affect these agencies can have on their lives.

Second, organizations are more responsive to consumers' needs when clients participate in decision making. Third, client participation helps to lessen the power imbalance between clients and agency staff. Fourth, participation can have therapeutic value to clients, increasing their coping skills and sense of well-being. In addition, participation in organizational decision making is a component of the recovery perspective and psychiatric rehabilitation (Cook & Hoffschmidt, 1993; Jacobson & Curtis, 2000). Thus, organizations that have adopted these perspectives would be expected to involve their clients in decision making.

Another reason to involve people with mental illness in organizational decision making is that participation fosters empowerment (Pilgrim & Waldron, 1998; Smith & Ford, 1986). Meaningful participation can result in both subjective and objective empowerment. It gives people a sense of control, and it can lead to tangible outcomes such as the creation of new services, improvement of existing ones, or increased access to services. In addition, Segal, Silverman, and Temkin (1995) argued that the ability to influence those organizations with which people with mental illness frequently interact is integral to their attaining empowerment. Considering that empowerment exists on a continuum, people with mental illness can experience a range of participation in organizational decision making, with empowerment increasing the more people with mental illness influence decision making. The level of participation can extend from no participation; to leaders providing information about pending decisions, with people with mental illness having only marginal opportunities for influence; to consultation in which agency leaders actively seek the opinions of people with mental illness and respond to them whether or not leaders accept clients' suggestions; to partnerships between staff and clients in which they reach decisions together as peers; to people with mental illness having complete control over decisions (Means & Smith, 1994; Peck et al., 2002).

Despite its empowerment potential, seemingly valid reasons for involving people with mental illness in organizational decision making, and successful examples of involvement, meaningful participation generally is not occurring. Bevilacqua (1995) stated that it is now politically correct to acknowledge the role of people with mental illness in organizational decision making; however, he believed the rhetoric of inclusion is far ahead of reality. Valentine and Capponi (1989) indicated, too, that a wide gap exists between the stated values of inclusion of people with mental illness in organizational decision making and actual practice. Barnes and Bowl (2001) and Peck et al. (2002) argued that results are mixed at best. On the positive side, Barnes and Bowl found that some organizations have changed policies and improved training to support increased participation. On the negative side, they found little evidence of attitudinal change on the part of mental health professionals supporting involvement. They also found

Table 7.1 Conditions for Empowering People With Severe Mental Illness Through Organizational Decision Making

Managed psychiatric symptoms—The person's psychiatric symptoms are managed to the degree required to meaningfully participate in organizational decision making.

Participation skills—The person has the skills needed to meaningfully participate in organizational decision making.

Psychological readiness—The person has the confidence, motivation, and willingness to meaningfully participate in organizational decision making.

Mutual trust and respect—Mutual trust and respect exist between the person with mental illness and those with whom he or she interacts in organizational decision making.

Reciprocal concrete incentives—The person with mental illness and individuals from the agency from which he or she receives services have concrete incentives to meaningfully participate together in organizational decision making.

Availability of choices—The person has choices of participation structures and programs through which to meaningfully participate in organizational decision making, has choices in what issues are being raised for consideration, and has choices of solutions to the problem under consideration.

Participation structures and processes—Structures and processes through which the person can meaningfully participate in organizational decision making exist.

Access to resources—The person has access to the resources needed to meaningfully participate in organizational decision making.

Supportive culture—The organization's culture supports meaningful participation of the person in organizational decision making.

that people with mental illness perceived that there has been too little change resulting from their participation. Peck et al., in describing efforts to enhance organizational participation in one region of England, noted that while a start had been made, changes were superficial and unlikely to ever result in significant increases in the power of people with mental illness. Application of the conditions for empowerment should shed some light on the reasons why participation has been inconsistent and how it can be improved. The conditions for empowerment, as they related to organizational decision making, are included in table 7.1.

MANAGED PSYCHIATRIC SYMPTOMS

One condition for empowering people with severe mental illness through organizational decision making is that the psychiatric symptoms of the person are managed to the degree necessary to meaningfully participate. Participation requires some ability to concentrate and screen out irrelevant information, for instance, when participating in committee meetings with staff; to process information, for example, when trying to understand the nature of a particular problem within an organization; and to make logical choices, such as when weighing the merits of policy options. The symptoms of many people are managed enough to participate in organizational decision making, although some people are incapable of doing so at particular times. In addition, the process of participation in organization decision making, itself, can produce stress and a possible reemergence of psychiatric symptoms (Barnes & Wistow, 1994). Therefore, some people who begin the participation process may need supports during times of stress, to be excused from some activities, or to discontinue participation altogether.

Some behaviors associated with psychiatric symptoms, such as periodic rocking or pacing, may not affect the cognitive ability of people with mental illness to participate, but other participants may find these to be disruptive or misinterpret them as disinterest in the process (Valentine & Capponi, 1989). Those responsible for the participation process can take two approaches to contend with this. One is to work with people with mental illness to reduce or eliminate these behaviors when participating in meetings with others. Another is to provide training to others participating in the process about symptoms of mental illness, behaviors associated with those symptoms, and behaviors that actually are side effects of psychotropic medications (Vandergang, 1996).

PARTICIPATION SKILLS

A second condition for empowerment is that the person with mental illness has the skills needed to meaningfully participate in organizational decision making. While required skills will vary by type of decision-making activity, people with mental illness often will need interpersonal skills; public speaking skills; writing skills; assertiveness skills; conflict resolution skills; negotiating skills; skills to read a budget; skills to function in formal boards, including operational knowledge of Robert's Rules of Order; or other skills (Pilgrim & Waldron, 1998; Rowe, Benedict, & Falzer, 2003). Many people with mental illness lack these skills and will need considerable training in order to participate (Means & Smith, 1994; Staples, 1999). Means and Smith (1994) pointed out that skill deficits exist, in part, because people with mental illness are not accustomed to being asked to participate in organizational decision making. In addition, Barnes and Bowl (2001) were highly critical of mental health organizations because they often spend an extensive amount of time training staff and others to participate but fail to think about providing the same level of training to the people with mental illness they ask to participate. In fact, many people, with and without mental illness, need training in many of the above skills areas to participate effectively in organizational decision making.

In-house staff typically provide training for people with mental illness on participating in organizational decision making, if training is provided at all. This training is often informal, not systematic, and not thorough enough relative to the level of participation the organization expects. Noticeably absent from the professional literature are accounts of in-house training to support skill development for participation in organizational decision making. There are, however, accounts of two excellent training programs that prepared people with mental illness to participate in community nonprofit boards. One program consisted of a 16-week, 2 hour-per-week program (Bullock, Ensing, Ally, & Weddle, 2000). The other training program met twice weekly for 3 hours each meeting for 7 weeks (Rowe et al., 2003). Both programs contained didactic and experiential components. The latter program also included a 6-month internship on a board in which a board member was assigned to the individual as a mentor.

Skills can improve through actual experience, not just through formal training. Pilgrim and Waldron (1998), for instance, found that people with mental illness who worked directly with program managers to improve the organization's mental health services enhanced their ability to work with others in a group setting; to negotiate with managers through written, telephone and in-person techniques; to review progress; and to develop new strategies for change. Finally, training can not only improve skills but also enable people with mental illness to experience subjective empowerment. Bullock et al. (2000) used an instrument developed by Rogers, Chamberlin, Ellison, and Crean (1997) to measure empowerment among trainees of a leadership program. They found that empowerment increased after completion of the training program, and that this higher level of empowerment remained when people were reevaluated 6 months later.

PSYCHOLOGICAL READINESS

A third condition for empowerment is that the person with mental illness has the psychological readiness to meaningfully participate in organizational decision making. Many people with mental illness are not psychologically prepared to participate, owing in large part to feelings of powerlessness and learned helplessness. Wilson (1996) stated that this reluctance was associated with "a lack of self-confidence, a feeling that they cannot contribute anything of value, a fear of failure, and a feeling of social isolation" (p. 80). In addition, some types of structures and processes for participation, such as serving on nonprofit boards of directors, can be daunting and complex for anyone, especially for some people with mental illness (Barnes & Bowl, 2001). Also, clients' prior unproductive attempts to influence organizational decision making can decrease their motivation to participate in future activities. Barnes and Bowl (2001) determined that these negative experiences can produce misunderstanding and anxiety and reinforce feelings of powerlessness.

Agencies can take several actions to increase the psychological readiness of people with mental illness to participate in organizational decision making. According to Staples (1999), mental health professionals must help people with mental illness increase their self-respect, confidence, and sense of control before they can be expected to want to participate. Achieving this requires that people with mental illness receive personal support, training, and the provision of other resources (Carling, 1995; Means & Smith, 1994). The two intensive training programs previously identified gave people with mental illness both the skills and the initial confidence to participate (Bullock et al., 2000; Rowe et al., 2003). In addition, some people with mental illness need ongoing encouragement to maintain their participation because their situations and needs change over time (Carling, 1995). Carling (1995) described supports to maintain participation. "The particular kinds of support that are needed depend on each individual's needs and experiences, but they may include indepth orientation and explanation of the process; clarifying expectations; providing feedback about a person's participation; confidence building; ongoing review of events and issues of concern; and so forth" (p. 278).

MUTUAL TRUST AND RESPECT

A fourth condition for empowerment is that mutual trust and respect exist between the person with mental illness and those with whom he or she interacts in organizational decision making. People with mental illness must trust that their voices will be heard, that actions they recommend will be enacted or at least considered, and that there will be no negative repercussions for critical comments. Those with whom consumers interact in organizational decision making must trust that consumers have the ability to contribute and will do so in a constructive way. People with mental illness understandably may be skeptical that mental health professionals will be willing to share power with them. Speaking from the position of mental health professionals, Williams and Lindley (1996) stated, "We can reasonably expect service users to be ambivalent about the merits of collaborating with those involved in service provision. They may have well founded doubts about whether we are willing, or able, to use our power to serve any interests other than our own" (p. 7). There also may be legitimate fear of reprisal from treatment staff or residential managers if clients voice opinions that reflect negatively on them or the areas for which they are responsible (Barnes & Bowl, 2001).

Staples (1999) offered several methods through which individuals who interact with people with mental illness can demonstrate trust and respect. Some were to "listen carefully to the consumer,... enable consumers to identify their own needs and to define problems,... ask questions rather than telling consumers what to do, . . . share expertise and opinions without imposing them, manipulating for agreement or creating deference" (pp. 132–133). Conversely, Williams and Lindley (1996) provided examples of means whereby mental health professionals can, and do, subvert the development of trust and respect in organizational decision making by keeping people with mental illness "in their place" (p. 11). Some of these included not explaining the purpose of the meeting and rules governing participation, calling clients by their first names and everyone else by their surnames, routinely using jargon, providing clients with only a limited amount of time to speak at the end of meetings, allowing key parties to reach agreement on decisions before the meeting, and interrupting clients and then speaking for them.

In light of the examples provided by Staples (1999) and Williams and Lindley (1996), staff need to be conscious of the manner in which they communicate and how their interactions demonstrate respect, or the lack thereof, and promote, or hinder, trust and thus affect meaningful client participation. Staff, in particular, need to be able, and willing, to point out to each other disruptive communication in order to correct it. To further promote trust and respect, the organizational decision-making process should include a formal evaluation of the implementation of efforts to meaningfully involve people with mental illness (Kent & Read, 1998). Comprehensive evaluations should examine the quality of interactions between consumers and other participants, the adequacy of resources provided, and the changes that have resulted from participation. This requires getting responses from both people with mental illness and other participants using a range of qualitative and quantitative techniques.

RECIPROCAL CONCRETE INCENTIVES

A fifth condition is that the person with mental illness and individuals from the agency from which he or she receives services has concrete incentives to meaningfully participate together in organizational decision making. There is growing acceptance that both people with mental illness and agencies benefit from such participation (Gerhart, 1990). Participation provides an acceptable means for clients to express dissatisfaction with services and operations and to have some effect on improving them (Atkinson & MacPherson, 2001; Barnes & Wistow, 1994). Furthermore, participation can result in tangible improvements for clients. Longo et al. (2002), for example, stated that the members council of a long-term psychiatric hospital was responsible for improvements in physical conditions at the hospital, including paved sidewalks and better lighting, and the institution of an identification badge that facilitated clients' ease of movement throughout the hospital. Clients also may receive some financial benefits for participation. Carling (1995) encouraged organizations to pay people with mental illness for the time they spend participating in agencywide activities to improve services. Ryan and Bamber (2002), however, cautioned against paying people with mental illness to participate, fearing these individuals can become dependent on these funds and unintentionally may try to exclude others from participating to retain this income. In addition, participation in the process itself can be empowering to people with mental illness if the experience has been successful (Pilgrim & Waldron, 1998; Smith & Ford, 1986). Conversely, poor experiences can be disempowering and be a disincentive for future participation. Finally, people with mental illness can participate for therapeutic value. Participation can improve problem-solving skills, organizational skills, coping mechanisms, self-esteem, and self-confidence (Gerhart, 1990; Katan & Prager, 1986; Pilgrim & Waldron, 1998; Smith & Ford, 1986).

Despite these incentives to participate in organizational decision making, many people with mental illness will choose not to participate in most types of decision-making processes. People are much more likely to want to participate in their treatment planning than in organizational decision making (Peck et al., 2002). One can speculate that the benefits of treatment planning are much more personal and immediate than participation in organizational decision making. This latter participation can take months or even years to affect change, and, unless there is a good feedback mechanism, clients may never know what effect, if any, their participation had on decisions. People with mental illness who reside in long-term psychiatric hospitals are much more likely to participate in organizational decision making than people living in acute care hospitals or those living in the community (Barnes & Wistow, 1994; Beeforth et al., 1990). People in long-term hospitals have greater incentives because both the quality of their mental health services and their environment are affected by organizational decision making. People hospitalized in acute psychiatric hospitals have less incentive because they are living there for only a short period of time and may never return. People who receive community-based services may not feel that participation is a priority, particularly if they are satisfied with their services, and other aspects of their lives are going well. Regardless of living situation, another reason why some people with mental illness choose not to participate is the perceived disconnect between their personal lives and organizational policy (Staples, 1999). They may not understand that changes in services and procedures can affect them personally. Consequently, helping people with mental illness to make a connection between organizational services, policies, and procedures and their personal lives can be an important first step toward participation. It is noteworthy that the reluctance of people to become involved in organizational decision making certainly is not limited to those with mental illness and often is not a result of mental illness. Rather, it is endemic to much of society. As examples, many parents do not become involved in their children's schooling by attending school board meetings, teacher conferences, or parent-teacher association meetings; and many residents do not join or participate in the neighborhood associations that could improve their own lives and those who live around them.

Concrete incentives for staff to meaningfully participate with people with mental illness in organizational decision making and to support them in this endeavor also exist. Most important, people with mental illness have special knowledge about services, service operations, and service needs that others do not have (Valentine & Capponi, 1989). Tapping into this special knowledge through participation in organizational decision making is one of the most important means for mental health professionals to develop services that are responsive to clients' needs (Katan & Prager, 1986; Kent & Read, 1998; Salzer, 1997). As Gerhart (1990) stated, "Their experiences and perceptions are invaluable for fitting services to the needs of agency clients.... The contribution of consumers can set the direction for new service delivery policies and enrich existing services" (p. 66). In addition, just as the therapeutic value of participation can be an incentive for people with mental illness to participate in this process, it also can be an incentive for staff to meaningful participate. It can be another resource for people with mental illness to learn, test, or further develop new skills and to increase confidence and self-esteem. Gerhart summarized this position, "The clinician may not have to look beyond the agency to involve the client in meaningful work and activities that are not only of therapeutic value to the client but also of benefit to others" (p. 66).

AVAILABILITY OF CHOICES

A sixth condition for empowerment is that the person with mental illness has choices in at least three areas. First, alternative solutions to problems that people with mental illness are asked to address in organizational decision making should exist. Ideally, people with mental illness should be included in the process of identifying alternative courses of action, as opposed to staff presenting them with a predetermined list. Staff making available to clients only one actual course of action or attempting to direct clients to an already selected alternative invalidates the meaningfulness of the process. It also is disempowering because it magnifies the limitations placed on clients (Barnes & Bowl, 2001). If agency leaders already have selected a course of action, they should explain this to people with mental illness without any pretense of seeking their contribution. Second, people with mental illness should have choices in what issues are raised for consideration for action. Rather than always asking people with mental illness to react to issues raised by agency leaders, people with mental illness, too, should have the authority to put items on the agenda for discussion (Means & Smith, 1994). Third, people with mental illness should have choices of structures and processes through which they can partici- pate in organizational decision making. People may be more comfort- able participating in some activities than in others. While some people may not wish, for instance, to participate on an ongoing agency com- mittee, they may be willing to attend a forum with other clients and staff to address a particular issue or to complete a mail questionnaire asses- sing clients' service needs. Offering people choices will increase the total number of people who ultimately choose to participate (Carling, 1995).

PARTICIPATION STRUCTURES AND PROCESSES

A seventh condition for empowerment is that structures and processes through which people with mental illness can participate in organi- zational decision making exist. At least four facets are relevant.

Multiple Decision-Making Structures

Many different types of such structures exist. One type consists of people with and without mental illness working together as peers in groups, including agency boards of directors, advisory boards, task forces, and committees (Barnes & Bowl, 2001; Carling, 1995; Vandergang, 1996). In such groups, Carling (1995) recommended that people with mental illness hold at least half of the seats. A second type of structure consists of a group of agency clients interacting with leaders in a variety of ways to influence organizational decision making. This client group may be referred to as a consumer council, user council, patient advisory committee, or some other name (Barnes & Wistow, 1994; Beeforth et al., 1990; Linhorst, Eckert, Ha- milton, & Young, 2001; Longo et al., 2002). A third structure includes forums between clients and agency leaders during which information is shared, concerns are identified and possibly prioritized, and alternative solutions discussed (Starkey & Leadholm, 1997). These typically are not decision-making bodies, although they can provide opportunities for people with mental illness to contribute to decision making through the opinions and information they provide to leaders. These meetings can be held on a regular basis, such as quarterly, or as staff or people with mental illness identify issues. Fourth, people with mental illness may influence organizational decision making through participation in program evalu- ation and performance improvement activities. A more focused discussion of this type of participation is reserved for chapter 10. Fifth, formal grievance systems and advocacy programs can influence organizational decision making (Olley & Ogloff, 1995). While they usually address indi- vidual client issues, they can identify systemic problems that require changes in organizational policies to rectify. Finally, people with mental illness may be able to influence organizational policy through informal means, typically personal conversations, letters, or telephone calls to clinical staff who then share that information with agency leaders, to agency leaders themselves, to individuals within the mental health system who have some oversight of the organization, or to federal or state governmental officials.

People with mental illness should have a range of options for participation. As Lord et al. (1998) stated based on their work with clients in organizational decision making, "We learned that genuine consumer participation can happen and that many strategies are required for it to occur in a constructive, meaningful manner" (p. 337). Traditional decision-making structures, such as boards and committees, may be inadequate because they can be intimidating to people both with and without mental illness, and some people with mental illness cannot accommodate to their high level of structure (Barnes & Bowl, 2001). Agencies may need to develop unconventional structures to solicit client participation. Means and Smith (1994), for example, found that unstructured open meetings with people with mental illness and staff were particularly good at identifying issues to be placed on the agenda, and that smaller, more structured meetings were better for developing plans and designing and overseeing implementation. Table 7.2 summarizes the structures through which people with mental illness can participate in organizational decision making.

Explicit Agreements on Participation

Regardless of the type of structure used to promote client involvement in organizational decision making, explicit agreement should exist

Table 7.2 Structures and Processes Through Which People With Severe Mental Illness Can Participate in Organizational Decision Making

- People with mental illness work together with nonconsumers as peers on agency boards of directors, advisory boards, task forces, or committees
- A group of agency clients interacts with leaders through a consumer council, a user council, a patient advisory committee, or some other similarly named client group
- Forums between clients and agency leaders during which information is shared, concerns are identified and possibly prioritized, and alternative solutions are discussed
- Program evaluation and performance improvement activities
- Formal grievance systems and advocacy programs that can identify systemic problems that require organizational decisions to rectify
- Informal means, such as personal conversations, letters, or telephone calls to clinical staff, to agency leaders, to individuals within the mental health system who have some oversight of the organization, or to federal or state governmental officials

between clients and staff on two issues. One issue is the clients' level of decision-making authority. As stated in the chapter introduction, client participation can range from minimal influence, to consultation, to collaboration, to clients having complete decision-making control (Means & Smith, 1994; Peck et al., 2002). The second issue is identification of the content areas and the phase or phases of decision making in which people with mental illness will be involved. Ideally, clients should have input into agenda setting and participate in decision making surrounding program and policy development, implementation, and evaluation in all major areas that directly affect them (Means & Smith, 1994; Staples, 1999).

In some instances, the level of decision making and areas of involvement, such as a clients serving on an agency board of directors and having voting power on all issues that come before the board, are set and ongoing. In many instances, however, selections of the level of decision-making power and areas of involvement are made on an issue-by-issue basis. In fact, Barnes and Bowl (2001) argued that decisions on clients' level of power and the issues they are to address should be made in a dynamic, negotiated process. Failing to have an explicit, written, negotiated agreement can lead to confusion on the part of both staff and clients and to the disempowerment of clients. Glasman (1991) provided an example of such a written agreement, which existed between a patient council and the management of a mental health organization in Holland that identified those issues clients could decide and those about which management would seek the advice of clients but would not be obligated to enact. To further promote client involvement in organizational decision making, Kent and Read (1998) recommended that organizations have formal written policies that specify the means through which people with mental illness can influence decision making. The lack of knowledge on the part of both clients and staff about means for participation is a significant obstacle to clients' participation. Written policies that outline participation options lessen this knowledge gap.

Representation by People With Mental Illness

While decisions surrounding the level of power and issues to be addressed are critical, other aspects of decision making are important as well. One question is the extent to which people with mental illness can, and should, represent other clients. Some mental health professionals have discounted the opinions of clients serving on boards and committees by stating that the opinions expressed by these clients do not represent those of most other clients. The issue of representation is complex because there is not one client opinion; clients have a great diversity of opinions (Valentine & Capponi, 1989). Views are likely to vary, for instance, between clients who currently are in long-term hospitals; those who are living in the community, are receiving disability income, and are frequently hospitalized; and those who are living in the community, are working full-time, and have not been hospitalized for years (Forbes & Sashidraran, 1997). If representation is expected, then people with mental illness should be given the means to systematically gather the views of other clients within the organization though forums, telephone surveys, questionnaires, or other means. In reality, people with mental illness cannot be expected to represent all client opinions without such efforts, just as one family member of a person with mental illness on a board of directors cannot be expected to represent all family views, and one case manager on a committee cannot be expected to represent the views of all case managers. Each individual on decision-making structures brings his or her own experiences, talents, and opinions to the decision-making body. Working together on a common purpose, this diversity of perspectives enriches the decision-making process.

Sustainability of Consumer Involvement

Another concern is the sustainability of involvement of people with mental illness on boards of directors, committees, consumer councils, or other structures. Vandergang (1996) surveyed mental health organizations in Canada and found that three fourths had difficulty sustaining client participation, as attendance was inconsistent and turnover was high. This was related to many factors such as the inclusion of too few clients, frustration on the part of clients who lacked decision-making control and believed their contribution was not valued, the fact that staff expectations exceeded the ability of the clients who were participating, and the staff's unwillingness to alter structures to better accommodate people with mental illness. Vandergang suggested that when participation is poor, agencies need to reexamine their commitment to client participation, identify obstacles, and make changes, including modifying structures and increasing resources to support participation, as needed. She also stated that it may not be necessary for individual clients to sustain long-term involvement for organizations to benefit from client participation.

ACCESS TO RESOURCES

An eighth condition for empowerment is that the person with mental illness has access to the resources needed to meaningfully participate in organizational decision making. People with mental illness can benefit from a range of resources.

Training

First, it is essential that people with mental illness have access to training to prepare them for participation (Means & Smith, 1994). As indicated in the previous discussion of participation skills, many people with mental illness will need training to improve their skills pertaining to interpersonal relations, public speaking, writing, assertiveness, conflict resolution, negotiation, and functioning in formal boards, among other activities (Pilgrim & Waldron, 1998; Rowe et al., 2003). Also previously described by Bullock et al. (2000) and Rowe et al. (2003) were two intensive training programs to prepare people for participation on boards, with the former consisting of 32 hours of training over 16 weeks and the latter including 42 hours of training over 7 weeks. Organizations should strive to provide this level of intensive training to people with mental illness for selected types of involvement, particularly serving on boards of directors. More limited training, however, may be more feasible for both organizations and clients yet still maximize client participation. Limited training can be as simple as a meeting with clients before the initial involvement and then briefly processing the event afterward to gauge the client's comfort level, to identify areas in which the client may need additional training, and to answer any questions that client may have about the activity. To facilitate ongoing skill development and support, people with mental illness can benefit from the assignment of mentors participating in the decision-making process, as was done as part of the training described by Rowe et al. It is noteworthy that the provision of training and assignment of mentors often occurs with participants without mental illness who are new to organizational decision making, especially those without prior experience with the type of decision-making process they have just entered.

Financial Compensation

Another resource to promote participation among people with mental illness is financial compensation. This can include payment for time people with mental illness spend in meetings, such as Carling (1995) recommended, as well as compensating them for their expenses related to participation such as child care, transportation, meals, and similar direct costs (Valentine & Capponi, 1989). This same consideration for financial compensation also should apply to required training, particularly if the training is extensive. The training described by Rowe et al. (2003), for instance, paid participants $10 for each class meeting, of which there were 14, and $20 for each board meeting attended during the 6-month internship that was part of the training. Ryan and Bamber (2002) strongly encouraged agencies to set written policies on compensation. Informal policies, or no policies at all, can lead to inconsistency in compensation and create tension between those responsible for disbursement and people with mental illness. In a survey of 46 mental health organizations in England, Ryan and Bamber found that only 20% had written policies. Ryan and Bamber then provided an excellent set of guidelines for the development of such policies, citing almost 50 points to consider, organized into seven categories. For example, the authors suggested considering the following: What forms of participation are reimbursable? What expenses are paid? Who is eligible to participate and receive compensation? What are the liability issues associated with compensation? How are the funds administered and audited?

Logistical Resources

A third set of resources is logistical in nature. These resources are associated with recruiting people to participate, notifying them of dates and times of activities and submitting reminders, arranging for transportation if needed, assembling meals if meeting during meal times or snacks if meeting at other times, and many more logistical tasks. Staff typically provide these resources, although clients of the organization may be able to offer substantial support. The amount of resources will vary depending on the activity. Those who participate on boards on a regular basis may need no logistical resources beyond what nonclient members receive. Other activities may require substantial amounts of money and staff hours. For instance, holding a forum between staff and clients to discuss how to contend with cuts in governmental funding could require expenditures for postage to mail notification letters to clients, for staff overtime pay to transport some clients to the meeting, for babysitting services, for written handouts, and for refreshments, to name only a few.

Staff Resources

Staff, too, need resources. One type is training for all levels of staff, including paraprofessionals, clinical staff such as psychiatrists, administrators, and people from outside of the organization who may participate on boards with people with mental illness (Vandergang, 1996). The content of training will vary by the party being trained but typically should include the advantages to people with mental illness and the organization when involving them, overcoming the stigma that promotes people with mental illness as being too ill to make a meaningful contribution, symptoms of mental illness and how they may be manifested when clients participate, ways to encourage and promote client participation during meetings, and things to avoid that may stifle client participation (Beeforth et al., 1990; Kent & Read, 1998; Starkey & Leadholm, 1997; Williams & Lindley, 1996). When possible, people with mental illness should be involved in this training as the actual trainers or as guest speakers (Vandergang, 1996). Staff also usually need the resource of time, especially frontline staff who may be responsible for notification and transportation of clients, and managers responsible for organizing such events.

Written Materials and Consultation

A final resource for both staff and people with mental illness is written materials and consultation that provide direction on how to develop, implement, and evaluate methods to involve people with mental illness in organizational decision making. The professional literature, some of which already has been cited, can assist with this process, and organizations should review this literature as part of the process of developing decision-making structures. It would be helpful, though, for more organizations to share their experiences in the professional literature and at conferences, including both positive and negative experiences, so that others can learn from them. In addition, a number of organizations publish manuals on various aspects of involvement. For instance, the National Consumer Supporter Technical Assistance Center (2001), in conjunction with the National Mental Health Association, published the manual entitled *How to Develop and Maintain a Consumer Advisory Board*. Also, formal or informal consultation may be available. In Holland, for example, the National Association of Patients' Councils was started in 1981 to provide technical support to local organizations that were interested in starting patient councils. Ideally, local agencies that have had success in involving their clients in organizational decision making would be willing to share their experiences and assist other agencies, either formally or informally.

SUPPORTIVE CULTURE

A final condition for empowering people with severe mental illness through organizational decision making is that the organization's culture supports meaningful participation. Despite tremendous recent progress in the inclusion of people with mental illness in organizational decision making, some mental health organizations and individuals continue to resist such involvement (Barnes & Bowl, 2001). While there are many reasons for this, Vandergang (1996) argued that one of the main reasons was that organizations failed to create an environment or culture throughout which participation was ingrained. Some staff continue to believe their power, authority, and perhaps value are threatened by client participation. This particularly is likely to occur among psychiatrists and other professionals and organizations that have adopted the medical model as their primary approach to working with people with mental illness (Barnes & Wistow, 1994; Kent & Read, 1998).

The creation of a supportive organizational culture requires strong leadership from management (Bargal, 2000). Without such leadership, participation is likely to be inconsistent, if it occurs at all. In their study of patient councils throughout Great Britain, Beeforth et al. (1990)

concluded that variance in their effectiveness was related to the level of management support, with those that were highly effective having strong management support. There are several steps that organizational leaders can take to create a supportive culture. The first is to adopt the recovery perspective or psychiatric rehabilitation, both of which strongly support the participation of people with mental illness in organizational decision making (Cook & Hoffschmidt, 1993; Jacobson & Curtis, 2000). The second is to provide staff with needed training. This training should include highlighting advantages to people with mental illness and the organization when involving them and addressing the stigma that suggests people with mental illness are too ill to meaningfully contribute. To better target training to those who most need it, Kent and Read (1998) recommended administering to staff at various time intervals surveys that measure attitudes toward various aspects of client empowerment, including participation in organizational decision making, and evaluating levels of meaningful client participation in decision making in order to be able to target groups of professionals or programs that may be in need of specialized training. The third step is to empower staff members, which includes involving them in organizational decision making (Staples, 1999). It is highly unlikely that staff would support client participation in organizational decision making if they, themselves, are not also involved. In particular, flat organizational structures that incorporate participatory management techniques promote empowerment of staff and clients (Gutiérrez, GlenMaye et al., 1995). The fourth is to provide the previously mentioned range of resources that facilitate client participation and staff support of that participation. The allocation of resources sends a strong message to both clients and staff that meaningful participation is important. The final step is to promote a supportive culture by encouraging organizational leaders to meaningfully involve people with mental illness in organizational decision making in their own interactions with clients, thus exemplifying how it should be done. Other staff is unlikely to involve them if organizational leaders do not do so themselves.

CASE STUDIES

To increase understanding of the opportunities for, and limitations to, the empowerment of people with mental illness through organizational decision making, empowerment is examined again through two cases studies, one among people with mental illness residing in a public psychiatric hospital that provides long-term care and treatment (Linhorst et al., 2005; Linhorst et al., 1999), and the other among those who are residing in the community and receiving services from a publicly funded community mental health agency (Kryah et al., 2003).

Empowerment Among Clients in a Psychiatric Hospital (SLPRC)

Degree of Empowerment

A low-to-moderate degree of empowerment occurred through client participation in organizational decision making at SLPRC. In some instances, staff provided clients with information about decisions that already had been made, and clients had the opportunity to provide comments, which staff incorporated to make small modifications. In other instances, staff consulted with clients about particular issues and enacted their suggestions. Furthermore, in a limited number of instances, a partnership developed between staff and clients, and together they reached agreement on decisions. In no instances did clients have decision-making control.

Objective empowerment outcomes, that is, instances when clients actually affected decisions, occurred primarily through the consumer council. The consumer council was a group of approximately 12 clients who represented clients in the hospital's four residentially based treatment programs. It typically met twice monthly to discuss hospitalwide policy, programmatic, and environmental issues. The consumer council was facilitated by a staff person from the quality management department who devoted at least half of her time to working with the council, advocating for and following up on issues it raised, and overseeing the hospital's client grievance system. Changes in which clients were involved, primarily through the consumer council, included an increase in the diversity of pastoral services offered to clients, an extension of curfew time for evening grounds privileges, an increase in the client spending budget, an increase in the choice of personal care products available to clients, an increase in the food choices offered in the cafeteria, the enforcement of smoking policies among clients and staff, an increase in the number of vending machines, and a decrease in prices at the client canteen. Other outcomes included a range of environmental issues, such as the construction of a roof over the pavilion in hospital's interior courtyard, the purchase of patio furniture for the cottages, and placement of pay telephones and mailboxes in the hospital's secured areas. In addition, subsequent to the study, hospital leaders incorporated the consumer council into the regular policy review process. Clients' participation in policy review led to content changes in policies related to photographing of clients with family members, dietary issues, client access to medical records, and client access to books. Their participation also led to revisions in the procedures in other policies that had helped to streamline those procedures, to simplify their language, and to make them more consistent with actual practice. Evidence existed that another objective empowerment outcome, the expansion and standardization of visiting hours at the hospital, occurred through the client grievance system. Prior to the client filing the grievance, unit directors set the visiting hours for each program, and hours were shorter in some programs than in others.

In addition to these objective empowerment outcomes, some clients, including clients who served on the consumer council and other clients who were aware of the consumer council's activities and accomplishments, experienced subjective empowerment as a result of the consumer council. Subjective empowerment was lessened by the lack of knowledge on the part of some clients and staff about the consumer council and its accomplishments. Some clients in each focus group had not heard of the consumer council, and those who did could name few, if any, accomplishments. Staff were much more familiar with the consumer council than clients, but it, too, could name few, if any, accomplishments.

Application of Conditions for Empowerment

Given its importance to organizational decision making, application of the conditions for empowerment is directed toward the consumer council. Despite the high levels of unmanaged psychiatric symptoms that are found in a hospital that provides long-term care, the consumer council maintained a membership of approximately 12 clients who had their symptoms managed to the degree they could meaningfully participate in decision making. While there was some turnover among members owing to discharge or increases in psychiatric symptoms, there always was a core group of members who wanted to participate, who enjoyed participation, and who believed they were helping out all clients within the hospital. This latter sentiment is particularly important, since genuine concern for others is an important part of recovery. The biggest incentive for clients to participate was that most clients resided in the hospital an extended period of time, as the average length of hospitalization was approximately 6 years. Thus, they had a personal stake in improving life within the hospital. Staff, too, had concrete incentives to participate with the consumer council in decision making. Suggestions of the consumer council led to meaningful improvements in the clients' day-to-day lives. The consumer council also provided staff who worked on the residential units with another option for dealing with concerns that clients brought to them; that is, they could suggest to clients that they contact the consumer council to help resolve their matter. In addition, some staff noticed that participation in the consumer council had therapeutic benefits for some clients.

A lack of availability of choices of issues and policy alternatives hampered greater empowerment. This occurred in part because many clients passively accepted undesirable situations rather than defining them as addressable problems. Some clients also lacked the ability to creatively generate alternative solutions. These challenges were mitigated, in part, by the staff liaison who worked with the consumer council and by members gaining decision-making experience. Financial limitations also decreased choices. Missouri, like most states, had limited state dollars for mental health services. Thus, some alternatives were not possible, particularly for the expansion of services that were most popular with clients, including paid work opportunities on hospital grounds and trips into the community. Further limiting choices, many important decisions were made at a level above hospital administrators by the central office of the Missouri Department of Mental Health and by the Missouri legislature. Thus, the consumer council concentrated its efforts on issues that improved the daily lives of clients within the hospital rather than expansion of treatment services, modifications to discharge and release policies, or similar major decisions over which they, and, in most cases, hospital administrators, had little control.

SLPRC clients had at least some decision-making influence because structures and processes for involving them existed, the consumer council being the primary one. Over time, hospital leaders incorporated the consumer council into the hospital's formal organizational structure. The consumer council reported directly to the hospital's rights and ethics committee, which was chaired by the same person who served as the staff liaison to the consumer council. That committee had the authority to bring issues directly to the hospital's executive committee. In addition, the consumer council became part of the routine review of hospital policies. A policy committee reviewed the consumer council's suggestions and could submit them to the executive committee. Also, the individual who was superintendent at the time of the study met at least quarterly with the consumer council to discuss concerns and share information.

The resource that was critical to the success of the consumer council was the staff liaison. She worked effectively with clients to help them select issues, process information, and make decisions without providing undue influence. She also worked effectively with staff to advocate for changes suggested by clients. Another resource was the training that the staff liaison provided to clients to prepare them to participate on the consumer council and to work with staff in work groups. Staff from the quality management department also provided some training on how to work with clients on committees to staff, in particular to individuals who chaired committees and work groups that included clients. Yet another resource was time for administrators, particularly the superintendent, to meet with and engage clients in decision making. This recently significantly decreased in Missouri, as superintendents are now responsible for two or more mental health facilities within a region. Thus, the amount of time to meet with staff or clients is much more limited. Finally, another important resource was the consumer council newsletter, which began after the study was completed. It helped to address the previously identified lack of information many clients and staff had about the consumer council and its accomplishments. It discussed issues the consumer council was addressing, provided updates on past issues, and shared information about the hospital that was of interest to clients. The newsletter was written primarily by clients and was typed by a client who was paid for the work. The newsletter became an important source of information for clients, and also, unexpectedly, for staff.

Over time, the consumer council became part of the organizational culture. It took at least 4 years for it to gain acceptance by staff. Some staff still did not believe that clients should be involved in organizational decision making, although they were in the minority. This evolution occurred because the consumer council produced thoughtful suggestions, initial misconceptions held by staff about the role of the consumer council were later clarified, staff become more comfortable working with the consumer council and other clients on committees, staff saw the benefits to clients and the organization from client participation, and some executive committee members provided strong leadership in its support.

At least two changes could significantly alter the consumer council's effectiveness. First, the elimination of the staff liaison position would certainly be damaging or even fatal to it. A significant decrease in time allocated to the position, or someone who did not share the strong commitment or possess the high level of skills of the current liaison assuming the position, could greatly reduce its effectiveness. The second potentially damaging change would be a change to leadership that no longer valued client participation in organizational decision making.

Empowerment Among Clients of a Community Agency (BJC-BH)

Degree of Empowerment

The level of involvement of BJC-BH clients in organizational decision making consisted primarily of clients receiving information from staff and having some opportunity to influence changes, and staff consulting with clients and enacting some of their suggestions. There were few, if any, situations identified that reflected a partnership between staff and clients working as peers to reach agreement on decisions, and there were no instances in which clients had decision-making control. In terms of objective empowerment outcomes, staff indicated that in recent years, the agency made the following changes based upon client suggestions: BJC-BH created new staff specialist positions in the areas of entitlements and other resources, housing, and employment to increase client access to these services; the time it took to get appointments with psychiatrists was decreased; the psychosocial rehabilitation center associated with one of the four BJC-BH locations was moved to a building with more space; service hours were expanded at one site; and new practitioners were recruited in underserved areas.

While staff could list some changes that resulted from clients' participation in decision making, clients in the focus groups could not list any instances in which their input resulted in policy, practice, or procedural changes. They did state, however, that they could express their views through three means, including client satisfaction surveys, informal conversations with case managers and supervisors, and, to a much less frequent extent, voicing complaints to the BJC Provider Relations Service. Having the means to voice their opinions despite not recalling any successful change efforts may have resulted in a limited degree of subjective empowerment, however.

Application of Conditions for Empowerment

Conditions for empowerment internal to clients were not met for some clients. Staff believed that psychiatric symptoms prevented some clients from participating at times when they were severe and unmanaged, and that some clients routinely functioned at such a low level that they did not ever have the capability to meaningfully participate in organizational decision making. Staff also indicated that some clients lacked the reading and cognitive skills to understand some of the more complex policy issues. Others lacked the confidence to participate, were intimidated by the thought of participating with staff in activities not directly related to their treatment, did not believe it was their role to participate, did not want to "rock the boat" or appear negative about the agency since they were dependant on its services, or did not believe that their participation would make a difference. Despite these limitations, whenever a site held an activity to involve clients in organizational decision making, sufficient numbers of clients who had the capacity to provide meaningful information attended.

Many of the conditions external to clients were not met either. Clients indicated there were two major limitations to their participation in organizational decision making. Clients believed they lacked knowledge of BJC-BH policies and the current policy issues and had limited choices to affect organizational decision making. Many staff members agreed with this. One administrator also indicated that the state budget crisis drove the agency planning process, leaving little room for client input and further limiting choice. Most clients also lacked concrete incentives to participate. Unlike clients hospitalized at SLPRC, interaction with BJC-BH was just one part of their lives, and it was a small part for some people. Thus, staff indicated that participation was not a priority for many BJC-BH clients. As a concrete incentive for staff to involve clients in decision making, administrators stated their belief that involving clients in organizational decision making was necessary to continually improve service delivery.

A different set of structures and processes were needed to involve clients in organizational decision making at BJC-BH than at a hospital. Unlike SLPRC, which had 200 clients living in one location, BJC-BH had 5,000 clients who were served through four sites spanning rural, suburban, and urban areas. As indicated above, clients said they provided input into organizational decision making through client satisfaction surveys, informal conversations with case managers and supervisors, or voicing complaints with the BJC Provider Relations Service. Staff added several other means of participation. Clients sit on the two BJC-BH advisory boards, one that exists for the three St. Louis sites and one for the rural site. The advisory board for the rural site had active client participation, and a client chaired the board at the time of the study. The bylaws of the St. Louis advisory board indicated that clients should hold at least three positions, although in practice only one client usually attended. It is noteworthy that none of the clients in the focus groups identified the advisory boards as a means whereby they could participate in organizational decision making. When asked about the board, some clients stated they did not know it existed, while others who were aware of it did not know who the client representatives were, or if they even could contact them if they had concerns. As another means of involvement, on one occasion, a BJC-BH staff person, who also was a consumer of mental health services, trained a group of clients to conduct telephone surveys with a random sample of BJC-BH clients to assess their service needs. Some sites also periodically invited clients to attend open forums, forums on specific topics, or open houses. One site, for instance, held a focus group with clients to get additional information about why clients rated an item low on a satisfaction survey and how satisfaction could be increased. At the one site that is associated with a psychosocial rehabilitation center, staff said clients expressed concerns through the staff liaison to the center, and directly to the site director, who had regular meetings with clients at the center. With the exception of client satisfaction surveys that were routinely done by an outside party for all four sites, there was considerable variation across the sites in what activities they held and how often they held them. In reviewing options to increase consumer participation in organization decision making after the study, the BJC-BH director decided to create a consumer council for the St. Louis area that would report directly to him. The director selected this structure because it provided him with easy access to an interested and available group of clients to consult with on special issues and to solicit volunteers to participate on committees with staff.

BJC-BH committed considerable resources to involve clients in decision making. Most of these resources were devoted to the quarterly client satisfaction survey. The agency also allotted staff time to organize and attend forums and related meetings and to transport clients. The agency typically provided refreshments for the forums and made available information handouts. The agency found that it took a large amount of staff time and financial resources to hold these forums.

The BJC-BH culture is one that supports the concept of clients being involved in organizational decision making yet has had difficulty in operationalizing that support into active participation. A large number of clients spread over a wide geographic area and limits on time and money largely prevented the agency from implementing an ongoing, multifaceted plan for involving clients in organizational decision making.

GUIDELINES FOR PROMOTING EMPOWERMENT THROUGH ORGANIZATIONAL DECISION MAKING

The professional literature and the two case studies support the idea that people with severe mental illness can participate in organizational decision making when conditions for empowerment are met. The following guidelines are offered to promote their participation:

1. *Contend with symptoms of mental illness.* One approach is to work with people with mental illness to reduce or eliminate behaviors that can be disruptive when participating in meetings with others. Another is to provide training to other participants about symptoms of mental illness, behaviors associated with those symptoms, and behaviors that actually are side effects of psychotropic medications.

2. *Be cognizant of the emergence of new symptoms.* The process of participation in organizational decision making, itself, can produce stress and a possible reemergence of psychiatric symptoms. Some people who begin the participation process may need support during times of stress, to be excused from some activities, or to discontinue participation altogether.

3. *Provide skill training and mentoring to enhance participation.* Some people with mental illness will need skill training, and possibly mentoring, to enhance the skills required to participate effectively in organizational decision making. People many need training to improve interpersonal skills; public speaking skills; writing skills; assertiveness skills; conflict resolution skills; negotiating skills; skills to read a budget; skills to function in formal boards, including operational knowledge of Robert's Rules of Order; or other skills areas.

4. *Promote the willingness of people with mental illness to participate.* This can be done by providing personal support, encouragement, and training; by clarifying expectations; and by helping people to see the connection between organizational services, policies, and procedures and their personal lives.

5. *Establish trust and respect.* Individuals who interact with people with mental illness can demonstrate trust and respect by actively listening to consumers, by asking questions, by sharing opinions without imposing them, by explaining the purpose of meetings and rules governing participation, by providing consumers with adequate time to speak during meetings, by permitting clients to speak for themselves, and by many other means.

6. *Recognize the benefits of clients' participation to the agency.* The special knowledge about services, service operations, and service needs that people with mental illness possess can help mental health professionals to develop services that are responsive to clients' needs, and participation can be a therapeutic resource whereby clients develop new skills and increase confidence and self-esteem.

7. *Promote active, meaningful involvement.* People with mental illness should be able to place issues on the agenda rather than always reacting to issues that others have brought before them and have alternative policy solutions for each issue they are addressing rather than others directing them to a solution that already has been selected.

8. *Offer a range of participation structures.* Options include people working together as peers in groups, including agency boards of directors, advisory boards, task forces, and committees; working in client groups, such as consumer councils, user councils, or patient advisory committees; working with agency leaders; working in forums between clients and agency leaders during which information is shared, concerns are identified, and alternative solutions are discussed; and participating in program evaluation and performance improvement activities.

9. *Make explicit agreements on level of involvement.* Explicit agreement should exist between clients and staff on clients' level of decision-making authority, which can range from minimal influence, to consultation, to collaboration, to clients having complete decision-making control, and on the areas of decision making in which people with mental illness will be involved.

10. *Monitor the level of ongoing client participation.* When participation is poor, agencies need to reexamine their commitment to client participation, identify obstacles, and make changes as needed, including modifying structures and increasing resources to support participation.

11. *Provide financial compensation in some instances.* This can include payment for time people with mental illness spend in training and meetings, as well as compensation for expenses such as child care, transportation, meals, and similar direct costs.

12. *Provide the necessary logistical resources.* These are associated with recruiting people to participate, notifying them of dates and times of activities, arranging for transportation if needed, assembling meals if meeting during meal times or snacks if meeting during meeting times, and many more. Clients of the organization may be able to offer substantial logistical support.

13. *Provide staff with time to facilitate participation.* Staff, including frontline staff responsible for notification and transportation of clients, managers responsible for organizing such events, and staff who work directly with client in organizational decision-making activities, need the resource of time to meaningfully involve clients in organizational decision making.

14. *Provide training to all levels of staff.* Training will vary by party, but it typically can include the advantages of participation to people with mental illness and the organization, overcoming the stigma that promotes people with mental illness as being too ill to make a meaningful contribution, symptoms of mental illness and how they may be manifested when clients participate, ways to encourage and promote client participation during meetings, and things to avoid because they may stifle client participation. When possible, people with mental illness should be involved in this training as the actual trainers or as guest speakers.

15. *Utilize written materials and consultation.* Written materials and consultation, derived from the professional literature, conference presentations, advocacy groups, local mental health agencies, and other sources, can provide direction on how to develop, implement, and evaluate methods to involve people with mental illness in organizational decision making.

16. *Create a supportive organizational culture.* This requires strong leadership from managers, which is reflected in their adopting the recovery perspective or the psychiatric rehabilitation model, providing clients and staff with needed training, involving staff in organizational decision making, providing the range of resources needed to facilitate client participation and staff support of that participation, and exemplifying client involvement by meaningfully involving people with mental illness in organizational decision making in their own interactions with clients.

8

Empowerment Through Planning and Policy Making

The mental health and support services that people with severe mental illness receive are determined largely by planning and policy making that takes place at a level above the agencies from which they receive services, including local planning boards, state governments, and federal organizations (Mechanic, 2001). Individual agencies, of course, have latitude in the services they offer, and they engage in some service innovation. However, planning and policy making, in particular within state governments and the federal government, set the parameters for the range, type, and amount of services most agencies are able to offer. Given its importance, there is growing recognition that people with mental illness should participate in this planning and policy-making process.

There are many examples of the meaningful involvement of people with mental illness in planning and policy making. An early example of involvement in policy making was Elizabeth Parsons Ware Packard's successful campaign to change Illinois' civil commitment law. Her husband involuntarily committed Packard to an Illinois public asylum between 1860 and 1863. The revised Illinois civil commitment law for which she advocated became a model for other states (Sapinsley, 1991). In addition, Clifford Beers, who was hospitalized for 3 years in the early 1900s, founded what is now known as the National Mental Health Association (NMHA) (Dain, 1980; NMHA, n.d.-b). This organization has a long history of involvement in mental health planning and policy making at the state and federal level. More recently, people with mental illness in New York influenced the state's policy on the use of restraints and seclusion (Fisher, Penney, & Earle, 1996). People with mental illness, working along with other stakeholders, also played significant roles in several states in shaping the components of managed care plans that were part of public mental health systems (Koyanagi & Belivacqua, 2001). As another example, in several local communities and states, people with mental illness helped to promote the development of services for people with the co-occurring disorders of mental illness and substance abuse by helping to organize advocacy efforts, raising community awareness of issues, and sharing their experiences about the need for, and benefits of, services for co-occurring disorders (U.S. DHHS, 2003).

Participation in planning and policy making can be empowering for people with severe mental illness from several perspectives. Participation in the process itself can lead to subjective empowerment outcomes; that is, it gives participants a sense of control. In addition, it can lead to objective empowerment outcomes in the form of new or improved policies, programs, and resources that are essential for empowerment. Finally, Segal et al. (1995) argued that involvement in the political process by people with mental illness is central to empowerment because it seeks to influence the social structures in which they live.

Despite the stated intentions of government officials to involve people with mental illness in planning and policy making and their potential for empowerment, meaningful participation has been sporadic, at best. In a survey of states, researchers found that states varied widely in the extent to which they involved people with mental illness in policy making and called upon state mental health authorities to make a greater commitment to participation (Geller, Brown, Fisher, Grudzinskas, & Manning, 1998). Bevilacqua (1995) stated that it is politically correct for planners and policy makers to recognize their participative role but concluded their participation was more rhetoric than reality. McCade and Unzicker (1995) found that tokenism rather than meaningful participation was prevalent, arguing that policy makers would sometimes carefully select consumers they knew would support their positions in order to project a commitment to consumer participation without jeopardizing their positions. Davidson and Hoge (1996) attributed the absence of meaningful participation, despite verbal support, to a lack of consensus about the nature and extent of participation by people with mental illness in policy making.

Despite this lack of success, the President's New Freedom Commission on Mental Health (2003) recently stated that participation by people with mental illness in service planning should be a priority and called upon policy makers to increase opportunities for participation. Application of the conditions for empowerment assists in understanding the gap between the rhetoric and reality of the participation of people with severe mental illness in planning and policy making and

Table 8.1 Conditions for Empowering People With Severe Mental Illness Through Planning and Policy Making

Managed psychiatric symptoms—The person's psychiatric symptoms are managed to the degree necessary to meaningfully participate in planning and policy making.

Participation skills—The person has the skills needed to meaningfully participate in planning and policy making.

Psychological readiness—The person has the confidence, motivation, and willingness to meaningfully participate in planning and policy making.

Mutual trust and respect—Mutual trust and respect exist between the person with mental illness and those with whom he or she interacts in planning and policy making.

Reciprocal concrete incentives—The person with mental illness and other involved parties have concrete incentives to meaningfully participate together in planing and policy making.

Availability of choices—The person has choices of what issues are being raised for consideration and choices of solutions to those issues.

Participation structures and processes—Structures and processes through which the person can meaningfully participate in planning and policy making exist.

Access to resources—The person has access to the resources needed to meaning-fully participate in planning and policy making.

Supportive culture—The culture supports meaningful participation of the person in planning and policy making.

ways to bridge this gap. Table 8.1 summarizes the conditions for empowerment as they apply to planning and policy making.

MANAGED PSYCHIATRIC SYMPTOMS

One condition for empowerment of people with severe mental illness through planning and policy making is that the person's psychiatric symptoms are managed to the degree necessary to meaningfully participate. During times of severe symptoms, some people may be unable to participate because they cannot, for instance, concentrate or screen out irrelevant information during planning board meetings, process complex policy information; or make logical, constructive choices between policy options. Periodic unmanaged symptoms also may require that people miss some planning or policy meetings, thereby affecting meeting continuity and lessening their ability to influence decisions (Bowl, 1996). In addition, the stress of participation, such as when testifying before a legislative committee, can increase symptoms. Therefore, people with mental illness must weigh their level of involvement with the possible symptoms that may result from it (Hess et al., 2001). Participation does not always cause symptoms, however. In fact, the opposite may occur. For some people with mental illness, participating in planning and policy making actually can help them deal more effectively with stress in their daily lives (Reisch, 2002). People with mental illness can minimize debilitating symptoms by selecting methods of participation that match their interests and abilities, by clarifying their role in the process, and by receiving adequate training.

PARTICIPATION SKILLS

A second condition for empowerment is that the person with mental illness has the skills required to meaningfully participate in planning or policy making. Participation in planning and policy making requires a wide range of skills. First, they must possess the oral and written communication skills, interpersonal skills, and assertiveness skills to effectively interact with different people including, but not limited to, state mental health officials, local service providers, state or federal legislators, members of planning boards, and other consumers whom they may be representing. They also need analytic and problem-solving skills to understand complex issues, to assist in developing creative solutions, and to weigh policy options. Most people with mental illness can gain the required participation skills if they have access to needed training.

Unfortunately, many people with mental illness receive no skills training to promote participation. In his study of local mental health service planning boards in England, Bowl (1996) found, for example, that the majority of local boards provided no training to participants with mental illness. There are, however, examples of model training programs. Training programs to promote participation in organizational decision making described by Hess et al. (2001) and Rowe et al. (2003), as introduced in chapter 7, also taught some of the skills required for planning and policy making. In addition to formal training programs, mental health professionals can play a prominent training role by working with individual clients. Reisch (2002), for instance, noted that one component of legislative advocacy for social workers is to provide the skills people with mental illness need to testify at legislative hearings and to lobby individual legislators. Later discussions on resources for empowerment include additional ways in which people with mental illness can improve their planning and policy-making abilities.

PSYCHOLOGICAL READINESS

A third condition for empowerment is that the person with mental illness has the psychological readiness, that is, the confidence, motivation, and willingness, to meaningfully participate in planning and policy making. People with mental illness who are psychologically ready to participate typically have had skill training, which increases confidence, and have had prior positive experiences. These positive experiences can occur even if they were not able to sway policy positions to those consistent with their viewpoint. As Barnes and Bowl (2001) found, for example, people with mental illness who were on local housing committees in England were eager to continue to participate in planning and policy making because they perceived that they were listened to and respected, and they believed they had improved perceptions held by nonconsumer participants about the abilities of people with mental illness.

Conversely, the lack of psychological readiness to participate can have its roots in poor skills, the lack of confidence, and adverse prior experiences. The director of a Missouri mental health advocacy organization believed that consumers' feelings of inadequacy were the single greatest factor limiting the participation of people with mental illness in policy making and advocacy. Also, Peck et al. (2002) reported that people with mental illness serving on a local planning board were disillusioned with the process, in part, because they could not set the agenda. They wanted to focus on operational issues in mental health organizations, while the rest of the board believed its purpose was to address larger issues. Still other people with mental illness simply may have no interest in planning and policy making. Peck et al. (2002) found that people with mental illness are much more interested in participating in treatment planning, which immediately and directly affects them, than in organizational decision making or policy making. It is important to place this finding in context. This lack of interest among some people with mental illness is consistent with many Americans who have no interest in local, state, or national policy issues; who do not educate themselves about positions held by public officials and those running for public office; and who do not vote regularly.

MUTUAL TRUST AND RESPECT

A fourth condition for empowerment is that mutual trust and respect exist between the person with mental illness and those with whom he or she interacts in planning and policy making. People with mental illness must trust that other participants in the planning and policy-making process will listen to their opinions and value their contributions. This sometimes does not happen, as participants may ignore consumers' opinions or even offer insulting or condescending remarks (McCabe & Unzicker, 1995). Likewise, planners and policy makers may not trust or respect people with mental illness when consumer participants engage in behaviors that typically are not found in planning and policy-making meetings, such as deviating from established meeting agendas or interrupting presentations to confront statements (Church,

1996). Mutual trust and respect are in large measure associated with the perceived quality of the process of participation, as some people with mental illness are satisfied with their participation when they believe their opinions were listened to and respected (Barnes & Bowl, 2001). Planners and policy makers demonstrate ultimate trust and respect when they act on consumers' suggestions.

RECIPROCAL CONCRETE INCENTIVES

A fifth condition is that the person with mental illness and other involved parties have concrete incentives to meaningfully participate together in planning and policy making. Incentives for people with mental illness to participate can include gaining positive feelings of accomplishment, increasing confidence, meeting new people, learning new skills, and improving services and policies that directly affect them. People with mental illness must weigh these incentives against potential disincentives. These can include feelings of disempowerment if policy makers do not respect their opinions; expenditures of time they could spend on more pressing daily activities; financial expenses such as transportation, meals, child care, and lost wages; and the possible reemergence of symptoms if involvement is too stressful. Another disincentive associated with some aspects of planning and policy making is disclosure of a mental illness. Because of continued stigma about mental illness, many people with mental illness do not want to share their stories. One Missouri mental health official indicated that adoption of the recovery perspective has reduced the willingness of some people to identify themselves as having a mental illness and participate in advocacy efforts. Instead, they want to put their mental illness behind them and resume normal life activities not associated with their illness.

The primary incentive for planners and policy makers to involve people with mental illness is that consumers have unique experiences to contribute that can improve the products of planning and policy making. Broner, Franczak, Dye, and McAllister (2001) rejected that belief that knowledge from experts should drive the mental health policy–making process. Instead, they advocated for policy making based on a consensus model because the contribution of both experts and service users creates new knowledge that can better inform the process than that of experts alone. In the development of New York's restraint and seclusion policy, for instance, people with mental illness who reviewed a draft of the proposed policy raised several issues that the task force, which included no mental health consumers, had not considered, and they offered their own recommendations to address these issues. Fisher et al. (1996) summarized the value of their contribution. "They [task force members] found, perhaps more than they had anticipated, that the recipients had crucial first-hand information, different perspectives, and a sensitivity based on their experiential knowledge which contributed substantially to policy discussions about restraint and seclusion'' (p. 550).

In addition, personal stories told by people with mental illness can be an effective resource for mental health advocacy groups when trying to persuade legislators to expand services or at least not to drastically cut services, the latter of which is more likely to occur in today's current state budget crises. One Missouri mental health advocate provided examples that personal testimonies offered by people with mental illness at legislative committee hearings were important to deflecting proposed major cuts in the state mental health budget in 2002 and for obtaining additional funding in prior years to make available the new psychotropic medications to larger numbers of Missourians. People with mental illness can provide mental health advocates with other resources including making telephone calls, writing letters, and organizing advocacy trips to the state capital, to name a few. A third incentive for mental health professionals to involve people with mental illness in planning and policy making is that involvement can have therapeutic value. If people with mental illness are provided the necessary skill training and resources, and if planners and policy makers meaningfully involve them, participation in planning and policy making can improve skills, increase confidence, and reduce psychiatric symptoms.

Disincentives for planners and policy makers to meaningfully involve people with mental illness also exist. Involving people with mental illness (or other stakeholders for that matter) lessens the chance of getting one's own service or policy option selected in the form desired. In addition, it requires additional time to involve more people in the planning and policy-making process and often requires a financial commitment to assure that participants are able to attend.

AVAILABILITY OF CHOICES

A sixth condition for empowerment is that the person with mental illness has choices in at least three areas. These choices are similar to those listed in chapter 7 on organizational decision making. First, people with mental illness should be participants in setting the direction of policies. As Davidson and Hoge (1996) noted, however, it is uncommon for people with mental illness to do so. Instead, they typically are asked to accept the policy directions that policy makers present to them and then may be invited to comment on the details of plans. A second choice type is associated with people with mental illness being part of the process in which potential policy solutions are identified and debated when particular planning or policy issues are raised. As with the first choice type, people with mental illness often are asked to respond to predetermined plans without having the opportunity to explore or offer alternative solutions. Third, people with mental illness should have some choice in the structures and processes through which they can affect planning and policy making. Some people may be comfortable testifying before a legislative committee, while others may prefer to serve on a planning task force with mental health professionals and other consumers, while still others may be willing only to write letters to legislators from their home.

When people with mental illness are not given the above choices or are excluded from the planning or policy-making process altogether, they must decide what, if any, action to take. Fisher et al. (1996) provided an excellent example of a policy-making situation at the state level in which people with mental illness were excluded from the process but assertively and effectively requested that the policy be revisited and participated in revising that policy into one that they could support. In the case study, the New York mental health commissioner convened a task force to revise the state's policy and procedures on the use of restraints and seclusion. The task force included a wide range of mental health professionals but no one with mental illness. The state had an office of consumer affairs, and it would have been reasonable to inform its director of the task force, and possibly to invite her to participate or to recommend other people with mental illness for membership. In fact, she was not notified, and she become aware of the task force only after it ceased meeting and submitted a complete draft report. The director and several consumer groups protested not being included and strongly objected to components of the report. Amid this vocal concern, the commissioner asked task members to reconvene and meet with those consumers who had concerns. The group of concerned consumers met with task force members, and, in addition, developed their own set of recommendations, which they presented to the task force and discussed as a group. The task force ultimately incorporated most of the recommendations into the final report and believed the state's new restraint and seclusion policy was improved considerably as a result of the consumer participation.

PARTICIPATION STRUCTURES AND PROCESSES

A seventh condition for empowerment is that structures and processes through which the person with mental illness can meaningfully participate in planning and policy making exist. People with mental illness, as any other citizen, have many ways by which they can influence planning and policy making. People can lobby for particular pieces of legislation or policy changes by letter writing, telephoning, or e-mailing legislators and other public officials; by arranging face-to-face meetings with them; by testifying at legislative committee hearings and other public forums; by writing position papers; by serving on local, state, or national planning boards; by joining advocacy groups; by getting to know and work with legislative staff; by monitoring the promulgation and implementation of rules following the passage of legislation; by participating in political campaigns; by initiating or participating in lawsuits; and by voting (Ezell, 2001; Haynes & Mickelson, 2002). While many of these activities and others are performed by individuals, they often are conducted by organized groups. While not diminishing the importance of individual actions, attention is focused primarily on organized group structures and processes through which people with mental illness are most likely to participate in planning and policy making.

Before discussing these structures and processes, it is important to identify issues that arise when people with mental illness participate in them. These issues are similar to those identified in chapter 7 on participation in organizational decision making. They are presented briefly here, and readers are encouraged to refer back to that chapter for more detailed discussion. First, since people with mental illness vary widely in their abilities, interests, time availability, and comfort levels, they should have a range of opportunities for participation. Second, there should be explicit agreement among all parties as to the function of the activity in which people with mental illness are participating and the level of decision-making authority they hold. With some structures, such as ongoing advisory boards, this typically is clear, while in many other settings, the function and level of decision-making authority are decided as issues arise. Peck et al. (2002) provided an example of a local planning board that asked people with mental illness to participate. The board's function was not clearly communicated to people with mental illness, who assumed the board could intervene in individual agency issues, when, in fact, it dealt only with boarder planning and resource allocation issues. This misunderstanding led to considerable frustration on the part of both consumers and nonconsumers. Third is the issue of representation by participants with mental illness of the larger population of consumers. Participants' opinions should be accepted as valid. If representation is sought, then resources need to be provided to obtain representative samples through survey methods. Fourth, sustainability of participation can be an issue. Inconsistent participation by people with mental illness can be related to many factors, including smaller numbers of consumers than of nonconsumers, consumers believing their views are not respected or appreciated, and a lack of flexibility in the logistics of holding meetings that does not accommodate their disabilities or schedules (e.g., holding meetings during the day or running 4-hour meetings), to name a few. A final issue outlined in the previous chapter is the level of support nonconsumers

Table 8.2 Structures and Processes Through Which People With Severe Mental Illness Can Participate in Planning and Policy Making

- State and regional planning boards
- Task forces and other ad hoc assemblies
- Advocacy groups
- State offices of consumer affairs
- Employment in senior management positions with state mental health authorities
- Consumer groups
- Mental health agencies
- Voting

provide to consumers when interacting with them in meetings. There are many ways in which nonconsumers can intentionally or unintentionally subvert the meaningful participation of people with mental illness, such as key parties making decisions before meetings are held and providing consumers with little time to speak. Having identified these major issues, attention is now turned to the structures and processes by which people with mental illness are most likely to participate in planning and policy making. Table 8.2 lists these major structures and processes, which are discussed below.

State and Regional Planning Boards

One means of participating in planning and policy making is for people with mental illness to serve on planning boards. In fact, the federal government, through the State Mental Health Planning Act of 1986 (Public Law 99-660) and its most recent reauthorization (Public Law 102-321), requires states to develop comprehensive state mental health service plans through planning councils that include people with mental illness, families of those with mental illness, and other stakeholders in order to receive federal mental health block grant funds. When this law was passed, nationally prominent mental health consumer advocates were cautiously optimistic that it could increase the voice of people with mental illness in planning mental health services, provided it was implemented as intended (Chamberlin & Rogers, 1990). To date, however, no studies could be found that evaluated the extent to which these councils actually shape state mental health policies and services, whether people with mental illness are regularly participating on them, and whether their participation is meaningful. Given the reported experiences of other types of planning councils, it is reasonable to assume that the meaningfulness of consumer participation varies widely across states.

The experience of the Missouri Department of Mental Health (MDMH) provides one example of how states have met the requirements of the federal planning law. It established the State Advisory

Council for its Division of Comprehensive Psychiatric Services in 1977. It revised its bylaws to comply with the 1986 federal planning law and now includes 25 members, of which 13 must be people with mental illness or family members, with members serving 3-year terms. In practice, seven slots are now designated for people with mental illness and six slots for family members, which substantially increased the number of consumer slots that typically were filled by consumers. These slots, however, sometimes go unfilled. For example, when last in contact with the staff liaison to the council, three consumer slots and one family slot were vacant. The council meets six times each year and, in concert with local mental health boards, is responsible for advising the MDMH Division of Comprehensive Psychiatric Services regarding the development of models of services and long-range planning and budgeting priorities; identifying statewide needs, gaps in services, and movement toward filling gaps; providing education and information about mental health issues; and monitoring, evaluating, and reviewing the allocation and adequacy of mental health services within the state. To increase participation in the planning process, the Division of Comprehensive Psychiatric Services used to operate five Regional Advisory Councils, which also included people with mental illness. MDMH recently eliminated these regional councils, however, because of the state's budget crisis. It had provided staff support to these regional councils and paid for travel and other expenses related to the councils' activities. In addition to these federally required state planning boards, many local communities have mental health planning boards that include people with mental illness. Orrin (1997) reported, for example, that Michigan revised its state mental health law in the mid-1990s to require that each county within the state include at least two people with mental illness on its community mental health board.

Task Forces and Other Ad Hoc Assemblies

Another means for people with mental illness to participate in planning and policy making is by serving on task forces and similar structures developed on an ad hoc basis to address particular issues. Ad hoc groups that included people with mental illness have had success in some states, for instance, in overseeing the development, implementation, and evaluation of contracts between managed care companies and state mental health authorities (Bazelon Center, 1998; Sabin & Daniels, 1999). Unfortunately, the experiences of people with mental illness when participating in these types of structures are not always positive. Bowl (1996), for example, stated that people with mental illness served along with professionals and politicians on local housing and social service committees in England. He found that some consumers did not feel comfortable enough in these meetings to share their opinions, that meetings were held at times and locations that were not convenient for the consumer members, and there was little effort by committee leaders to facilitate consumer participation. Consumers instead preferred to hold forums comprised of consumers that had some professional support, during which they studied particular issues and developed plans to lobby for their positions. As a second example, Church (1996) described the involvement of people with mental illness in public hearings held by a legislative subcommittee in various locations in Ontario, Canada to obtain consumer feedback on proposed legislative changes that would affect them. Committee members wanted to discuss only the 14 points of the legislative changes. Many consumers wanted to raise other issues and some strongly challenged the basis for some of the 14 points. Overall, consumer leaders did not find the meetings useful, stating they "considered it rude for professionals/bureaucrats to expect partnership from them when meetings were hosted in environments which were not survivor-friendly, on topics which were not survivor-generated, using documents and language which were not survivor-accessible" (p. 40). Some subcommittee members, too, were dissatisfied with the interaction in some of the meetings, differing on meaning and significance of the consumer input; some even found their interactions with the consumers to be "confusing, unexpected, perhaps frightening" (p. 38). As a final example, Fisher et al. (1996) described the involvement of people with mental illness in a task force to revise a state's restraint and seclusion policies. As previously described in this chapter, people with mental illness were not asked to participate on the original task force and were allowed to participate only after protesting components of the draft report. Consumers then worked with the task force or alone to revise the report. Consumers and most of the original task force members believed this participation resulted in an improved product.

Advocacy Groups

Advocacy groups are another mechanism through which people with mental illness can participate in planning and policy making. While one typically thinks of people with mental illness participating in mental health advocacy groups, opportunities also exist to join advocacy groups that focus on other policy areas that affect the lives of people with mental illness, such as housing or employment. Some mental health advocacy groups have national organizations, as well as state and local affiliations. Other advocacy groups are found only at the state or local levels. The following are four prominent national advocacy groups that provide at least some advocacy for adults with severe mental illness and involve consumers in various ways in their organizations.

National Mental Health Association

One is the National Mental Health Association (NMHA, n.d.-c). NMHA was started in 1909 by Clifford Beers, a person with severe mental illness, and is the first and oldest consumer-led organization. It is a broad-based organization that addresses a wide range of mental health and illness issues, and adults with severe mental illness are just one of the populations it serves. In addition to the national organization, it now has over 340 affiliate organizations nationwide. One of its many functions is to engage in policy advocacy at the national, state, and local levels through its national organization and local affiliates. It stresses consumer participation and empowerment in all aspects of its organizations. For instance, people with mental illness are some of its leaders and staff and participate in policy advocacy. To support the participation of people with mental illness in planning and policy making, NMHA operates the Advocacy Resource Center. This center offers state and local affiliates training on coalition building and strategy development and provides a range of technical resources including legislative analyses, model legislation, legislative alerts, and connections to experts on specific topics, to name a few.

Considerable variation exists among the NMHA affiliates. The largest affiliate is the Mental Health Association of Southeastern Pennsylvania (MHASP), founded in 1951, which serves the city of Philadelphia and the four surrounding counties (MHASP, n.d.). Its president is a mental health consumer and a leader in the national consumer movement. MHASP employs over 250 people, many of whom are people with mental illness. It provides a range of treatment, vocational, residential, and support service programs, as well as family and community education and policy advocacy. Most of its advocacy occurs through its Office of Policy Development. It also created the Involved Consumer Action Network (ICAN) of Pennsylvania to promote the active involvement of people with mental illness in policy development and the planning and delivery of services. Among other things, ICAN provides training and information, and advocates for people with mental illness to serve on governmental committees and boards of directors of service agencies. The president also is active in policy advocacy, frequently serving on national committees and providing testimony to legislative bodies at the federal and state levels. In contrast to MHASP is the Mental Health Association of Greater St. Louis (MHAGSL, n.d.), founded in 1945. It serves St. Louis City and the surrounding six counties. It has a small paid staff and relies heavily on volunteers. It provides no direct treatment or vocational services as does MHASP, but it instead offers a range of educational activities; provides information and referral services; serves as a local clearinghouse for self-help groups; cosponsors the St. Louis Empowerment Center, a self-help and drop-in center for adults with severe mental illness; and makes available a limited number of support services. Its mission also is to serve as a voice in shaping public policy, which it does primarily through its Systems Building and Advocacy Program. The MHAGSL director takes the lead on advocacy initiatives, frequently serving on policy committees and testifying before legislative bodies. People with mental illness are involved in policy advocacy primarily by testifying at legislative committee hearings and meeting with legislators.

National Alliance for the Mentally Ill

A second major national mental health advocacy organization is the National Alliance for the Mentally Ill (NAMI, n.d.-b). NAMI was created in 1979 by two mothers of adult children with mental illness. While NMHA addresses a range of issues associated with mental health and illness, NAMI focuses on people with severe mental illness and offers a range of educational, self-help, support, and advocacy services. NAMI and its over 1,200 state organizations and local affiliates have become a highly effective lobbying body that advocates for research on severe mental illnesses and treatment for people with severe mental illness. NAMI operates the Policy Research Institute, which provides information on policy issues, offers action alerts, provides technical assistance to state organizations and local affiliates, develops position papers, and engages in many other activities. NAMI also provides training to consumers on the basics of the political system and legislative advocacy.

While some regard NAMI as representing primarily the views of family members, NAMI has made special efforts over the past two decades to more fully incorporate people with mental illness into the organization. One major step in this direction was the creation of the NAMI Consumer Council in the mid-1980s. Its stated purpose is to promote the involvement of people with mental illness in NAMI at the national, state, and local levels by contributing to advocacy issues and program development. The consumer council is comprised of a voting and nonvoting representative from each state and meets annually at NAMI's national convention. The consumer council's director is a voting member of the NAMI national board of directors. Second, at the beginning of 2002, NAMI formed a task force, comprised of consumer council members and the body that represents the presidents of the state organizations, to provide recommendations to assist NAMI to move toward full inclusion of people with mental illness in the organization. Among the many recommendations, the report stated that a standard for participation of consumers in programs, advocacy, and education was needed for all affiliates; that various means be used to promote a cultural change within NAMI that is more accepting of consumer inclusion; that every state organization have a consumer council; and that financial support be provided to assure inclusion of consumers (National Consumer Council, 2002). Third, NAMI created the Office of Consumer Affairs in July 2002, which provides staff support to the consumer council, conducts consumer education and support programs, makes available targeted technical assistance to states and affiliates, and offers training to develop consumers' leadership skills.

Variation exists in the size and activities of the 50 state and 1,200 local NAMI organizations, just as they do among NMHA affiliates. For example, wide variation in the extent to which state organizations have developed consumer councils exists. To promote their development, NAMI identified three states—Florida, Illinois, and Indiana—as having model state consumer councils (NAMI, n.d.-c). Variation in consumer inclusion exists within individual states, too. For instance, the director of NAMI St. Louis, one of the five largest affiliates in the United States and serving seven counties and having over 2,000 members, said it did not involve consumers within the organization nearly as much as other affiliates within Missouri.

National Association of State Mental Health Program Directors

A third major mental health advocacy group is the National Association of State Mental Health Program Directors (NASMHPD, n.d.-a), which is comprised of the directors of state mental health authorities. Its primary function is to advocate for their collective interests at the national level. NASMHPD identifies relevant policy issues, disseminates research findings and best practices, provides consultation and technical assistance, and fosters collaboration among organizations with related interests. NASMHPD has promoted the involvement of people with mental illness in planning and policy making, among other things. In 1989, it issued a position statement that recognized the contribution that people with mental illness can make to program development, policy formulation, program evaluation, education of mental health professionals, and the provision of mental health services (NASMHPD, 1989). In addition, in 1993, NASMHPD aided in the development of the National Association of Consumer/Survivor Mental Health Administrators (n.d.), which is comprised of people with mental illness who serve in leadership positions within state mental health authorities. This organization offers a forum to help members represent the interests of people with mental illness within the context of the state bureaucracies in which they work, provides technical assistance to state mental health authorities wishing to develop offices of consumer affairs, and generally seeks to increase the participation of people with mental illness in all facets of the public mental health system.

Campaign for Mental Health Reform

A fourth major advocacy organization is the Campaign for Mental Health Reform. Unlike the three previous organizations that are broad-based and have long histories, this organization was created in 2003 to take advantage of the momentum generated by the final report of the

President's New Freedom Commission on Mental Health (Campaign for Mental Health Reform, 2003). It supports the commission's recommendations and is working to promote their legislative enactment. It was created by four major mental health advocacy groups: the NMHA, NAMI, NASMHPD, and the Bazelon Center for Mental Health Law. They sought to present a unified voice within the mental health community following the release of the commission's report. To broaden its base, these four members also invited a wide range of other groups representing providers of mental health services, professional associations, other organizations with special interests such as children's issues, and consumer groups.

Offices of Consumer Affairs

Other structures through which people with mental illness can participate in planning and policy making are offices of consumer affairs and state mental health authorities as employees in senior management positions. Fisher et al. (1996) argued that people with mental illness who are in senior management positions are most effective when they serve as internal change agents. They described what this entails. "The role of the change agent is to question the dominant paradigm, raise disturbing questions, present possible alternatives, and encourage others in the organization to look with fresh vision at old ways of doing things" (p. 552). NASMHPD strongly urged states to develop offices of consumer affairs to promote the involvement of people with mental illness in policy making at the state level and offered core elements of such a structure (NASMHPD, n.d.-b). These elements included the involvement of people with mental illness in establishing the office and hiring its director, the director being a consumer of mental health services, the director being a member of the senior management team, the provision of ongoing support to the director and the office, the director serving as a system change agent, and continuation of contact with people with mental illness by senior management staff who are not consumers. Rogers (1993a) outlined a more comprehensive set of guidelines for operating these offices. In addition, the National Association of Consumer/Survivor Mental Health Administrators wrote a 43-page manual detailing how states could start and operate offices of consumer affairs within their state mental health authorities (Jorgensen & Schmook, 2000).

   The number of states hiring people with mental illness into senior management positions appears to be increasing. In the mid-1990s, Geller et al. (1998) conducted a survey of all 50 states, the 5 U.S. territories, and the District of Columbia and found that approximately half reported that a paid position for a consumer existed with its central office, although the survey did not indicate the level of the position. The National Association of Consumer/Survivor Mental Health

Administrators (n.d.), comprised of consumers who are senior managers within state mental health authorities, currently lists members from 46 states. The Alabama Department of Mental Health and Mental Retardation started the first office of consumer affairs in 1990, and by 1993 they existed in at least 14 states (Rogers, 1993b). Jorgensen and Schmook (2000) reported that 26 states had offices of consumer affairs in 2000.

While the number of offices of consumer affairs and senior managers who are consumers is growing, not all people with mental illness support their development. Geller et al. (1998) reported, for instance, that when one state mental health authority approached consumer and family organizations about creating staff positions within its central office to be filled by consumers and family members, the organizations declined the offer and instead opted to take the designated funds in order to add staff positions within their organizations. Also, in interviews with leaders of statewide consumer groups and directors of offices of consumer affairs conducted early in the development of these offices, Rogers (1993b) found that opinions were mixed. On the positive side, some believed that these offices helped to change the attitudes of senior managers who were not consumers to one that was more understanding of consumers' needs and the effects of policies on consumers, and that they put consumers in formal decision-making structures where they could influence the policy agenda and policy development. On the negative side, some individuals believed that state mental health authorities created offices of consumer affairs to coopt the consumer voice, that the positions were token appointments, that senior managers who were not consumers often stopped communicating with consumer groups after the development of the offices, and that some directors of offices of consumer affairs did not have enough contact with consumers or consumer groups to be able to truly represent consumer interests. Other individuals argued that the most effective consumer advocacy occurred when it came both from inside the state bureaucracy in the form of offices of consumer affairs and from outside of the state mental health systems in the form of strong statewide consumer organizations.

In Missouri, for example, the director of the office of consumer affairs is in a senior management position and a member of the MDMH executive committee. The position was created in 1996, and consumers participated in the hiring of its director. Formal duties of the office include representing consumer and family views in policy making, aiding people to access services, and ensuring that client rights are protected. Currently, the most time consuming duty of the office is fielding telephone calls and complaints from people with mental illness, with developmental disabilities, or with substance abuse problems. Staff reductions within the office due to state budget shortfalls led to a reduction in the frequency of face-to-face meetings with consumers from across that state, thereby making it more difficult for the director to identify current consumer issues and to represent consumers' views. The director instead is relying more on consumer views presented in open forums and hearings and from telephone calls that the office receives. This lack of face-to-face time is particularly problematic since the only statewide consumer organization ceased to exist in 2001.

Consumer Groups

In addition to people with mental illness working alongside non-consumers on state and regional planning boards, on task forces, in advocacy groups, and as senior managers within state mental health authorities, they also can engage in planning and policy making through their own consumer-run organizations and advocacy groups. Most consumer organizations have one or both of two functions: self-help and working toward political change (Chamberlin, 1990). People with mental illness band together to provide a united front for advocacy purposes, just as do other people with common characteristics, such as psychiatrists through the American Psychiatric Association or directors of state mental health authorities through NASMHPD. Chamberlin (1990), a leader in the consumer movement, expressed the rationale for creating separate organizations for advocacy comprised solely of consumers. "At present, many groups exist that claim to speak 'for' patients, that is, to be patients' advocates. Even the American Psychiatric Association claims this role, as does the National Alliance for the Mentally Ill. . . . However, a basic liberation principle is that people *must* speak for themselves" (p. 334).

Frese (1998) classified leaders of consumer organizations into two basic types. One type promotes greater respect of, and control for, people with mental illness (referring to themselves as consumers), seeks to empower consumers, and advocates for improved mental health and social services. The other type considers themselves to be psychiatric survivors; devalues treatment, particularly involuntary treatment; and focuses advocacy more on human rights issues than service issues. Frese also found that the former type is much more likely to work collaboratively with nonconsumer groups than is the latter type. The two most notable advocacy groups reflecting these types have been the National Mental Health Consumers Association and the National Association of Psychiatric Survivors, both of which began in the mid-1980s. Representatives from one or both of these groups played prominent roles in obtaining federal funding and other support for consumer self-help activities; for a stronger role for consumers in federal protection and advocacy organizations; for passage of federal legislation such as the State Mental Health Planning Act of 1987, the Fair Housing Amendments Act of 1988, and the Americans with

Disabilities Act of 1990; and for NASMHPD promoting consumer involvement in state policy making (Carling, 1995). Both of these organizations have disbanded in recent years for reasons described as organizational difficulties. However, many of their leaders remain active in policy advocacy today (Frese, 1998).

A new group of national consumer organizations has emerged in recent years. The core members of the Campaign for Mental Health Reform, described above, invited four consumer organizations to join in their advocacy efforts. Three of these groups are the National Mental Health Consumers' Self-Help Clearinghouse (n.d.), the National Empowerment Center (n.d.), and the Consumer Organization and Networking Technical Assistance Center (n.d.), also known as CONTAC. All three are technical assistance centers funded in part by the federal Substance Abuse and Mental Health Services Administration's (SAMHSA) Center for Mental Health Services and provide a wide array of resources to mental health consumers. Some of these resources include maintaining a library of educational, training, and skill development materials; assisting in the development and implementation of consumer programs that includes on-site consultation; holding national training events, teleconferences, and conferences; publishing newsletters; offering information and referral services; and disseminating public policy and political information and materials to assist consumers become involved in the political process. The fourth invited organization was the Depression and Bipolar Support Alliance (n.d.). This grassroots organization, and its state and local affiliates, also engages in a range of activities including providing information and referral services, operating over 1,000 support groups across the country, publishing educational materials, hosting national and international conferences, and advocating at the national level and state levels for social policies that support people with mental illness. Most of the staff of these four consumer organizations are people with mental illness, and their leaders actively serve on national and state boards and committees.

In addition to these national consumer organizations, numerous consumer-run statewide and local advocacy organizations exist. A number of entities, such as the National Mental Health Consumers' Self-Help Clearinghouse and the National Empowerment Center, maintain databases of state and local consumer organizations, although no database is complete because of the high rate at which some organizations are disbanding and new ones are forming. Some evidence also exists that state mental health authorities are including state and local consumer groups in decision making. Respondents to Geller et al.'s (1998) mid-1990 survey of all 50 states, the 5 U.S. territories, and the District of Columbia reported that 90% of the mental health authorities had regular contact with consumers groups from their jurisdiction and 90% had meetings as needed. It should to be pointed out, however, that the survey did not describe the nature, quality, and outcomes of consumers' participation. At a minimum, it appears consumer organizations are at least getting a voice in planning and policy making in many instances.

Mental Health Agencies

Another mechanism through which people with mental illness may be able to participate in planning and policy making is involvement in the agencies from which they receive services. Although little has been written about this scenario, at least three possibilities for involvement exist. First, local or state mental health authorities may contact mental health agencies to obtain recommendations of clients who may be interested in serving on boards or committees, or testifying at legislative hearings. Second, clients do not live in a vacuum. They often hear about proposed policy changes in the mass media, particularly when mental health budget cuts are proposed. They are likely to discuss with their case managers their concerns about the possible affects of the proposed changes on their services. Case managers are in an ideal position to provide their clients with information about the proposals; where they can obtain additional information; and how they can express their opinions to state mental health authorities, legislators, and other governmental officials. Such actions on the part of case managers or other staff within the agency can help to relieve clients' stress by giving them accurate information about possible actions and their effects; can empower clients by giving them a voice in the decision-making process by writing letters or making telephone calls in support of, or opposition, to proposals; and can improve clients' advocacy skills. Third, many agencies actively participate in the planning and policy-making process by providing public officials with information useful for decision making. Agencies may ask for volunteers among their clients, for instance, to participate in a mental health lobby day at the state capital, to share their stories along with agency staff at legislative committee hearings, or to write down their experiences about the effect of mental health services on their lives that agency staff can then give to legislators. These types of actions require that agencies are proactive in providing consistent information to consumers and in creating ways to involve them in planning and policy making.

Voting

A final mechanism through which people with mental illness can participate in planning and policy making is voting. While it is not a structure for participation as were the proceeding ones, voting deserves mention because of its potential benefits and limitations. One benefit is that voting can promote the social inclusion of people with mental illness into the larger community by involving them in one of the most symbolic acts of citizenship in the United States (Nash, 2002). This especially can be meaningful for people with mental illness residing in long-term psychiatric hospitals by providing them with a normalizing experience that puts them in contact with something important that extends beyond the hospital (Weiner & Wettstein, 1993). Second, voting, and activities associated with being an informed voter, can have therapeutic value for people with mental illness residing in hospitals and in the community (Duckworth et al., 1994; Hanrahan, Matorin, & Borland, 1986). Discussing the various candidates and issues on the election ballot can help improve concentration, increase self-esteem, and provide clients with a lesson in delayed gratification. In recognition of the potential benefits of voting to people with mental illness, some mental health facilities have organized voting drives (Hanrahan et al., 1986). Federal legislation also has sought to increase voter participation among people with disabilities, including those with mental illness, and other vulnerable populations. The Americans with Disabilities Act of 1990 addressed some access issues related to voting, and the National Voter Registration Act of 1993 required that public agencies offer voter registration.

Despite the potential benefits of voting and federal initiatives to expand voter access to people with mental illness, many do not vote. Schriner, Ochs, and Shields (1997) concluded that the last suffrage movement is voting rights for people with mental illness. Limitations on voting by people with mental illness are attributable primarily to states' restrictions (Hemmens, Miller, Burton, & Milner, 2002; Schriner et al., 1997). In the Unites States' system of federalism, states retain substantial authority for establishing voter qualifications. In a survey of state statutes, Hemmens et al. (2002) found that as of 1999, 37 states had chosen to limit the voting rights of at least some people with mental illness, which is an increase of 4 states from 1989. No states that had voting prohibitions in 1989 eliminated them during this 10-year period, and 4 states that previously did not limit voting added prohibitions. In terms of type of restriction, the investigators found that 19 states had general restrictions against people with mental illness; 12 states restricted anyone who the courts had declared to be incompetent, including people with mental illness; and 6 states restricted both groups. In practice, some have argued that unless a person has been found incompetent, most states allow people with mental illness to vote; therefore, efforts should be made to encourage people with mental illness to register to vote (National Consumer Supporter Technical Assistance Center, 2002). Schriner et al. (1997) passionately argued for increasing voting rights to people with mental illness and cognitive disabilities. If states insist on having such laws, they recommended that qualifying tests should be objective and apply to all people who seek to vote. As an example, they stated that the test could be the ability to provide name, address, age, and assurance of citizenship.

ACCESS TO RESOURCES

An eighth condition for empowerment is that the person with mental illness has the resources needed to meaningfully participate in planning and policy making. At least six types of resources exist.

Written Materials

In recent years there has been a large increase in the amount and type of resources available to people with mental illness and advocacy groups to promote consumer participation in a wide range of planning and policy-making activities. Manuals and related written material are now available on topics such as involving consumers in developing and overseeing public managed care contracts (Bazelon Center, 1998; Koyanagi & Belivacqua, 2001); creating consumer advisory boards (National Consumer Supporter Technical Assistance Center, 2001); starting consumer councils to participate in planning of mental health services (U.S. Department of Veterans Affairs, 2000); and many others. Consumers, too, have written manuals on such topics as the development and operation of consumer organizations (Harp & Zinman, 1994) and consumer involvement in policy making (Orrin, 1997). In addition, the National Consumer Supporter Technical Assistance Center (2002, n.d.) launched the National Voter Empowerment Project and provides many resources through its Web site on how to organize voting drives to register people with mental illness. There also are general works on policy development and advocacy that could be applied to mental health planning and policy making (e.g., Ezell, 2001; Haynes & Mickelson, 2002; Jansson, 2003; Richan, 1996; Schneider & Lester, 2001). In addition, the Web sites of all the national major mental health advocacy groups and consumer organizations previously identified offer a considerable amount of policy material, including proposed legislation and legislative alerts, how to contact legislators and other governmental officials, overviews and examples of lobbying methods, and links to other policy-related Web sites, to name a few.

Education and Training

Another set of resources is education and training. To be effective advocates, many people with mental illness, as do many nonconsumer Americans, need education about the planning, policy making, and legislative processes and training on methods of advocacy. This can be accomplished through extensive, formal training programs similar to those described by Hess et al. (2001) and Rowe et al. (2003); by less intensive formal training; and by on-the-job training provided, for example, by pairing less experienced consumers with more skilled and experienced consumer or nonconsumer advocates.

Time to Participate

Time also is a valuable resource. People with mental illness need the time to be trained and to engage in the actual planning and policy-making activities. Similarly, people who serve as trainers need the time to effectively educate and train people with mental illness. In addition, all parties need enough time together in planning and policy-making sessions in order for a dialogue through which people with mental illness can meaningfully contribute to the process to occur (Fisher et al., 1996).

Liaisons to Consumer-Run Organizations and Work Groups

A resource important to some consumer-run organizations and work groups are liaisons from the state or local mental health authority. Two assets that consumers have found to be particularly useful are liaisons' knowledge of how the mental health system operates and their ability to connect consumers with important individuals within it (Bowl, 1996). The liaison function can especially be difficult to enact because it must be able to provide assistance, guidance, and resources without being invasive or interfering (Bowl, 1996). Chapter 11 includes more information about liaisons when discussing consumer-run organizations.

Logistical Resources

Many people with mental health illness also will need logistical support to participate in planning and policy making. This may include periodic meeting space, a permanent office space, office supplies, or written materials. It also may include provision of, or reimbursement for, child care; lodging; meals; or transportation to, for instance, polling locations in order to vote, training sessions, or legislative committee hearings. Because many people with mental illness have low incomes, it also may be appropriate to reimburse them for their time, particularly when they must miss work to participate. McCabe and Unzicker (1995) reported, for example, that members of Wisconsin's statewide consumer policy-making council were paid meal, travel, and lodging expenses and $150 for 2-day meetings, and people with mental illness were paid $10 per hour when participating in work groups and task forces sponsored by the state mental health authority. Some agencies that wish to support their clients' participation in planning and policy making may find that rigid accounting systems complicate the process by which they pay consumers' expenses. Church (1996) related the difficulties that clients of one agency experienced when arranging for reimbursement for their experiences to participate in regional forums conducted by a legislative subcommittee. The agency's accounting system was designed to reimburse expenses, not to provide up-front payment or cash advances for them. Most of the clients, however, could not afford to pay their own expenses and be reimbursed later. After much discussion between staff and clients and considerable ill feelings, some staff members finally agreed to allow clients to charge their expenses on the staff members' personal credit cards, with staff hoping to get reimbursed at a later time.

Financial Resources

All of the resources described above require financial commitments. Geller et al. (1998) found that many states were willing to provide some financial support to consumer organizations and consumer involvement in planning and policy making, and that several states provided substantial financial support. In addition, SAMHSA's Center for Mental Health Services, including its Community Support Program, is widely recognized for its leadership and substantial technical and financial support for consumer organizations and consumer participation in planning and policy making (Frese, 1998; Lefley, 1996; McCabe & Unzicker, 1995). It remains to be seen, though, how the current governmental fiscal crisis will affect the ability of the federal government and state governments to provide enough resources to promote meaningful involvement of people with mental illness in planning and policy making.

SUPPORTIVE CULTURE

A final condition for empowering people with severe mental illness through planning and policy making is that the culture supports meaningful participation. Relevant cultures include those of mental health professional organizations; the organizations from which people with mental illness receive services; mental health and support service advocacy groups; state mental health authorities; local, state, and federal governments; and the larger societal culture that permeates all others. A culture is supportive of consumers' involvement in policy and planning when it values their opinions and contributions; when leaders automatically invite consumers to participate in planning and policy making along with other stakeholders; when participation structures and processes are modified to accommodate the needs of some people with mental illness; when it provides the resources necessary for people with mental illness to meaningfully participate; and when, in general, it does not accept the stigmatized view that people with mental illness are incapable of, or are not interested in, participation in planning and policy making.

Strong leadership is essential for developing such a supportive culture. Leaders can assume the strengths perspective, which views people with mental illness as having the capabilities to make contributions to many areas, including planning, policy making, and advocacy (Hess et al., 2001; Schneider & Lester, 2001). Leaders also can require that people with mental illness have the opportunity for participation, and that decision-making structures and processes accommodate them. This involvement, even when initially resisted by nonconsumers, eventually can alter the culture to one that is supportive of consumer participation (Bowl, 1996; Fisher et al., 1996). In addition, leaders can allocate available resources to increase opportunities for meaningful participation. Finally, leaders can serve as role models to other staff as to how to respectfully engage people with mental illness in planning and policy making.

Many organizations are going to have to change their cultures to meaningfully involve people with mental illness in their planning, policy making, and advocacy efforts. A NAMI task force report on integrating people with mental illness in its national, state, and affiliate organizations exemplifies the critical and extensive self-examination that many organizations will have to go through to be inclusive (National Consumer Council, 2002). It first acknowledged that it would have to change its culture. While this change effort is still in the beginning stages, the report acknowledged that some NAMI members throughout its organizations did not fully value consumer participation. Consequently, the report outlined a number of recommendations to facilitate a cultural change. Some of the recommendations included developing guiding principles and setting specific standards for consumer membership, governance, and program participation including involvement in advocacy by members dialoguing with consumers using structured approaches if necessary, by educating its members about recovery, by developing consumer leadership, by establishing the national NAMI consumer council as a model for best practice for state organizations, by conducting outreach to consumers organizations, by facilitating structured feedback on the barriers that continue to discourage consumer members, and by other approaches. Other advocacy organizations and state mental health authorities may need to engage in similar extensive, long-term processes to ensure their organizations include people with mental illness and provide them with opportunities to meaningfully contribute to planning and policy making.

CASE STUDIES

To increase understanding of the opportunities for, and limitations to, the empowerment of people with mental illness through planning and policy making, empowerment is examined through the usual two case studies, one among people with mental illness residing in a public psychiatric hospital that provides long-term care and treatment (Linhorst et al., 1999), and the other among those who reside in the community and are receiving services from a publicly funded community mental health agency (Kryah et al., 2003). A third case study is added to this chapter to further exemplify the resources needed to develop statewide consumers organizations, the difficulties in maintaining them, and the contributions they can make to state planning and policy making.

Empowerment Among Clients in a Psychiatric Hospital (SLPRC)

Degree of Empowerment

SLPRC clients were not empowered through planning and policy making. There was no evidence that they influenced, or even participated in, planning or policy making that extended beyond the boundaries of the hospital. In addition, few, if any, SLPRC clients voted in public elections. Missouri law prohibits from voting people with legal guardians and people convicted of most crimes, among other groups. The state attorney general has rendered the opinion that clients found NGRI fall into the convicted group even though they have been acquitted of their crimes; thus, they cannot vote. This lack of influence through participation in planning and policy making and voting is noteworthy because of the tremendous effect that MDMH policies and state and federal laws have on SLPRC clients and clients of other long-term MDMH psychiatric hospitals.

Application of Conditions for Empowerment

Several conditions for empowering people with severe mental illness were not met related to SLPRC clients participating in planning and policy making. Chief among them was a lack of structures and processes through which SLPRC clients could participate. They had no connections with advocacy groups or with the MDMH central office through which they could voice their views. Several organizations potentially could have sought to involve SLPRC clients but did not do so. One was Missouri Protection and Advocacy. Unlike some states' Protection and Advocacy organizations, Missouri's has chosen to focus primarily on individual client issues rather than on policy making. Two other advocacy organizations, NAMI St. Louis and the MHAGSL have chosen to focus heavily on planning and policy making related to community services and special populations residing in the community, such as children's services and people with mental illness who enter the criminal justice system. People residing in the long-term MDMH hospitals have not been a priority for them, and neither organization makes contact with SLPRC clients on a routine, or even ad hoc, basis to discuss policy issues with them and represent their views in the planning and policy making arena.

Consumer-run organizations, of which there are two primary ones in the St. Louis area, also potentially could have represented the views of SLPRC clients. Both focus more on self-help than on policy advocacy, however, and neither have developed a working relationship with SLPRC clients. At the time of the study, Missouri had a statewide consumer organization, the Missouri Mental Health Consumer Network, which participated in a range of planning, policy making, and advocacy activities. However, it too maintained no contact with people with mental illness residing in the MDMH long-term hospitals. A final entity that potentially could solicit information from clients residing in long-term hospitals and represent their views in planning and policy making was the MDMH central office. The office of consumer affairs within the central office would be the logical option through which to involve clients. However, as stated above, although the office's director would like to routinely meet with clients in all MDMH hospitals in order to represent their views in planning and policy making, other duties prevent her from taking the time needed to make these routine visits.

Another condition that was not met was the existence of concrete reciprocal incentives. From one perspective, SLPRC clients had concrete incentives to participate. They potentially could play a role in statewide planning and policy making in order to improve, expand, or create new programs and services at the hospital, and to change laws that could facilitate their release into the community. However, such involvement typically does not result in immediate or direct gains and can be time consuming. In fact, when the consumer council started, members included in their bylaws that they would focus only on hospitalwide issues, rather than expend their energies on issues external to the hospital. If a process was readily available to the consumer council members through which they could participate in policy making, such as representatives from local advocacy groups holding quarterly meetings at the hospital with the consumer council, they likely would take advantage of that opportunity.

Parties other than consumers did not have concrete incentives to involve SLPRC clients in planning and policy making. For legislators and other elected officials, SLPRC clients could not vote, were not aligned with advocacy groups, and could not contribute time or money to political campaigns. For advocacy groups, including consumer-run organizations and the MDMH central office, the development of the best possible mental health services to address the needs of people with mental illness who were hospitalized should have been a concrete incentive to involve them. Clients could have provided some assistance with advocacy efforts, such as writing letters that described the benefits of the mental health services they have received and additional services they needed, and assisting with mailings of advocacy materials. Despite the potential incentives, these groups did not perceive that hospitalized clients had anything concrete to offer them in their advocacy, planning, and policy-making efforts. One can speculate, too, that a lack of resources contributed to the failure of these organizations to involve SLPRC clients. Even if these groups recognized some or all of the benefits of participation by SLPRC clients, they may have perceived that the benefits would not have outweighed the time, energy, and money needed to involve them.

Conditions internal to clients could have played a role in limiting SLPRC clients' participation in planning and policy making. Unmanaged psychiatric symptoms and poor skills of many of the clients may have prevented their meaningful participation in planning and policy discussions. Based on the abilities demonstrated by the consumer council members and other SLPRC clients in organizational decision making, however, one can speculate that enough clients would have had the psychiatric stability and been able to learn the skills required to participate in planning and decision making with consumer groups or advocacy organizations. One also can speculate that sufficient numbers of clients would have had the psychological readiness, that is, the motivation, willingness, and confidence, to participate in planning and policy making had they had reasonable access to advocacy groups and policy makers.

Empowerment Among Clients of a Community Agency (BJC-BH)

Degree of Empowerment

Some BJC-BH clients were empowered through their participation in planning and policy making. Some clients were involved by means of letter and e-mail writing to state legislators and other state officials. Some clients did this on their own and others with the assistance of BJC-BH staff. Also, at least two instances were reported in which BJC-BH clients had written letters to editors about mental health policy proposals that were published in local newspapers. Second, some clients attended the annual Mental Health Awareness Day at the state capital to lobby for mental health legislation and support services. Third, some clients were involved in mental health policy making and advocacy through participation in other organizations, including NAMI St. Louis, the St. Louis Empowerment Center, the MHAGSL, various psychosocial rehabilitation centers, and the Missouri Mental Health Consumer Network. Fourth, some clients shared their stories with BJC-BH staff that were then used in BJC-BH educational efforts with state legislators and other public officials. In 2002, for instance, BJC-BH compiled these stories in a booklet that staff used to educate public officials about the value of services received by clients. Fifth, some BJC-BH clients testified at legislative committee hearings about mental health issues. Finally, some clients said they voted.

Most clients who participated in these activities experienced subjective empowerment. They felt very good about their experiences and believed that had contributed, even in a small way, to the effort to improve mental health and support services. Clients who did not directly participate in advocacy efforts, but who were aware of other clients who had done so, may have experienced a moderate degree of subjective empowerment based on the pride they felt that other clients within the agency had been involved. Clients who did not participate in advocacy activities and were unaware of the efforts of other clients experienced no empowerment.

Clients' participation may have achieved some short-term objective empowerment outcomes. Most people from the individual interviews and the focus groups believed that client participation in policy advocacy had a positive effect, such as personalizing mental illness and providing legislators with a better understanding of the potential for recovery if adequate services are provided. Others, however, believed that some legislators did not respect the opinions of people with mental illness who testified before them in committee hearings. Finally, clients, in concert with others, achieved some long-term objective empowerment outcomes in the form of improved services, increased funding, or smaller cuts during times of fiscal constraint. However, Missouri's mental health system falls well short of meeting the treatment and rehabilitation needs of its citizens, as do the mental health systems of all other states.

Application of Conditions for Empowerment

A number of limitations internal to some clients were identified, including psychiatric symptoms that periodically were unmanaged, low educational and intellectual levels that made it difficult to understand complex policy issues, and a lack of oral and written communication skills. In addition, some clients were too overwhelmed with meeting daily needs to have the time and energy to participate, possessed feelings of hopelessness and helplessness, believed their voice did not make a difference, lacked confidence in their advocacy abilities, or were not interested in policy making or politics, just as many nonconsumers are not interested. Other clients were still in the acceptance and adaptation stages of the recovery process and were not yet comfortable with publicly advocating. Some clients also lacked knowledge of the general planning and policy-making process, the effect that policies had on them, how to stay up to date on important legislative issues, or how to get involved. Other limitations were external to clients. Some clients lacked the resources to participate in advocacy activities, including transportation and childcare. In addition, while many staff viewed clients' participation in advocacy as having therapeutic value and the potential to be empowering, some staff believed there was a lack of clarity within the agency about the proper role of staff in involving clients in advocacy, as well as the level of importance it had relative to other staff tasks.

Some staff and clients also believed that client participation in planning and policy making had decreased considerably following the departure of a BJC-BH staff member who, among other duties, participated in a wide range of planning and policy-making activities at the local and state levels, and who also was a mental health consumer. This dynamic individual usually was the person who helped to rally BJC-BH staff and clients around advocacy issues, who represented consumer perspectives, and who got other consumers involved in planning and advocacy efforts. BJC-BH administrators reported they did not refill this position because it had been a unique one, and that it would have taken a special person to continue with the activities in which she was involved at her level of involvement. They also indicated they continue to employ people with mental illness in a wide range of positions within the agency, and they plan to further involve clients in planning and policy making through the creation of a consumer council and other means. Finally, the stigma associated with mental illness also had an effect. Some clients were unwilling to engage in advocacy activities that required them to identify themselves as consumers, and some legislators and other participants discounted clients' opinions because of the stigma.

The Missouri Mental Health Consumer Network

The third case study is that of the Missouri Mental Health Consumer Network, which existed from 1988 to 2001 and served as an important mechanism through which people with mental illness could participate in planning and policy making at the state level. Its mission was to represent and empower mental health consumers and promote awareness of mental health issues in order to improve mental health services in Missouri. It especially sought to expand consumer participation in state and local service planning and policy development. Before the development of the Consumer Network, people with mental illness had minimal influence on planning and policy making. MDMH had not yet created its Office of Consumer Affairs, consumers had few slots in the MDMH's State Advisory Council and five Regional Advisory Councils, and there was no organization of consumers that represented their interests. In the mid-1980s, efforts were made to start a statewide consumer organization, but they were unsuccessful and eventually discontinued. These meetings were loosely structured, nonproductive, and unsatisfying to participants. Out of these meetings, however, a core group of consumers that was committed to developing a statewide consumer organization arose. Realizing the lack of involvement consumers had in planning and policy making, MDMH approached this smaller group about assisting them with forming a statewide organization. To obtain statewide representation, psychosocial rehabilitation centers were asked to elect representatives, which eventually totaled 30 people. To defuse any undue influence, MDMH approached Missouri Protection and Advocacy about collaborating on the project. Missouri Protection and Advocacy funded the director's position and provided office space the first couple of years. The consumer work group, with assistance from MDMH, obtained a small grant from the National Institute of Mental Health to offset some of the start-up expenses. The work group met monthly. The initial meetings were facilitated by the MDMH staff member assigned to serve as a liaison, although eventually consumers assumed responsibility for setting the agenda and running the meetings. The work group soon incorporated as a nonprofit corporation under the name of the Missouri Mental Health Consumer Network.

Consumers described the development of the Consumer Network during its first 3 years as occurring in three stages. In the initial phase, it developed the organization's mission, structure, and operational rules. Members also began to develop good working relationships and in some cases friendships. In addition, members had to struggle with the stigma associated with mental illness, because they had publicly identified themselves as having a mental illness by their association with the Consumer Network. By the end of this first phase, they began to view themselves as having the potential to hold at least some power and to be an effective organization. Consumers described the organization's second phase as the fighting phase. This occurred as members began to make and implement specific plans to carry out its mission. Continued participation in the Consumer Network during this period was too stressful for some people, who had to resign. Looking back on this time period, members believed their struggles were necessary and promoted individual growth and a much clearer direction for the organization. The third phase in the organization's early period was developing ongoing relationships and gaining credibility with MDMH and other advocacy groups, which it accomplished by the third year. By this time, members had to prioritize their areas of involvement because requests for participation began to exceed their capability.

The Consumer Network experienced problems like any new organization. Three issues stood out in particular. First was the development of local chapters. The statewide organization wanted strong local chapters to increase its ability to carry out its mission, to provide opportunities to greater numbers of consumers to be involved in planning and policy making, and to develop leadership for the statewide organization. The development of these local chapters was complicated because Missouri is large geographically, has a racially and economically diverse population, and largely is rural, with the exception of two large cities on opposite ends of the state. The Consumer Network quickly formed 18 chapters, although even this number did not cover many rural areas. In its haste to develop as many chapters as possible, it did not have the resources to provide sufficient technical assistance to develop structured organizations with strong leadership. By the latter part of the 1990s, only 11 chapters remained.

A second issue was financial instability. While consumers were appreciative of the assistance provided by MDMH and Missouri Protection and Advocacy, they sought to develop an independent funding source so they could be a fully independent body. Throughout its life, the Consumer Network received small federal grants from the National Institute of Mental Health and SAMHSA. At least two attempts to create consumer-run small businesses to fund the organization never materialized despite considerable efforts, including the hiring of a part-time business development consultant. Consumer Network engaged in some fundraising but with minimal results. They also received some funding from the MDMH including contracts to carry out particular activities. Together these sources did not meet organizational needs, and financial problems always plagued the Consumer Network.

A third issue, which was its most serious, was variability in leadership and management of the Consumer Network over time. There was a continual struggle experienced by the Consumer Network members, its board of directors, and staff within MDMH as to how much direction and oversight MDMH should provide. The consumers and MDMH were sensitive to MDMH "taking over" the organization. Considerable resources were expended to provide training to Consumer Network staff and its board in order for the Consumer Network to operate independently. In November 1995, for example, 10 Consumer Network board members attended a 2-day retreat to develop more effective leadership skills and strengthen the organization. A more intensive training effort occurred a couple of years later when the Consumer Network agreed to work with the director of a local mental health advocacy organization to provide mentoring to the Consumer Network director and its board of directors. A year or so after that, the Consumer Network experienced a rapid turnover of directors, and allegations of fiscal and managerial mismanagement arose. At the request of MDMH executive staff, one of the Consumer Network board members, a former MDMH staff person, agreed to serve as interim director for 3 months at the beginning of 2000 in order to resolve its administrative difficulties and stabilize the organization. Later in 2000, the Consumer Network board voted to assign oversight of its administrative and fiscal management to a local mental health advocacy organization that previously had provided mentoring services. This level of assistance also failed to stabilize the organization. Amid an additional turnover of directors and new allegations of problems, the Consumer Network board of directors voted to end the organization in 2001.

Despite the ongoing problems experienced by the Consumer Network, particularly during its latter years, it was respected by many people within the mental health community, had become integrated into MDMH decision-making structures, and had many accomplishments. The following is a sample of some its activities: First, the Consumer Network participated in a wide range of legislative advocacy activities. As examples, two Consumer Network members testified for 1 hour before legislators of the Mental Health Budget Appropriation Committee regarding the needs of people with mental illness. MDMH executive staff received a call from the House staff person the following week to say how impressive the consumer testimony was and how important it was to the legislators. Members also testified against a proposed bill that was before the Senate committee that would have eliminated the right of persons found NGRI to reside in a "least restrictive environment." Next, members held a peaceful demonstration in front of the state capital to protest a proposed large cut in the MDMH budget and organized its members from across the state to telephone their state legislators. As an additional example, members issued position papers and later met with the governor's office staff and key legislators regarding health care reform and the state's plan to seek a Medicaid waiver to expand mental health services.

In a second area of involvement, Consumer Network members participated in statewide program and service planning. For instance, members served on many MDMH planning committees including the System Redesign Steering Committee, Consumer Satisfaction Implementation Team, and State and Regional Advisory Committees, to name a few. Members also participated in the development of strategic plans that the governor required of all state departments and in the planning of a system of mental health crisis services. Next, members had input into creating the MDMH office of consumer affairs. Two consumers and two MDMH staff attended an office of consumer affairs national meeting in another state in 1995, and consumers were on the committee to hire the office's director. As a final example, MDMH applied for a federal technical assistance housing grant. Eight states were chosen for a pre–site selection visit. Consumer Network members were on the panel and well represented in the audience. The site visitors spoke highly of the level of consumer involvement, which greatly contributed to Missouri's selection for technical assistance. MDMH included two members on the task force to develop the housing plan.

Finally, Consumer Network members participated in many other types of activities. For example, they attended annual mental health lobby days at the state capital and took the lead on planning some of them. The Consumer Network also contracted with MDMH to hold a state conference for consumers and cosponsored other conferences. Next, the Consumer Network joined the Missouri Protection and Advocacy in a lawsuit against MDMH that sought to force the state to create additional housing for people with mental illness who were homeless. As yet another example, to educate professionals about consumer issues, members participated in statewide conferences held by recreational therapists, social workers, and psychiatrists, and they made presentations in university classes in professional programs.

The disbanding of the Consumer Network left a void in consumer participation in planning and policy making within the state. People with mental illness still have a policy advocate in the Office of Consumer Affairs, but a significant amount of time has been diverted in recent years away from meeting with consumers and representing their views in statewide planning and policy making. They still have representation on the State Advisory Committee, but the five Regional Advisory Committees have been eliminated. People with mental illness may become involved in planning and policy making through their affiliations with advocacy groups and their service providers, although these organizations vary in the extent to which they include consumers in advocacy efforts. One MDMH official stated that Consumer Network members provided a voice that often was not heard elsewhere. Compared to consumers who participated in other advocacy organizations, Consumer Network members tended to have more severe mental illnesses, were less affluent, were more likely to be receiving disability incomes, tended not to have supportive family members if they had any family at all, and raised issues that other consumers in other forums did not raise. Despite the best efforts of all participants—consumers, MDMH staff, and mental health advocacy groups—people with mental illness lost their representation by a peer organization in planning and policy making. Although some consumers have talked about starting a new statewide consumer organization, to date there have been no firm plans to do so. Moreover, in this era of tight state and federal budget, it is unlikely that sufficient resources to create a new organization and implement it will be forthcoming any time soon.

GUIDELINES FOR PROMOTING EMPOWERMENT THROUGH PLANNING AND POLICY MAKING

This discussion in this chapter illustrates the opportunities for empowerment through planning and policy, as well as the limitations that exist to this endevor. The following guidelines are offered to promote empowerment:

1. *Reduce psychiatric symptoms resulting from participation.* People with mental illness can minimize debilitating symptoms by selecting methods of participation that match their interests and abilities, by clarifying their role in the process, and by receiving adequate training.
2. *Teach planning and policy-making skills.* Some people with mental illness will need training to improve their oral and

written communication skills, interpersonal skills, assertive-ness skills, and analytic and problem-solving skills. These skills can be enhanced through formal training classes, or more in-formal individual training and mentoring.

3. *Recognize the incentives for participation.* Incentives for people with mental illness may include gaining positive feelings of ac-complishment, increasing confidence, meeting new people, learning new skills, and improving services and policies that directly affect them. Incentives for others to involve people with mental illness are the facts that their participation can improve the products of planning and policy making; consumers' per-sonal stories can be an effective resource for mental health ad-vocacy groups with legislators; and consumers can be a resource for making telephone calls, writing letters, organizing advocacy trips to the state capital, and other activities.

4. *Promote planning and policy choices.* People with mental illness should be part of the process through which issues are raised and potential policy solutions are identified and debated, rath-er than being asked only to react to the details of planning and policy proposals that others developed without their partici-pation.

5. *Promote knowledge of, and access to, a wide range of participation structures.* This includes state and regional planning boards, task forces and other ad hoc assemblies, advocacy groups, state offices of consumer affairs, employment in senior management positions within state mental health authorities, consumer groups, and mental health agencies.

6. *Advocacy groups should incorporate consumers into their planning and policy-making activities.* Established advocacy groups are in ideal positions to provide consumers with opportunities for involvement in planning and policy making through modifi-cation of their existing structures and processes.

7. *Mental health agencies should educate their clients about planning and policy-making issues and opportunities.* Case managers, in particular, can provide their clients with information about proposed policy changes; where they can obtain additional information; and how they can express their opinions to state mental health authorities, legislators, and other governmental officials. This can help to relieve clients' stress by giving them accurate information about possible actions and their effects, can empower clients by giving them a voice in the decision-making process, and can improve clients' advocacy skills.

8. *Offer resources to support participation.* These can include edu-cation and training on the legislative process and advocacy skills, staff from mental health organizations serving as liaisons

to consumer advocacy groups, and logistical and financial support.

9. *Develop a culture supportive of participation.* Leaders can develop supportive cultures by adopting the strengths perspective, by requiring that people with mental illness have the opportunity for participation, by accommodating decision-making structures and processes to their needs, by allocating the resources necessary for meaningful participation, and by serving as role models to other staff as to how to respectfully engage people with mental illness in planning and policy making.

9

Empowerment Through Employment

Employment serves many important functions within most societies (Noble, 1998). First, it provides an essential source of income for nearly all people. Employment income, when adequate, allows individuals to meet their basic needs, offers them choices in the selection of goods and services, and promotes independence. In the United States, employment also is the principal means through which nonelderly adults obtain health insurance. In addition, employment plays a critical role in determining social class and social standing within communities. Moreover, it is an important means through which people develop social relationships. Finally, employment status can affect individuals' sense of self-esteem and self-identification. Knisley, Hyde, and Jackson (2003) articulated the social importance of employment. "In our society we define ourselves as well as others by what we do—our work. Work is an essential element of our participation and acceptance in our communities" (p. 140).

Many have recognized the critical role of employment to the empowerment of people with disabilities, including those with severe mental illness (Beverly & Alvarez, 2003; Provencher, Gregg, Mead, & Mueser, 2002; Stein, 2000). When employment provides an adequate income, it affords people with mental illness a range of consumer and lifestyle choices. Employment also promotes empowerment by increasing financial independence. People with mental illness who do not work often rely on income from government disability programs or financial support provided by family members and others. Many who receive disability checks do not have control over their finances.

Instead, their checks are assigned to representative payees, who may be legal guardians, community service providers, or others, to oversee the distribution of this income. Some of these individuals use this financial control as leverage for coercion of people with mental illness (Cogswell, 1996; Stavis, 1994). Thus, having one's own source of income through employment frees individuals of at least one source of coercion. Almost as significant as the economic contributions of employment to empowerment are the interpersonal and social benefits of employment, particularly to individuals' subjective sense of empowerment. As Warner (2000) stated, "Work is central of the development of self-esteem and in shaping the social role of the mentally ill person. . . . Lacking a useful social role, many people with mental illness face lives of profound purposelessness" (pp. 71–72). Finally, Provencher et al. (2002) concluded that employment plays an important role in the recovery process of many people with mental illness by promoting a sense of self-empowerment and self-actualization. O'Day and Killeen (2002) summarized the importance of employment to people with severe mental illness:

> Employment provides financial independence and integration into the community. It also improves social status, provides social support, enables workers to make a contribution, and increases self-worth. Additionally, and most significantly for people with psychiatric disabilities, employment is a critical element to their recovery. It boosts self-esteem, provides a sense of purpose and accomplishment, and allows people to enter or re-enter the mainstream after psychiatric hospitalization. (p. 560)

Despite its potential, many people with severe mental illness are not empowered through employment for essentially two reasons. First, unemployment among people with mental illness is pervasive. Reports of the percentage of working-age adults with mental illness who are not employed vary from 50% to 95%, with 85% being most commonly cited (Fabian, Abramson, & Willis, 2003; Henry, Barreira, Banks, Brown, & McKay, 2001; President's New Freedom Commission on Mental Health, 2003; Stefan, 2002; Warner, 2000; Weinstein & Hughes, 2000). Bianco and Shaheen (2001) believed that lower reported rates of unemployment are inaccurate because they fail to account for the many people with mental illness who have given up on employment and thus are no longer included in official unemployment figures. In contrast, Stefan (2002) argued that high reported rates of unemployment are inaccurate because they fail to capture many people with mental illness who are employed but who are not receiving services from the public mental health system from which rates of employment often are determined. She reported that rates of employment of people with mental illness are much higher when samples are taken from the general population. Despite variation in the reported rates of unemployment, there is general agreement that people with mental illness are less likely to be employed than people with most other types of disabilities and are much less likely to be employed than the general public (Stefan, 2002; Weinstein & Hughes, 2000).

Another measure of the lack of employment is the extensive use of disability income programs among people with mental illness. People with mental illness are the single largest diagnostic category among recipients of Supplemental Security Income (SSI), constituting 35% of SSI recipients, and they constitute 28% of Social Security Disability Insurance (SSDI) recipients (President's New Freedom Commission on Mental Health, 2003). O'Day and Killeen (2002) reported that people with mental illness represent the fastest growing population of SSI and SSDI recipients. Once receiving a disability income, people are unlikely to return to employment. Warner (2000) cited a U.S. government report that found that among all recipients, not just those with mental illness, only 1% of SSI recipients and a half of 1% of SSDI recipients will ever terminate benefits because of a return to full-time employment.

A second reason for the lack of empowerment through employment is that even if people with mental illness are employed, their income often is not sufficient to raise them out of poverty. Schur (2002) found that people with disabilities, including those with mental illness, who are employed are much more likely than people without disabilities to engage in what he called nonstandard work, including temporary jobs, part-time jobs, and independent contracting. Nonstandard work usually pays lower salaries and has fewer, if any, benefits. This has led many mental health advocates to argue for providing people with mental illness with access to good paying jobs, permanent jobs, and those with benefits, rather than simply helping them to become employed (Bianco & Shaheen, 2001). The effects of poverty on people with mental illness are devastating, regardless of whether poverty is caused by no income, by the low incomes provided by disability income programs, or by underemployment. In her study of empowerment of people with mental illness, Manning (1999) found that poverty was critically related to the absence of empowerment. She recounted the effect of poverty on the lives of those she interviewed. "Economic status affected living conditions, social status, health and well-being and access to resources and opportunities. Basic issues such as transportation, medical and dental care, telephones and adequate food and clothing were constant problems in the lives of the consumers interviewed" (p. 108). People with mental illness may experience subjective feelings of empowerment from employment even if it does not lift them out of poverty. For objective empowerment to occur, however, employment must provide people with sufficient financial resources to raise them out of poverty.

Table 9.1 Conditions for Empowering People With Severe Mental Illness Through Employment

Managed psychiatric symptoms—The person's psychiatric symptoms are managed to the degree necessary to participate in a specific job at a specific time.

Participation skills—The person possesses the skills required to participate in a particular job.

Psychological readiness—The person has the confidence, motivation, and willingness to seek employment and maintain a particular job.

Mutual trust and respect—The person with mental illness and his or her employer have the necessary level of mutual trust and respect for the person to participate in a job.

Reciprocal concrete incentives—Concrete incentives exist for the person with mental illness to obtain and maintain employment and for employers to hire and retain people with mental illness.

Availability of choices—The person has choices of jobs that are meaningful to him or her.

Participation structures and processes—The person has structures and processes through which he or she can obtain and maintain employment.

Access to resources—The person has access to the resources needed to obtain and maintain employment.

Supportive culture—The cultures of the work setting and of the mental health organization from which the person receives services are supportive of the employment of the person with mental illness.

Stefan (2002) argued that most people with mental illness want to work, that most people with mental illness can work, and that many people with mental illness are working. However, many factors undermine the employment potential of people with mental illness. Some limitations exist within the individuals, but most exist in the social and economic environments in which people with mental illness live (Kirsh, 2000; Mowbray, Leff, Warren, McCrohan, & Bybee, 1997; Noble, 1998; US DHHS, 1999). Application of the conditions for empowering people with mental illness helps to increase understanding of these limitations and to identify guidelines for increasing employment opportunities for people with mental illness. Table 9.1 summarizes the conditions for empowerment as they apply to employment.

MANAGED PSYCHIATRIC SYMPTOMS

One condition for empowering people with severe mental illness through employment is that the person's psychiatric symptoms are managed to the degree necessary to participate in a specific job at a specific time. Unquestionably, unmanaged psychiatric symptoms interfere with the ability of some people, during some periods of their lives, to obtain and maintain employment, and they are one contributing factor to high unemployment rates among people with mental illness (Baron &

Salzer, 2002). Symptoms of mental illness can affect people's ability to concentrate, to process information, to make logical decisions on the job, to maintain constructive interpersonal relationships with work colleagues and supervisors, to manage routine job stress, and to work long hours (Bianco & Shaheen, 2001; Stefan, 2002). In a study of the effect of symptoms on employment among people with mental illness participating in a supervised work program, 70% indicated that symptoms affected their social skills, 63% said they affected their work performance, 42% said they affected their work motivation, 35% said they affected their ability to follow tasks and instructions, 34% said they affected their compliance with work standards, and 27% said they affected their personal presentation (Banks, Charleston, Grossi, & Mank, 2001) These responses illustrate the wide ranging consequences symptoms may have. They also exemplify the differential effect of symptoms on employment, as most individuals did not experience all the potentially negative consequences. Another study sought to identify the effects of four categories of symptoms on employment among a sample of people with schizophrenia who were employed (Slade & Salkever, 2001). They found that negative symptoms of schizophrenia, such as dulled emotions and attention impairment, had the greatest affect on employment. Major depression also negatively affected the employment of a substantial number of people with schizophrenia. The two remaining categories had much less influence on employment. These were positive symptoms, such as hallucinations, delusions, and illogical thoughts, and the side effects of medication. It is important to note that individuals' psychiatric diagnoses and level of psychiatric symptoms alone are not useful for predicting employment success. As Stefan (2002) stated, "simply knowing that an individual has a psychiatric diagnosis tells an employer little, if anything, about that individual's talents, abilities, and difficulties in the work arena, and whether and to what extent the psychiatric condition affects work performance" (p. 10).

While psychiatric symptoms clearly affect employment, employment can affect symptoms. For some people with mental illness, the stress and anxiety of seeking and maintaining employment can lead to an exacerbation of psychiatric symptoms, as well as the onset of physical problems (Nobel, 1998). For others, however, employment actually may improve psychiatric symptoms and promote recovery. Lehman (1995), for example, reviewed employment studies and found that employment was associated with medication compliance and a reduction in symptoms. Warner (2000) reported employment was associated with better functioning but did not always lead to symptom reduction. Mueser et al. (2003) found that employment could be particularly beneficial to the recovery process for people with the co-occurring disorders of mental illness and substance abuse by providing additional motivation to reduce or eliminate their substance use.

Multiple approaches often are necessary to help people with mental illness who are seeking employment, or who are employed, to manage their psychiatric symptoms. For many people, these will include taking psychotropic medication and adjusting medication levels as symptoms arise and dissipate. Some people with mental illness also may benefit from learning stress reduction and symptom management techniques. Others may be able to contend with symptoms by obtaining jobs that allow them to take selected breaks during the work days, to temporarily reduce work hours, or to flex their work schedules when symptoms arise. Peer support programs also can help to reduce symptoms and maintain employment (O'Day & Killeen, 2002).

PARTICIPATION SKILLS

A second condition for empowerment is that the person possesses the level of skills required to participate in a particular job. A wide range of skills, including oral and written communication skills, social skills, problem-solving skills, and skills associated with particular jobs or professions, may be necessary for jobs. In some cases, skill deficits are a function of the mental illness itself (Spaulding et al., 2003). For others, early onset of their mental illness interrupted their formal education (Unger, 1998).

One approach to promoting employment when skill deficits exist is to selectively match people with mental illness to jobs that are compatible with their current skill levels and the work environment. Ford (1995) stated that employers might be willing to accept some skill deficits, such as poor social skills, among highly productive workers that they would not accept from workers who performed marginal work. She also stated that skill levels required for one position may be very different than for another. She cited the example that one would need more advanced social skills to work as a receptionist than to work in a warehouse. Another approach is for people with mental illness to improve their skills. Participation in psychiatric rehabilitation can address many of these skill deficits (Anthony et al., 2002; Cook & Hoffschmidt, 1993; Weinstein & Hughes, 2000). People with mental illness can attend to other skill deficits by resuming participation in formal education activities, which may include programs to obtain one's high school equivalency certificate, vocational schools, or college (Unger, 1998). Upcoming discussions of the conditions participation structures and processes and access to resources include additional information on resources to improve skills needed for employment.

PSYCHOLOGICAL READINESS

A third condition for empowerment is that the person has the confidence, motivation, and willingness to seek employment and maintain a particular job. Despite its potential benefits and the fact that many people with mental illness can and do work, some people with mental illness and their families may not be ready for, or interested in, employment. In one study, for example, researchers sampled a small group of people with mental illness and family members and had them rank-order 12 outcomes, of which employment was 1 (Cradock, Young, & Forquer, 2002). Researchers indicated that vocational outcomes were not highly valued by either group. While this sample may not reflect the attitudes of the larger population of people with mental illness, it does illustrate that some people value outcomes other than employment, and that other people in their lives may not promote employment and even may discourage it.

People with mental illness may not be psychologically ready for employment for several reasons. One reason is the presence of stigma. People with mental illness may internalize the erroneous beliefs that they are incompetent and incapable of many life roles, including being employed (Link & Phelan, 1999). Consequently, they may not even imagine they are capable of employment, or, if they do think about it, they may not have the confidence to take the steps necessary to obtain employment. Internalization of a stigma is more likely to occur when people with mental illness have had repeated failed experiences with employment and perceive they do not have the opportunities and resources needed to reenter the workforce (Bianco & Shaheen, 2001). In addition, if people with mental illness are experiencing learned helplessness, one effect is their lack of involvement in employment (Flannery et al., 1996). Until they begin to perceive they can regain control over aspects of their lives, it is unlikely they will be psychologically ready to consider employment and take the steps necessary to prepare for it. Further impeding the willingness to work among people with mental illness receiving disability incomes is the fear of being without any income or health insurance should their employment end for any reason (Ford, 1995). This fear is not an irrational one, as will be discussed in the upcoming condition, reciprocal concrete incentives.

At least four actions can be taken to increase the readiness of people with mental illness to work. One is for mental health professionals to talk about employment with their clients. Evidence exists that some mental health professionals underestimate the potential of their clients to work and thus often do not raise the issue for discussion (Bianco & Shaheen, 2001). If their clients are receiving disability benefits, part of that discussion should include accurate information about how employment will affect their benefits. A second action is to provide opportunities for people with mental illness to gain confidence in their potential to work. This can be done in many ways, such as encouraging people to participate in volunteer work or psychosocial rehabilitation clubhouse work programs (Jackson, 2001; Woodside & Luis, 1997). A third action to assist people with mental illness is to find employment that matches their work interests. People are much more willing to seek and maintain employment if it is something in which they are interested (Mueser, Becker, & Wolfe, 2001). Finally, mental health organizations should celebrate their clients' successes with employment and share them with other clients who are working and with those who are not. Such success stories help to motivate employed people to maintain their jobs and offer encouragement to those who are not working that they, too, may be able to be employed.

MUTUAL TRUST AND RESPECT

A fourth condition for empowerment is that mutual trust and respect exist between the person with severe mental illness and his or her employer. One aspect of this from the perspective of people with mental illness is whether to disclose to employers and coworkers that they have a mental illness. Many people with mental illness are fearful of disclosing their mental illness and choose not to do so (Dalgin & Gilbride, 2003). Dalgin and Gilbride (2003) identified some of the reasons for not disclosing. These included concern that employers may not hire them if they disclosed their mental illness during the initial job interview, that employers may more closely supervise or monitor them if they disclosed, that disclosure may isolate them from coworkers, that they may lose their jobs if they disclosed, that disclosure may limit their opportunities for promotion within the company, and that, if they disclosed, they may have to work harder than other employees to gain the respect of their employer and coworkers. Potential benefits to disclosure may include employers being willing to provide a flexible work environment, to offer assistance if symptoms develop, to offer feedback on their job performance as it may relate to mental illness, and to offer emotional support (Gowdy, Carlson, & Rapp, 2003; Rollins, Mueser, Bond, & Becker, 2002). One study of disclosure found that when mental health professionals openly discussed the potential benefits and drawbacks to disclosure, people with mental illness were more likely to disclose their mental illness (Gowdy et al., 2003).

When people with mental illness disclose their mental illness, they are trusting that employers will respect their work abilities even though they have a mental illness, will not limit their job duties or promotional opportunities solely on the basis of having a mental illness, and will support them if symptoms arise that interfere with some aspect of their job duties. Some people with mental illness who currently are managing their symptoms and experiencing recovery may never need to disclose their mental illness. Others may choose not to disclose the mental illness at time of employment, but at a later time after a trusting and respectful working relationship has been established with employers should the need arise for employer support and flexibility in the work environment. In still other instances, however, people with mental illness must blindly trust their potential employer. The decision to disclose a mental illness during job interviews may be preferable and even necessary when people with mental illness have to explain large gaps of unemployment or when transitioning from part-time employment of long duration to full-time employment. Trust and respect of employers may be enhanced if other people with mental illness already are working at the place of employment, and employers and coworkers have treated those employees with respect. The identification of such employers may happen informally through word-of-mouth communication. Alternatively, people with mental illness may be directed to such employers by mental health or vocational professionals who have working relationships with them and have first-hand knowledge and experience that those employers have been respectful to people with mental illness.

Employers must overcome stigmatized views of people with mental illness in order to trust and respect them as potentially capable employees. Among other things, these stigmatized views may include perceptions that people with mental illness may be violent in the work place, that their mood may be unstable, and that they may engage in unusual behaviors in the workplace (Bianco & Shaheen, 2001). Gilbride, Stensrud, Vandergoot, and Golden (2003) identified characteristics of employers who are likely to trust and respect people with disabilities. Although they did not explicitly include people with mental disabilities, their conclusions still appear to be relevant. The characteristics included the employer focusing on the individual's strengths and matching job requirements to those strengths, soliciting information from individuals about their abilities to perform certain job functions, focusing on essential job functions, and offering internships to allow individuals to test their interest and abilities in particular jobs and then often hiring them after they successfully completed their internships. The question then becomes how to convince employers to look beyond individuals' mental illness to instead view them as potentially capable, productive employees.

Ideally, employer trust of, and respect for, people with mental illness and other diverse populations already is part of the culture of the organization. In most instances, however, people with mental illness themselves, or mental health or vocational rehabilitation professionals who may be assisting them to obtain employment, will have to take the initiative to promote employer trust and respect. People with mental illness can do this by providing employers with references from past employers or from educational, vocational, or rehabilitation programs if they have had a stable work history. People with mental illness also may promote employer trust and respect by openly discussing their mental illness, its potential affects on employment, and how each can promote successful employment. Professionals can promote trust and respect among employers by dispelling the myths associated with mental illness, by discussing the strengths of the individuals for whom they are advocating, by offering to provide ongoing support and consultation to the employer, and by providing employers with the names of other employers with whom the professionals have provided support services for other employees with mental illness.

RECIPROCAL CONCRETE INCENTIVES

A fifth condition for empowerment is that concrete incentives exist for the person with mental illness to obtain and maintain employment and for employers to hire and retain people with mental illness. For people with mental illness who are not working, the decision as to whether to seek employment often is a calculation of incentives and disincentives. As Cook and Burke (2002) wrote, "people with schizophrenia make work decisions by weighing the relative 'costs' and 'benefits' of paid work within their own individual economic and psychosocial contexts" (p. 551). Warner (2000) elaborated on this calculation process, stating, "Like everyone else, people with psychiatric disabilities balance several factors to optimize their income. The decision to work is based on three counter-balancing factors: (1) the economic return; (2) the stress and effort involved; and (3) the satisfaction derived from the work" (p. 79). Employers, too, weigh the incentives and disincentives to hiring people with mental illness. A discussion of each follows.

Employment Incentives and Disincentives for People With Mental Illness

At least three incentives for people with mental illness to seek and maintain employment exist. First, employment has the potential to increase their income beyond what they are receiving from disability incomes or other sources, and to move them out of poverty. Second, it can decrease psychiatric symptoms, improve functioning, and promote recovery (Lehman, 1995; Provencher et al., 2002; Warner, 2000). Third, it can provide them with a useful social role, increase their social networks, and promote a sense of self-empowerment and self-actualization (O'Day & Killeen, 2002; Provencher et al., 2002; Warner, 2000).

Disincentives to employment for people with mental illness also exist. Economic disincentives include the potential loss of income and health care benefits for people receiving disability incomes (O'Day & Killeen, 2002). For those people who have no income or who are receiving substantial support from family members or other sources, any amount of money earned through employment would be beneficial. People with disability incomes, however, may not necessarily experience an economic gain from employment, and employment may jeopardize their access to health insurance. It is widely recognized that U.S. social benefit programs for people with mental illness are structured in such a way as to create substantial economic disincentives to employment (Baron & Salzer, 2002; Noble, 1998; O'Day & Killeen, 2002; President's New Freedom Commission on Mental Health, 2003). These same employment disincentives also exist in many other countries (O'Flynn & Craig, 2001; Turton, 2001; Warner, 2000). For example, Warner (2000) reported that in Great Britain, the annual value of a disability pension, housing subsidy, and free medication received by the average person with mental illness amounted to approximately $22,000 of tax free income, while a full-time minimum wage job there paid approximately $15,000 per year of taxable income.

Employment Disincentives Under SSI

In the United States, the two primary disability income programs used by people with mental illness are SSI and SSDI. SSI is a federally funded cash benefit paid to people who are elderly, blind, or have a disability, including mental illness, and who have limited income and resources (Social Security Administration, 2004). In 2004, the monthly benefit was $564. States have the option to fund an increase in the monthly payment. In 2002, 24 states added to the federal payment, which then was $545. However, 13 of these 24 states added less then $50, and the average monthly SSI payment across all states in 2002 was $595. To be eligible, recipients' assets (e.g., cash, stocks, bank accounts, and real estate excluding one's home) cannot exceed $2,000. Limited exceptions to the $2,000 asset limit exist. One is the Plan for Achieving Self-Support, which allows employed SSI recipients to set aside assets in excess of $2,000 to meet specific, time-limited, job-related goals such as college or a vocational program. In 39 states, SSI recipients are eligible for Medicaid, a joint federal-state health insurance program that provides medical benefits, including selected medications, hospital benefits, and outpatient services. The other 11 states have different eligibility requirements for Medicaid than for SSI. Missouri, for example, has Medicaid asset limits of $1,000 rather than the $2,000 limit under SSI.

    Employment affects the monthly amount of income of virtually all people with mental illness who receive SSI (Social Security Administration, 2004). SSI recipients can earn up to only $85 monthly without it affecting the amount of their checks. Some expenses required for employment, such as psychotropic medication, may reduce the amount of income that is included in the calculations. When employment exceeds the calculated limit for that individual, his or her SSI check will be reduced $1 for every $2 of income that exceeds that amount. Recipients must notify the Social Security Administration when this occurs so that their checks can be reduced by the appropriate amount. In recent years, federal law was modified to permit states to extend Medicaid to former SSI recipients who are employed. Medicaid continues after SSI checks have stopped, provided that Medicaid benefits are needed to remain in employment, that recipients are unable to obtain medical coverage through their employer or purchase health insurance on their own, that they meet all other requirements for SSI including the continuation of the disability and resource limits, and that recipients' income is under the state threshold amount. States set their own threshold amounts, which vary widely. For example, in 2004, the lowest state threshold was $18,719 in Alabama and the highest was $42,390 in Connecticut.

The employment disincentives under this program lie less with the amount of the net income gain (employment income plus the reduced SSI check) than with the program's implementation, the ripple effects of having a monthly income that often changes, limits on savings accounts, the potential loss of Medicaid, and monthly reports to multiple parties. Often, there is a delay of months between the time recipients report their income to the Social Security Administration and the months in which their checks are reduced (O'Day & Killeen, 2002). The result is that SSI "overpayments" must be deducted from future checks. It is not uncommon, then, for people with mental illness to attempt work, to lose their jobs, and to have no income for several months because their SSI checks are reduced or eliminated because of overpayments resulting from employment. Because resource limits are so low ($2,000 for SSI and $1,000 for Medicaid in states such as Missouri), people are not allowed to save money for this potential interim period between job loss and the resumption of their SSI checks. In addition, people who receive federal housing subsidies and other social benefits, such as food stamps, must report income changes to those respective offices so those offices can change benefits accordingly by, for example, increasing the monthly rent and reducing the amount of food stamps for the next month. Medicaid continues for some people, but only under the criteria defined above, which vary widely across states. All these factors, then, serve as disincentives to employment, severely limiting SSI recipients' economic motivation to work.

Employment Disincentives Under SSDI

SSDI is the other major disability program. SSDI is a federal income program for people who are blind or have a disability, including mental illness (Social Security Administration, 2004). Unlike SSI, SSDI recipients must have paid into the social security system while being employed, benefit amounts vary according to length of employment and amount paid into the social security system, and there are no resource limitations. People with mental illness who experienced the onset of symptoms early in their adult lives may never have worked and thus would not be eligible for SSDI. People who have worked a limited amount of time may receive both SSDI and SSI if their SSDI check is under amount of the state's SSI payment and the individual meets all SSI criteria, including income and resource limitations. After a 2-year waiting period for most people, SSDI recipients are eligible for Medicare, a federal health insurance program for SSDI and social security retirement recipients, which pays for selected hospital and outpatient services, as well as selected medications under an expansion of Medicare that is scheduled for implementation in 2006.

Employment affects people receiving SSDI very differently than those on SSI (Social Security Administration, 2004). SSDI recipients are granted a 9-month trial work period, during which they can receive the full amount of their SSDI check regardless of how much they earn. These trial work months do not have to be consecutive and are considered on a rolling 60-month basis. In 2004, a trial work month was identified when an individual earned more than $580 in a particular month. After people have completed their trial work months, one of two things can happen to their SSDI checks. If employment income usually was under $810 per month (under 2004 guidelines), which is consider substantial gainful activity (SGA), then SSDI checks most likely will continue as long as their income remains under the SGA level. If monthly income usually exceeded the SGA level of $810, then SSDI checks end after a 3-month grace period. If SSDI checks end, they can restart within 36 months of the end of the trial work period during any month they fell below the SGA level. In addition, SSDI has a quick restart benefit that enables former recipients to restart their benefits without a new application within 5 years of receiving their last SSDI check. Former SSDI recipients remain eligible for Medicare for at least 93 months after their last trial work month, as long as they continue to have a disability.

SSDI regulations are most favorable to SSDI recipients who work part-time and to those working in low paying jobs. As long as their monthly income is under $580 (for 2004), trial work months do not start, and as long as monthly income is under SGA $810 (for 2004), most recipients will be able to continue to receive their full SSDI checks even though their trial work months have expired, so long as they continue to have a disability. The primary work disincentives apply to those who earn more than the SGA level. For many of these people, their monthly income from employment will never exceed the monthly income earned from working part-time and receiving their disability check. There also may be general anxiety related to no longer having a guaranteed monthly check, even if it can be restarted within the first 5 years of receiving their last SSDI check (O'Day & Killeen, 2002).

Decreasing Work Incentives Under SSI and SSDI

Positive changes have been made in the SSI and SSDI programs in recent years, particularly the extension of Medicaid and Medicare for a period of time after checks cease and the resumption of checks without requiring a new application process for 5 years. Disincentives remain, however (O'Day & Killeen, 2002). Some advocates and policy makers continue to push for further revisions in the two disability income and medical insurance programs (Bianco & Killeen, 2001; President's New Freedom Commission on Mental Health, 2003; Warner, 2000; White House Domestic Policy Council, 2004). Some of the suggested changes include improving access to medical benefits to individuals who leave SSI and SSDI for employment, particularly increasing or eliminating the Medicaid state threshold amounts; increasing the monthly SGA limit under SSDI to at least $1,000 from its current level of $810; and making work requirements under SSI the same as those under SSDI. A second needed step is to educate people with mental illness, family members, and mental health and rehabilitation professionals about the changes in regulations that recently have occurred so the people with mental illness can make informed choices about whether or not to seek employment. Many people are unaware of these changes or do not understand them (Bianco & Shaheen, 2001; O'Day & Killeen, 2002). As Baron and Salzer (2002) stated, "although Congress has made important changes in the SSI/SSDI systems to soften the disincentives to employment, the myths surrounding the punitive and arbitrary decisions of the Social Security Administration are powerful enough to dissuade a great many people from seriously pursuing financial independence" (p. 592).

Weighing of Economic Incentives and Disincentives Against Other Factors

As Warner (2000) indicated, people with mental illness often weigh potential economic incentives and disincentives from employment against other factors. While employment can promote recovery, the responsibilities associated with working and maintaining needed benefits can produce anxiety and a reemergence of psychiatric symptoms that people may not readily be able to manage. Repeated failed attempts at employment can decrease self-esteem and self-worth. Moreover, while employment can increase social networks, not everyone who works is accepted by their coworkers, and some individuals in the workplace may be isolated or subjected to overt antagonism and ridicule.

Employer Incentives and Disincentives for Hiring People With Mental Illness

In addition to people with mental illness needing incentives to seek and maintain employment, so too do employers need incentives to hire and retain people with mental illness. The foremost incentive to hire people with mental illness is that employers potentially have access to needed employees. By arbitrarily not hiring people with mental illness, employers eliminate an entire pool of employees that could fill their labor needs. Second, in some employment situations, mental health or vocational rehabilitation professionals may provide on-site or off-site support services to the employee with mental illness to lessen the chance of job turnover and possibly even guarantee that the position will be filled by another qualified candidate. Third, employers can reduce recruitment costs by using free national job referral services that include people with disabilities, such as the Employer Assistance Referral Network and Ticket to Hire (Social Security Administration, 2004). Fourth, in some instances, employers can receive tax credits for hiring people with disabilities, including those with mental illness. One example is the Work Opportunity Tax Credit, which targets nine groups that have barriers to employment (U.S. Department of Labor, n.d.). Two of these groups are likely to have substantial numbers of people with mental illness, including SSI recipients and people with disabilities who have completed a state or federal rehabilitation program. Fifth, it is possible that a particular employer may get positive publicity within its community for hiring people with disabilities. A final incentive for employers to hire people with mental illness is to avoid violation of, and prosecution under, the Americans with Disabilities Act (ADA), which, among other things, prohibits employment discrimination against people with mental illness.

Employers may have disincentives, as well as incentives, to hire people with mental illness. These disincentives are rooted, in part, in stigmatized views of people with mental illness and isolated negative experiences that reinforce these views. As examples, an employer may believe that hiring a person with mental illness could jeopardize the physical safety of coworkers and customers, that the person's mannerisms may disrupt the work environment, or that customers may not patronize the business if they learn that a person with mental illness works there. A range of actions is needed to overcome employer disincentives and to promote incentives. Better and ongoing public education surrounding mental illness, as well as the capabilities of people with mental illness, is vital to dispel the stigma of mental illness. Also, the provision of support services to workers with mental illness and employers can decrease some disincentives. In addition, enhanced tax credits and better enforcement of the ADA can increase employment (Baron & Salzer, 2002). Greater publicity of existing tax credits, the free national employer referrals services, and ADA requirements are necessary for them to be maximally effective (White House Domestic Policy Council, 2004).

Societal Incentives for People With Mental Illness to Work

While the focus of discussion has been on concrete incentives for people with mental illness and employers, it is important to note that incentives for people with mental illness to be employed exist at the societal level as well. Beverly and Alvarez (2003) believed that "as a result of discrimination against disabled persons in education and in the labor market, society receives few benefits from the talents of disabled individuals. Many disabled persons are able to work and live in independent settings, yet they are often directed to welfare systems rather than to labor markets" (p. 27). Likewise, the President's New Freedom Commission on Mental Health (2003) concluded, "The loss of productivity and human potential is costly to society and tragically unnecessary" (p. 29).

AVAILABILITY OF CHOICES

The sixth condition for empowerment is that the person with mental illness has choices of jobs that are meaningful to him or her. Many people with mental illness have the necessary level of education, job experience, and recovery from their mental illness to enjoy a wide range of employment opportunities. Unfortunately, many others do not. For these individuals, the choice is often between not working and working in an entry-level position with little hope of advancement or getting out of poverty (Carling, 1995). This limited view of employment choices is widespread throughout society. As Mowbray, Leff et al. (1997) stated, "Vocational opportunities are often conceptually limited, in the minds of service providers, consumers, and the public, to lower-level service occupations ('food and filth') or to blue collar positions in industry" (pp. 342–343). Such choices, of course, are not meaningful, nor do they offer real choices. Gilson (1998) wrote, "To offer scaled-back options, limited opportunities, or inadequate support is not choice; it is a continuation of practices of domination and paternalism" (p. 11). People with mental illness need choices that include a range of employment opportunities that pay well, that include benefits, and that provide career opportunities (Mowbray, Leff et al., 1997). For some individuals who lack education, training, and a strong work history, obtaining one's desired job choices may have to include long-range plans to develop the required qualifications (Gilson, 1998).

Obtaining even low-level jobs in today's economy may be difficult for people with mental illness. As Baron and Salzer (2002) noted:

> Those with serious mental illness often have the same labor market liabilities as other non-disabled workers, limiting their employment prospects to the secondary labor market [low pay, poor career path] without regard to their disability; that is, for some their race, gender, social networks, and educational level may diminish their prospects, independent of their illness. (p. 593)

Similarly, Noble (1998) indicated that people with mental illness must compete with other disadvantaged people, including people receiving welfare benefits who are mandated to work under the Temporary Assistance for Needy Families program and legal and illegal immigrants, for these secondary labor market jobs.

Creating meaningful employment choices requires work at multiple levels, ranging from national policy, to state policy, to individual employers. Social policies in the areas of labor, immigration, social welfare, and education, among others, affect employment opportunities. It is important for mental health advocates to align themselves with other groups to advocate for employment-related policies that benefit all disadvantaged groups, as well as to advocate for policies targeted specifically to people with mental illness (Draine, Salzer, Culhane, & Hadley, 2002). Given the U.S. system of federalism and the increasingly important role that states play in social policy development, it is important that advocacy efforts are directed both to the federal government and to state governments (Linhorst, 2002b). For example, if the political will to enact innovative job training programs does not exist at the federal level, these programs may be passable within individual states.

At the same time that changes are being sought at the federal and state social policy levels, action to develop meaningful jobs for people with mental illness is needed at the individual level. Rapp's (1998) general principles for community resource development have utility for demonstrating how to approach employers to hire people with mental illness for jobs of their choice. One principle is to emphasize advantages or rewards, which may include the employer getting a competent, dedicated worker; mental health or rehabilitation professionals providing on-site or off-site support for these employees; and employers experiencing satisfaction knowing they helped someone who really wanted to work find work. A second principle is using comprehensible, clear, nontechnical language with employers when dispelling myths of mental illness and describing psychiatric symptoms, treatments, or available support services. A third principle is to show compatibility of values. The fact that these individuals want to leave government disability programs to become financially independent is entirely consistent with values of individual responsibility and autonomy to which many employers can relate. A fourth principle is to cite proven results. This can include discussing the vocational successes of the individual for whom a job is being sought and providing references to support it, of other people with mental illness participating in a particular mental health or vocational program, or of people with mental illness in general. A fifth principle is to allow for a trial period. This can include an employer agreeing to hire an individual on a short-term probationary period, or hiring other individuals from a particular mental health or vocational program if the first person is successful. A sixth principle is to link the employment message to influential others.

This may include, for instance, referencing President Bush's desire to see that all Americans be given the opportunity to work in jobs for which they qualify, or referring them to other employers who have worked with people with mental illness.

PARTICIPATION STRUCTURES AND PROCESSES

A seventh condition for empowerment is that the person with mental illness has structures and processes through which he or she can obtain and maintain employment. As will be discussed, in some instances, participation in these structures and processes is an end in itself, while in other instances, participation prepares people with mental illness for future jobs that are more aligned with their job choice and career goals. Supported employment is the structure that research supports as providing the best employment outcomes. Some argue, however, that a range of employment options should be available to people with mental illness (Carling, 1995; Henry et al., 2001; O'Flynn & Craig, 2001). People who may not be willing to participate in supported employment may be willing to participate in another employment activity that eventually can lead to the type of employment they ultimately desire. Seven employment structures and processes are considered below.

Structures and Processes Available to All People Seeking Employment

Many people with mental illness will be able to obtain employment without assistance from special programs for people with mental illness or from mental health or vocational rehabilitation professionals. They use the same structures and processes for accessing employment that people without disabilities use. Examples of such structures and processes include searching job advertisements in newspapers or Internet sites; registering with state-operated employment services, private job search companies, or individual headhunters; using employment services offered through their colleges if they were college graduates; and networking with friends and former colleagues who may be working in their desired fields. People with mental illness who access these structures and processes typically are well into the recovery process, possess the skills to conduct job searches and obtain employment on their own, have a work history, are confident in their abilities to obtain employment, and would like the option not to disclose their mental illness to their employers or coworkers at time of employment.

Supported Employment

In its most general sense, supported employment refers to the provision of support services to help people with mental illness obtain and maintain employment. Using this broad definition, most of the structures and process that follow are considered by some to be supported employment (Baer, 2003). There is growing acceptance, however, of the application of the term to refer to the provision of support to an individual to locate a competitive job of his or her choice in an integrated setting, and to provide ongoing support to that individual in the amount and duration needed to maintain that job (Bond et al., 2001). Bond et al. (2001) listed five critical components of supported employment based upon their review of the relevant research:

[1]   The agency providing supported employment services is committed to competitive employment as an attainable goal for its clients with severe mental illness. . . .

[2]   Supported employment programs use a rapid job search approach to help clients obtain jobs directly, rather than providing lengthy preemployment assessment, training, and counseling. . . .

[3]   Staff and clients find individualized job placements according to client preferences, strengths, and work experiences. . . .

[4]   Follow-along supports are maintained indefinitely. . . .

[5]   The supported employment program is closely integrated with the mental health treatment team. (p. 315)

Examples of ongoing supports include on-site visits or telephone calls to the employee, employer, or coworkers; written evaluations with information provided by some combination of the employee, the employer, coworkers, the person providing support, and family members; off-site support provided to employees in their homes, in restaurants, or in other locations; and support from other people with mental illness who are employed, which often is provided in the form of peer support groups (Ford, 1995). These support services can be provided by vocational rehabilitation agencies, by mental health organizations, or by independent supported employment agencies (Ford, 1995).

There is substantial evidence that supported employment, coordinated with psychiatric services, results in better outcomes than other employment models for people with severe mental illness, particularly in obtaining and maintaining permanent, competitive employment (Bond et al., 2001; Bond, Drake, Mueser, & Becker, 1997; Lehman, 1995; Salyers, Becker, Drake, Torrey, & Wyzik, 2004). It is noteworthy that these better outcomes are not associated with specific characteristics of people with mental illness, such as age, gender, type of mental illness, number of prior hospitalizations, or education (Bond et al., 2001). Not all supported employment programs, however, generate the same level of positive outcomes. Like any program, they must be implemented properly. Gowdy et al. (2003) compared supported employment programs operated by mental health organizations that had high rates of employment with those that had low rates of employment and found that those programs with high success rates had several differentiating characteristics. First, case managers had a structured system for initiating conversations with clients about the possibility of working, they used a strengths-based approach to guide discussions, and they openly dealt with clients' fear about working. Second, case managers had developed excellent working relationships with the state vocational rehabilitation program staff. Consequently, their clients were able to obtain program services in a timely manner and to receive a high degree of support from vocational rehabilitation staff, particularly when they experienced problems on the job. Third, case managers openly discussed with clients the advantages and disadvantages of whether they should disclose their mental illness to employers and seek accommodations. As a result, clients were much more likely to disclose their mental illness and receive accommodations, while clients at low-success sites were much more likely to reduce employment options rather than disclose their mental illness. Fourth, employers received frequent support and a wide range of types of support. Finally, clients felt comfortable asking for help, whether from mental health professionals, vocational rehabilitation staff, or employers, and were confident that they would get needed assistance.

Transitional Employment Positions

Transitional employment positions are time-limited jobs, typically 6–9 months, in competitive, integrated work environments (Henry et al., 2001; Jackson, 2001). They are designed to help people with mental illness test their ability to work and to begin to develop a positive work history. People often work several different transitional employment jobs as springboards to permanent positions. Transitional employment positions can be for one person or a group of people within a particular setting. Program staff learn the job duties, selects and trains the people who are to work in the transitional employment job, and actually works the job if clients are unable to do so themselves. As such, employers are guaranteed workers in areas for which they may have difficulty hiring and retaining employees.

Consumer Businesses and Self-Employment

Many people with mental illness have started their own businesses, and self-employment can be a sound alternative for others (Allen & Granger, 2003; Bianco & Shaheen, 2001). Self-employment can be a particularly important employment alternative in rural areas and other locations with high unemployment rates and low job availability (Bianco & Shaheen, 2001). It also offers people a high degree of independence and flexibility, which some people with mental illness may need. In addition, Allen and Granger (2003) argued that it is the most empowering form of employment because people with mental illness are running the companies themselves, rather than working for others. Small businesses are now an essential part of the U.S. economy. As such, federal, state, and local governments are providing a substantial amount of assistance to those individuals who are willing to try to develop such business enterprises. In addition to the support that is available to anyone trying to start a business, many people with mental illness may need additional support of various types from mental health and vocational rehabilitation professionals to maximize their potential for success (Allen & Granger, 2003). The disadvantages to consumer businesses and self-employment, are, of course, that they may require substantial start-up capital, they are highly risky ventures, they can require substantial number of work hours to be successful, and they can be very stressful (Bianco & Shaheen, 2001). Many small businesses fail, which can result in substantial financial losses to those involved, as well as damage the self-esteem and confidence of the people with mental illness involved in them.

Social Enterprises

Social enterprises are businesses operated in the open market that are established for the sole purpose of providing employment opportunities to groups of people who have experienced chronic unemployment, have disabilities, or have other disadvantages that affect their employability (Bianco & Shaheen, 2001). They offer industry-scale competitive wages and may hire individuals without disabilities to provide a more integrated work setting. Social enterprises are much more common in Europe and Canada, where they typically are referred to as social firms, than they are in the United States (O'Flynn & Craig, 2001; Warner, 2000). Examples of social firms operating in Italy, for example, include hotels, restaurants, transportation services, building renovation companies, large cleaning companies, and horticulture businesses (Warner, 2000). Social enterprises are structured in such a way as to be able to provide substantial amounts of support and to allow individuals to learn job skills. Some individuals work in social enterprises without aspirations of other employment, while others use the experience to build an employment record that allows them to get a different job of their choice.

Sheltered Workshops

Sheltered workshops are organizations designed to provide work opportunities to people with disabilities, including mental illness. They have been highly criticized in recent years because they typically are segregated settings in which only people with disabilities are employed; they do not pay competitive wages but base wages on productivity, which can be far less than minimum wage; many of the work activities are simulated tasks, with little real work value; and few participants typically move on to competitive employment (Young, 2001). Despite these disadvantages, some continue to support their existence (O'Flynn & Craig, 2001; Young, 2001). Young (2001) argued that they can be modified to become a viable employment option. He provided a case study of a sheltered workshop that was modified by hiring some individuals without disabilities, by encouraging mental health professionals to appear on-site, by having only real work activities, and by making transition to competitive employment an explicit goal of the program.

Volunteer Work

A final structure and process for accessing employment is volunteer work. While it, by definition, is not employment, some argue that volunteer work can be a meaningful and valuable first step toward employment for many people with mental illness (Harp, 1994; Woodside & Luis, 1997). People who volunteer can learn new job skills, can increase their confidence in their potential to work, can get a sense of satisfaction from helping others, and can directly or indirectly get jobs as a result of the volunteer experience (Woodside & Luis, 1997). Harp (1994), who has a mental illness and became a national leader in the mental health consumer movement, was a strong proponent of volunteering, based on his own positive experience. After being pushed, in his view, by vocational rehabilitation professionals to take a job that was not satisfying to him and had no opportunities for career advancement, he eventually quit that job and began volunteering in an advocacy organization doing the type of work he always had hoped to do. He described this volunteer work as being his own individualized program of vocational rehabilitation, which eventually led to full-time, permanent employment and a career as a mental health advocate.

Table 9.2 summarizes the seven structures and processes for accessing employment just discussed.

ACCESS TO RESOURCES

An eighth condition for empowerment is that the person has access to the resources needed to obtain and maintain employment. The previously described structures and processes, particularly supported employment, can, themselves, be considered important resources for employment, but there are many others as well. Common types of resources that promote employment of people with mental illness are discussed below.

State Vocational Rehabilitation Agencies

The federal government, through the Rehabilitation Services Administration in the U.S. Department of Education, provides states with

Table 9.2 Structures and Process Through Which People With Severe Mental Illness Can Enter or Maintain Employment

Structures and process available to all people—Examples include searching job advertisements in newspapers or Internet sites, registering with various types of employment services, and networking with friends and former colleagues who may be working in their desired fields.

Supported employment—The provision of support to an individual to locate a competitive job of his or her choice in an integrated setting, and to provide ongoing support to that individual in the amount and duration needed to maintain that job.

Transitional employment positions—Time-limited jobs, typically 6–9 months, in competitive, integrated work environments that are designed to help people with mental illness test their ability to work and begin to develop a positive work history.

Consumer businesses and self-employment—Starting one's own business can be a sound alternative, particularly in rural areas and other locations with high unemployment rates and low job availability. It also may offer some people needed independence and flexibility.

Social enterprises—Businesses operated in the open market that are established for the sole purpose of providing employment opportunities to groups of people who have experienced chronic unemployment, have disabilities, or have other disadvantages that affect their employability. They offer industry-scale competitive wages and may hire individuals without disabilities to provide a more integrated work setting.

Sheltered workshops—Work opportunities for people with disabilities, including mental illness, that exist in segregated settings in which they employ only people with disabilities. They base wages on work productivity, which can be far less than minimum wage. Many of the work activities are simulated tasks, with little real work value, and few participants typically move on to competitive employment.

Volunteer work—Working in unpaid positions can be a meaningful and valuable first step toward employment for some individuals. People who volunteer can learn new job skills, can increase confidence in their potential to work, and can directly or indirectly lead to paid employment.

funds, in an 80%-20%, federal-state match, to establish vocational rehabilitation programs for people with disabilities (Fabian et al., 2003). State vocational rehabilitation agencies serve many different types of people, including those with mental illness. Vocational rehabilitation staff can provide counseling, vocational training, job development, and job placement, as well as purchase a range of educational and vocational resources, including supported employment, from other providers. Some of these services can be highly valuable to people with mental illness who are seeking employment and may find it difficult to obtain similar services from other sources (Ford, 1995).

State vocational rehabilitation agencies have been highly criticized for their work with people with mental illness (Harp, 1994; Noble, 1998; Noble, Honberg, Hall, & Flynn, 1997). First, services are designed to be time limited under the assumption that people, once trained and placed, will succeed in their jobs. In fact, the measure of success for vocational rehabilitation agencies is 90 consecutive days of employment. However, many people with mental illness will need ongoing support (Fabian et al., 2003; Noble et al., 1997). Second, despite legislation to the contrary, many vocational rehabilitation agencies continue to selectively choose their clients, focusing primarily on those people who are most employable in the shortest amount of time, which typically are not people with mental illness (Fabian et al., 2003; Noble et al., 1997). Third, many vocational rehabilitation administrators and counselors have an inadequate understanding of mental illness, its affect on employment, and the services people with mental illness need to be employable (Fabian et al., 2003; Noble et al., 1997). Fourth, state vocational rehabilitation agencies often have failed to work cooperatively with mental health programs and other agencies that may be involved with their clients (Fabian et al., 2003; Noble et al., 1997). Fifth, vocational rehabilitation agencies focus on entry-level positions and do little to support advancing education and helping people build careers (O'Day & Killeen, 2002).

Many suggestions about ways to improve the services that people with mental illness receive through state vocational rehabilitation agencies have been offered. First, additional funding is needed so that vocational rehabilitation agencies can provide people with mental illness with the long-term resources that many need to obtain and maintain employment (Bond et al., 2001; Bond & Resnick, 2000). Second is to provide mental health training to vocational rehabilitation staff, as well as to provide training to mental health professionals about the availability and limitations of vocational rehabilitation services for their clients (Fabian et al., 2003). A third suggestion is to modify the incentive structure to encourage state vocational rehabilitation counselors to work with people with mental illness (Noble et al., 1997).

Ticket to Work

The Ticket to Work, a component of the federal Ticket to Work and Work Incentives Improvement Act of 1999, is a program that provides selected people with disabilities who are receiving SSI or SSDI with a ticket or voucher that they can use to purchase vocational, rehabilitation, or support services from an employment network to enhance their potential for employment. This program is voluntary for both people seeking services and service providers. If sufficient numbers of service providers choose to join the employment network, this program has the potential to increase the range of service choices for people with mental illness beyond what they have been able to receive through state vocational rehabilitation agencies. In fact, the Ticket to Work program was established, in part, in response to the failure of these agencies to meet the employment needs of people with mental illness (Knisley et al., 2003). The program is being phased in nationally over a 3-year period beginning in 2002.

One early process evaluation study of Ticket to Work, released in March 2003, reported that many potential providers were reluctant to join the employment network (Livermore et al., 2003). Potential providers cited a variety of reasons, including insufficient reimbursements for services provided; concern about their ability to be able to document clients' earnings over the extended amount of time required for reimbursement, which ranges from 9 months to 5 years, depending on the payment option they selected; and potential restrictions on their ability to mingle Ticket to Work funds with funds received from other sources. The report also indicated that only a small percentage of people who were eligible to obtain services through Ticket to Work actually used them, although it did not offer an explanation for this. By February 2003, 13,109 people had received tickets and had assigned them to agencies to receive services. This total represented far less than 1% of all eligible individuals in the states included in the first phase of implementation. Another criticism came from members of the President's New Freedom Commission of Mental Health (2003). They found the Ticket to Work program created financial disincentives for employment network providers to offer services to people with severe mental illness because, historically, they have been less likely to be leave SSI and SSDI for full-time employment than other disability groups. Because providers can choose the clients they will accept, commission members were concerned that people with severe mental illness would be underserved by Ticket to Work.

Mental Health System

The mental health system plays a vital role in promoting employment among people with mental illness. As their primary role, mental health programs provide the treatment and rehabilitation that many people with mental illness need in order to be able to work. Knisley et al. (2003) listed other important roles that state and local mental health authorities can play. These included employing people with mental illness in their own agencies; making referrals to vocational and employment support services; operating vocational and employment programs; funding or operating residential programs that include vocational components; planning or funding employment services; and serving a regulatory function by defining employment services as reimbursable, monitoring their implementation, and including employment as an important outcome measure.

Despite their potential, many people believe that mental health programs do not do enough to promote employment among their clients. Ware and Goldfinger (1997) argued that mental health programs in general, and the psychiatric rehabilitation field in particular, have not focused enough attention on issues of poverty. Bond et al. (2001) noted that community mental health centers devote only a very small percentage of their funds to employment services. Rapp (1998) believed that the mental health system itself was a barrier because it overrelied on vocational services it provided, rather than utilizing the wide range of services and employment opportunities that exist outside the mental health system. More specifically, Noble (1998) reported that mental health programs do not make sufficient numbers of referrals to state vocational rehabilitation programs. Finally, O'Day and Killeen (2002) found that mental health professionals, particularly psychiatrists, have not sufficiently encouraged their clients to test their boundaries of stress and explore vocational and employment options. In light of these criticisms, Bianco and Shaheen (2001) called upon mental health programs to make employment a priority and operationalize that priority by "articulating employment as a major component of its mission, seeking funding, establishing new partnerships, providing staff training, and dedicating resources" (p. 42). Despite the benefits of employment to clients' mental health and quality of life, many mental health organizations will be not be able to dedicate the resources needed to greatly influence the unemployment rates of their clients in this era of limited mental health funds and program closures. Many programs, instead, are focusing on what they believe their core mission to be, that is, providing psychiatric services.

Supported Education

In the U.S. labor market, having a college education greatly increases the chances of a person living outside of poverty. While some people with mental illness have a college education and advanced degrees, many others do not. For some, completing a college education is an important first step toward obtaining employment that is meaningful to them, that offers career opportunities, and that provides a reasonable standard of living. Some people, however, face substantial barriers to furthering their education. The results of one study of the experiences of colleges students who had mental illness are particularly enlightening (Megivern, Pellerito, & Mowbray, 2003). Almost half of the 35 students in the study reported an increase in symptoms that affected their school performance, including an inability to concentrate, fatigue, paranoia, hostility, irritable moods, and social isolation. Students who reported that psychiatric symptoms increased but did not interfere with their educational effort indicated that support from their psychiatrists, teachers, or study group partners was of great assistance. The 35 students in the study left and returned to school a total of 118 times.

Almost one third of the occurrences of leaving school were associated with psychiatric symptoms. Eleven of the 35 students eventually graduated after multiple enrollments. Most of the students did not disclose their mental illness to faculty, staff, or students. Most students also did not use campus counseling services or services from the disability office. Furthermore, they stated they received little support to further their education from their mental health workers.

To increase the chances of educational success, supported education is emerging as an important resource for at least some people with mental illness who are seeking to further their education (Mowbray, Brown, Furlong-Norman, & Soydan, 2000; Unger, 1998; Wells-Moran & Gilmur, 2002). Supported education seeks to improve their access to a college education and their retention in college programs. According to Unger (1998), supported education can consist of one or a combination of models. One model consists of a self-contained classroom on a college campus that includes only people with mental illness. The curriculum can consist of materials to orient its students to the college's educational requirements, career opportunities and their respective educational requirements, resources available on campus, working with faculty and other students, and adjusting to college life. Instructors, who can be employees of mental health programs or the college, continue to provide participants with encouragement and support as participants move into the general curriculum, if they choose to do so. A second approach is to provide on-campus support to people with mental illness enrolled in the regular curriculum that is provided through the college's disability office, through the college's counseling services, or by a community mental health provider who has an office on campus. A third approach is to provide mobile support, whereby a person with mental illness enrolls in a college of his or her choice, and a designated mental health professional provides support on campus or in other settings designated by the student. Regardless of the model used, one important issue is whether to officially disclose the presence of a mental illness in order to receive an accommodation under the Americans with Disabilities Act. Unger provided many examples of difficulties that people with mental illness may experience and the accompanying accommodations to address them. Students, for example, may receive assistance from college staff to register for classes, to apply for financial aid, or to select classes. As a second example, if taking notes and concentrating are problems, students may be able to take a symptom management class, attend a special study skills class, use a tape recorder in class, be assigned a note taker, obtain textbooks on tape, or get a tutor.

Title I of the Americans With Disabilities Act

The legislative intent of Title I of the ADA was to promote employment among people with disabilities, including those with mental illness.

Federal legislators passed it in recognition that employers' stigmatized views of people with mental illness and other disabilities unfairly prevented them from obtaining employment, when, in fact, they were capable of working the jobs for which they applied (Miller, 2000). While the law does not require that employers hire people with disabilities, it does seek to prevent discrimination based solely on disability. Employers are required to consider hiring applicants with disabilities and to provide reasonable work accommodations to assist them to carry out job functions. To receive work accommodations, people with mental illness must disclose their mental illness to employers and discuss the need for accommodations with them. This disclosure and discussion can take place at the time of hire or during the course of employment when symptoms arise that may require an accommodation to maintain employment.

Some have argued that the ADA has failed to achieve its purpose. For instance, the President's New Freedom Commission on Mental Health (2003) concluded, "The Americans with Disabilities Act (ADA) has not fulfilled its potential to prevent discrimination in the workplace. Workplace discrimination, either overt or covert, continues to occur" (p. 34). Similarly, Stefan (2002) wrote, "When it comes to psychiatric disabilities, it would be fair to conclude that the ADA has failed to provide a remedy against employment discrimination" (pp. 19–20). Several reasons account for this. First, Miller (2000) and Wilkinson and Frieden (2000) aptly pointed out there are inherent limitations to civil rights legislation affecting social attitudes and practices deeply engrained in culture, and the ADA is no exception. As such, one cannot expect that legislation alone can change employment practices, at least in the foreseeable future. Second, the ADA does not apply to businesses with less than 15 employees; consequently, it does not have jurisdiction over many employment opportunities. Third, some people with mental illness are unwilling to identify themselves as "being disabled," and as such, do not avail themselves to the protections that the ADA may offer them (Dalgin & Gilbride, 2003). Fourth, even if some people with mental illness are willing to accept the disability label, they still may choose not disclose their mental illness to their employers for a wide variety of reasons, which previously were discussed (Dalgin & Gilbride, 2003; Stefan, 2002).

Fifth, many people with a severe mental illness who disclose their illness may not have a disability under the ADA (Petrila & Brink, 2001). Court cases beginning in 1999 have greatly narrowed the definition of disability from its uncorrected state to its corrected state, the latter of which for people with mental illness may be, for instance, when symptoms are managed with medication. Petrila and Brink (2001) concluded, "Even the most serious mental illness might not be presumed to be a disability under the ADA. Instead, the individual must demonstrate specifically how the illness in its corrected state substantially limits major life activities" (p. 630). Finally, even if their mental illness is found to be a disability, the likelihood is small that people with mental illness will get a satisfactory resolve of their grievance if they choose to file a complaint. Among people with all disability types, Moss, Ullman, Starrett, Burris, and Johnsen (1999) found that only 15.7% of the complaints filed through March 31, 1998 resulted in some benefit to people who filed the complaint, and only 1.7% of the complaints resulted in being hired or reinstated into jobs. They also found that people with mental illness filed only a small percentage of all complaints (10.7%). Their benefit rate (13.6%) was slightly lower than that of all disability types, and people with schizophrenia had even lower benefit rates. Moss et al. (1999) cautioned that these data do not capture voluntary compliance by employers who chose to adopt nondiscriminatory practices based upon passage of the ADA, which is difficult to quantify. While the ADA is not a panacea for employment of people with mental illness, it provides a resource that should be considered carefully.

Family Medical Leave Act

Another federal law that may be a resource to employed people with mental illness is the Family Medical Leave Act (FMLA). FMLA requires employers to permit their employees to take to up to 12 weeks of unpaid medical leave each year if a serious medical condition arises that affects their ability to perform the job (Stefan, 2002). During their leave, employers must continue the employer's contribution to group health insurance coverage. When employees return from leave, employers must reinstate them in the former positions or in equivalent positions. Employees must work at the company for 1 year to be eligible for the leave. FMLA applies to all public organizations and most private businesses with 12 or more employees. In most instances, people with mental illness would be eligible to take unpaid leave under FMLA if their psychiatric symptoms became unmanaged to the level that they were unable to perform their job duties, as documented by a psychiatrist. FMLA is independent of the ADA. Even if employees with mental illness did not have disability as defined under the ADA, they still may be eligible for FMLA.

Social Support

Interpersonal relationships at work settings can be a source of both stress and support for anyone, including people with mental illness (Rollins et al., 2002). Positive social interactions and social supports within the workplace can be critically important to the employment success of people with mental illness (Banks et al., 2001). Ideally, those workplace social interactions occur naturally, either formally, such as

during new employee orientation, or informally, such as while coworkers celebrate an on-the-job success (Ford, 1995). Interventions may
be needed with the person with mental illness, the employer, or coworkers to establish social supports for those people with mental illness who are unable to do so themselves. This especially may be
necessary for employees diagnosed with schizophrenia, because they
are likely to have fewer positive social interactions with coworkers than
are those with other types of mental illness (Banks et al., 2001). Selected
coworkers may be willing to provide a range of workplace supports,
such as modeling workplace behaviors in specific situations, assisting
with completing tasks, providing task and skill training, evaluating
work performance and offering suggestions for improvement, and
advocating on the employee's behalf to supervisors and other coworkers (Ford, 1995). Social support also can be provided off work sites
by family members, friends, and mental health and vocational rehabilitation professionals. Finally, underutilized sources of support are
peer support and self-help services (Bianco & Shaheen, 2001; Ford, 1995).
Employees with mental illness, themselves, especially have noted the
value of peer support to their employment success (O'Day & Killeen,
2002).

Staff Resources

While the previously identified resources are for people with mental
illness, it is important to note that staff, too, may need resources to
support the employment of people with mental illness. Staff especially
needs training. Fabian et al. (2003) noted, for example, that mental health
professionals and vocational rehabilitation professionals need cross
training to better understand their respective areas of expertise and how
to work together to better support the employment of people with
mental illness. Both types of staff need to be educated about the capability of many people with mental illness to work and the importance of
employment to the recovery process. They also need training on how to
conduct vocational assessments specific to people with mental illness, to
use a strengths-based approach to employment planning and career
development, to work with employers to develop new job opportunities,
to understand the details of employment incentives and disincentives of
SSI and SSDI, and to provide on-site and off-site support services. These
are just a few of the training needs. Staff also need the time to meaningfully engage their clients in discussions of employment interests and
possibilities in order to ensure they have the information needed to make
informed choices about employment. Staff, too, need time away from
the office to work with their clients on the job sites, if necessary, to
provide the support clients need to maintain their employment.

Table 9.3 summarizes the various types of resources that support
people with mental illness obtaining or maintaining employment.

Table 9.3 Resources to Assist People With Severe Mental Illness to Obtain or Maintain Employment

Supported employment and other employment programs—Assist people to develop the confidence and employment skills and to obtain employment, and may provide ongoing supports to maintain employment.

State vocational rehabilitation agencies—Funded through an 80%-20% federal-state match, state vocational rehabilitation agencies provide counseling, vocational training, job development, and job placement, as well as purchase a range of educational and vocational resources from other providers, including supported employment.

Ticket to Work—A federal program that provides selected people with disabilities who are receiving SSI or SSDI with a ticket or voucher that they can use to purchase vocational, rehabilitation, or support services from an employment network to enhance their potential for employment.

Mental health programs—Provide the treatment and rehabilitation that many people need to be able to work, employ people with mental illness in their own agencies, make referrals to vocational and employment support services, operate vocational and employment programs, provide disability and employment information, discuss work incentives and disincentives, and give emotional support.

Supported education—Seeks to improve access to, and retention in, college programs. Can include information and emotional support provided on campus or in off-campus sites.

Title I of the Americans with Disabilities Act—Prevents employment discrimination based solely on disability. Employers are required to consider hiring applicants with disabilities and to provide reasonable work accommodations to assist them to carry out job functions. To receive work accommodations, people must disclose their mental illness to employers and discuss the need for accommodations with them.

Family Medical Leave Act—Requires employers to permit their employees to take to up to 12 weeks of unpaid medical leave each year if a serious medical condition that affects their ability to perform the job arises. During their leave, employers must continue their contribution to group health insurance coverage. When employees return from leave, employers must reinstate them in the former positions or in equivalent positions.

Social support—Deliberate on-site interventions may be needed with the person with mental illness, the employer, or coworkers to establish social supports. Social support also can be provided off work sites by family members, friends, mental health and vocational rehabilitation professionals, and peer support and self-help services.

SUPPORTIVE CULTURE

A final condition for empowering people with severe mental illness through employment is that the cultures of the work setting and of the mental health organization from which the person receives services are supportive of the employment of the person with mental illness.

The workplace culture is a significant factor in the success of employment of people with mental illness (Kirsh, 2000). Gilbride et al. (2003) identified seven characteristics of employment cultures that support the employment of people with disabilities:

1. Employers include people with disabilities with all workers and treat them equally.
2. Employers welcome diversity; they are egalitarian and inclusive.
3. Employers' management style is more personal and flexible.
4. Employers focus on a worker's performance, not his or her disability.
5. Senior management expects and rewards diversity.
6. Employers are comfortable providing accommodations to all their employees.
7. The organization provides "cafeteria style" benefits. (p. 133)

It takes time and strong leadership to overcome the stigma surrounding people with mental illness to develop a workplace culture that supports their employment, such as the one above.

The culture of the mental health organization from which people with mental illness receive services also significantly affects employment (Gowdy et al., 2003). Many people with mental illness have experienced a lack of support to pursue their vocational goals from mental health professionals (O'Day & Killeen, 2002; Secker, Grove, & Seebohm, 2001). A supportive mental health organization is one that establishes employment as a priority and includes it in its mission; that strongly believes in the potential of their clients to be employed, a belief that is held by all staff, not just employment staff; that openly engages in formal and informal conversations with their clients about their potential for employment and provides them with the information they need to make informed choices about employment; that uses research-based, best practice approaches; and that provides staff with the time and training to maximize employment opportunities for their clients (Bianco & Shaheen, 2001; Gowdy et al., 2003; Knisley et al., 2003). The development of such a culture is enhanced through the adoption of the recovery perspective and the strengths perspective (Anthony, 1993; Rapp, 1998; U.S. DHHS, 1999).

CASE STUDIES

To increase understanding of the opportunities for, and limitations to, the empowerment of people with mental illness through employment, empowerment is examined through two cases studies, one among people with mental illness residing in a public psychiatric hospital that provides long-term care and treatment, and the other among those residing in the community who are receiving services from a publicly funded community mental health agency.

Empowerment Among Clients in a Psychiatric Hospital (SLPRC)

Degree of Empowerment

Beginning in the mid-1990s, a small client work program at SLPRC was expanded, under the direction of a new hospital superintendent, to become an integral part of the range of treatment and rehabilitation services available to clients. At the time of the focus groups in 1998, 60% of the 240 clients were participating in some type of paid work activity. One client was employed part-time in the community, while the remaining clients were employed in a range of jobs on hospital grounds. The employment program continued to grow, and by mid-2004, approximately 80% of the 200 clients were engaged in some form of paid employment. On average, they worked 11 hours weekly, although the number of hours ranged from 7.5 to 19.5. Approximately 65% of the employed clients worked in a sheltered workshop operated on hospital grounds. The hospital had production contracts with a number of community businesses. As is common in sheltered workshops, clients were paid on the basis on their work productivity. Approximately 27% of other clients were integrated with hospital employees in a wide range of hospital departments, including accounting, dietary, housekeeping, quality management, and others. Clients were paid an hourly rate based upon the prevailing wage for that position within state government, which was at least the state's minimum wage. In some instances, selected clients actually received a higher hourly pay rate than the psychiatric aides who worked in their residential unit because the clients' positions were rated higher within the state merit system. The remaining 8% of employed clients worked in the community, either in vocational rehabilitation programs or in competitive part-time positions.

On one level, those clients who participated in paid employment experienced little, if any, objective empowerment. They worked only part-time while in the hospital and earned relatively small amounts of money; most clients never had the opportunity to work in the community while hospitalized; and few, if any, clients had full-time jobs arranged when they left the hospital. Within the context of living in a long-term hospital, however, some clients experienced objective empowerment to a limited degree. If clients did not have a source of income, the hospital provided them with $30 monthly that they could spend on items such as cigarettes, sodas, and snacks. For many clients, then, their employment resulted in a substantial increase in spendable income, which could have improved their quality of life while hospitalized. They used the increased funds from their employment for additional personal care items, for recreation, to start and maintain savings accounts for their use in the community when released from the hospital, and for other items. Some clients who worked also experienced subjective empowerment. These clients took great pride in their work, they learned new jobs skills, and they increased their confidence to be able to work when leaving the hospital; in addition, the hospital employment was the first time in many years that some clients had worked. Not all clients who worked, however, experienced subjective empowerment. For some, it merely was a way to pass the time and have some extra spending money. Clients who did not participate in employment experienced neither objective nor subjective empowerment.

Application of the Conditions for Empowerment

In relationship to the internal conditions for empowerment, for a limited number of clients, their psychiatric symptoms were so severe that they were unable to participate in any type of work activities. Most clients, however, were able manage their symptoms to engage in some type of employment. Many clients also lacked the range of skills required for employment. Various treatment and rehabilitation activities helped clients to develop skills that could be transferred to employment. Clients learned others skills on the job site, either from client work program staff in the sheltered workshop or from regular hospital employees in the various departments in which clients worked. In addition, many clients initially lacked the psychological readiness to work. For some of these clients, confidence in their potential to work increased as their severe psychiatric symptoms subsided and they made progress in other aspects of their treatment and rehabilitation. For others, seeing other clients work and reap the financial benefits was a motivating factor to participate in employment themselves.

With regard to environmental conditions, considerable mutual trust and respect existed between clients and client work program staff and between clients and nonclinical hospital employees. It developed quickly between clients and staff from the client work program. This staff exhibited strong leadership, believed in the ability of clients to work, and demonstrated a clear commitment to creatively maximize employment opportunities for clients. Clients observed this and trusted that staff would do everything to assist them to obtain their employment goals. It took more time, however, for hospital employees to trust and respect the clients who were assigned to work in their areas. Many employees had had limited contact, if any, with clients, and held society's stigmatized views of clients, particularly those related to fear of violence and perceptions of the hospitalized clients as being incapable of any type of productive activity. Trust and respect increased among hospital employees as they heard about positive experiences from employees in other departments and had the opportunity to work directly with clients in their own departments.

Concrete incentives for clients to want to work and for hospital employees to work with them did exist. From clients' perspective, employment increased spending money, it was an opportunity to test and develop vocational skills, and it offered hope that they could be employable when they returned to life in the community. For NGRI clients, the fact that they were employed, either at the hospital or in the community, was viewed positively by criminal court judges when clients sought conditional releases to return to the community. Hospital employees also had concrete incentives to work with clients. Most hospital departments had sizeable staff reductions in recent years during the state's budget crisis. While client labor was never a sizable portion of the workforce within departments, many of the departments came to recognize the valuable contribution that clients made. The hospital's clinical staff also had incentives to support client employment. Many staff observed the positive influence that employment had on clients' psychiatric symptoms, level of functioning, and confidence.

Clients' employment choices were limited, of course, by being hospitalized. Some clients could not get the approval of legal guardians, or overseeing criminal court judges in the case of NGRI clients, to avail themselves to employment opportunities in the community. Choices also were limited in the hospital. Clients and staff in many of the focus groups identified the need to expand employment options. Subsequently, some success has been achieved in recent years to increase the number of work opportunities in regular hospital departments. The client work program was a vital employment structure. All educational and employment activities flowed through that program. Its staff offered clients educational and vocational assessment and prevocational programs, operated the sheltered workshops, served as liaisons to hospital departments where clients worked, trained hospital employees to supervise client workers in their departments, provided basic educational courses, assisted clients to apply for grants and take college courses, and facilitated clients' involvement with the state vocational rehabilitation agency either during hospitalization or as they prepared for discharge into the community.

Despite severe cutbacks in financial resources experienced in recent years by all Missouri Department of Mental Health psychiatric hospitals and community mental health programs, the hospital was able to retain a core group of client work program staff. However, it has not always been able to provide all the services it normally offered on an ongoing basis. For example, the program employed a special education teacher to run the educational testing and remedial education programs, but when the employee retired, the hospital was unable to refill the position, and education programs had to be greatly curtailed. The client work program has tried to creatively develop new resources. For instance, to increase the number of clients who took college classes, the client work program assisted clients to apply for federal grants to pay for community college courses that were offered over the local public television station. Staff accompanied client students to the college bookstore to buy their books and supplies and to take the midterm and final examinations, which must be done on campus. Because staff went with clients, it was not necessary for NGRI clients to get a court order to allow them to participate. In the spring of 2004, for instance, three NGRI clients took college courses through this avenue. The client work program also was exploring the possibility of helping students to access online college courses through the Internet to further increase their educational options.

Finally, since the mid-1990s, the hospital culture has progressed slowly to one that now values and supports the employment of clients. Clients now expect there to be a range of employment opportunities, and departments, for the most part, welcome client workers and appreciate their contribution. This culture was promoted, in part, by the adoption of psychiatric rehabilitation as a model to guide treatment and rehabilitation, by strong leadership from executive staff, and by client work program and many clinical staff who recognized the contribution work made to the recovery of SLPRC clients.

Empowerment Among Clients of a Community Agency (BJC-BH)

Degree of Empowerment

A survey of BJC-BH clients conducted in 2002 found that 75% were not employed; 15% were competitively employed without support services; 6% were sporadically employed; 3% were involved in employment-related activities such as supported employment, sheltered workshops, or volunteer work; and less than 1% were retired and not seeking employment. Anecdotal evidence suggested that some BJC-BH clients had careers that paid them a livable income. Other clients worked full-time in low-paying jobs that kept them in poverty. Still other clients received SSI or SSDI, and they occasionally tried to work part-time to increase their income but had little hope that they ever would work full-time and end their disability payments. Finally, another group of clients had not worked in many years and had no intention of attempting to work. As such, the degree of clients' objective empowerment varied with job status. Those clients who worked full-time, especially in higher paying career positions, likely experienced higher degrees of objective empowerment, while other clients who worked part-time or who did not work experienced little, if any, objective empowerment through employment. Some clients who worked also may have experienced a degree of subjective empowerment from their employment, regardless of the amount and type of employment, particularly when they viewed it as part of the recovery process.

Application of Conditions for Empowerment

The mental illness of at least some BJC-BH clients was too unmanaged to permit them to work. Some clients also lacked the social skills, the communication skills, the problem-solving skills, or the educational skills to work. In addition, some clients lacked the motivation and confidence to work. Even when clients aspired to work, many did not follow through with steps needed to begin the employment process. One BJC-BH employment specialist estimated that clients did not show up for 40% of appointments. Some clients and staff discussed the substantial disincentives for employment that were associated with the potential loss of SSDI, SSI, and health benefits should they be unable to maintain employment. They held these perceptions despite recent changes to these programs to decrease work disincentives. Some clients and staff also discussed the limited job opportunities open to clients, particularly those jobs that would result in an improved income beyond that which disability income and other social services could provide.

BJC-BH had an established structure to promote employment among its clients. The agency staff included five employment specialists who were dispersed across its four offices. Their function was to explore with clients options for employment, training, and education; to discuss the benefits and risks of employment; to refer clients to other vocational resources; to help clients to locate jobs; and to provide employment supports to some clients. BJC-BH, itself, was a recognized vendor of supported employment services. Employment specialists helped clients to access a wide range of resources. They referred some clients to BJC-BH entitlement specialists, and others directly to the local social security administration office, to discuss in detail the effect of employment on their income and support benefits. They also had excellent working relationships with the local state vocational rehabilitation agency. Many times, in fact, vocational rehabilitation workers interviewed clients at the BJC-BH office to facilitate clients' ease of access to their services. Some clients also participated in prevocational and employment-related activities through psychosocial rehabilitation centers. Still other clients chose volunteer work as a way to explore and improve their employment skills.

The culture of BJC-BH reflected the ambiguity of employment of people with mental illness that exists in the United States and many other countries. On the one hand, BJC-BH valued and attempted to promote employment among its clients. This was exemplified by adopting the recovery perspective and the psychiatric rehabilitation model, both of which support employment; by funding five positions dedicated entirely to facilitating client employment; and by identifying engagement in meaningful, productive employment-related activities as a desired client outcome. On the other hand, variability existed in the rate at which case managers promoted employment among their clients. Some case managers apparently discussed employment with clients only when clients, themselves, raised the issue, rather than engaging clients in a discussion that it could be a viable option for them. Similarly, rates of referral of clients to employment specialists varied widely among case managers.

GUIDELINES FOR PROMOTING EMPOWERMENT THROUGH EMPLOYMENT

As is discussed, many people with severe mental illness *do* work, and many others *can* work when certain conditions are met. The following guidelines were derived from the previous discussion of the application of the conditions for empowering people with mental illness through employment:

1. *Understand the relationship between psychiatric symptoms and employment.* Psychiatric diagnoses and level of symptoms are poor predictors of employment success. Many people with severe mental illness who experience symptoms can, and do, work. Employment can cause an increase in symptoms, but it also can promote recovery, increase medication compliance, improve functioning, reduce substance abuse, and foster social relationships.
2. *Overcome skill deficits.* Skill deficits can be overcome by carefully matching individuals' skill levels to particular jobs, or by improving skills through participation in psychiatric rehabilitation, vocational programs, or college education. People with mental illness in long-term hospitals should receive skill development applicable to employment, and should have opportunities for employment while hospitalized.
3. *Assist clients to develop the confidence and motivation to work.* Many people with mental illness have accepted the stigmatized view that they are incapable of employment. Actions to promote readiness for employment include initiating open discussions of the benefits and risks to employment, encouraging some clients to participate in volunteer work or clubhouse programs as a way to test and develop their work skills, listening to clients' job preferences and working with them to obtain those jobs, and celebrating and publicizing clients' employment successes.
4. *Discuss the incentives and disincentives to employment.* Such open discussions should include up-to-date information on

the effect of employment on disability income and medical benefits, as well as the potential of employment to promote recovery or increase symptoms and to increase individuals' social networks and self-esteem or further isolate them.

5. *Advocate for social policies that create incentives and remove disincentives to employment.* These include modifications to SSDI and especially to SSI to further remove disincentives and extend medical benefits, financial incentives to employers to hire people with mental illness, and publicity about the employability of people with mental illness to lessen the effects of stigma.

6. *Promote access to a range of job choices that are meaningful to them.* Rather than focusing on simply getting jobs, people with mental illness should have access to jobs that pay livable wages and lift them out of poverty, have benefits, and offer career opportunities. This will require that mental health advocates join broad-based coalitions to advocate for social policies that promote employment opportunities for all Americans, as well as advocating for social policies and programs that specifically benefit people with mental illness.

7. *Take advantage of resources that promote employment.* These may include resources made available through state vocational rehabilitation agencies and mental health programs, as well as the community resources available to all people who seek employment.

8. *Consider increasing education as a means to career development.* Many people with mental illness will not be able to rise out of poverty unless they obtain additional formal education or vocational training. Supported education services should be made available to those who need and want them.

9. *Make supported employment services available.* Research has found that of all the employment models, supported employment most frequently results in obtaining and maintaining permanent, competitive employment.

10. *Make available a range of employment structures and processes.* For those people who are not ready or willing to engage in supported employment, a range of other employment structures and processes should be available to them. These may include transitional employment positions, consumer businesses and self-employment, social enterprises, modified sheltered workshops, and volunteer work.

11. *Establish social supports to promote and sustain employment.* Supports can be provided formally or informally on job sites by employers and coworkers, or off-site by mental health or vocational rehabilitation professionals, family members, or

friends. An underutilized resource is peer support, which can be provided through a range of informal and formal means.

12. *Discuss the benefits and risks of disclosing one's mental illness to employers and coworkers.* People with mental illness need to understand the potential benefits and risks to disclosure of their mental illness, and the circumstances under which disclosure may be most beneficial with the least amount of risk. This includes, but is not limited to, disclosing one's mental illness to seek work accommodations under Title I of the ADA and unpaid leave under the FMLA when psychiatric symptoms arise.

13. *Provide resources to staff.* Mental health and state vocational rehabilitation staff need a range of resources to facilitate employment. Especially needed is training in a wide range of areas. Staff members also need the time to engage their clients in meaningful conversations about aspects of employment and to provide support services when needed.

14. *Establish workplace cultures that support the employment of people with mental illness.* This includes the culture of the site at which people are employed, as well as the culture of the mental health organization from which people receive services. A supportive culture within mental health organizations establishes employment as a priority, strongly believes in the potential of clients to be employed, openly engages in formal and informal conversations with clients about their potential for employment, uses best practice approaches to employment, and provides staff with the time and training to maximize employment opportunities for its clients.

10

Empowerment Through Research

Research, for the purposes of this chapter, refers to the systematic study of social phenomenon. Stages in this process include identifying a research question; developing the research design, including deciding what data to collect and how to collect it; collecting the data; analyzing and interpreting the data; disseminating findings; and, in some instances, facilitating action based on the results. This depiction of research refers to four types of activities. One type is basic research, which essentially is research to increase knowledge without a particular application, such as understanding how people with severe mental illness subjectively experience recovery, in mind at the time of the study. A second type is applied research, which is research conducted with a specific purpose, such as gaining a better understanding of the stigma toward people with mental illness in order to develop educational programs to reduce it, in mind. A third type is evaluation research, which seeks to understand the operation of, or identify the outcomes resulting from, a particular social policy, program, or intervention in order to improve performance or assess its success. Examples of evaluation questions include whether the passage of mental health insurance parity legislation in a state resulted in more people receiving mental health services; why case managers were referring few clients to the agency's supported employment program; and whether participation in self-help groups affected psychiatric hospitalizations, level of functioning, or quality of life among a sample of people with mental illness. A fourth type of research is performance improvement, which uses techniques of continuous quality improvement or total quality

management to monitor important organizational activities and outcomes in order to improve organizational performance. One example is
monitoring the rates of restraint use in a psychiatric hospital, and then,
if rates were determined to be outside of acceptable parameters,
studying the process and making changes to reduce them.

People with severe mental illness, historically, have not been involved in research, except possibly as research subjects, that is, researchers collected information from them or about them. Over the past
several decades, however, some people with mental illness have begun
to participate in multiple stages of the research process, and, in some
instances, have led research projects themselves (Campbell, 1997; Linhorst & Eckert, 2002; Rapp et al., 1993). This increased involvement is
associated, in part, with the advent of the mental health consumer
movement and the development of new models of evaluation. As
people with mental illness have assumed greater participation in their
treatment and the organizations from which they received services,
it was a logical progression to seek greater participation in research-
related activities (Beresford & Evans, 1999). At about the same time as
the consumer movement developed, new models of research, evaluation, and performance improvement that included powerless populations in multiple stages of the process evolved. These models included
participatory action research (Whyte, 1991), utilization-focused evaluation (Patton, 1997), empowerment evaluation (Fetterman, 2001), and
continuous quality improvement and total quality management (Mason & Soreff, 1996).

The potential for empowerment through participation in research
increasingly has been recognized and discussed for people with mental
illness and others (Beresford & Evans, 1999; Dullea & Mullender, 1999;
Evans & Fisher, 1999; Fleming & Ward, 1999). It is empowering, in
part, because it allows people to speak for themselves, to choose to
investigate those areas that are important to them, and to evaluate and
improve policies and services that affect them. Disagreement as to
when people with mental illness are empowered through research
exists. Evans and Fisher (1999), for instance, emphasized the importance of people with mental illness serving as researchers and controlling the research process. They wrote, "We argue for recognition
of the role of service users as researchers in their own right, not merely
as participants in research processes designed by professionals, and for
the role of user controlled research as a means of increasing the power
of service users over the way their experiences are defined" (p. 349).
Similarly, Carrick, Mitchell, and Lloyd (2001) identified three levels of
research involvement, with the degree of empowerment varying by the
type of involvement. The types of involvement included consultation,
where researchers ask the opinions of people with mental illness about

the research process; collaboration, which is a partnership between the researcher and people with mental illness wherein power is shared; and user-controlled research, where people with mental health involve professionals in specific aspects of the research process only if they choose to do so. They concluded that user-controlled research was most empowering and consultation was least empowering. Others have noted, however, that simply being able to share one's story as a research subject without participating in other stages of the research process can itself be empowering (Hutchinson, Wilson, & Wilson, 1994; Linhorst, 2002a; Peled & Leichtentritt, 2002; Sullins, 2003). Still others view the empowerment potential of research as existing on a continuum. Beresford and Evans (1999) identified eight aspects of the research process (e.g., origins of research and benefits from research) and provided a continuum of involvement for each, ranging from most empowering to not empowering. From their perspective, empowerment increases as consumers increasingly control each aspect of the research process.

While people with mental illness have increased their involvement in research in recent years, few examples exist of people with mental illness controlling the research process (Evans & Fisher, 1999). Instead, most people with mental illness continue to rely on those directing the research process to invite them to participate in one or more research stages and to share power with them. Even when researchers invite people with mental illness to participate in the research process, they may intentionally or unintentionally exert control (Dullea & Mullender, 1999; Mason & Boutilier, 1996). In addition, people with mental illness may experience feelings of powerlessness if they assumed that participation in the research process would lead to a change in circumstances, when, in fact, it did not (Linhorst, 2002a; Race, Hotch, & Packer, 1994; Townsend, Birch, Langley, & Langille, 2000). Finally, more than just not being empowered through research, people with mental illness have a long history of being coerced into participating in research and experiencing other unethical research practices (Dresser, 2001). Dresser (2001) and Peled and Leichtentritt (2002) highlight the importance of continuing to ensure that research with people with mental illness is conducted in an ethical manner.

Carrick et al. (2001) took a realistic view of empowerment through participation in research. "I believe the research process should empower where possible, and at the very least should not disempower" (p. 220). Application of the conditions for empowerment provides direction for determining how to empower, and how not to disempower, people with mental illness through research. Table 10.1 includes the conditions for empowerment as they apply to empowerment through research.

Table 10.1 Conditions for Empowering People With Severe Mental Illness Through Research

Managed psychiatric symptoms—The person's psychiatric symptoms are managed to the degree necessary to meaningfully participate in a specific research process.

Participation skills—The person possesses the necessary skills to meaningfully participate in a specific research process.

Psychological readiness—The person has the confidence, motivation, and willingness to meaningfully participate in a specific research process.

Mutual trust and respect—The person with mental illness and any researchers without mental illness with whom they may work have the necessary level of mutual trust and respect to meaningfully participate together in a research process.

Reciprocal concrete incentives—Concrete incentives exist for the person with mental illness to participate in research processes and for researchers and other participants to meaningfully work with him or her.

Availability of choices—The person has choices of research processes in which to meaningfully participate.

Participation structures and processes—The person has structures and processes through which to meaningfully participate in a research process.

Access to resources—The person has access to the resources needed to meaningfully participate in a research process.

Supportive culture—The culture surrounding the research process is supportive of the meaningful participation of the person with mental illness.

MANAGED PSYCHIATRIC SYMPTOMS

One condition for empowering people with severe mental illness through research is that the person's psychiatric symptoms are managed to the degree necessary to meaningfully participate in a specific research process. Participation as a research subject, as well as in other aspects of the research process such as analyzing and interpreting data and report writing, require that people be able to concentrate, to process information, and to make logical decisions. Severe psychiatric symptoms can limit these cognitive processes. In addition, the experience of participation in research can be stressful and lead to the onset of symptoms. Boothroyd (2000) surveyed people with mental illness who had provided information as part of an evaluation of a behavioral health managed care program and found that almost 9% reported feeling anxious as a result of participation. He also found that people who were experiencing higher levels of symptoms at the time of the study reported higher anxiety levels. Also, Morrell-Bellai and Boydell (1994) presented a case study of six people with mental illness who administered questionnaires as part of a research project. Two of the six individuals were unable to complete the data collection process because of the onset of symptoms and directly related those symptoms to their research participation. Similarly, Reeve, Cornell, D'Costa, Janzen, and Ochocka (2002) reported that their research project included three research assistants who had mental illness and were involved in all stages of the research process. One of the three research assistants had to be hospitalized during the project because of an increase in psychiatric symptoms.

While research participation can produce psychiatric symptoms in some individuals, many people with mental illness view the research experience positively and believe it can promote their recovery. In the Boothroyd (2000) study introduced in the previous paragraph, greater than 91% of participants did not experience any anxiety from providing information in the study, 96% reported their experience was positive, and 86% said they would participate in a similar research project again. In the above Morrell-Bellai and Boydell (1994) study, the four participants who completed the project stated they believed the experience had promoted their recovery, as did all three participants in the Reeve et al. (2002) study. The consumer researchers from the two studies experienced a great sense of accomplishment for their participation, during which they did not experience symptoms they could not manage. The experience even was positive for the one consumer researcher in the Reeve et al. study who was hospitalized. He experienced his shortest hospitalization ever and was able to rejoin the project. Reeve et al. described the challenge to involving people with mental illness in research and being mindful of the potential for symptoms. "It's a balance between empowering and giving responsibility to consumers, without overwhelming them" (p. 408). Stress that can lead to the onset of severe psychiatric symptoms can be minimized by providing people with the skills needed to succeed, by providing encouragement and emotional support, and by conducting research in a supportive culture, all of which will be discussed in upcoming conditions for empowerment.

PARTICIPATION SKILLS

A second condition for empowerment is that the person possesses the skills necessary to meaningfully participate in a specific research process. Researchers need a range of interpersonal and technical skills. They first need to be able to effectively communicate and interact with the research subjects; with other researchers involved in the project; and others related to the project, such as funders and administrators. They also need the technical skills to write research proposals, to design research studies, to analyze data, and to write reports (Townend & Braithwaite, 2002). Some people with mental illness will obtain these skills through graduate school education, and, indeed, there are a growing number of highly trained and educated researchers who have a severe mental illness (Kaufmann, 1996). Most people, with or without a mental illness, never will achieve this level of research training. It is possible, however, to provide skill training to enable many people to meaningfully participate in most, if not all, of the stages of the research process. Fetterman (1996), for instance, argued that powerless people can learn the basic skills required to conduct evaluations if provided with the proper training and support. Morrell-Bellai and Boydell (1994) offered this advice when hiring research assistants who have mental illness. "Consumer-employees require adequate training and remuneration, feedback on their performance, and opportunities to provide input and effect decision making. . . . In the event that they have little or no previous research experience, the work should be presented as a training experience" (pp. 105–106). Ochocka, Janzen, and Nelson (2002) described the training provided to three people with mental illness who had no research experience and were part of a research team along with two university professors and two student research assistants. The university professors initially provided the consumer research assistants with formal training sessions on many different topics, such as the type of evaluation approach they were employing in the study, how to conduct interviews with research subjects, and methods of analyzing data. Much of the training occurred, though, informally as on-the-job training as the research project was taking place. Time was built into the research process to allow this to happen.

PSYCHOLOGICAL READINESS

A third condition for empowerment is that the person has the psychological readiness, that is, the confidence, motivation, and willingness to meaningfully participate in a specific research process. Many people with mental illness will lack the confidence to be research subjects, and especially to participate in other stages of the research process as a researcher. If they have internalized stigmatized views of mental illness, they, themselves, may believe their views have no value, and that they are incapable of learning how to participate in the research process, even with training. They also may have experienced repeated failures in completing tasks and, consequently, may lack the confidence to become involved in something seemingly as daunting as research. Others may be unwilling to participate because they believe that mental heath professionals or professional researchers should be responsible for such undertakings (Dullea & Mullender, 1999). Finally, people may be so overwhelmed with the tasks of daily living that participation in research is not a priority, regardless of the benefits they may receive directly or indirectly (Sullins, 2003).

To become psychologically ready to participate in research, many people with mental illness will need an explanation of what research is, what roles they can play in the process, and what they have to contribute. Offers of training, open discussions of the potentially positive and negative effects of involvement on psychiatric symptoms, and the provision of emotional support may be needed before some people will be willing to take a chance on becoming involved in a research project. Dullea and Mullender (1999) stressed the importance of timing to the engagement of people in research. They recommended initiating a call for research participation when an issue of genuine concern has arisen for which the systematic collection of data may add to the discussion. Finally, Townsend et al. (2000) summed up their approach to getting people with mental illness psychologically ready to participate in research as "invitation, encouragement, and guidance" (p. 35).

MUTUAL TRUST AND RESPECT

A fourth condition for empowerment is that the person with mental illness and any researchers or other participants without mental illness with whom they work have the necessary level of mutual trust and respect to meaningfully participate together in the research process. People with mental illness are more likely to agree to serve as research subjects when they respect the abilities of the researchers and they trust the researcher to maintain confidentiality, if that is an issue, and to use the information for the purposes described to them. Similarly, people with mental illness are more likely to serve as researchers when they trust and respect those with whom they will be working to share power and meaningfully involve them in the research process, and to provide them with the training and support needed to make a meaningful contribution. Researchers without a mental illness must respect the contribution that people with mental illness can make as research participants and as researchers, and trust them to contribute to the best of their ability. Campbell (1997) highlighted the importance of mutual trust and respect. "Mental health consumers have moved rapidly to be involved in the design and implementation of quality management in psychiatric systems of care. The growth and acceptance of such partnerships in accountability over the last decade show the potential for progress when researchers and consumers/survivors work together in relationships of mutuality and respect" (p. 361). Morrell-Bellai and Boydell (1994) stated the result when mutual trust and respect do not exist. "Even when consumers are paid for their involvement, the experience can be very disempowering if they are not viewed as equals by their professional co-workers" (p. 99).

The adoption of particular models of research, evaluation, and performance improvement helps to promote mutual trust and respect among participants. These models include participatory action research (Whyte, 1992), utilization-focused evaluation (Patton, 1997), empowerment evaluation (Fetterman, 2001), and continuous quality improvement and total quality management (Mason & Soreff, 1996). While these models differ in some regards, all support the belief that everyone involved in a particular issue, problem, or program has something meaningful to contribute to the research and resolution processes. Dullea and Mullender (1999) summarized this belief in relationship to one of these models. "Participatory [action] research is based on the belief that people can do research. They are capable of gathering data, analysing them, and using them to take action based on the research findings, even in a world where what constitutes knowledge is normally defined by the 'experts' " (p. 84).

These models also place the responsibility to facilitate an atmosphere of mutual trust and respect in the research process on the lead researcher. Nelson, Ochocka, Griffin, and Lord (1998) provided general means whereby such an atmosphere is created. These include recognizing members' contributions; sharing power in the research process; and acknowledging that expertise is created, in part, by the lived experiences of people with mental illness. Ochocka et al. (2002) offered these additional suggestions: Researchers should avoid research jargon when possible, promote discussion and actively listen to everyone's opinion, openly negotiate differences of opinion, and seek consensus when possible. Consumer research assistants who worked on a study as part of a team with university researchers and college students articulated how they experienced this process (Reeve et al., 2002). "It was very empowering to be asked about my opinions and positions. The leaders shared the power through seeking consensus and including all team members in decision-making. It was a work environment that respected and responded to differences among team members. It became a team effort, not dictated by a director" (p. 406). Another consumer research assistant stated, "I felt I was empowered to play an important role in forming the interview questions. I felt I was a valued partner. If I had concerns, I could raise them; and not only just raise them, but the concerns would be taken seriously as well. Often, people would thank me for my comments" (p. 406). Such successful efforts to promote mutual trust and respect took time and substantial effort. As Ochocka et al. (2002) noted, "Our process of relationship building was slow and incremental, continuously nurtured and occasionally tested. Through open and honest communication, disagreements and frictions were overcome" (p. 384).

RECIPROCAL CONCRETE INCENTIVES

A fifth condition for empowerment is that concrete incentives exist for the person with mental illness to participate in research processes and for researchers and other participants to meaningfully work with him or her. At least seven concrete incentives for people with mental illness to participate in research exist. The type of benefit will vary, in part, by whether the person is a research subject or a researcher. One concrete incentive is that research participation gives people a voice to share their experiences and to express their needs (Evans & Fisher, 1999; Hutchinson et al., 1994). This sharing, among other things, can lead to an improvement in the quality of mental health services they receive (Boll, 1995). A second incentive is that participation may permit people with mental illness to set a research agenda that is meaningful to them. One study found, for example, that many of the research priorities of people with mental illness were in areas where current research was limited (Thornicroft, Rose, Huxley, Dale, & Wykes, 2002). A third incentive for participation is the possibility of experiencing increased self-esteem, empowerment, and enjoyment for participating in a meaningful activity (Hutchinson et al., 1994; Morrell-Bellai & Boydell, 1994; Reeve et al., 2002). A fourth incentive is that participation can promote recovery and personal development (Hutchinson et al., 1994; Morrell-Bellai & Boydell, 1994; Reeve et al., 2002; Townend & Briathwaite, 2002). A fifth incentive is that participation as a researcher will likely result in learning new skills, including vocational skills (Morrell-Bellai & Boydell, 1994; Reeve et al., 2002). A sixth incentive is that people may be paid for their participation (Morrell-Bellai & Boydell, 1994). Research subjects may be paid a small stipend of $10 or $20, for instance, for contributing information. People with mental illness who are researchers may be able to earn a full-time, livable wage from this activity. Others may earn less but still receive competitive wages. For example, the three people with mental illness who worked as research assistants with university researchers and graduate students earned the same amount of money as the graduate students (Reeve et al., 2002). Finally, Carrick et al. (2001) identified that some people with mental illness participate in research for altruistic reasons, knowing that the research eventually may improve knowledge about mental illness or mental health services.

People with mental illness also have disincentives to participate in research. One disincentive is the fear of experiencing increased psychiatric symptoms, although as previously discussed, many people with mental illness will not experience increased, unmanageable symptoms (Boothroyd, 2000; Morrell-Bellai & Boydell, 1994; Reeve et al., 2002). Second, people with mental illness participating in evaluation and performance improvement projects associated with the organization from which they are receiving mental health services may be concerned that any information they share that reflects negatively on the organization, or specific individuals within it, may not be kept confidential, and, as a result, they may experience negative repercussions. Finally, while many people with mental illness may be willing to serve as a research participant for altruistic reasons, some will be unwilling to do so if they do not see a direct benefit to their participation (Carrick et al., 2001). This is particularly likely to occur when people with mental illness participated previously in research that failed to result in the changes they anticipated (Linhorst, 2002a; Race et al., 1994; Townsend et al., 2000).

Researchers without mental illness and others who may be involved in the research process also have concrete incentives to work with people with mental illness on research projects. One incentive is to meet accreditation standards. Bodies that accredit mental health organization, such as the Commission on Accreditation of Rehabilitation Facilities, the Joint Commission on the Accreditation of Healthcare Organizations, and the National Committee for Quality Assurance, require evidence that organizations are involving their clients in quality management and performance improvement activities (Fox, 2000). This requirement typically can be met by their clients serving as research subjects, rather than being involved in other stages of the research process. A second incentive is that participation in research by people with mental illness can result in improved service delivery (Boll, 1995; Fox, 2000). Such participation can help to clarify the mission and goals of the organization, improve the quality of the service delivered, and make the service more responsive to changing client needs. A final incentive is that participation of people with mental illness throughout the research process can improve the quality of the research (Morrell-Bellai & Boydell, 1994; Rogers & Palmer-Erbs, 1994; Townend & Braithwaite, 2002). Such involvement especially can maximize the quality of information received from participants and reduce errors in data analysis and interpretation by providing a view of the data from the perspectives of people both with and without mental illness.

Potential disincentives for involving people with mental illness also exist throughout the research process. One disincentive is the added time it takes to meaningfully involve them. It can take substantial amounts of time to properly train people for specific tasks within the research process, to provide them with emotional support, and to meaningfully involve them in decision making. A second disincentive for some researchers is the relinquishing of at least some of their power in the research process. They must be willing, as Beresford and Evans (1999) phrased it, to work "with" people with mental illness rather than "on" them (p. 673).

Townend and Braithwaite (2002) believed that the benefits of the participation of people with mental illness far outweigh any disincentives. They wrote, "We argue that service user researchers are essential to the future evolution of mental health research and the practice developments that should arise from its findings. Users must be recognized as drivers, designers and deliverers of research if the desired outcome is to improve the quality of people's lives" (p. 119). Taking it one step further, Carrick et al. (2001) argued that to maximize their own benefits, people with mental illness and researchers need each other. "Scientific rigour is of little value if results are unintelligible or irrelevant to the users that they are supposed to help. But without the trained researcher's scientific rigour results risk being uninterpretable and are less likely to be brought to a wider audience including those who may be able to affect useful change" (p. 224).

AVAILABILITY OF CHOICES

A sixth condition for empowerment is that the person has choices of research processes in which to meaningfully participate. Throughout this chapter, having the choice of participation in multiple stages of the research process and not just as research subjects, which many researchers and mental health advocates support, has been stressed (Beresford & Evans, 1999; Evans & Fisher, 1999; Fleming & Ward, 1999; Ochocka et al., 2002; Townend & Braithwaite, 2002). This section discusses each of the research stages and the roles that people with mental illness can play in them (Linhorst & Eckert, 2002). Many people who are highly trained researchers that lead independent research and evaluation projects have a mental illness (Kaufmann, 1996). Most people with mental illness, however, will be collaborators with researchers and other participants in the research and will be involved in evaluation and performance improvement associated with the organizations from which they receive services. It is from the perspective of people with mental illness serving as collaborators in evaluation and performance improvement that the stages of the research process are discussed.

Pose Evaluation Questions

At least two benefits exist when people with mental illness are able to pose questions for evaluation and performance improvement. First and foremost, the focus of evaluation may change (Corrigan & Garman, 1997). People with mental illness bring unique perspectives to the identification and definition of problems (Thornicroft et al., 2002). Second, people with mental illness are more likely to accept ownership of organizational problems and work toward viable solutions when they can raise questions and actively participate in the evaluation process (Boll, 1995). The formal process of evaluation and performance improvement then can become a feasible alternative through which to raise organizational concerns.

People with mental illness can initiate evaluation questions on their own if they are knowledgeable of the evaluation or performance improvement processes and have a structure for communicating their ideas. Researchers or professional staff sometimes, though, may need to work with them to identify areas for evaluation. Townsend et al. (2000) indicated that this can happen by reframing statements made by consumers into research questions, such as "What interests me is..." or "We need to find a way to convince the government (community, others) that our housing (employment, etc.) programs make a difference..." (p. 27). Boll (1995) provided an example in which a committee of three consumers and two staff in a psychosocial rehabilitation center developed a list of evaluation questions and then worked together as an evaluation team to gather data, analyze the findings, and implement corrective action. In addition, Rapp et al. (1993) advocated for the use of focus groups to help people with mental illness develop research and evaluation questions.

Develop the Evaluation Design

People with mental illness are capable of providing input into the design of evaluation and performance improvement efforts (Beresford & Evans, 1999; Boll, 1995; Durbin, Goering, Wasylenki, & Roth, 1995; Koch, Lewis, & McCall, 1998). Their level of contribution will depend, in part, on their research knowledge, experience, and skill levels. In outcome studies, for example, people with mental illness may not be able to make significant contributions to discussions of study design, such as those about whether to use pre-experimental, quasi-experimental, or experimental designs. They may be able to contribute, however, to the discussion of which outcomes to measure and how to measure them. Their involvement may be most useful in the logistical and pragmatic aspects of evaluation design, such as pretesting data collection instruments, planning for the recruitment of evaluation participants, and selecting optimal times for data collection.

Collect Data

The most typical role for people with mental illness in the evaluation process has been to provide information as "subjects" in the data collection process. For example, they may complete consumer satisfaction questionnaires, provide outcome data, offer their perspectives in process evaluations, or have their medical records reviewed. In addition to this important role, many people with mental illness can collect data or at least assist with the data collection process (Boll, 1995; Rapp et al., 1993; Townsend et al., 2000). Depending on the evaluation methods employed, people with mental illness can perform a variety of tasks. They may be able to serve as interviewers, which can increase response rates and improve the quality of the data collected (Durbin et al., 1995; Morrell-Bellai & Boydell, 1994). They also may be able to distribute and collect written questionnaires. In addition, they may be able to assist respondents who have difficulty reading or understanding written questionnaires complete them. Finally, they may be able to enter results into computerized databases or type out transcripts of recorded interviews.

Analyze and Interpret Data

Data analysis and interpretation is the stage of the evaluation process in which one attempts to understand and draw conclusions from the data. Involving people with mental illness in this process helps to avoid errors in interpretation and results in a more comprehensive portrayal of the subject matter (Morrell-Bellai & Boydell, 1994). As with evaluation design, the role played by people with mental illness will vary by the type of evaluation and by their knowledge and skill levels. In quantitative outcome evaluations, some people with mental illness may have the ability to statistically analyze and interpret data, but most will not. Their greatest contribution to data analysis and interpretation typically will be the assignment of meaning to the collected data from their perspective.

Dissemination of Findings

People with mental illness may write the evaluation or performance improvement report itself, write sections of the report, or review drafts of the report written by others and recommend modifications (Beeforth et al., 1990; Boll, 1995). They also may write up findings for client or staff newsletters or for publication in the professional literature (Townsend et al., 2000). In addition, people with mental illness may make oral presentations of the findings to other clients, staff, or administrators of the organization, and at professional conferences (Pratt & Gill, 1990; Townsend et al., 2000). The actual level of participation in the dissemination of findings is likely to be a function of the extent to people with mental illness initiated the project, their level of collaboration with staff, and their writing and oral presentation abilities.

Act Upon the Findings

Given the applied nature of evaluation and performance improvement, it seemed appropriate to include taking action based upon the evaluation findings as a step in the process in which people with mental illness should be involved. They can contribute in at least two ways (Boll, 1995; Race et al., 1994; Rapp et al., 1993). First, they can offer policy and program alternatives to address areas for improvement identified in evaluation reports. In many instances, they may know best what changes are needed to resolve problems. Their participation in this area typically will be collaborative with staff, particularly for large-scale changes, as consumers may not have all the information or the authority required to make final selections. As with data interpretation, their greatest contributions usually will be identifying alternatives and describing from their perspective the merits of each alternative that they or others offer. A second contribution people with mental illness can make is to facilitate and monitor the change process. They often have the most to gain from the enactment of policy or program changes and thus have a vested interest in seeing the process through to its successful conclusion.

PARTICIPATION STRUCTURES AND PROCESSES

A seventh condition is that the person with mental illness has structures and processes through which to meaningfully participate in various stages of the research process. For purposes of discussion, structures and processes are considered separately.

Participation Structures

Two types of formal structures exist through which people with mental illness can participate in research. First are structures with memberships comprised entirely of people with mental illness. Based upon their reviews of a number of evaluations of community mental health programs, Durbin et al. (1995) concluded that consumer councils and advisory groups provide a functional structure through which people with mental illness can participate in all stages of the research process. In some cases, these structures already may exist within the mental health organization, and its members can assume the research task as another of its duties. In other cases, it may be necessary to create a new consumer group specifically for the purpose of research. Fox (2000), for example, described the creation of a consumer advisory board specifically for the purpose of becoming part of the organizational performance review process. Since the agency served both people with mental illness and those with mental retardation, the board consisted of four members with each disability type. A manager of the quality improvement department served as the liaison to the advisory board. As a second example, Blackwell, Eilers, and Robinson (2000) described the creation of a small agency that was staffed entirely by people with mental illness for the purpose of conducting client satisfaction focus groups with clients of the local mental health agencies. The agency, which was funded by the local mental health authority, was created as a separate agency with its own budget to ensure a degree of independence and impartiality. The authors noted that the findings from these consumer evaluations helped to increase accountability among the local agencies and led to a number of service improvements.

A second type of structure is mixed groups comprised of people with mental illness, researchers, and other involved parties. This type of structure can take many forms. Koch et al. (1998) described the creation of a statewide work group comprised of people with mental illness, family members of consumers, mental health agency representatives, and staff from the state mental health authority's central office. Its purposes were to design a statewide community outcomes system and to follow its implementation. Ochocka et al. (2002) provided an example of a research team that consisted of two university researchers, two graduate students, and three people with mental illness who served as research assistants. The team's research purpose was to understand the process of change that three community mental health agencies had undergone when moving to an empowerment model of service delivery. Nelson et al. (1998), too, recommended the research team approach, but believed that some research projects warranted oversight by a research steering committee. These steering committees also can be comprised of people with mental illness, researchers, and others. Their responsibilities can range from providing input into the various stages of the research process to making decisions about the research design and process. Psychosocial rehabilitation centers using the clubhouse model are prime candidates to conduct program evaluation using research teams. In one clubhouse, a committee of three consumers and two staff developed a list of evaluation questions that consumers and staff from the various units of the clubhouse used for self-evaluation. After 3 months, each work unit provided oral and verbal reports of their findings and offered recommendations for improvement. As a second example, Townsend et al. (2000) reviewed 25 small program evaluation projects conducted at a clubhouse over a 2-year period. A research committee comprised of 8 to 12 members, most of whom were consumers, met weekly to review the status of projects, to discuss findings, and to identify topics for new projects, among other things. Consumer membership was somewhat fluid, and over the 2-year period, approximately half of the 120 consumers participated in one or more meetings.

It is important to note that structures such as consumer councils and research teams are not without their challenges. First, they may be difficult to create, or they may break down and become nonfunctional. It may be difficult to recruit people with mental illness to serve on advisory boards and research teams when existing structures are not available (Durbin et al., 1995). Also, Sullins (2003) disbanded a research team after two meetings. She, as the researcher, decided to implement most of the research stages herself and shifted the contribution of people with mental illness to providing meaningful data. A second challenge is that the inclusion of people with mental illness in these structures does not guarantee their participation will be valued by others. Fox (2000), for example, was quite open that the primary goal of forming a consumer advisory board was to meet contract requirements mandating that consumers have input into the quality management process. He stated that the creation of the board was the quickest and least expensive way to gain compliance, and that obtaining meaningful information from the board was only secondary. Similarly, Nelson et al. (1998) wrote that working in groups with others does not ensure that people with mental illness will have a voice in the research process. Researchers and others must still be willing to share power. Developing clear principles to guide the process, delineating the scope of responsibility for structures, and adopting a consensus model of decision making help ensure that the participation of people with mental illness in research processes will be meaningful.

Participation Processes

As stated before, research is most empowering when conducted by people with mental illness, themselves. Often, however, this is not possible, and people with mental illness must collaborate with researchers and others. In collaborative models of research, the degree of empowerment experienced by people with mental illness is directly related to the level and quality of their participation in the various stages of the research process. Over the past couple of decades, approaches to research that emphasize the meaningful participation of people with mental illness and other powerless populations in the evaluation and research process have evolved. As stated before, these approaches include participatory action research (Whyte, 1992), utilization-focused evaluation (Patton, 1997), empowerment evaluation (Fetterman, 2001), and continuous quality improvement and total quality management (Mason & Soreff, 1996). These approaches hold as core beliefs that anyone involved in an activity has something meaningful to contribute to its evaluation, and the role of the researcher or evaluator is to facilitate the involvement of others in the process. In describing the application of participatory research, for instance, Mason and Boutilier (1996) wrote, "It is a distinctive approach to research which emphasizes the equalization of power between researcher and research subject/object.... Participatory researchers assert that everyone has legitimate knowledge and can be an active contributor toward the creation of new knowledge.... Therefore in participatory research the relationship of researcher to subject alters to one of collaboration among equal participants" (p. 146). Similarly, Fleming and Ward (1999) wrote in relationship to social action, the British version of participatory research, "It is the responsibility of researchers to set in motion a process of participation whereby people identify and define their needs and work on common issues that can become agendas for change.... The research methods should reflect non-elitist principles and enable users to empower themselves to make decisions and control outcomes" (p. 375).

People with mental illness who are unable to participate in multiple stages of the research process may still be able to experience some level of empowerment by providing information as research subjects. Many have argued that the use of qualitative research methods provides the greatest opportunity for empowering research subjects (Nelson et al., 1998; Peled & Leichtentritt, 2002). Within the range of qualitative research methods, the use of ethnographic interviews (Hutchinson et al., 1994; Rapp et al., 1993) and focus groups (Linhorst, 2002a; Race et al., 1994; Rapp et al., 1993) especially are empowering. These approaches allow people to tell their stories and to contribute information about their experiences in their own words in ways that are largely unstructured by the researcher (Hutchinson et al., 1994; Nelson et al., 1998).

ACCESS TO RESOURCES

An eighth condition for empowerment is that the person with mental illness has access to the resources needed to meaningfully participate in the research process. One resource needed by most people with mental illness is training to develop their research skills for each stage of the research process (Townend & Braithwaite, 2002). This can be accomplished through formal training prior to and during the research process, as well as through informal training and mentoring throughout process (Ochocka et al., 2002). Townend and Braithwaite (2002) and Evans and Fisher (1999) took training one step further and argued for funding for competitive scholarships and fellowships so that more people with mental illness can develop the academic-based research skills to conduct research independently. A second resource is emotional support and encouragement throughout the research process (Morrell-Bellai & Boydell, 1994). Consumer-only groups, such as consumer councils and advisory groups, can be a source of mutual support. The research team, itself, can provide support as well, which Ochocka et al. (2002) demonstrated. People with mental illness also may get this support from friends, relatives, or mental health professionals with whom they frequently interact. Third, many people with mental illness will need a range of logistical resources. Morrell-Bellai and Boydell (1994) and Ochocka et al. (2002) recommended that consumer researchers have a supportive work environment, and preferably have their own office space when working on research teams on long-term projects. Other logical resources may include compensation for transportation, child care, and meals, especially when people are not being paid for their contributions to the research project.

Researchers and others participating with people with mental illness in research processes also may need resources. Some will need training on how to work effectively with people with mental illness (Fossey, Epstein, Findlay, Plant, & Harvey, 2002; Townend & Braithwaite, 2002). This training can include the effects of mental illness and medication on individuals' performance, the need to provide skill training to consumer researchers, and the importance of providing emotional support and encouragement, among other topics. Second, everyone will need the resource of time (Durbin et al., 1995; Ochocka et al., 2002). It takes considerable time to develop working relationships with participants, to provide training to people to ensure they have the skills required for meaningful participation, to provide emotional support, and to make decisions throughout the research process by consensus. Durbin et al. (1995) emphasized the importance of building time and resource requirements into research schedules and budgets to ensure that adequate resources will be available to best support people with mental illness when they serve as researchers.

SUPPORTIVE CULTURE

A final condition for empowerment is that the culture surrounding the research process is supportive of the meaningful participation of the person with mental illness. Cultural changes among researchers, mental health organizations, and research funders will be necessary for people with mental illness to reach their potential as participants in the research process (Townend & Braithwaite, 2002). A supportive culture requires that all research participants, including people with mental illness, themselves, put aside stigmatized views of people with mental illness as being incompetent, and instead view them as capable of learning new skills and participating in new activities that can empower them. It also entails the belief that people with mental illness have a right to evaluate the services they receive and the right to access the resources required for meaningful participation (Boll, 1995; Ochocka et al., 2002). Evans and Fisher (1999) extended rights to include the right of service users to establish the research agenda, not just to participate in the research process that others already established. Fetterman (1996) extended rights still further, expanding it to all people, when he argued for "the right of every citizen to use evaluation to foster improvement and self-determination within a context of social justice" (p. 383).

A supportive culture also promotes the use of research approaches that involve people with mental illness is all stages of the research process, such as participatory action research (Whyte, 1992), utilization-focused evaluation (Patton, 1997), empowerment evaluation (Fetterman, 2001), and continuous quality improvement and total quality management (Mason & Soreff, 1996). This requires a shift among many researchers, mental health organizations, and research funders that these approaches, which vary from traditional research paradigms, still can provide valid findings and are worth the extra time and money it usually takes to apply them in a meaningful manner.

Finally, a supportive culture provides the resources necessary for people with mental illness to meaningfully participate in research.

Researchers must take time to teach research skills to consumers, to involve them in decision making, and to provide emotional support. Researchers themselves also may need training on how to work effectively with people with mental illness. Mental health organizations must provide staff with the time to support people with mental illness in their research endeavors within the organization and to provide consumers with the logistical resources needed to allow them to participate. Research funders promote cultural change by funding projects specifically for consumer researchers and providing educational funds to allow more people with mental illness to develop the skills needed to become independent researchers.

CASE STUDIES

To increase understanding of the opportunities for, and limitations to, the empowerment of people with mental illness through research, empowerment is examined through two cases studies, one among people with mental illness residing in a public psychiatric hospital that provides long-term care and treatment (Linhorst & Eckert, 2002; Linhorst et al., 1999), and the other among those residing in the community who are receiving services from a publicly funded community mental health agency (Kryah et al., 2003).

Empowerment Among Clients in a Psychiatric Hospital (SLPRC)

Degree of Empowerment

Some limited opportunities for SLPRC clients to participate in various types of research existed. Occasionally, researchers from outside the hospital asked SLPRC clients to participate in social research projects. The evaluation of client empowerment conducted by the author at this hospital is one such example. In that study, one third of clients volunteered to participate in focus groups. Clients also participated through the consumer council, which reviewed draft focus group questions and suggested revisions, offered suggestions as to where and when to hold the focus groups, reviewed the final report, and made suggestions for improvement based upon the results, some of which were enacted. For example, one area for improvement was increased communication between clients and management. The consumer council suggested that the superintendent hold monthly meetings with the consumer council and periodically hold open meetings for all clients to attend, both of which the superintendent did.

SLPRC clients also recently began completing the annual national NRI/MHSIP Inpatient Consumer Survey. Response rates varied widely across units of the hospital. The hospital receives results for each unit of the hospital, as well as comparative statewide and national data. Staff from the quality management department analyzed results and presented them to executive staff, to unit directors, and to the consumer council. To date, the administration has not enacted any major changes based upon this data.

Next, SLPRC clients participated in research activities through the hospital's performance improvement system. This system uses the principles of continuous quality improvement and total quality management to identify areas for improvement, to develop improvement strategies, and to monitor improvement efforts. The collection of data is a critical component of this system, as is the formation of performance improvement teams to develop and monitor improvement efforts. SLPRC clients provided data as part of this process and served on improvement teams when the issue directly affected them. On average, three performance improvement teams are created annually, of which one typically includes SLPRC clients as part of the team. As one example of a performance improvement team, the consumer council expressed concern to the quality council, which oversees the performance improvement system, about the lack of partnerships between clients and staff in some interactions. In response, the quality council created the partnership performance improvement team to further investigate this issue and to make recommendations for improvement. The team consisted of 10 staff and 10 clients representing the various areas of the hospital. The team identified eight areas of the hospital in which partnerships existed (e.g., individual therapy and the client work program), and two general areas in which they did not exist, including the operation of the wards and cottages and treatment team meetings. For the latter two areas in which partnerships did not exist, the team identified client barriers, staff barriers, and organizational barriers to partnerships. The team concluded their final report with recommendations for improvement. Initially, administrators did not act on this report. However, the committee that oversees the provision-of-care function recently agreed to place the issue back on its agenda and reexamine the report.

Finally, clients participated in other small research projects that did not fit the above categories. For instance, one client conducted a weekly survey of environmental conditions at the hospital and issued a report to the environmental committee, which then assigned responsibility for correction to the appropriate maintenance or housekeeping unit. As another example, clients were concerned about the number of scheduled client activities in the gymnasium that were cancelled because staff was using it for meeting space. They kept records of the number of cancellations and presented the report to administrators. Consequently, scheduling of client and staff activities was better coordinated, and the number of cancellations was greatly reduced.

Based upon clients' involvement in research in these four areas, some clients were empowered through participation in research. Most of those clients who were directly involved in the various research activities, particularly clients serving on the consumer council and partnership performance improvement teams, experienced subjective empowerment by participating. Additional clients may have experienced some subjective empowerment by completing the annual inpatient survey and participating in the focus groups that were part of the empowerment study, although the level of empowerment experienced would likely be less than that gained through participation in those research activities in which clients played greater roles. Some objective empowerment also was realized because of tangible changes that resulted from some of the research activities, although not all projects led to improvements. Subjective empowerment was not experienced by more clients because many clients lacked knowledge of these projects and their results; however, the recent creation of a client newsletter has helped to improve the communication of information of this type.

Application of Conditions for Empowerment

Several conditions that promoted the level of empowerment that existed were at least partially met. A sufficient number of clients had their symptoms managed to a degree that they could meaningfully participate in various research activities. A staff member from the quality management department worked informally with clients to provide them with needed levels of skills and support. Over time, most staff members came to trust and respect clients' contributions to the research activities, and, indeed, often requested their participation, particularly on performance improvement teams. Clients, too, came to trust the research process over time, as their contributions were respected and their recommendations were enacted sometimes. Incentives for clients to participate included having an opportunity to voice their opinions and the possibility that positive change may result because of their participation. At least some staff was motivated to participate because client involvement helped to meet accreditation requirements, improved the research process, and was one additional means to engage clients in therapeutic activities. In addition, while most clients served as research subjects, clients had choices for participation in other stages of the research process. When considering all the projects together, clients participated in all stages of the research process. The existence of two major structures, the consumer council and the performance improvement system, were critical to clients' participation. Clients also received resources that enabled participation to occur, including informal training and emotional support from the quality management department and staff time to work with clients on research projects. Finally, over time, the hospital culture became supportive of clients' meaningful participation in research.

Empowerment Among Clients of a Community Agency (BJC-BH)

Degree of Empowerment

BJC-BH clients had multiple types of opportunities to participate in research as research subjects, but few opportunities to participate in other aspects of the research process. Some social research projects were conducted with BJC-BH clients, the author's empowerment study being one example. In that study, one focus group for clients was held at each of the agency's four sites, although no clients showed up for the focus group scheduled at one of the sites. In total, 25 clients participated in the focus groups. Clients did not participate in any other aspect of this study, with the exception of one client who served on one of the BJC-BH advisory boards and was present when the board offered comments on the research proposal and later examined a draft copy of the final report. Clients also completed three client satisfaction surveys. One survey was given to new clients upon admission to the agency. Clients mailed the six-question survey anonymously, which resulted in a return rate of approximately 50%. Also, the agency's parent organization conducted a monthly telephone survey of a random sample of approximately 60 current BJC-BH clients. BJC-BH clients played a role in developing this survey instrument by participating in a series of focus groups about topic areas they believed should be reflected in the survey and by pretesting the draft version. In addition, the Missouri Department of Mental Health (MDMH) conducted an annual survey of all people with mental illness who receive services through publicly funded programs, including BJC-BH clients. BJC-BH staff gave the anonymous MDMH questionnaire to all its clients, of whom approximately 5% mailed the form back to MDMH.

Another means for clients to participate in research as research subjects was through community forums that involved BJC-BH staff, clients, other mental health providers, and community residents. For several years, they were held annually, although they occurred with less frequency in recent years. During these events, in addition to clients having the opportunity to contribute in the open sessions, staff sometimes held focus groups just with clients on various issues. The purpose of these events was to allow the various parties to share opinions about the quality of services provided, to identify unmet needs, and to make suggestions for improvements. A number of meaningful programmatic changes, such as the creation of specialist staff positions in the areas of housing, entitlements, and employment, grew out of these forums. Finally, a number of special research projects arose when client perspectives were needed. For example, as part of a strategic planning process, a BJC-BH employee, who was a mental health consumer, trained 12 clients to conduct a telephone survey of clients to assess their treatment, rehabilitation, and support service needs.

Some clients may have experienced subjective empowerment as a contributor of information through written and telephone surveys and through forums and focus groups. Some objective empowerment existed, too, because client information led to some service improvements. Among the factors that limited empowerment were the facts that only approximately half of the 5,000 BJC-BH clients ever completed written surveys or were contacted for telephone surveys, few clients ever participated in stages of the research process other than as research subjects, and none of the clients who participated in the focus groups were aware of any improvements that resulted from information clients provided.

Application of Conditions for Empowerment

The degree of empowerment was limited primarily because clients served almost exclusively as research subjects, with little opportunity to participate in other aspects of the research process. Only two examples in which clients were involved in activities other than as research subjects were identified. BJC-BH did, however, provide substantial resources to involve clients as research subjects. Resources were expended to provide all clients with the opportunity to complete satisfaction surveys after their initial contact with the agency, to survey a random sample of current clients on a monthly basis, and to involve clients in a limited number of forums and focus groups. When incidents of client participation in aspects of research other than as subjects occurred, the agency provided resources to support those endeavors. For example, the needs assessment in which clients telephoned other clients required substantial staff time and financial resources. The BJC-BH employee who organized the activity provided several rounds of training to the 12 clients serving as interviewers, which included didactic information and role playing. The telephone interviews occurred over several evenings. Follow-up interviews were held with all interviewers to process their experiences and to remind them to keep all information confidential. The client interviewers were paid $10 per hour for their training and work time, the agency paid any child care costs incurred by clients, staff provided transportation to meetings for most of the 12 clients, and refreshments were served at each meeting.

The psychiatric symptoms of sufficient numbers of clients were managed to the degree the clients could respond to surveys or participate in forums. In addition, the agency provided clients with the skills and assistance to participate in the limited number of instances in which clients served in research capacities other than as research subjects. Contributing to clients' trust was the fact that the employee who led some of the research efforts was a consumer and was particularly sensitive to clients' needs, abilities, and potential to serve as research subjects and as consumer researchers. Finally, an agency culture that valued clients' contribution to the research process as research subjects existed. The involvement of clients in other aspects of the research process was not part of the culture. When it occurred, it resulted primarily from the leadership of an employee who openly identified herself as a consumer.

GUIDELINES FOR PROMOTING EMPOWERMENT THROUGH RESEARCH

As has been discussed, people with severe mental illness increasingly have been involved in all stages of the research process, and there is a growing group of highly trained research professionals that has a severe mental illness. The following guidelines are offered to further promote the empowerment potential of participation in research, evaluation, and performance improvement.

1. *Promote the participation of people with mental illness in all stages of the research process.* The traditional role for people with mental illness in research has been as research subjects. They can, however, make significant contributions to each stage of the process, ranging from forming research questions to disseminating and acting upon findings.

2. *Educate research professionals and other participants as to the benefits of consumer participation.* Participation can result in improved service delivery and in services that are responsive to changing consumer needs. Participation in multiple stages of the research process can improve the quality of research, in part, by maximizing the quality of information received from participants and by reducing data interpretation errors.

3. *Educate people with mental illness about the benefits to their participation.* These benefits can include gaining an opportunity to share their experiences and to express their needs, initiating research projects that are important to them, learning new skills, receiving financial compensation, increasing their self-esteem and sense of empowerment, and promoting their own recovery and personal development.

4. *Discuss the potential effects of research participation on psychiatric symptoms.* For a small number of people, participation in research may promote the onset of psychiatric symptoms or increase the severity of existing symptoms. This is more likely to happen when people are already experiencing severe symptoms or stress, in which case they should carefully consider whether they should participate. For most people, however, participation will not negatively affect symptoms, and it even can promote recovery.

5. *Incorporate flexibility into the research process.* When possible, flexibility should be incorporated into the level of participation in the research process so that if symptoms arise, people with mental illness can reduce or stop their involvement, either temporarily or permanently.

6. *Provide skill training to people with mental illness.* Training can include formal training sessions and more informal training and mentoring that takes place throughout the research process. Training should address interpersonal skills and technical research skills.

7. *Provide training to people who will be working with people with mental illness.* Some researchers may need training to work effectively with people with mental illness. This training can include the effects of mental illness and medication on individuals' performance, the need to provide skill training to consumers, and the importance of providing emotional support and encouragement.

8. *Create a trustful, supportive, and respectful research environment.* This can be accomplished, in part, by recognizing each participant's contributions, by sharing power throughout the research process, by avoiding research jargon when possible, by promoting discussion and actively listening to everyone's opinions, by openly negotiating differences of opinion, by seeking consensus when possible, by offering ongoing emotional support and encouragement, and by allowing time for relationships to develop.

9. *Develop structures through which people with mental illness can participate in research.* Ideally, people with mental illness will be part of a research team comprised of professional researchers and other involved parties. They also may participate through groups composed solely of people with mental illness, such as consumer councils and advisory groups.

10. *Adopt research approaches that promote empowerment.* Approaches such as participatory action research, utilization-focused evaluation, empowerment evaluation, and continuous quality improvement and total quality management hold as core beliefs that anyone involved in an activity has something meaningful to contribute to its evaluation, and that the role of the researcher or evaluator is to facilitate the involvement of others in the process. In addition, qualitative research methods should be used whenever possible.

11. *Provide the resources needed to meaningfully involve people with mental illness in research.* One important resource is the allocation of enough time for people to be properly trained, for emotional support and encouragement to be provided,

and for consensus-based decision making. Another is financial compensation for the involvement of people with mental illness as research subjects, as research assistants, or as researchers. A third is funding for scholarships and fellowships for more people with mental illness to be able to develop academic-based research skills to become independent researchers. In some instances, people with mental illness also will need a range of logistical resources to participate, such as transportation, child care, meals, and lodging.

12. *Develop a research culture that supports the meaningful participation of people with mental illness.* Such a culture helps all research participants to overcome stigmatized views of people with mental illness as being incapable of activities such as research, views participation in research by people with mental illness as a right, uses research approaches that support empowerment, and provides the resources necessary for meaningful participation.

11

Empowerment Through Service Provision

Over the past three decades, people with severe mental illness increasingly have served as providers of mental health services in the United States and internationally (Carling, 1995; Meagher, 1996). This has its origins dating back to the 1920s when Harry Sullivan, who directed an inpatient unit in a psychiatric hospital, hired former patients who had recovered to work as psychiatric aides, and to the 1950s when many psychiatric hospitals adopted therapeutic community models that incorporated mentoring, support, and collaborative decision making among the patients (Davidson et al., 1999). The more recent influences were the expatient and consumer movement that began in the 1960s, the development of community support and psychiatric rehabilitation programs that expanded in the 1970s, and the publication of Chamberlin's seminal book in 1978 that argued for consumer-provided services and offered guidance on how to establish and operate them (Moxley & Mowbray, 1997).

People with mental illness can provide a wide range of services. Davidson et al. (1999) grouped these services into three types. First are mutual support groups through which people with mental illness voluntarily gather to share their experiences with mental illness, and in the process, reduce social isolation and assume the role of helpers. Groups have their own routines and models of dealing with problems, and are led by people with mental illness, not mental health professionals. Examples of mutual support groups for people with mental illness include local affiliations of Schizophrenics Anonymous; Recovery, Inc.; GROW, Inc.; Emotions Anonymous; and the Depression and

Bipolar Support Alliance, as well as many local groups without national or state affiliation. Second are consumer-run services, which can include drop-in centers, residential programs, outreach services, and vocational programs. While these, too, are built around the notion of mutual support, consumer-run services typically are offered by paid staff comprised of people with mental illness, through private nonprofit corporations that are independent of traditional mental health organizations. Third are people with mental illness who serve as providers of services in traditional mental health agencies. They can work in positions created specifically for people with mental illness or in regular positions that can be filled by consumers or nonconsumers.

Many have argued that mutual support groups, consumer-run programs, and traditional mental health services offered by consumer-providers should be part of the range of services available to people with mental illness. For example, the National Association of State Mental Health Program Directors (1989), comprised of the directors of state mental health authorities, endorsed people with mental illness serving as employees of traditional mental health programs and recommended that funding be increased to expand consumer-run mental health programs and mutual support groups. Also, the Surgeon General's 1999 mental health report included consumer-operated programs and consumer self-help and advocacy activities as part of the range of mental health services that should be available to adults with severe mental illness (U.S. DHHS, 1999). Similarly, in 2003, the President's New Freedom Commission on Mental Health (2003) promoted consumer-run agencies and the hiring of people with mental illness into a variety of treatment and rehabilitation settings.

Service provision can be empowering to people with severe mental illness in several ways. For all three types of consumer-provided services, people with mental illness are empowered through having opportunities to help themselves and others (Mowbray & Moxley, 1997). This can alter their definition of disability, so that they can see their own potential to help others and can learn from others' examples that it is possible to successfully cope with symptoms and problems to take control of their own lives (Segal et al., 1993). Having role models is especially important to this empowerment process, whether they are peers in mutual support groups, leaders in consumer-run programs, or consumer-providers in traditional mental health agencies (Manning, 1999; Mowbray & Moxley, 1997). Participation in consumer-run programs can be another form of empowerment when it involves all members in decision making using democratic management styles (Chamberlin, 1994; Hardiman & Segal, 2003; Segal, Silverman, and Temkin, 1993). It is the sharing of responsibility and power that makes this participation empowering (Mead, Hilton, & Curtis, 2001). Leaders in consumer-run organizations also are empowered through the official positions they hold (Manning & Suire, 1996). Serving as consumer-providers, too, can be empowering. Manning and Suire (1996) illustrated this in relationship to people with mental illness who worked as case management aides. "Consumer case manager aides experienced empowerment resulting from their employment through legitimacy, including being treated 'like other staff'; material symbols, such as a desk and name plate; and status symbols, such as access to clients' records" (p. 940).

Despite its potential, empowerment may not occur through service provision. Consumer-run organizations have the same power issues as any other type of organization (Chamberlin, 1978; Mead et al., 2001). Harp (1987) observed instances in which consumers oppressed their own members in self-help organizations. Consumer-run organizations may adopt the same nondemocratic hierarchical structures that are found in many traditional mental health organizations (McLean, 1995). In addition, many people with severe mental illness do not participate in mutual support groups. Davidson et al. (1999) found, for instance, that only approximately one third of people with mental illness participate in such activities, and many of those individuals do not continue long term. Finally, people with mental illness working as service providers in traditional mental health organizations may be dissatisfied with their employment experiences and find them to be actually disempowering (Carling, 1995). This often is associated with staff of mental health organizations holding stigmatized views of consumer-providers and engaging in discriminatory behavior toward them (Fisher, 1994b; Manning & Suire, 1996). Such professionals cannot get beyond the label of mental illness to view their coworkers as capable individuals who have a unique contribution to make toward the recovery of others with mental illness.

Application of the conditions for empowering people with mental illness provides guidance for making service provision an empowering experience. Table 11.1 summarizes the conditions for empowerment as they apply to mental health service provision. Consideration is given to conditions related to participation in mutual support groups and consumer-run organizations, and to paid positions within consumer-run organizations and as service providers in traditional mental health organizations.

MANAGED PSYCHIATRIC SYMPTOMS

One condition for empowering people with severe mental illness through service provision is that the person's psychiatric symptoms are sufficiently managed to meaningfully participate in self-help activities through mutual support groups or consumer-run programs, or in paid positions within consumer-run organizations or traditional mental

Table 11.1 Conditions for Empowering People With Severe Mental Illness Through Service Provision

Managed psychiatric symptoms—The person's psychiatric symptoms are sufficiently managed to meaningfully participate in self-help activities through mutual support groups or consumer-run programs, or in paid positions within consumer-run organizations or traditional mental health agencies.

Participation skills—The person possesses the skills required to meaningfully participate in self-help activities, or in paid positions within consumer-run organizations or traditional mental health agencies.

Psychological readiness—The person has the confidence, motivation, and willingness to meaningfully participate in self-help activities, in paid positions within consumer-run organizations, or in traditional mental health agencies as service providers.

Mutual trust and respect—People with mental illness have the necessary level of mutual trust and respect to meaningfully participate together in consumer-run organizations or in mutual self-help activities; mutual trust and respect exist between consumer-providers in traditional mental health agencies and their coworkers; and mutual trust and respect exist between consumer-run organizations and mutual self-help groups and traditional mental health agencies.

Reciprocal concrete incentives—Concrete incentives exist for people with mental illness to meaningfully participate in mutual self-help activities and consumer-run organizations, for the mental health system to support them, for people with mental illness to serve as consumer-providers, and for traditional mental health organizations to hire them.

Availability of choices—The person with mental illness has meaningful choices of consumer-provided mental health services, including mutual support groups, services provided by consumer-run organizations, and services offered by consumer-providers in traditional mental health agencies.

Participation structures and processes—Structures and processes exist to promote shared decision making within consumer-run organizations, for referring people with mental illness to mutual support activities and consumer-run programs, and for recruiting consumers to work as service providers in traditional mental health agencies.

Access to resources—People with mental illness have access to the resources needed to meaningfully participate in self-help activities, or in paid positions within consumer-run organizations or traditional mental health agencies.

Supportive culture—The culture surrounding public policy making, professional mental health organizations, consumer-providers, consumer-run organizations, and mutual self-help activities is supportive of consumer service provision.

health agencies. Some people may experience symptoms that are too severe to meaningfully participate in self-help activities (Davidson et al., 1999). Others, however, may be able to participate, despite experiencing symptoms, because many self-help programs, such as consumer-run drop-in centers, place less stress and demands on attendees and can be a more accepting environment than those operated by nonconsumer professionals

(Mowbray, 1997). Participation in consumer-run programs and mutual support groups even may reduce symptoms. Although research is limited in this area, it can be stated generally that participation does not make symptoms worse and may improve symptoms, reduce hospitalizations, and increase self-esteem (Davidson et al., 1999; Simpson & House, 2002; Solomon & Draine, 2001).

People with mental illness who are paid staff in consumer-run organizations and service providers in traditional mental health organizations will need symptoms managed to the degree that they can complete the requirements of their positions. Some people, during parts of their lives at least, will not be able to achieve this level of managed symptoms. In addition, symptoms may reemerge for some people because of the act of becoming employed, as discussed in chapter 9. They also may experience additional stress, and the possible reemergence of their symptoms, specifically related to their roles as service providers. Mowbray (1997) noted, for example, that consumers working in mental health programs may feel overly responsible for those with whom they work, which can cause excessive worry and sleeplessness. She also identified that service provision may produce memories of unresolved traumatic events, which can trigger symptoms. Mowbray concluded, however, that symptoms are most likely caused by consumer-providers being treated poorly and without respect by nonconsumer coworkers, by being given too much responsibility without adequate training, and, in general, by working in an environment that does not offer adequate supports. It is important to note, though, that most consumer-providers are not negatively affected by their jobs (Simpson & House, 2002). In fact, it can promote their continued recovery by providing an opportunity for personal growth and development and meaningful employment (Carlson, Rapp, & McDiarmid, 2001; Manning, 1999; Salzer & Shear, 2002).

PARTICIPATION SKILLS

A second condition for empowerment is that the person possesses the skills required to meaningfully participate in self-help activities, or in paid positions within consumer-run organizations or traditional mental health agencies. From one perspective, people with mental illness who participate in self-help activities do not need special skills. As Bassman (2001) stated, "The self-help phenomenon is one of possibilities, where people of vastly different skills and abilities try to use and make the best out of whatever individual members have to contribute" (p. 24). From another perspective, people with mental illness can maximize the benefits they receive from participation in self-help activities by increasing their skill levels. Skill improvement will vary by the type of activity and the existing skill levels of participants. Some participants in mutual support groups, for instance, may benefit from improved listening and communication skills. Likewise, participants of a drop-in center may need to further develop their assertiveness skills and oral communication skills to effectively contribute their opinions to the operation of the program. In both of these examples, skill development can be facilitated by the group process itself or by instruction that is more formal. In fact, one of the benefits of participation in mutual support groups and consumer-run programs is skill improvement (Davidson et al., 1999).

People with mental illness who work as paid staff in consumer-run organizations or as service providers in traditional mental health agencies also need a range of skills. In the former case, these include leadership skills, as well as budgeting, management, fundraising, planning and other skills needed to operate a program or agency. In the latter instance, they need the skills to provide their assigned service activities. Some people with mental illness already have the education and experience to move into positions such as these. Others may need some combination of college education, training, continuing education, and mentoring to successfully fill them (Davidson et al., 1999). Many types of skill development initiatives have been identified. Paulson (1991), for example, described a university's master of social work program that made a special effort to recruit and support people with mental illness to become social workers in mental health organizations. Bentley (2000) and Jasper (1997) each provided examples of training directed toward helping people with mental illness to develop the skills needed to work in consumer-run organizations. Others have described skill training to work as service providers with people with mental illness who were homeless (Fisk & Frey, 2002), to facilitate greater participation of people with mental illness in community leisure and recreation activities (Gammonley & Luken, 2001), to provide case management services (Sherman & Porter, 1991), and to work with people with mental illness who were hospitalized and nearing discharge to facilitate their reentry into the community (Turner, Korman, Lumpkin, & Hughes, 1998). As such, it is not unexpected that many people with mental illness have reported that the development of new skills was a benefit of working in paid positions in consumer-run programs and in traditional mental health organizations (Carlson et al., 2001; Manning, 1999; Mowbray & Moxley, 1997).

PSYCHOLOGICAL READINESS

A third condition for empowerment is that the person has the psychological readiness (e.g., confidence, motivation, willingness) to meaningfully participate in mutual support groups, in consumer-run program, or in traditional mental health agencies as service providers.

The greatest single barrier to participating in any of these activities may be people with mental illness internalizing the stigmatized view that they are incompetent to help each other. People with mental illness who enter paid positions in consumer-run or traditional mental health organizations also must overcome perceptions of their being incapable of employment in general. In addition, some will have to contend with their own feelings of incompetence as they work with nonconsumers as peers in traditional mental health organizations.

Several steps can be taken to help people with mental illness overcome self-perceptions of incompetence and consider participating in one or more of the three types of service provision. One is application of the strengths perspective and the recovery perspective. The strengths perspective can assist people with mental illness to view their own experiences with mental illness and with the mental health system as strengths for helping others contend with their illnesses and access needed services (Rapp, 1998). Similarly, the recovery perspective supports the belief that people who are experiencing recovery can help others in their own recovery, and it encourages participation in self-help activities (Anthony, 1993). Application of these perspectives must include conversations about the advantages of, and concerns with, consumer service provision in order to identify and dispel stigmatized views that may be preventing people with mental illness from accessing needed services. Second, people with mental illness involved in all three consumer service provision areas can serve as role models that others, too, can be service providers (Davidson et al., 1999; Manning, 1999). Third, people with mental illness should be encouraged to visit multiple mutual support groups and consumer-run programs in order to find one that best meets their needs (Salzer & Mental Health Association, 2002). Finally, offers of training and support can be essential to helping people with mental illness overcome feelings of incompetence, particularly as they consider paid employment in consumer-run and in traditional mental health program as service providers. Without training and support, many people will not be willing to enter such positions or be able to succeed in them.

Assuming that people with mental illness can overcome self-perceptions of incompetence, the availability of mutual support groups and consumer-run programs may increase their psychological readiness to engage in services. For some people with mental illness, it may be easier and less anxiety provoking to accept mental health and support services from other consumers working as providers in traditional mental health agencies (Mowbray, 1997). Also, people with mental illness who fear being coerced into treatment from traditional mental health providers may be more willing to accept services from mutual support and consumer-run programs (Segal, Hodges, & Hardiman, 2002).

MUTUAL TRUST AND RESPECT

A fourth condition for empowerment is that people with mental illness have the necessary level of mutual trust and respect to meaningfully participate together in mutual support groups and consumer-run programs, that mutual trust and respect exist between consumer-providers and their coworkers in traditional mental health agencies, and that mutual trust and respect exist between consumer-run organizations and traditional mental health agencies. Mistrust and a lack of respect can occur between people with mental illness in mutual support groups and consumer-run programs. Mowbray (1997) identified that some people with mental illness who have accepted stigmatized views of themselves and their peers may believe that only mental health professionals can help them, and thus reject any of the three types of consumer-provided services. She also found that when people with mental illness move into paid staff positions within consumer-run or traditional mental health programs, their peers may no longer trust them because of their new status as paid staff. Several things can be done to improve mutual trust and respect among people with mental illness. First, application of the strengths perspective and the recovery perspective can give consumers confidence to provide services, as well as to accept that others with mental illness can be service providers to them. Also, paid consumer-providers in traditional mental health programs can be role models, demonstrating that people with mental illness can be effective providers of mental health services. In addition, some people with mental illness may benefit from discussions of the research on the success of consumer-provided services. The latter concern of people not trusting peers who are hired into paid service-provider positions typically resolves itself over time if the new consumer-providers treat their former peers with respect, include them in decision making, and use their position to advocate for consumers' interests.

A lack of mutual trust and respect also can exist between consumer-providers and their nonconsumer coworkers in traditional mental health agencies. Coworkers especially are likely to mistrust and disrespect their consumer-provider coworkers (Mowbray, 1997). It can be difficult for nonconsumer coworkers to avoid accepting some of the stigmatized view of people with mental illness (Solomon & Draine, 1998). In fact, Fisher (1994b) argued that mental health professionals are discriminatory and stigmatizing toward people with mental illness, which carries over to their interactions with consumer-providers. Conversely, consumer-providers may not trust that coworkers and administrators will treat them fairly, be inclusive of them, or give them the support they need to be successful. Training and supervision of nonconsumer staff are essential to their developing trust and respect for the consumer-providers with whom they may work. This is especially needed because the formal training that most mental health professionals receive does not value the ideology surrounding consumer provision of mental health services, and it does not educate them about the benefits to their clients of receiving consumer-provided services (Constantino & Nelson, 1995; Salzer & Mental Health Association, 2002). To maximize the effectiveness of training, Simpson and House (2002) recommended that people with mental illness serve as trainers or cotrainers. Good supervision of nonconsumer staff also is needed to build trust and respect (Salzer & Mental Health Association, 2002; Zipple et al., 1997). This supervision begins with open acknowledgment of conflicts and discomfort that may be associated with stigmatized views, and then development of strategies to contend with them. Mental health organizations can address consumer-providers' mistrust by hiring multiple consumer-providers to demonstrate that the organizations value their contribution and to create opportunities for peer mentoring and formally organized peer support (Fisher, 1994b; Manning & Suire, 1996). Providing quality supervision is another means to help consumer-providers to cope with difficulties they may experience in their relationships with their coworkers and to develop trust in, and respect for, the organization and its staff (Solomon & Draine, 1998; Zipple et al., 1997).

Finally, mutual trust and respect is important between mutual support groups and consumer-run organizations and traditional mental health agencies. In their study of the relationship between self-help organizations and mental health professionals, Constantino and Nelson (1995) found that achieving mutual respect was their highest priority. Chamberlin (1978) indicated that each consumer-run program must decide what the relationship should be between itself and the traditional mental health system. On the one hand, if that relationship is too close, the consumer-run program may be coopted by the mental health system and lose its unique identity, qualities, and benefits (Kasinsky, 1987; Salzer & Mental Health Association, 2002). On the other hand, most consumer-run programs rely on the traditional mental health system for financial support, for referrals to their programs, for meeting space, for technical assistance, and for other resources (Constantino & Nelson, 1995; Davidson et al., 1999). Avoiding overinvolvement requires that mental health organizations trust and respect the ability of people with mental illness to be service providers when given adequate training and resources, and that people with mental illness trust that mental health organizations can offer them support without assuming that these organizations want to control them. Trust can be built through education of mental health professionals about the abilities of consumers to be service providers and the unique contributions they can make to the continuum of available mental health services (Salzer & Mental Health Association, 2002; Salzer, Rappaport, & Segre, 2001; Solomon & Draine, 1998). Mutual trust and respect also can be promoted by having leaders from consumer-run programs and traditional mental health agencies sit on the boards of directors of each others' organizations or by interacting through other formal structures (Chinman, Kloos, O'Connell, & Davidson, 2002).

RECIPROCAL CONCRETE INCENTIVES

A fifth condition for empowerment is that concrete incentives exist for people with mental illness to meaningfully participate in mutual support groups and consumer-run organizations, for the mental health system to support those activities, for people with mental illness to serve as consumer-providers, and for traditional mental health organizations to hire them. Numerous incentives for people with mental illness to participate in mutual support groups and consumer-run programs exist. At its most basic level, participation puts people into the role of helper, which they may never have held before. As Bassman (2001), a mental health consumer, stated, "Being for once in the position to help others feels good and increases self-esteem. . . . You are able to rethink your professionally adjudicated label of incompetence" (p. 24). A second incentive is access to the services that these programs offer that traditional mental health programs may not make available. In their study of new attendees at self-help and traditional programs, Segal, Hodges et al. (2002) found people with mental illness went to self-help programs to increase their socialization opportunities or to access specific self-help services that the programs offered. In contrast, people went to the community mental health centers to obtain medication and to receive formal counseling. A third incentive is that participation may result in positive outcomes. As previously stated, the limited amount of outcome research has found that participation may improve symptoms, reduce hospitalizations, and increase self-esteem (Davidson et al., 1999; Simpson & House, 2002; Solomon & Draine, 2001). Mowbray and Moxley (1997) identified other benefits to participation as well. These included receiving social support and nurturance; having opportunities for organizational decision making not available in traditional mental health agencies; and having an increased sense of hope, confidence, and personal empowerment because of being able to help others and being in the presence of consumers serving in leadership and provider roles.

Disincentives for people with mental illness to participate in mutual support groups and consumer-run programs also exist. People with mental health illness may not have easy access to self-help services that do not exist in close proximity, or they may experience transportation problems. Participation in such services also may identify individuals as mental health consumers who would rather not be identified as such, particularly those living in rural areas (Bjorklund & Pippard,

1999). In addition, people with mental illness simply may not need the services that available programs offer, particularly if they are well into recovery. For instance, a person who is employed, has a strong support system, and has symptoms managed by medication may not feel a need to engage in mutual support groups or consumer-run programs.

The traditional mental health system, comprised of mental health providers, state mental health authorities, and funders, also has incentives to help sustain mutual support groups and consumer-run programs. First, contrary to the view held by some, studies have found that, in general, people with mental illness who participate in mutual support groups and consumer-run programs are more likely, rather than less likely, to participate in traditional mental health services than those who do not participate in these consumer-provided activities (Kessler, Mickelson, & Zhao, 1997). Thus, mental health system support of these consumer programs can increase utilization of traditional services as well. Second, as stated above, the limited available research has found that mutual support groups and consumer-run programs have positive mental health outcomes. Participation does not make symptoms worse and may improve symptoms, reduce hospitalizations, and increase self-esteem (Davidson et al., 1999; Simpson & House, 2002; Solomon & Draine, 2001). A third incentive is that mutual support groups and consumer-run programs can augment traditional mental health services for reasonable costs. This is particularly important in an era of limited resources during which many public mental health systems are reducing services. Chinman et al. (2002) noted that mutual support groups, for example, compliment traditional mental health services with very little additional costs to the mental health system. Consistent with this, Bassman (2001) reported that when New York initiated a managed care Medicaid pilot program, self-help and empowerment services were one of five mandated types of services, and were included because of their anticipated cost savings.

Disincentives for mental health systems to support participation in mutual support groups and consumer-run programs also exist. One disincentive is ideological. Fisher (1994b) stated that support of self-help programs is inconsistent with the medical model of mental health practice. "The medical model, which is an illness paradigm, . . . conflicts with the healing paradigm of the consumer/survivor movement" (p. 68). Similarly, Salzer et al. (2001) identified that "professional-centrism" is a barrier to support of self-help programs by some professionals. They use this term to refer to the perception that "professional services and expertise are the central effective components of a mental health system" (p. 2). They continued, "Self-help groups may be perceived as less helpful than professionally-led groups because professionals devalue the importance of the benefits associated with self-help, . . . thereby ignoring the unique benefits of self-help groups" (p. 2).

The other disincentive for the mental health system to support mutual support groups and consumer-operated programs is financial. Most funding for consumer-run programs comes from state mental health authorities (Davidson et al., 1999). Overall, states allocate far less than 1% of their budgets to such programs (Mead et al., 2001). With many states cutting their mental health budgets, it is unlikely that they will be able to increase funding for these services, despite their relative low cost. Holter, Mowbray, Bellamy, MacFarlane, and Dukarski (2004) believed that the current level of evaluation findings did not yet warrant expansion beyond current levels. "In our budget-conscious, managed care-oriented, re-stricted economy, mental health services which are not validated face severe disadvantages in terms of expansion, or even maintenance of their funding base. . . . Thus, it appears that, without effectiveness research, consumer-run services are unlikely to move beyond the very limited funding they now receive" (p. 48).

Incentives for people with mental illness to serve as service providers in traditional mental health agencies also exist. For instance, Carlson et al. (2001) identified benefits as being increased self-esteem, increased personal growth and development, skill development, reduced hospi-talizations, and stable employment. Salzer and Shear (2002) summa-rized the benefits as being the satisfaction of helping others in their recovery process, moving forward with one's own recovery, increased social approval, professional growth, and having an enjoyable job. Similarly, Mowbray and Moxley (1997) noted skill development, con-tinued recovery, greater independence, new friends, satisfaction of helping others, and improved self-perception as being benefits.

People with mental illness considering employment as service pro-viders must offset these potential benefits against potential disincen-tives. First, some of the jobs that agencies make available to people with mental illness offer low pay and status, provide little decision-making autonomy, and have no opportunities for advancement (Mowbray, 1997; Mowbray et al., 1996; Solomon & Draine, 1998). Mowbray et al. (1996) described the consequences that some consumers experience when placed in such positions. "Growing expectations about the qual-ity of work life and more assertiveness evolving from feelings of em-powerment may result in heightened dissatisfaction with their employment status" (p. 60). In addition, consumer-providers may lose their peer support, particularly when hired by agency from which they and their friends receive services (Fisher, 1994b). Relationships with nonconsumer coworkers may not develop to replace this lost support (Mowbray, 1997). Also, consumer-providers may have to contend with nonconsumer coworkers who do not accept them and endure resent-ment; hostility; and exclusionary, distant, and guarded behavior (Mowbray, 1997; Mowbray & Moxley, 1997). Finally, if people with mental illness who consider working as service providers are receiving a disability income and medical benefits, they will have to consider the effect of the employment on these benefits.

Mental health agencies considering hiring people with mental illness into service positions also face incentives and disincentives. An incentive to hire a service provider who is a consumer is that their presence can help staff to identify and dispel their prejudices, and improve attitudes toward, and interactions with, clients (Carlson et al., 2001). Second, such hirings can provide meaningful employment opportunities to people with mental illness (Mowbray et al., 1996). Third, they can serve as role models to agency clients (Davidson et al., 1999). Mowbray and Moxley (1997) described the importance of this function. "Consumer-providers act as role models and provide inspiration to others that rehabilitation is a real possibility. This addresses motivational issues and helps recipients move forward in their own process of recovery. Consumers report feeling a sense of personal empowerment, knowing that others can and do succeed, even with symptoms" (p. 507). Finally, consumer-providers can contribute to improvement in the quality of services provided by the agency and expand consumer participation in organizational decision making (Mowbray & Moxley, 1997). Disincentives for mental health agencies hiring consumers also exist. One is that it often is difficult to recruit qualified people with mental illness, particularly those who have the educational requirements to fill regular staff positions (Mowbray, 1997). Also, agencies will need to alter their training and supervision of both consumer and nonconsumer staff to promote good working relationships and openly deal with the discomfort that both consumer and nonconsumer staff may experience in working together. Both Mowbray and Moxley (1997) and Carlson et al. (2001) argued that agencies can address these disincentives, and that the benefits far outweigh the effort required to create a work environment that supports consumer-providers.

AVAILABILITY OF CHOICES

A sixth condition for empowerment is that the person with mental illness has meaningful choices of consumer-provided mental health services, including mutual support groups, services provided by consumer-run organizations, and services offered by consumer-providers in traditional mental health agencies. For people who specifically want them, it is important to clarify what constitutes, and does not constitute, consumer-run services. In the area of mutual support groups, support groups that include consumer participants but are led by nonconsumer professionals are not considered consumer-operated activities, even though consumers may provide support to each other (Davidson et al., 1999). Also, there are programs that state they are consumer-run, when, in fact, nonconsumers have informal or direct control over major decisions (Zinman, 1987). For example, psychosocial rehabilitation clubhouses require consumer participation in all phases of operation (Wang, Macias, & Jackson, 1999). While some clubhouses claim to be consumer-run, two prominent mental health consumers argued strongly that consumers do not hold the power in them (Chamberlin, 1978; Zinman, 1987). Finally, people with mental illness who work as service providers are considered to be consumer-providers only if they disclose their mental illness to their clients and to at least some other staff within the program (Salzer & Mental Health Association, 2002). If they do not disclose, there is minimal benefit to their clients and to their agencies. A more detailed discussion of each of the three types of consumer-provided services follows.

Mutual Support Groups

In recent years, the number of mutual support groups specifically for people with severe mental illness has grown dramatically, with some activities having state, national, or international affiliations. Some mutual support groups are open to people with any type of mental illness, such as Recovery, Inc. (n.d.), GROW, Inc. (Davidson et al., 1999), and Emotions Anonymous (n.d.). Other groups are directed toward people with a specific mental illness, such as Schizophrenics Anonymous (n.d.) and the Depression and Bipolar Support Alliance (n.d.). Still others are for people with the co-occurring disorders of substance abuse and mental illness, such as Double Trouble in Recovery (n.d.) and Dual Recovery Anonymous (n.d.). All of the above groups have national or international affiliations, and the number of U.S. chapters ranges from 100 to over 1,000. In addition to these affiliated groups, many local communities have developed groups that exist only in that community. The approaches and cultures of these groups can vary widely, and consumers should have the opportunity to try different ones to find the group or groups with which they are most comfortable.

Despite the large number of mutual support groups available nationally, some consumers may not have access to any groups, particularly in rural areas. Several things can be done to increase consumers' access to mutual support groups. One is to ensure that people with mental illness are aware of those mutual support groups that already exist in their areas. It is particularly important for consumer-run programs, mental health professionals, and mental health advocacy groups to be knowledgeable about those resources, and then make that information widely available to consumers. Next, mental health consumers themselves, as well as mental health professionals and mental health advocacy groups, can organize groups if none or insufficient numbers of groups exist within a given community. Some of the organizations listed above, such as Double Trouble in Recovery (n.d.) and Schizophrenics Anonymous (n.d.), for instance, assist individuals with starting groups. Finally, Bjorklund and Pippard (1999) advocated strongly for increased use of the Internet to provide mutual support activities, which, they said, can be a valuable resource especially for people living in rural areas. Some support groups, such as the Depression and Bipolar Support Alliance (n.d.), have online support groups, and many consumer-run programs are beginning to offer them as well (Bjorklund & Pippard, 1999).

Consumer-Run Programs

Nationally, the number and type of consumer-run programs has greatly increased as well. Carling (1995) summarized the types of services that consumers are providing, which included self-help and mutual support groups; outreach services; drop-in centers; traditional mental health treatment services; crisis response services and alternatives to hospitalization; housing and homelessness services; employment, training, and rehabilitation services; rights protection and advocacy; and case management services. The most common type of consumer-run service is the drop-in center (Holter et al., 2004). Mowbray, Robinson, and Holter (2002) completed a study of 32 of Michigan's 33 drop-in centers. In addition to being a place for consumers to socialize, they found that centers varied widely in the range of specialized services they offered. Specialized services offered by at least half of the centers included making a telephone available, assisting with finding employment, collecting clothing, and providing a mailing address. They also varied widely in their operating budgets and in the hours of operation. Almost all of the centers were underfunded and struggled financially. While drop-in centers may be the most common service, a limited number of consumer-run programs provide traditional mental health services as well (Carling, 1995). Carling gave an example of one consumer-run program that hired psychiatrists, who also were consumers, to provide traditional psychiatric services. He also cited an example of a consumer-run program that handled the discharge and community placement of a group of long-term residents of a state psychiatric hospital that the local mental community mental health agency was unable to accomplish.

As with mutual support groups, some people with mental illness may not be aware of, or have access to, consumer-run services. Therefore, it is important for people with mental illness, mental health professionals, and mental health advocacy groups to publicize information about them. In addition, mental health consumers, mental health professionals, and mental health advocacy groups can work together to create consumer-run programs to fill unmet needs. As well as advocating for the use of the Internet for mutual support, Bjorklund and Pippard (1999) believed that consumer-run programs could use it to expand the services they offer at a reasonable cost.

Consumer-Providers in Traditional Mental Health Agencies

A third means for people with mental illness to serve as service providers is through paid positions in traditional mental health agencies. Research on consumer-providers has consistently found that people with mental illness can effectively provide mental health services (Davidson et al., 1999). Moreover, they have provided many types of services. Mowbray, Moxley, Jasper, and Howell (1997), for example, assembled reports on individuals' experiences as consumer-providers in traditional mental health agencies, which included working in the areas of peer counseling, respite services, housing supports, advocacy in inpatient settings, and case management. Others have reported on consumers' experiences in assisting hospitalized individuals adjust to community living (Turner et al., 1998), providing outreach services to people who are homeless (Fisk & Frey, 2002), serving on a mobile crisis unit (Lyons, Cook, Ruth, Karver, & Slagg, 1996), serving as case management aides (Sherman & Porter, 1991), and working as a psychiatrist (North, 1987).

Mental health agencies can expand choices for people with mental illness to serve as service providers by creating positions specifically for consumers or by hiring consumers into regular positions that can be filled by either consumers or nonconsumers. Mowbray et al. (1996) argued against the practice of creating special positions for people with mental illness. "Hiring consumers into specially identified positions, such as PSS [peer support specialists] may be inherently problematic. It could be argued that creating a programmatic culture in which there are dual tracks for professionals and consumer workers will only foment divisiveness, raising equity and justice issues" (p. 64). Others, however, have reported positive experiences by staff and consumer-providers with service positions created for people with mental illness (Sherman & Porter, 1991).

PARTICIPATION STRUCTURES AND PROCESSES

A seventh condition for empowerment is that structures and processes exist for promoting shared decision making within consumer-run organizations, for referring people with mental illness to mutual support groups and consumer-run programs, and for recruiting consumers to work as service providers in traditional mental health agencies. Each aspect of the condition is discussed below.

Shared Decision Making

People with mental illness can be empowered not only through the services they receive from consumer-run programs, but also through their participation in operational decision making. Therefore, it is critical that consumer-run programs develop structures and processes that maximize opportunities for all consumers to participate in decision making. This is difficult to achieve, however. Consumers can oppress their own members in consumer-run programs, and it is not unusual for a core group of members to make most of the decisions (Chamberlin, 1978; Harp, 1987). In other words, consumer-run organizations have the same power issues as any other organization (Mead et al., 2001). Ziman (1987) articulated the problem:

> Unfortunately, the mental patient movement has had difficulty in achieving a community of equal partners, groups whose members all exercise equal power.... Alternative ways of relating and governing are difficult to sustain amidst a culture that propagates hierarchy. We have all internalized the ways society, and especially the mental health system, governs. We, too often, replicate them in our own client-run alternatives. (p. 182)

Ideally, consumer-run organizations adopt a consensus or collective decision-making approach that involves all members, rather than hierarchical structures in which decisions are made by leaders with little or no input from members (Chamberlin, 1978, 1994). In their quest not to adopt hierarchical structures, some organizations develop no decision-making structures and processes, which can lead to crisis within the organization. As Meagher (1996) noted, "Lack of adequate structure is one underlying cause of crisis. A very common element of fledgling consumer groups is the almost obsessive determination to avoid a formal structure" (p. 42).

The extent to which organizations can adopt true consensus approaches depends on at least two factors. One is the size of the organization, in terms of the number of programs it operates, the amount of members, and the size of the paid staff (Carley, 1994). The larger the organization, of course, the more difficult it is to implement consensus approaches to decision making. The other factor is the degree to which the organization has tasks it must complete. The greater the number of specific tasks, the most likely it is that a hierarchical approach will be employed because of its efficiency for task completion. McLean (1995) provided an example in which funding of a consumer-run program was contingent on achievement of certain goals. She concluded, "Hierarchical distinctions and unequal power distribution may be inevitable in situations where certain individuals have been hired to handle administrative details and may be discharged if they do not" (p. 1068). Ultimately, the degree to which consumer-run programs are able to use collective decision-making processes to empower its members will depend on its leadership, regardless of whether leadership emanates from assigned leaders who are paid staff or from informal leaders that exist among its membership. It is very difficult, however, for leaders to facilitate the membership to shape its own programs, and still meet any external expectations that may exist (McLean, 1995).

Referrals to Mutual Support Groups and Consumer-Run Programs

Both people with mental illness themselves and professionals can, and should, refer people with mental illness to mutual support groups and consumer-run programs. Currently, the majority of referrals of people with mental illness come from informal sources, such as other consumers, friends, and family members (Chinman et al., 2002; Davidson et al., 1999). This is an appropriate referral source that should be encouraged to continue. Also, consumer-run programs can make their participants aware of mutual support groups and other consumer-run programs from which they may benefit. Similarly, people with mental illness who serve as service providers in mental health agencies should take advantage of opportunities to make referrals.

In addition to informal and consumer-generated referrals, it is important that mental health professionals increase their referrals to mutual support and consumer-run programs. In their review of studies of these programs, Davidson et al. (1999) found that professionals referred between 20% to 35% of participants. Segal, Hardiman, and Hodges (2002) offered a rationale for professionals increasing their referrals:

> It is critical that community mental health agencies recognize and appreciate the role of self-help agencies in long-term maintenance and support.... While many services cannot be provided by the community mental health agencies because of time, cost, and case-load limitations, clients should not go without these services when they are available at nearby self-help agencies. (p. 1152)

More professionals may not be referring people with mental illness to mutual support groups and consumer-run programs for at least three reasons (Chinman et al., 2002). One is that professionals may not know about the available groups. Second, some professionals may not believe that these consumer-run activities are beneficial. There appears to be a small, but significant, minority of professionals that do not support these activities. One survey of professionals found that 16% indicated they would try to convince people with mental illness who were participating in self-help activities to seek professional services instead (Salzer et al., 2001). However, those professionals who do make referrals tend to do so repeatedly. This same survey of professionals found that 92% of professionals who make referrals would do so again (Salzer et al., 2001). Third, some professionals may view people with mental illness as incapable of service provision through mutual support groups and consumer-run programs.

Chinman et al. (2002) offered the following suggestions to promote greater referrals by professionals to mutual support groups and consumer-run programs. First, and possibly most important, professionals need information about their effectiveness; their potential to be a valuable resource to their clients; and their importance as a component of the overall mental health system of treatment, rehabilitation, and support. Another is to educate professionals about the availability of mutual support groups and consumer-run programs in their service areas. Consistent with this, Hardiman and Segal (2003) argued that professions have a responsibility to learn about these potential resources for their clients. Chinman et al. (2002) also suggested that mental health organizations incorporate referrals to self-help activities into their formal referral structure to ensure that these referrals are not overlooked. Next, they cited the creation of opportunities for increased interactions between professionals and self-help activities. As examples, professionals may be able to attend some mutual support groups that allow nonconsumers as guests, and consumer-run programs can hold open houses for professionals to showcase their activities. Finally, they recommended that traditional mental health organizations incorporate consumers who participate in mutual support groups and consumer-run programs into their administrative structure through mechanisms such as service on boards of directors, advisory boards, and committees in order to increase professionals' knowledge of, and comfort with, consumers and the activities and programs they represent.

Finally, Noordsy, Schwab, Fox, and Drake (1996) noted that referring people with mental illness to mutual support groups and consumer-run programs involves more than simply giving them the contact information. Using referrals of people with the co-occurring disorders of mental illness and substance abuse to self-help programs as an example, Noordsy et al. (1996) offered the following five guidelines. These included suggesting self-help programs as one of a range of available treatment options; offering to initially go with consumers to programs as they try to find one with which they are comfortable; treating the mental illness, substance abuse, and skill deficits so that consumers are in a better position to function in self-help programs; backing off of referrals to self-help programs if consumers are not receptive initially and discussing referrals again at later stages of treatment; and encouraging people with co-occurring disorders to attend mutual support groups and consumer-run programs that have experience working with co-occurring disorders in order to achieve the best possible fit.

Recruitment of Consumer-Providers

It can be difficult to recruit people with mental illness to be service providers in traditional mental health agencies. At least two factors may account for this. Some believe there is a shortage of qualified consumers, particularly those with the educational credentials that certain positions require (Mowbray, 1997; Zipple et al., 1997). It also may be difficult to recruit consumer-providers, not because they do not exist in sufficient supply, but because properly qualified and credentialed professionals are unwilling to disclose that they have a mental illness. Regardless of the reason, it usually will be necessary to develop special recruitment processes. Carling (1995) recommended developing affirmative action plans to guide the recruitment of consumer-providers. The plan can set hiring goals, which, for instance, one agency set at 15% (Zipple et al., 1997). Plans should include posting announcements in traditional places, such as newspapers and job service companies, and include a statement that consumers are preferred. It also should include targeted announcements placed in areas where people with mental illness may congregate, such as the locations of mutual support groups and consumer-run programs. In addition, Zipple et al. (1997) suggested contacting consumer-run programs, nonconsumer mental health advocacy groups, and vocational service providers. Although they did not list this, the professional organizations associated with mental health service providers can be contacted as well. Zipple et al. stressed that recruitment of consumer-providers from among these consumer and nonconsumer organizations should not be viewed as isolated one-time hirings, but as an ongoing process. They recommended that mental health agencies identify an employment liaison to maintain ongoing relationships with these organizations in order to expedite the hiring of consumers when vacancies arise. To further facilitate the hiring of consumer-providers, mental health organizations already should have identified accommodations that may be possible and discuss those with job candidates. It also is helpful to have consumer-providers already hired at the agency participate in the job interviews and share their work experiences (Carling, 1995). Both of these actions can make interviewees more comfortable, and they demonstrate to job candidates that the agency values consumers' contributions. Despite these efforts to recruit qualified consumer-providers, people meeting the expected levels of experience and education may not be located. In some instances, agencies may have identified consumers that did not meet all requirements but demonstrated potential. If this occurs, it may be possible to hire them anyway, and then assist them to obtain additional education or provide them with in-house training, supervision, and mentoring so they eventually can fully perform all job functions.

ACCESS TO RESOURCES

An eighth condition for empowerment is that people with mental illness have access to the resources needed to meaningfully participate in self-help activities, or in paid positions within consumer-run organizations or traditional mental health agencies. When consumer provision of services fails, it often is the result of insufficient resources dedicated to the situation (Mowbray & Moxley, 1997). In many instances, both consumers and nonconsumers will need at least some resources for consumer service provision to be successful. A discussion of the most important resources follows.

Training, Supervision, and Support for Consumer-Providers

Some consumer-providers, but certainly not all, will need training, supervision, and workplace accommodations (Davidson et al., 1999). Training can take several forms. It can include consumers pursuing college degrees (Paulson, 1991). It also can include didactic training provided by the agency. One agency, for example, provided consumers with 180 hours of didactic training as part of their preparation to help people who were hospitalized to transition to community living (Turner et al., 1998). In another program, consumers received 300 hours of didactic training to become case management aides (Sherman & Porter, 1991). A third type of training is on-the-job training, which often follows didactic training. The program cited above by Turner et al. (1998) required a 320-hour apprenticeship program working in agencies, which followed the 180 didactic training. After an initial 11-day orientation, another program paired newly hired consumer-providers with nonconsumer staff members until they were ready to work independently, which typically was approximately 8 weeks (Zipple et al., 1997). A fourth type of training is continuing education. One program, for instance, offered weekly workshops and paid for professional conferences for both consumer and nonconsumer staff (Zipple et al., 1997).

In addition to training, many consumers who serve as service providers will need ongoing, consistent supervision (Mowbray et al., 1996; Solomon & Draine, 1998). As Zipple et al. (1997) stated, "Good supervision is essential to the success of any employee in a mental health organization. This is particularly true for employees who have significant histories as mental health consumers" (p. 414). It is important that supervision not become "treatment" for the consumer-provider (Solomon & Draine, 1998). It can be difficult for some supervisors to view consumer-providers first as providers rather than as consumers, although these are two entirely separate functions that should not overlap. Also, some argue that consumer-providers should only be supervised by other consumers (Fisher, 1994b), while others believe that if a consumer-supervisor is not available, a nonconsumer supervisor should be located from outside the agency (Salzer & Mental Health Association, 2002). Regardless of who provides supervision, several content areas should be included. Supervisors should assist consumer-providers to identify ways to incorporate their experiences and perspectives as consumers into their work with agency clients and to benefit the agency as a whole (Carling, 1995). Supervision also should address issues that arise as a result of their dual roles as consumers and providers and the role confusion that can arise (Carlson et al., 2001). This includes helping them sort out their new relationship with their friends with mental illness who may be clients of the agency at which they are working and with their nonconsumer coworkers who may be having a difficult time adjusting to their presence. Supervision, too, should assure that consumer-providers can properly assess consumers' potential and do not hold expectations that are not appropriate for their clients (Solomon & Draine, 1998). Associated with this, supervision should also help consumer-providers deal with the anxiety, disappointment, and frustration they can experience when their clients do not meet their expectations.

Finally, some consumer-providers can benefit from other types of support. One type is peer support. Agencies that have multiple consumer-providers can create opportunities for them to get together to provide mutual support (Carling, 1995; Salzer & Mental Health Association, 2002; Solomon & Draine, 1998). In addition, some consumer-providers may need workplace accommodations. Common accommodations may include leaves for mental health and medical problems, and options for flexible work schedules as their symptoms may change (Carling, 1995). Developing workplace accommodations for mental illnesses can be difficult, requires creativity, and is a highly individualized process (Zipple et al., 1997).

Technical Assistance and Leadership Development for Consumer Service Activities

Other resources are related to the creation of mutual support groups and consumer-run programs. Mental health agencies can provide some resources needed to create and operate these programs. They can sponsor programs, offer meeting space, assist with starting bookkeeping systems and personnel files, help with organizing groups of consumers, and assist with the many issues that arise when trying to start new activities and programs (Mowbray & Moxley, 1997; Salzer & Mental Health Association, 2002). One of the most important contributions that mental health organizations can make is to help to develop consumer leaders, individuals who then can go on to establish consumer-run programs and mutual support groups, among other activities (Jasper, 1997). This can be a time-consuming process, but one that is vital to promoting consumer involvement in service provision.

People with mental illness can, and have, provided technical assistance and leadership training to their peers. The first major example of this was Chamberlin's (1978) book that included instruction on how people with mental illness could start consumer-controlled services. Many other less noteworthy, but still highly useful, guides written by people with mental illness on developing consumer-run activities have been written by Budd, Harp, and Ziman (1987), Harp and Ziman (1994), and Meagher (1996), to name a few. People with mental illness received a substantial boost in their ability to provide technical assistance to their peers wishing to create consumer-operated activities when the Community Support Program, now affiliated with the federal government's Center for Mental Health Services, funded three national self-help technical assistance centers. The National Empowerment Center (n.d.) and the National Mental Health Consumers' Self-Help Clearinghouse (n.d.) were funded in 1992, and the Consumer Organization and Networking Technical Assistance Center (n.d.) was funded in 1998. All three centers are led by people with mental illness, and most, if not all, of their staff members are consumers as well. While they provide a range of services that vary somewhat across the three centers, all three provide technical assistance to consumers who wish to develop consumer-run services and programs. Some of the assistance includes providing written information about the many topics that relate directly to starting and operating programs, providing opportunities for networking between consumer-run programs, holding national conferences where consumers can get together to share ideas, and consulting directly with individual consumer organizations including making site visits.

Training and Supervision for Nonconsumer Staff

Nonconsumer staff members also have a need for training and supervision to ensure they are maximizing consumers' ability to engage in service provision. Training should address the contribution that consumers can make to service provision, the research support for it, mutual support groups and consumer-run programs available to their clients, how they can support consumer-providers, and how to properly supervise consumer-providers without creating a therapeutic relationship (Salzer & Mental Health Association, 2002; Salzer et al., 2001; Solomon & Draine, 1998). When possible, people with mental illness should provide at least part of this training (Simpson & House, 2002). Nonconsumer staff also need supervision in order to openly address any concerns or discomforts they may have about working with consumer-providers (Zipple et al., 1997).

Financial Resources

Financial resources are needed in multiple areas to support consumer service provision. First is funding for consumer-run programs. Inadequate funding may be the single greatest impediment to the maintenance and expansion of consumer-run programs. As an example, in their study of consumer-run drop-in centers, Mowbray et al. (2002) found they often were underfunded, and that centers reported funding as their primary problem. Funding is needed to pay for all the expenses of any organization, including salaries, building expenses, supplies, insurance, and many other costs. Being able to bill for consumer-run services through Medicaid managed care contracts and other health insurance plans could greatly increase the number of consumer-run programs (Bassman, 2001). Traditional mental health agencies also need funding to be able to provide quality training to consumer-provider and nonconsumer staff to maximize their participation. Finally, greater funding is needed for research and evaluation on consumer service provision in order to improve service provision and to legitimate it (Holter et al., 2004).

SUPPORTIVE CULTURE

A final condition for empowering people with severe mental illness through service provision is that supportive cultures exist related to public policy making, professional mental health organizations, consumer-providers, consumer-run organizations, and mutual self-help activities. A supportive culture at the public policy level would include increased funding for national centers that provide technical assistance to people with mental illness as service providers, such as the National Empowerment Center (n.d.) and the National Mental Health Consumers' Self-Help Clearinghouse (n.d.); requirements that consumer-run services be included in the range of services that are available to people with mental illness through public funding, including public Medicaid managed care contracts; increased research on the effectiveness of consumer-run services and mutual support groups; and increased anti-stigma education that includes the capability and value of people with mental illness providing services to their peers as part of the educational message.

The establishment of a supportive culture within traditional mental health organizations is vital to consumer service provision because of their role in serving as a setting for consumer-providers, and providing technical support, financing, and referrals to consumer-run programs and mutual support groups. Establishing a support culture requires eliminating, or at least minimizing, the misconception held by many mental health professionals that people with mental illness cannot participate in service provision (Fisher, 1994b; Sherman & Porter, 1991). Agency leaders set the tone for creating a supportive culture (Solomon & Draine, 1998). This begins with establishing agency mission, vision, and values that reflect and support consumer service provision (Mowbray & Moxley, 1997). It also can be facilitated by hiring people with mental illness in both clinical and administrative positions, especially upper level administrative positions, and offering consumer-employees opportunities for education and advancement (Carling,

1995; Mowbray et al., 1996). In addition, a supportive culture offers consumer-providers reasonable accommodations, includes consumer-providers in all meetings and social events in which nonconsumer staff are involved, trains nonconsumer staff on the benefits consumer service provision, and provides good supervision to both consumers and nonconsumer staff that includes open discussion of dual roles and role confusion (Carling, 1995; Carlson et al., 2001; Manning & Suire, 1996; Solomon & Draine, 1998).

Finally, the culture within consumer-run programs and mutual support groups must continue to be one that respects and values the participation of all members, and continually seeks ways to incorporate their views into decision making and service provision (Carley, 1994). This can be difficult to accomplish, particularly as consumer-run organizations increase in size and become more task oriented (McLean, 1995). Without the continual inclusion of members in collective decision making, consumer-run programs will lose much of their unique contribution to consumer empowerment.

CASE STUDIES

To increase understanding of the opportunities for, and limitations to, the empowerment of people with mental illness through service, empowerment is examined through two cases studies, one among people with mental illness residing in a public psychiatric hospital that provides long-term care and treatment (Linhorst et al., 1999), and the other among those residing in the community who are receiving services from a publicly funded community mental health agency (Kryah et al., 2003).

Empowerment Among Clients in a Psychiatric Hospital (SLPRC)

Degree of Empowerment

SLPRC clients experienced little empowerment through service provision. Only three examples of client provision of services were identified. Clients ran an Alcoholics Anonymous group as part of the hospital's substance abuse treatment and a smoking cessation group. Hospital policy required that staff members must be present at all activities to provide oversight, but they sat away from the group and did not participate. Some hospital employees joined the clients' smoking cessation group as peer participants, but not as leaders. In addition, the hospital chaplain developed a working relationship with a local community church. The deacons of that church trained hospital clients to serve as deacons at the hospital services. While the chaplain still conducted the service, clients took a leadership role in running the service. When clients assumed this larger role in services, client attendance increased dramatically. Empowerment opportunities were lacking in all other areas. There were no consumer-providers, that is, no clinical staff members who identified themselves as having a mental illness. There were no consumer-run programs within the hospital, and no community consumer-run programs had an affiliation with the hospital clients or programs.

Application of Conditions for Empowerment

Many SLPRC clients had neither the participation skills nor symptoms managed enough to function as service providers. Some others did so, however, as evidenced by their successfully leading the Alcoholics Anonymous and smoking cessation mutual support groups, and serving as deacons in religious services held at the hospital. Many clients also may not have had the psychological readiness to serve as service providers, lacking confidence in their abilities, having low self-esteem, or displaying apathy. Many clinical staff and administrators may not have trusted or respected the abilities of hospitalized clients to be service providers, even within mutual support groups. They also may not have seen any clinical benefit for consumer provision that would be beyond that which clients already were receiving through traditional treatment and rehabilitation services. In addition, there were no structures for involving community consumer-run programs that could facilitate SLPRC clients' service provision or provide services to SLPRC clients. Most importantly, the hospital culture was not supportive of client service provision. While the hospital had adopted a psychiatric rehabilitation orientation, this orientation was thus far limited to the potential of clients to learn new skills and to function with supports in the community. The medical model still was pervasive in the hospital, which typically does not support consumer provision of services. The recovery perspective and strengths perspective, which support consumer service provision, largely were absent from the hospital.

The potential existed for consumer service provision in several areas. One is to have clients lead, or at least co-lead, more mutual support groups. Most of the clinical programs offer groups, but they typically were psychotherapy or counseling groups led by staff. Second, discharged clients could be asked to return to the hospital to lead groups that focus on discharge planning and successful reentry into the community. Some discharged clients returned to the hospital to visit friends and engaged current clients in informal discussion about their community experiences. These informal interactions could be formalized to benefit more hospitalized clients. Third, the hospital could establish linkages with community consumer-run programs. Volunteers from programs of this type could, for example, lead mutual support groups on discharge planning and successful reentry into the community, and in doing so could serve as role models. Finally, the hospital could hire people with mental illness as service providers. This would help to change the hospital culture to one that is more supportive of client service provision, and these individuals could be role models demonstrating that recovery is possible. None of this will happen without strong leadership to facilitate a cultural change that includes educating both clients and staff about value of consumer service provision and the potential of some SLPRC clients to be service providers.

Empowerment Among Clients of a Community Agency (BJC-BH)

Degree of Empowerment

Many BJC-BH clients were empowered, or at least had the potential for empowerment, through consumer service provision. A range of mutual support groups and consumer-run programs were available to clients in the St. Louis area. Clients and staff generally were knowledgeable of them, some clients participated in them, and staff tended to refer clients to them. Also, BJC-BH collaborated with two other agencies to help start a consumer-run program called the St. Louis Empowerment Center. In addition, some of the regular clinical and case management staff had histories of mental illness. BJC-BH also hired consumers into paraprofessional positions through at least two programs. In one, the agency received a federal grant to hire consumers to work in a program for people who had a mental illness and were homeless. In the other, they hired two consumers who received training as community support specialists through a special Missouri Department of Mental Health program. Also, BJC-BH hired a person who was a consumer into a regular nonclinical position. That individual conducted needs assessments, evaluations, and quality management studies; wrote grants; served as a liaison to numerous community projects; and participated in many other activities. At the time she was employed, she was receiving a disability income, SSDI, which she gave up for full-time employment at BJC-BH. She worked there approximately 8 years, during which time she received a number of promotions and had the title of Coordinator of Community Development when she left the agency. While she was not in a consumer advocate position, many staff saw her as such, in a positive way, and perceived her as a leader in helping the agency to be more attentive to client needs and perspectives.

Application of Conditions for Empowerment

The relatively high level of client empowerment through service provision was attributable through meeting several conditions. One was that the BJC-BH culture was supportive of mutual support groups and consumer-run programs. The agency adoption of the recovery perspective and strengths perspective supported this culture. The agency incorporated the importance of mutual support groups and consumer-run programs into their training of new employees, and allocated staff time toward the development of a consumer-run program. Most clients and staff believed such services could be a useful resource for some clients, and staff routinely referred clients to them. Many clients had the level of managed symptoms and participation skills required to benefit from such services. BJC-BH took advantage of two opportunities to hire consumer-providers into special paraprofessional positions designated for consumers, although both were short-term ventures. The agency had few concrete incentives to maintain these positions after the initial funding ran out, and had no incentives to create new such programs. In particular, current funding streams did not allow the agency to bill for services provided by paraprofessionals, including those with mental illness. In addition, consumer-providers who worked out of specially designated positions typically were not treated by other staff as regular employees and did not develop the social relationships that frequently emerged among coworkers. Clients also had little incentive to participate in these specially created positions because they were part-time, low pay, carried no benefits, and did not allow for advancement within the agency. The agency believed that hiring consumers into regular service positions was much more beneficial to both the consumer-providers and the agency. These consumer-providers had a full range of benefits and opportunities for advancement. The agency received qualified workers who could use their mental health experience as a consumer to better support their clients and the agency, and it could bill for their services. Some staff members, who also were consumers, chose not to openly disclose their mental illness to clients and to most staff, although many did. While some nonconsumer staff members were apprehensive about having coworkers who were consumers, this typically dissipated after they worked together for a short period.

GUIDELINES FOR PROMOTING EMPOWERMENT THROUGH SERVICE PROVISION

Numerous guidelines for promoting the empowerment of people with severe mental illness through participating in mutual support groups and consumer-run programs, and serving as consumer-providers in traditional mental health organizations can be derived from the application of the conditions of empowerment through consumer service provision.

1. *Offer a range of options that includes consumer-provided services.*
   It is now generally accepted that mutual support groups, consumer-run programs, and services provided by people

with mental illness employed in traditional mental health agencies should be among the mental health service options available to people with severe mental illness.

2. *Treat symptoms of mental illness and teach participation skills.* Some people with mental illness will be unable to participate in, or fully benefit from, mutual support groups and consumer-run programs unless their symptoms are more managed and they obtain needed skills.

3. *Encourage people with mental illness to visit multiple self-help activities.* Mutual support groups and consumer-run programs vary considerably in their structure, focus, and atmosphere. Consumers should be encouraged to visit multiple sites to find those that best meet their needs and with which they are most comfortable.

4. *Create new consumer-provided services if service gaps exist.* Consumer organizations, traditional mental health agencies, and mental health advocacy groups should work together to develop mutual support groups and consumer-run programs in those communities that do not offer these services.

5. *Develop affirmative action plans to promote hiring people with mental illness as service providers.* Traditional mental health agencies should develop plans that set hiring goals, include targeted recruitment methods, identify available workplace accommodations, incorporate consumer-providers already at the agency into the hiring and interview process, and outline educational and training options to enable consumer-providers to meet all job functions if they cannot already do so when hired.

6. *Discuss the research on consumer-provided services.* Both people with mental illness and nonconsumer providers and administrators can benefit from discussions of the relevant research. This information can help dispel stigmatized views of consumers' abilities and provide guidance for anticipating potential problems and ways to overcome them.

7. *Offer training to consumers engaging in service provision.* For paid employees of consumer run programs, this should include training in leadership, strategic planning, budgeting, fundraising, and other skills needed to operate nonprofit organizations. Some consumer-providers in traditional mental health agencies may need a combination of college education, continuing education, in-house training, or mentoring. This training can be provided, in part, by traditional mental health agencies, as well as from successful consumer-run programs and from national consumer technical assistance centers.

8. *Offer training to nonconsumer employees in traditional mental health agencies.* Training should include the value of self-help

services to their clients; the availability of self-help services in the area; the process to refer clients to self-help services; the value to the agency of employing consumer-providers and how to support them; and for supervisors, how to properly supervise consumer-providers without "treating" them. Consumers should serve as trainers whenever possible.

9. *Offer supervision to both consumer-providers and nonconsumer employees of traditional mental health agencies.* Consumer-providers will need supervision on how to contend with uncooperative nonconsumer coworkers, and with their dual roles as employees and mental health consumers and the resulting role confusion that may occur. Supervision of non-consumer employees should openly address any concerns or discomforts they may have with consumer-providers.

10. *Properly fund consumer service provision.* This includes funding to operate consumer-run programs, to train consumer-providers and nonconsumer staff to maximize the benefits of having consumer-providers at the agency, and to conduct additional research on consumer-provided services to further improve and legitimate them.

11. *Consumer-run programs should adopt and maintain collective decision-making processes.* Part of empowerment through participation in consumer-run programs extends not just from the services received but from the process of all members participating in the program operation. Programs need to periodically monitor decision-making processes to ensure they are as inclusive as possible, given the size of the organization and its required tasks.

12. *Implement consumer service provision in long-term psychiatric hospitals.* Consumer service provision can occur in psychiatric hospitals through at least three means. Some hospital clients can be trained to lead mutual support groups. Also, consumers from community consumer-run programs can lead mutual support groups or offer other services to hospitalized clients. Finally, hospitals can hire consumers into regular staff positions.

13. *Establish a culture that supports consumer service provision.* In traditional mental health agencies, agency leaders are responsible for creating a supportive culture. This can be done by setting mission, vision, and values that reflect and support consumer service provision; by hiring consumers into clinical positions and upper-level administrative positions; by offering reasonable accommodations to consumer-providers; by including consumer-providers in all meetings and social activities; and by providing staff with training and supervision.

12

Creating and Living
Empowered Lives

EMPOWERMENT OPPORTUNITIES AND LIMITATIONS

The preceding seven chapters illustrate the diverse opportunities for empowering people with severe mental illness, including those living in the community and those residing in long-term public psychiatric hospitals. Some of the opportunities were associated with subjective empowerment, that is, feelings of increased power, control, or influence. This occurred through the process of participation itself, through mechanisms such as having a meaningful voice in the operation of a mental health organization through serving on its board of directors or helping other people and being helped by others through participation in a mutual support group. Other opportunities were empowering because of the objective, or tangible, short-term outcomes that resulted from participation, such as getting a college degree or learning the skills required to engage in legislative advocacy. Still other opportunities were empowering because they led to objective long-term outcomes, for example, obtaining a job of one's choice and raising oneself out of poverty or moving to safe, affordable housing in one's community of choice. Table 12.1 lists the opportunities for empowering people with severe mental illness described in chapters 5 through 11.

The preceding chapters also identify substantial limitations to empowerment. Chapter 2, A History of Powerlessness, highlighted the long-term nature of many limitations to empowerment; chapter 3, Individual Rights, Coercion, and Empowerment, identifies the coercive

Table 12.1 Opportunities for Empowering People With Severe Mental Illness

- Meaningful participation in treatment planning
- Selection and maintenance of one's housing of choice
- Meaningful participation in the control of one's housing
- Meaningful participation in decision making regarding service development and pragmatic aspects of program operation within the organizations from which one receives services through mechanisms such as boards of directors, task forces, committees, open forums, consumer councils, and program evaluation
- Meaningful participation in service planning and policy making at the local, state, or federal levels through mechanisms such as state and regional planning boards, task forces, advocacy groups, offices of consumer affairs within state mental health authorities, consumer groups, mental health agencies, and voting
- Employment that provides a livable wage and offers benefits including comprehensive health and mental health insurance coverage
- Meaningful participation in research, evaluation, and performance improvement activities in multiple stages of the research process
- Meaningful participation in mutual support groups
- Meaningful participation in consumer-run organizations as members or as paid staff
- Employment as service providers in traditional mental health organizations

use of power as a limitation to empowerment; and chapters 5 through 11 describe limitations to empowerment associated with particular empowerment opportunities. One of the most prominent limitations affecting all empowerment opportunities is the enduring stigmatized views of people with mental illness as being violent, irresponsible, incapable of making meaningful decisions, or unable to care for themselves. These views are held by many people within society, including some policy makers, mental health professionals, family members, and even people with mental illness themselves. A second prominent limitation is insufficient financial resources. Such funding limitations extend to needed mental health treatment, rehabilitation, and support services, including the new psychotropic medications that have greater efficacy and fewer side effects, safe and affordable housing, and supported employment, to name a few. A third prominent limitation to empowerment is unmanaged psychiatric symptoms. Despite recent advances in mental health treatment and rehabilitation, including the new psychotropic medications and supported employment, for example, some people with mental illness are incapable of being empowered, that is, taking full control over their own lives, because of ongoing or periodic unmanaged psychiatric symptoms. Table 12.2 includes these three and other potential limitations to empowering people with severe mental illness.

**Table 12.2 Potential Limitations to Empowering People With Severe
            Mental Illness**

- Stigmatized views of people with severe mental illness
- Insufficient financial resources to fund quality mental health treatment, rehabilitation, and support services
- Unmanaged psychiatric symptoms
- People with mental illness lacking participation skills and the access to needed skill training
- People with mental illness lacking confidence, motivation, or willingness to meaningfully participate
- Cultural, racial, or ethnic differences inhibiting communication and understanding needed for meaningful participation
- Lack of concrete incentives, or the presence of concrete disincentives, for people with mental illness to participate, or for others to meaningfully involve people with mental illness
- Lack of choices that are meaningful
- Lack of information needed to make informed choices
- Choice limitations placed on people with mental illness by criminal justice agencies, legal guardians, or other potentially coercive bodies
- Lack of knowledge about the legal rights of people with mental illness or how to seek redress if their rights are violated
- Lack of structures and processes for meaningful participation
- Lack of access to advocates to provide support, or to mediators to resolve disputes
- People with mental illness lacking knowledge of the benefits to them for meaningful participation
- Parties participating with people with mental illness lacking knowledge of the benefits to people with mental illness and to themselves for meaningfully involving people with mental illness
- Lack of logistical resources needed for participation, such as transportation or child care
- Parties interacting with people with mental illness lacking the skills to meaningfully involve them
- Insufficient time to meaningfully participate together
- People with mental illness lacking knowledge of the successes of other people with mental illness that could inspire them to participate
- Organizational leaders not providing the time, training, or resources to support meaningful participation, nor modeling meaningful participation in their own interactions with people with mental illness
- Culture surrounding the potentially empowering activity lacking support for meaningful participation by people with mental illness

CREATING THE CONDITIONS FOR EMPOWERMENT

Chapter 4 identifies nine conditions that typically are necessary for empowering people with severe mental illness and for this empowerment to be sustained long-term. These conditions then are applied in chapters 5 through 11 to various opportunities for empowerment. Many parties can contribute to creating the conditions for empowerment that address limitations to, and maximize opportunities for, empowerment. The parties and their role in empowerment will vary by the specific opportunity for empowerment. There are, however, at least six parties that are in positions to contribute to creating the conditions for empowerment opportunities. The parties and their general contributions follow.

People With Severe Mental Illness

As identified in the conceptualization of empowerment in chapter 1, one person cannot empower another. People with severe mental illness must act to empower themselves. They are, of course, more likely to take such actions when conditions for empowerment are met. Yet, there are actions people with mental illness can take to empower themselves, or at least to create the conditions over which they have at least some control. The following are a sample of these actions:

- Seek out ways to manage psychiatric symptoms, such as taking psychotropic medication, learning stress reduction and symptom management techniques, or a combination of the two.
- Improve skills through training, rehabilitation, or formal educational activities, and request assistance to improve skills when skill deficits exist in specific empowerment opportunities.
- Take advantage of those opportunities for empowerment that already may exist through treatment planning, housing, organizational decision making, planning and policy making, employment, research, service provision, or other opportunities not addressed in this book, and request, and in some instances insist upon, these opportunities when they currently do not exist.
- Request, and in some instances insist upon, meaningful choices that promote empowerment, whether they be, for example, policy alternatives while engaged in organizational decision making or choices of housing.
- Identify, and carefully weigh, concrete incentives and disincentives for part-time and full-time employment.
- Volunteer to participate in boards of directors, task forces, committees, open forums, consumer councils, or program evaluations in order to influence service development and pragmatic aspects of program operation within the organizations from which one receives services.
- Volunteer to participate in state and regional planning boards, task forces, advocacy groups, state offices of consumer affairs, consumer groups, or mental health agencies in order to influence

service planning and policy making at the local, state, or federal levels.

- Exercise one's right to vote, if eligible, and participate in the political process.
- Request, and in some instances insist upon, opportunities to participate in all stages of the research, evaluation, or performance improvement processes.
- Request, and in some instances insist upon, the resources needed for meaningful participation, which, depending on the situation, may include training, transportation, the presence of an advocate, peer support, or other resources.
- Consider participating in mutual support and consumer-run organizations, both to receive assistance and to help others.
- Value short-term empowerment outcomes that can lead to greater empowerment in the future, such as completing a training program in order to sit on the board of directors of a mental health agency or working part-time before seeking full-time employment.
- Selectively disclose one's mental illness to help dispel the stigma of mental illness.
- Share experiences of recovery to serve as role models and to offer hope to others with mental illness.

Mental Health and Other Direct Service Providers

Individuals who provide treatment, rehabilitation, and support services directly to people with severe mental illness have many opportunities to create conditions for empowerment. First and foremost, they do this through the provision of services many people with mental illness need to be empowered. They also do this through other direct interactions they have with people with mental illness, as well as their interactions with other service providers, family members, administrators, advocacy groups, policy makers, and researchers. The following are some of the actions service providers can take to create conditions for empowerment:

- Provide quality treatment and rehabilitation services to enable people with mental illness to manage their psychiatric symptoms and develop the skills needed to meaningfully participate in empowerment opportunities.
- Provide emotional support to people with mental illness and celebrate even small accomplishments to help them develop the confidence, motivation, and willingness to participate in empowerment opportunities.
- Meaningfully involve people with mental illness in treatment planning by carefully listening to their opinions, by providing

them with choices and with accurate information to make informed choices, by acting on their preferences when possible,
and by using techniques of procedural justice when working
with coerced individuals.

- Create time, or at least advocate for time, in one's schedule to
meaningfully involve people with mental illness in treatment
planning.
- Involve family members of people with mental illness in treatment, rehabilitation, and support services, to the extent that
people with mental illness can, and are able to, give permission
and in accordance with state and federal law.
- Develop good working relationships with other service providers so that people with mental illness can access needed
services in a timely manner.
- Reject the continuum of care housing model, and instead encourage those who cannot live independently to consider supported housing realizing, though, that some individuals may
choose housing options that offer less independence.
- Maximize opportunities for people with mental illness to participate in the control of their residential setting, particularly those
residing in long-term hospitals and other congregate settings.
- Encourage agency administrators to involve people with mental
illness in organizational decision making through various means,
and meaningfully engage them when working directly with
them, for example, on an agency task force.
- Educate people with mental illness about opportunities to participate in planning, advocacy, and policy-making activities at
the local, state, or federal levels.
- Raise the issue of employment to people with mental illness and
discuss its concrete incentives and disincentives.
- Identify opportunities for people with mental illness to participate in research, evaluation, and performance improvement activities, and advocate for their participation in all stages of the
process.
- Educate people with mental illness about the opportunities for,
and the benefits of, participation in mutual support and consumer-run organizations.
- Treat coworkers who have mental illness with respect, and
support their meaningful participation in the organization.
- Identify service gaps and communicate them to administrators.
- Participate in advocacy groups to promote the development of
the range of treatment, rehabilitation, and support services
needed by people with mental illness.
- Educate people with mental illness about their legal rights and
ways to seek enforcement of those rights if violated.

- Provide or advocate for the logistical resources, such as transportation, stipends, or child care, that some people with mental illness need in order to meaningfully participate in an empowerment opportunity.
- Speak out against stigmatized views of mental illness when opportunities arise with people with mental illness themselves, with coworkers, with other service providers, with administrators, with policy makers, and with the general public.

Mental Health and Support Service Administrators

Arguably the most important empowerment-related function for administrators of mental health and support service programs or agencies is to create an organizational culture that is supportive of, and provides opportunities for, empowerment of people with mental illness. Administrators can do this through their interactions with clients and staff, through the policies and procedures they establish, and through the models of engagement they adopt. Some actions to create conditions for empowerment are similar to those of direct service providers and are repeated below, while others are unique to the position of administrator.

- Create an organizational culture that is supportive of, and provides opportunities for, empowerment of people with mental illness.
- Engage in interactions with clients in ways that are empowering in order to provide a model for others within the organization.
- Ensure that clients are receiving quality treatment, rehabilitation, and support services to manage their psychiatric symptoms and develop the skills needed to maximize their opportunities for empowerment.
- Provide emotional support when directly interacting with clients, and celebrate even small accomplishments by, for example, listing the names of people who are in job training, are engaged in volunteer work, or who recently became employed in order to help all clients develop the confidence, motivation, and willingness to participate in empowerment opportunities.
- Ensure that a structure and process through which clients can meaningfully participate in treatment planning exist, that clients and staff have the necessary time available for this to occur, and that a process exists to resolve disputes that may arise between clients and staff during treatment planning.
- Involve family members of people with mental illness in planning, policy making, and evaluation at the agency level.
- Develop good working relationships with administrators of other service providers to facilitate clients' accessing needed services in a timely manner.

- If responsible for a residential setting, maximize opportunities for clients to meaningfully participate in decisions associated with its operation.
- Involve clients in organizational decision making through various means, and meaningfully engage them when working directly with them, for example, at a board of directors meeting.
- Educate people with mental illness about opportunities to participate in planning, advocacy, and policy-making activities at the local, state, or federal levels.
- Create opportunities for clients to participate in all stages of the evaluation or performance improvement process.
- Provide financial, technical, and logistical resources to assist people with mental illness to develop mutual support groups and consumer-run programs.
- Actively recruit service providers who have a mental illness, and provide them with the necessary support, supervision, and training to succeed within the organization.
- Identify service gaps and communicate them to policy makers.
- Participate in advocacy groups to promote the development of the range of treatment, rehabilitation, and support services needed by people with mental illness.
- Ensure that clients are aware of their legal rights and ways to seek enforcement of those rights if violated.
- Provide the logistical resources, such as transportation, stipends, or child care, that some clients need in order to meaningfully participate in empowerment opportunities.
- Speak out against stigmatized views of mental illness when opportunities arise with people with mental illness themselves, with coworkers, with service providers, with other administrators, with policy makers, and with the general public.
- Empower staff by involving them in organizational decision making in order to increase the likelihood that they will meaningfully empower clients.
- Adopt models of engagement, such as the recovery perspective, the strengths perspective, and psychiatric rehabilitation, as well as models for particular issues, such as supported housing, supported employment, and participatory action research, that support empowerment.

Mental Health Advocacy Groups

Mental health advocacy groups contribute to creating the conditions for empowerment through their direct interactions with people with severe mental illness and through their work on behalf of people with mental illness. The following is a list of some of the actions they can take to promote empowerment:

- Recognize the valuable contribution that people with mental illness can make to advocacy efforts, such as helping to prioritize policy issues and develop position statements, offering moving testimony at legislative committee hearings, or providing labor to do mailings to the group's membership about an important new topic.
- Recruit people with mental illness to be members of the advocacy group and to be paid staff in larger advocacy organizations.
- Provide structures and processes through which people with mental illness can meaningfully participate in the selection of advocacy topics, in forming positions on these topics, and in developing the advocacy strategies to promote these positions.
- Provide people with mental illness with a range of opportunities for participation in advocacy so they can select those activities that best match their interests and abilities and produce an amount of manageable stress.
- Provide people with mental illness with the skills to meaningfully participate in advocacy, such as how to write letters to elected officials or approach elected officials at a lobby day.
- Provide emotional support to people with mental illness to help them develop the confidence, motivation, and willingness to participate in advocacy.
- Provide the logistical resources that some people with mental illness need in order to participate, such as transportation, child care, and meals.
- Advocate for increased funding for treatment, rehabilitation, and support activities, as well as for funding in those areas that fall outside of the narrow definition of mental health services, such as housing and employment.
- Align with advocacy groups outside of mental health when advocating for more broad-based issues, such as housing, education, employment, and health care.
- Advocate for federal comprehensive mental health and substance abuse insurance parity legislation, and advocate for similar bills in state governments until a comprehensive federal law is passed.
- Advocate for funding mechanisms that reduce the disparities in access to treatment, rehabilitation, and support services across states, across social classes, and across racial and ethnic groups.
- Advocate for increasing the legal rights of people with mental illness, and especially for increased enforcement of existing rights.

- Speak out against stigmatized views of mental illness when opportunities arise with people with mental illness themselves, with service providers, with other advocacy groups, with policy makers, and with the general public.

Planners and Policy Makers

For purposes of this discussion, planners are identified as state or federal government employees responsible for developing and implementing policies and service systems, and policy makers are elected officials responsible for passing legislation. Both parties affect the conditions for empowerment primarily through creating service choices and by providing resources necessary for empowerment. Planners, and occasionally policy makers, also affect empowerment through direct interactions they may have with people with mental illness. Some of these actions mirror those of advocacy groups but warrant repeating.

- Planners and policy makers should recognize the valuable contribution that people with mental illness can make to planning and policy making, particularly at a time when most states are reducing services.
- Planners should provide structures and processes through which people with mental illness can meaningfully participate in planning and policy making.
- Planners should solicit participation from groups internal to state and federal departments, such as state offices of consumer affairs, and from consumer advocacy groups that exist outside of the formal system.
- Planners should provide people with mental illness with the technical and interpersonal skills to meaningfully participate in planning and policy making.
- Planners should provide emotional support to people with mental illness to help them develop the confidence, motivation, and willingness to participate in planning and policy making.
- Planners should provide the logistical resources that some people with mental illness need in order to participate in planning and policy making, such as transportation, child care, and meals.
- Planners and policy makers should redesign funding mechanisms and service systems to reduce the disparities in access to treatment, rehabilitation, and support services that currently exist across states, across social classes, and across racial and ethnic groups.
- Policy makers should enact increased funding for treatment, rehabilitation, and support activities, including mutual support and consumer-run programs, as well as funding in those areas that fall outside of the narrow definition of mental health services, such as housing and employment.

- Federal policy makers should enact a comprehensive mental health and substance abuse insurance parity law, and state policy makers should enact the same in their states until comprehensive federal legislation is passed.
- Policy makers should increase the legal rights of people with mental illness, and especially increase enforcement of existing rights.
- Policy makers should fund a range of safe and affordable housing options for people with mental illness and others who cannot afford this necessity.
- Policy makers should remove disincentives to employment for people with mental illness or others with disabilities receiving SSDI and especially SSI.
- Policy makers should increase funding for medical research, as well as for social research and evaluation to continue to develop and improve treatment, rehabilitation, and support services.
- Planners and policy makers should speak out against stigmatized views of mental illness when opportunities arise with people with mental illness themselves, with their peers, with service providers, with advocacy groups, and with the general public.

Researchers and Evaluators

Finally, researchers and evaluators contribute to creating the conditions for empowerment by adding to the body of knowledge needed to improve mental health treatment, rehabilitation, and support services by including people with mental illness in the research process, and by continuing to study the conditions under which the empowerment of people with mental illness is likely to occur. These three areas are expanded upon in the following list of actions that researchers and evaluators can take to promote empowerment among people with mental illness.

- Continue research to improve all aspects of mental health treatment, rehabilitation, and support services.
- Continue to develop evidenced-based practices, as is being done in new areas such as supported housing and treatment of the co-occurring disorders of mental illness and substance abuse.
- Continue to evaluate the effectiveness and efficiency of mutual support groups and consumer-run programs.
- Provide structures and processes through which people with mental illness can meaningfully participate in all phases of the research and evaluation process.
- Provide people with mental illness with the technical and interpersonal skills to meaningfully participate in research and evaluation.

- Provide emotional support to people with mental illness to help them develop the confidence, motivation, and willingness to meaningfully participate in research and evaluation.
- Provide the logistical resources that some people with mental illness need in order to participate in research and evaluation, such as transportation and financial compensation.
- Investigate how people with mental illness can better manage their psychiatric symptoms, as well as how unmanaged symptoms affect the quality of participation in various activities that have the potential for empowerment.
- Investigate the type and level of skills people with mental illness need to meaningfully participate in specific activities that can be empowering, and how best to enable them to gain those skills.
- Investigate the psychological factors that prevent the readiness of people with mental illness to engage in a potentially empowering activity, as well as ways to increase their confidence, motivation, and willingness to participate in that activity.
- Investigate how mutual trust and respect can be created or retarded in specific activities that can be empowering, and ways to promote mutual trust and respect.
- Investigate the perceived incentives and disincentives for people with mental illness and other parties to participate together in a potentially empowering activity, and identify ways to increase incentives and reduce disincentives among participants in that activity.
- Investigate those choices that should exist within a potentially empowering activity for participation to be meaningful, the information needed to make informed choices, and ways to maximize choices.
- Investigate the structures and processes that promote meaningful participation in a potentially empowering activity, and ways to create and maintain them.
- Investigate the resources—including peer support, advocates, training, and logistical resources, among others—needed to promote meaningful participation in a potentially empowering activity.
- Investigate ways to create a culture that is supportive of empowering people with mental illness within mental health organizations and within society, and especially methods of reducing stigmatized views of people with mental illness.

LIVING EMPOWERED LIVES

Amid the discussion throughout the book about the conditions for empowerment and creating those conditions, one should not lose sight of the book's purpose, which is to enable people with severe mental illness to live empowered lives. Living an empowered life does not mean that people with mental illness no longer experience psychiatric symptoms. It does not mean that they will have endless choices. It does not mean success in everything they do. It does not mean they never will experience stigma. Rather, people live empowered lives under the following conditions:

- When they have the treatment, rehabilitation, and support services they require to manage their symptoms.
- When they seek out the skills they need to meaningfully participate in activities that provide them with control and power over important areas of their lives, such as having the skills to plan their own treatment or to obtain and maintain employment that raises them out of poverty.
- When they have the confidence, motivation, and willingness to try new things that can further their control over their own lives, and they can withstand failed efforts without damage to their sense of self.
- When they do their part to develop relationships based on mutual trust and respect, in which parties listen to each other's opinions, respectfully disagree, and reach compromises.
- When they recognize the incentives to participate in activities that can increase their power and influence, and when they educate others about the value they add by working together.
- When they consider all their choices in potentially empowering situations and work to create new choices when they are lacking.
- When they use existing structures and processes to participate in opportunities to exert control and influence over their lives, and seek to create new ones if their voices are not being heard.
- When they take advantage of and leverage resources to maximize their ability to take control of their own lives and work to create resources when they are lacking in a particular area.
- When they openly oppose stigmatized views of mental illness and do not internalize them.

This state of people with mental illness living an empowered life is dynamic and situational. People with mental illness can be empowered in some areas of their lives and not others. An empowered life can change when the conditions for empowerment change, such as psychiatric symptoms becoming more unmanageable despite the best treatment efforts, or resources required to participate in an important activity becoming unavailable. Thus, it is incumbent upon all of us to continually work to create opportunities for empowerment, and to develop and maintain the conditions for empowerment so that these opportunities can be realized. People who are empowered lead fulfilling and productive lives despite having a mental illness, which in turn benefits society as a whole.

References

Ackerson, B. J., & Harrison, W. D. (2000). Practitioners' perceptions of empowerment. *Families in Society, 81*(3), 238–244.

Addington v. Texas, 441 U.S. 418 (1979).

Allen, J. B., Jr., & Granger, B. (2003). Helping people with psychiatric disabilities start and develop consumer-run businesses. In D. P. Moxley & J. R. Finch (Eds.), *Sourcebook of rehabilitation and mental health practice* (pp. 319–331). New York: Kluwer Academic/Plenum Publishers.

Allen, M. (1996). Separate and unequal: The struggle of tenants with mental illness to maintain housing. *Clearinghouse Review: Journal of Poverty Law, 30*(7), 720–739.

Allen, M. (2003). Waking Rip van Winkle: Why developments in the last 20 years should teach the mental health system not to use housing as a tool of coercion. *Behavioral Sciences and the Law, 21,* 503–521.

Allen, M., & Smith, V. F. (2001). Opening Pandora's box: The practical and legal dangers of involuntary outpatient commitment. *Psychiatric Services, 52*(3), 342–346.

American Nurses Association. (2001). *Code of ethics for nurses with interpretative guidelines.* Washington, DC: Author.

American Occupational Therapy Association. (2000). *Occupational therapy code of ethics-2000.* Retrieved on September 12, 2003 from http://www.aota.org/general/coe.asp.

American Psychological Association. (2002). *Ethical principles of psychologists and code of conduct.* Washington, DC: Author.

Anthony, W., Cohen, M., Farkas, M., & Gagne, C. (2002). *Psychiatric rehabilitation* (2nd). Boston: Center For Psychiatric Rehabilitation, Boston University.

Anthony, W. A. (1993). Recovery from mental illness: The guiding vision of the mental health service system in the 1990s. *Psychosocial Rehabilitation Journal, 16*(4), 11–23.

Appelbaum, P. S. (1994). *Almost a revolution: Mental health law and the limits of change.* New York: Oxford University Press.

Atkinson, J. M., & MacPherson, K. (2001). Patients' advocacy: The development of a service at the state hospital, Carstairs, Scotland. *Journal of Mental Health, 10*(6), 589–596.

Aviram, U. (1990). Community care of the severely mentally ill: Is social control a "necessary evil" in policy-making considerations? *Psychiatric Quarterly, 61*(2), 77–86.

Bachrach, L. L. (1983). An overview of deinstitutionalization. In L. Bachrach (Ed.), *Deinstitutionalization* (pp. 5–14). San Francisco: Jossey-Bass.

Bachrach, L. L. (1994). Residential planning: Concepts and themes. *Hospital and Community Psychiatry, 45*(3), 202–203.

Baer, R. (2003). Supporting the employment of people with serious mental illness. In D. P. Moxley & J. R. Finch (Eds.), *Sourcebook of rehabilitation and mental health practice* (pp. 363–377). New York: Kluwer Academic/Plenum Publishers.

Baer, R., Goebel, G., & Flexer, R. W. (1993). An interdisciplinary team approach to rehabilitation. In R. W. Flexer & P. L. Solomon (Eds.), *Psychiatric rehabilitation in practice* (pp. 63–78). Boston: Andover Medical Publishers.

Banks, B., Charleston, S., Grossi, T., & Mank, D. (2001). Workplace supports, job performance, and integration outcomes for people with psychiatric disabilities. *Psychiatric Rehabilitation Journal, 24*(4), 389–396.

Bargal, D. (2000). The manager as leader. In R. J. Patti (Ed.), *The handbook of social welfare management* (pp. 303–319). Thousand Oaks, CA: Sage.

Barker, P. (2001). The Tidal Model: Developing an empowering, person-centred approach to recovery with psychiatric and mental health nursing. *Journal of Psychiatric and Mental Health Nursing, 8,* 233–240.

Barnes, M., & Bowl, R. (2001). *Taking over the asylum: Empowerment and mental health.* New York: Palgrave.

Barnes, M., & Wistow, G. (1994). Learning to hear voices: Listening to users of mental health services. *Journal of Mental Health, 3,* 525–540.

Baron, R. C., & Salzer, M. S. (2002). Accounting for unemployment among people with mental illness. *Behavioral Sciences and the Law, 20,* 585–599.

Bartle, E. E., Couchonnal, G., Canda, E. R., & Staker, M. D. (2002). Empowerment as a dynamically developing concept for practice: Lessons learned from organizational ethnography. *Social Work, 47*(1), 32–43.

Bassman, R. (1997). The mental health system: Experiences from both sides of the locked doors. *Professional Psychology: Research and Practice, 28*(3), 238–242.

Bassman, R. (2001). Whose reality is it anyway? Consumers/survivors/ex-patients can speak for themselves. *Journal of Humanistic Psychology, 41*(4), 11–35.

Bazelon Center for Mental Health Law and the Legal Action Center. (1998). *Partners in planning: Consumer's role in contracting for public sector-managed mental health and addiction services.* Rockville, MD: U.S. Department of Health and Human Services, Substance Abuse and Mental Health Services Administration.

Beeforth, M., Conlan, E., Field, V., Hoser, B., & Sayce, L. (1990). *Whose service is it anyway? Users' views on co-ordinating community care.* London: Research Development for Psychiatry.

Beers, C. W. (1908). *A mind that found itself: An autobiography.* New York: Longmans, Green, and Company.

Belcher, J. R., & DeForge, B. R. (1997). The appropriate role of the state hospital. *Journal of Mental Health Administration, 24*(1), 64–71.

Bellus, S. B., Kost, P. P., & Vergo, J. G. (2000). Preparing long-term inpatients for community re-entry. *Psychiatric Rehabilitation Journal, 23*(4), 359–364.

Bentley, K. J. (2000). Empowering our own: Peer leadership training for a drop-in center. *Psychiatric Rehabilitation Journal, 24*(2), 174–178.

Beresford, P., & Evans, C. (1999). Research and empowerment. *British Journal of Social Work, 29*, 671–677.

Beverly, C., & Alvarez, A. R. (2003). Employment and empowerment of people with disabilities: A social development perspective. In D. P. Moxley & J. R. Finch (Eds.), *Sourcebook of rehabilitation and mental health practice* (pp. 27–36). New York: Kluwer Academic/Plenum Publishers.

Bevilacqua, J. J. (1995). New paradigms, old pitfalls. In L. I. Stein & E. J. Hollingsworth (Eds.), *Maturing mental health systems: New challenges and opportunities* (pp. 19–30). San Francisco: Jossey-Bass Publishers.

Bianco, C., & Shaheen, G. E. (2001). Employment. In C. Bianco & S. M. Wells (Eds.), *Overcoming barriers to community integration of people with mental illnesses* (pp. 37–48). Delmar, NY: Advocates for Human Potential.

Bianco, C., & Wells, S. M. (Eds.). (2001). *Overcoming barriers to community integration of people with mental illnesses.* Delmar, NY: Advocates for Human Potential.

Bjorklund, R. W., & Pippard, J. L. (1999). The mental health consumer movement: Implications for rural practice. *Community Mental Health Journal, 35*(4), 347–359.

Blackwell, B., Eilers, K., & Robinson, D., Jr. (2000). The consumer's role in assessing quality. In G. Stricker, W. G. Troy, & S. A. Shueman (Eds.), *Handbook of quality management in behavioral health* (pp. 375–386). New York: Kluwer Academic/Plenum Publishers.

Blaustein, M., & Viek, C. (1987). Problems and needs of operators of board-and-care homes: A survey. *Hospital and Community Psychiatry, 38*(7), 750–754.

Bloch, S., Chodoff, P., & Green, S. A. (1999). Appendix: Codes of ethics. In S. Bloch, P. Chodoff, & S. A. Green (Eds.), *Psychiatric ethics* (3rd ed.) (pp. 511–531). New York: Oxford University Press.

Bloom, J. D., & Williams, M. H. (1994). *Management and treatment of insanity acquittees: A model for the 1990s.* Washington, DC: American Psychiatric Press.

Boll, J. (1995). Member roles in program evaluation: A case study from a psychosocial clubhouse. *Psychiatric Rehabilitation Journal, 19*(1), 79–82.

Bond, G. R., Becker, D. R., Drake, R. E., Rapp, C. A., Meisler, N., Lehman, A. F., et al. (2001). Implementing supported employment as an evidence-based practice. *Psychiatric Services, 52*(3), 313–322.

Bond, G. R., Drake, R. E., Mueser, K. T., & Becker, D. R. (1997). An update on supported employment for people with severe mental illness. *Psychiatric Services, 48*(3), 335–346.

Bond, G. R., & Resnick, S. G. (2000). Psychiatric rehabilitation. In R. G. Frank & T. R. Elliot (Eds.), *Handbook of rehabilitation psychology* (pp. 235–258). Washington, DC: American Psychological Association.

Boothroyd, R. A. (2000). The impact of research participation on adults with severe mental illness. *Mental Health Services Research, 2*(4), 213–221.

Boothroyd, R. A., Poythress, N. G., McGaha, A., & Petrila, J. (2003). The Broward County Mental Health Court: Process, outcomes, and service utilization. *International Journal of Law and Psychiatry, 26*, 55–71.

Bowl, R. (1996). Involving service users in mental health services: Social services departments and the National Health Service and Community Care Act 1990. *Journal of Mental Health, 5*(3), 287–303.

Brakel, S. J. (1988). After the verdict: Dispositional decisions regarding criminal defendants acquitted by reason of insanity. *DePaul Law Review, 37*, 181–258.

Brazeal, S., & Finkle, J. (2001, April). Legislation opens new doors for economic renewal. *The American City and County, 116*(5), 38–39.

Breakey, W. R., Flynn, L., & Van Tosh, L. (1996). Citizen and consumer participation. In W. R. Breakey (Ed.), *Integrated mental health services: Modern community psychiatry* (pp. 160–174). New York: Oxford University Press.

Broner, N., Franczak, M., Dye, C., & McAllister, W. (2001). Knowledge transfer, policymaking and community empowerment: A consensus model approach for providing public mental health and substance abuse services. *Psychiatric Quarterly, 72*(1), 79–102.

Brown, M. A., & Wheeler, T. (1990). Supported housing for the most disabled: Suggestions for providers. *Psychosocial Rehabilitation Journal, 13*(4), 59–68.

Brown, P. (1985). *The transfer of care: Psychiatric deinstitutionalization and its aftermath.* Boston: Routledge and Kegan Paul.

Brown, T. J. (1998). *Dorothea Dix: New England reformer.* Cambridge, MA: Harvard University Press.

Browne, G., & Courtney, M. (2004). Measuring the impact of housing on people with schizophrenia. *Nursing and Health Sciences, 6*(1), 37–44.

Budd, S., Harp, H. T., & Zinman, S. (Eds.) (1987). *Reaching across: Mental health clients helping each other.* Sacramento, CA: California Network of Mental Health Clients.

Bullock, W. A., Ensing, D. S., Alloy, V. E., & Weddle, C. C. (2000). Leadership education: Evaluation of a program to promote recovery in persons with psychiatric disabilities. *Psychiatric Rehabilitation Journal, 24*(1), 3–12.

Callahan, L. A., & Silver, E. (1998a). Factors associated with the conditional release of persons acquitted by reason of insanity: A decision tree approach. *Law and Human Behavior, 22*(2), 147–163.

Callahan, L. A., & Silver, E. (1998b). Revocation of conditional release: A comparison of individual and program characteristics across four U.S. states. *International Journal of Law and Psychiatry, 21*(2), 177–186.

Campaign for Mental Health Reform. (2003). The Campaign for Mental Health Reform: A new advocacy partnership. *Psychiatric Services, 54*(11), 1475–1479.

Campbell, J. (1997). How consumers/survivors are evaluating the quality of psychiatric care. *Evaluation Review, 21*(3), 357–363.

Carley, M. (1994). The governance structure of mental health client-controlled programs. In H. T. Harp & S. Zinman (Eds.), *Reaching across II: Maintaining our roots: The challenge of growth* (pp. 16–19). Sacramento, CA: California Network of Mental Health Clients.

Carling, P. J. (1993). Supports and rehabilitation for housing and community living. In R. W. Flexer & P. L. Solomon (Eds.), *Psychiatric rehabilitation in practice* (pp. 99–118). Boston: Andover Medical Publishers.

Carling, P. J. (1995). *Return to community: Building support systems for people with psychiatric disabilities.* New York: Guilford Press.

Carlson, L. S., Rapp, C. A., & McDiarmid, D. (2001). Hiring consumer-providers: Barriers and alternative solutions. *Community Mental Health Journal, 37*(3), 199–213.

Carrick, R., Mitchell, A., & Lloyd, K. (2001). User involvement in research: Power and compromise. *Journal of Community and Applied Social Psychology, 11*(3), 217–225.

Center for Mental Health Services. (2003). State and county psychiatric hospitals, inpatient census, end of 2000. Retrieved August 11, 2003 from the U.S. Department of Health and Human Services, Substance Abuse and Mental Health Services Administration, National Mental Health Services Center, Center for Mental Health Services at http://mentalhealth.samhsa .gov/databases

Chamberlin, J. (1978). *On our own: Patient-controlled alternatives to the mental health system.* New York: Hawthorn Books.

Chamberlin, J. (1990). The ex-patients' movement: Where we've been and where we're going. *Journal of Mind and Behavior, 11*(3/4), 323–336.

Chamberlin, J. (1994). Direct democracy as a form of program governance. In H. T. Harp & S. Zinman (Eds.), *Reaching across II: Maintaining our roots: The challenge of growth* (pp. 13–15). Sacramento, CA: California Network of Mental Health Clients.

Chamberlin, J. (1996). Self-help: Living it, promoting it, and learning from it. *The Community Psychologist, 29*(3), 10–11.

Chamberlin, J. (1997). A working definition of empowerment. *Psychiatric Rehabilitation Journal, 20*(4), 43–46.

Chamberlin, J., & Rogers, J. A. (1990). Planning a community-based mental health system. *American Psychologist, 45*(11), 1241–1244.

Chinman, M., Kloos, B., O'Connell, M., & Davidson, L. (2002). Service providers' views of psychiatric mutual support groups. *Journal of Community Psychology, 30*(4), 349–366.

Chinman, M. J., Allende, M., Weingarten, R., Steiner, J., Tworkowski, S., & Davidson, L. (1999). On the road to collaborative treatment planning: Consumer and provider perspectives. *Journal of Behavioral Health Services and Research, 26*(2), 211–218.

Christian Michaels, S., Noll, G., & Wernet, S. P. (1999). Organizational reform in a community mental health center. In S. P. Wernet (Ed.), *Managed care in human services* (pp. 181–199). Chicago: Lyceum Books.

Church, K. (1996). Beyond "bad manners": The power relations of "consumer participation" in Ontario's community mental health system. *Canadian Journal of Community Mental Health, 15*(2), 27–44.

Clark, C. C., & Krupa, T. (2002). Reflections on empowerment in community mental health: Giving shape to an elusive idea. *Psychiatric Rehabilitation Journal, 25*(4), 341–349.

Cogswell, S. H. (1996). Entitlements, payees, and coercion. In D. L. Dennis & J. Monahan (Eds.), *Coercion and aggressive community treatment: A new frontier in mental health law* (pp. 115–125). New York: Plenum Press.

318

Commission on Accreditation of Rehabilitation Facilities. (n.d.). Official Web site. Retrieved on September 14, 2003 from http://www.carf.org.

Congress, E. P., & Sealy, Y. M. (2001). The role of social work ethics in empowering clients and communities. In R. Perez-Koenig & B. Rock (Eds.), *Social work in the era of devolution* (pp. 305–330). New York: Fordham University Press.

Constantino, V., & Nelson, G. (1995). Changing relationships between self-help groups and mental health professionals: Shifting ideology and power. *Canadian Journal of Community Mental Health, 14*(2), 55–70.

Consumer Organization and Networking Technical Assistance Center. (n.d.). Official Web site. Retrieved on June 10, 2004 from http://www.contac.org.

Cook, J. A., & Burke, J. (2002). Public policy and employment of people with disabilities: Exploring new paradigms. *Behavioral Sciences and the Law, 20,* 541–557.

Cook, J. A., & Hoffschmidt, S. J. (1993). Comprehensive models of psychosocial rehabilitation. In R. W. Flexer & P. L. Solomon (Eds.), *Psychiatric rehabilitation in practice* (pp. 81–97). Boston: Andover Medical Publishers.

Corrigan, P. W. (2001). Place-then-train: An alternative service paradigm for persons with psychiatric disabilities. *Clinical Psychology: Science and Practice, 8*(3), 334–349.

Corrigan, P. W. (2002). Empowerment and serious mental illness: Treatment partnerships and community opportunities. *Psychiatric Quarterly, 73*(3), 217–228.

Corrigan, P. W., & Garman, A. N. (1997). Considerations for research on consumer empowerment and psychosocial interventions. *Psychiatric Services, 48*(3), 347–352.

Corrigan, P. W., McCracken, S. G., & Holmes, E. P. (2001). Motivational interviews as goal assessment for persons with psychiatric disability. *Community Mental Health Journal, 37*(2), 113–122.

Corrigan, P. W., & Penn, D. L. (1999). Lessons from social psychology on discrediting psychiatric stigma. *American Psychologist, 54*(9), 765–776.

Corrigan, P. W., & Watson, A. C. (2002). The paradox of self-stigma and mental illness. *Clinical Psychology: Science and Practice, 9*(1), 35–53.

Council of State Governments. (1950). *The mental health programs of the forty-eight states: A report of the Governors' Conference.* Chicago: Author.

Coursey, R. D., Curtis, L., March, D. T., Campbell, J., Harding, C., Spaniol, L., et al. (2000a). Competencies for direct service staff members who work with adults with severe mental illnesses in outpatient public mental health/managed care systems. *Psychiatric Rehabilitation Journal, 23*(4), 370–377.

Coursey, R. D., Curtis, L., March, D. T., Campbell, J., Harding, C., Spaniol, L., et al. (2000b). Competencies for direct service staff members who work with severe mental illnesses: Specific knowledge, attitudes, skills, and bibliography. *Psychiatric Rehabilitation Journal, 23*(4), 378–392.

Cradock, J. A., Young, A. S., & Forquer, S. L. (2002). Evaluating client and family preferences regarding outcomes in severe mental illness. *Administration and Policy in Mental Health, 29*(3), 257–261.

Croft, S. & Beresford, P. (1992). The politics of participation. *Critical Social Policy, 35,* 20–44.

Crosby, C., Carter, M. F., & Barry, M. M. (1995). The care process: Care environments, care management and staff attitudes. In C. Crosby & M. M.

Barry (Eds.). *Community care: Evaluation of the provision of mental health services* (pp. 59–86). Brookfield, VT: Avebury.

Dain, N. (1980). *Clifford W. Beers: Advocate for the insane.* Pittsburgh, PA: University of Pittsburgh Press.

Dalgin, R. S., & Gilbride, D. (2003). Perspectives of people with psychiatric disabilities on employment disclosure. *Psychiatric Rehabilitation Journal, 26*(3), 306–310.

Daskal, J. (1998, June 15). *In search of shelter: The growing shortage of affordable rental housing.* Washington, DC: Center for Budget and Policy Priorities.

Davidson, L., Chinman, M., Kloos, B., Weingarten, R., Stayner, D., & Tebes, J. K. (1999). Peer support among individuals with severe mental illness: A review of the evidence. *Clinical Psychology: Science and Practice, 6*(2), 165–187.

Davidson, L., & Hoge, M. A. (1996). Hospital or community living? Examining consumer perspectives on deinstitutionalization. *Psychiatric Rehabilitation Journal, 19*(3), 49–58.

Davidson, L., Hoge, M. A., Merrill, M. E., Rakfeldt, J., & Griffith, E. E. H. (1995). The experiences of long-stay inpatients returning to the community. *Psychiatry, 58*, 122–135.

Davis, S. (2002). Autonomy versus coercion: Reconciling competing perspectives in community mental health. *Community Mental Health Journal, 38*(3), 239–250.

Deegan, P. E. (1997). Recovery and empowerment for people with psychiatric disabilities. *Social Work in Health Care, 25*(3), 11–24.

Denton, A., & Bianco, C. (2001). Housing. In C. Bianco & S. M. Wells (Eds.), *Overcoming barriers to community integration of people with mental illnesses* (pp. 27–36). Delmar, NY: Advocates for Human Potential.

Depression and Bipolar Support Alliance. (n.d.). Official Web site. Retrieved on June 8, 2004 from http://www.dpsalliance.org.

Deutsch, A. (1948). *The shame of the states.* New York: Harcourt, Brace and Company.

Deutsch, A. (1949). *The mentally ill in America: A history of their care and treatment from colonial times* (2nd ed.). New York: Columbia University Press.

Dillon, M. R. (1994). Consumer choice is the American way. In C. J. Sundram (Ed.), *Choice and responsibility: Legal and ethical dilemmas in services for persons with mental disabilities* (pp. 117–125). Albany, NY: New York State Commission on Quality Care for the Mentally Disabled.

Donaldson v. O'Connor, 493 F. 2nd 507 (5th Cir. 1974).

Double Trouble in Recovery. (n.d.). Official Web site. Retrieved on June 8, 2004 from http://www.doubletroubleinrecovery.org.

Dougherty, M. (2001). Measuring up: HCFA, Joint Commission show some restraint. *Journal of AHIMA, 72*(5), 64–65.

Dowdall, G. W. (1996). *The eclipse of the state mental hospital: Policy, stigma, and organization.* New York: State University of New York Press.

Draine, J., Salzer, M. S., Culhane, D. P., & Hadley, T. R. (2002). Role of social disadvantage in crime, joblessness, and homelessness among persons with serious mental illness. *Psychiatric Services, 53*(5), 565–573.

Draine, J., & Solomon, P. (2001). Threats of incarceration in a psychiatric probation and parole service. *American Journal of Orthopsychiatry, 71*(2), 262–267.

Dresser, R. (2001). Research participants with mental disabilities: The more things change.... In L. E. Frost & R. J. Bonnie (Eds.), *The evolution of mental health law* (pp. 57–74). Washington, DC: American Psychological Association.

Dual Recovery Anonymous. (n.d.). Official Web site. Retrieved on June 8, 2004 from http://www.draonline.org.

Dubois, B., & Miley, K. K. (1999). *Social work: An empowering profession* (3rd ed.). Boston: Allyn and Bacon.

Duckworth, K., Kingbury, S. J., Kass, N., Goisman, R., Wellington, C., & Etheridge, M. (1994). Voting behavior and attitudes of chronic mentally ill outpatients. *Hospital and Community Psychiatry, 45*(6), 608–609.

Dullea, K., & Mullender, A. (1999). Evaluation and empowerment. In I. Shaw & J. Lishman (Eds.), *Evaluation and social work practice* (pp. 81–100). Thousand Oaks, CA: Sage.

Durbin, J., Goering, P., Wasylenki, D., & Roth, J. (1995). Meeting the challenge: Field evaluations of community support programs. *Psychiatric Rehabilitation Journal, 19*(1), 19–26.

Elbogen, E. B., & Tomkins, A. J. (2000). From the psychiatric hospital to the community: Integrating conditional release and contingency management. *Behavioral Sciences and the Law, 18*, 427–444.

Ellison, M. L., Anthony, W. A., Sheets, J. L., Dodds, W., Barker, W. J., Massaro, J., et al. (2002). The integration of psychiatric rehabilitation services in behavioral health care structures: A state example. *Journal of Behavioral Health Services and Research, 29*(4), 381–393.

Emener, W. G. (1991). Empowerment in rehabilitation: An empowerment philosophy for rehabilitation in the 20th century. *Journal of Rehabilitation, 57*(4), 7–12.

Emotions Anonymous. (n.d.). Official Web site. Retrieved on June 15, 2004 from http://www.mtn.org/EA.

Estroff, S. E. (1981). *Making it crazy: An ethnography of psychiatric clients in an American community.* Los Angeles: University of California Press.

Evans, C., & Fisher, M. (1999). User controlled research and empowerment. In W. Shera & L. M. Wells (Eds.), *Empowerment practice in social work: Developing richer conceptual foundations* (pp. 348–369). Toronto: Canadian Scholars' Press.

Evenson, R. C., Holland, R. A., & Johnson, M. E. (1994). A psychiatric hospital 100 years ago: II. Patients, treatment, and daily life. *Hospital and Community Psychiatry, 45*(10), 1025–1029.

Everett, B. (2001). Community treatment orders: Ethical practice in an era of magical thinking. *Canadian Journal of Community Mental Health, 20*(1), 5–20.

Ezell, M. (2001). *Advocacy in the human services.* Belmont, CA: Brooks/Cole.

Fabian, E., Abramson, L., & Willis, S. (2003). State rehabilitation authorities and their role in responding to the employment needs of people with serious mental illness. In D. P. Moxley & J. R. Finch (Eds.), *Sourcebook of rehabilitation and mental health practice* (pp. 117–126). New York: Kluwer Academic/Plenum Publishers.

Fakhoury, W. K. H., Murray, A., Shepherd, G., & Priebe, S. (2002). Research in supported housing. *Social Psychiatry and Psychiatric Epidemiology, 37*, 301–315.

Farabee, D., Shen, H., & Sanchez, S. (2002). Perceived coercion and treatment need among mentally ill parolees. *Criminal Justice and Behavior, 29*(1), 76–86.

Ferleger, D. (1994). The place of "choice." In C. J. Sundram (Ed.), *Choice and responsibility: Legal and ethical dilemmas in services for persons with mental disabilities* (pp. 69–97). Albany, NY: New York State Commission on Quality Care for the Mentally Disabled.

Fetterman, D. M. (1996). Conclusion: Reflections on emergent themes and next steps. In D. M. Fetterman, S. J. Kaftarian, & A. Wandersman (Eds.), *Empowerment evaluation: Knowledge and tools for self-assessment and accountability* (pp. 379–384). Thousand Oaks, CA: Sage.

Fetterman, D. M. (2001). *Foundations of empowerment evaluation.* Thousand Oaks, CA: Sage.

Fisher, D. B. (1994a). A new vision of healing as constructed by people with psychiatric disabilities working as mental health providers. *Psychosocial Rehabilitation Journal, 17*(3), 67–81.

Fisher, D. B. (1994b). Health care reform based on an empowerment model of recovery by people with psychiatric disabilities. *Hospital and Community Psychiatry, 45*(9), 913–915.

Fisher, W. A., Penney, D. J., & Earle, K. (1996). Mental health services recipients: Their role in shaping organizational policy. *Administration and Policy in Mental Health, 23*(6), 547–553.

Fisk, D., & Frey, J. (2002). Employing people with psychiatric disabilities to engage homeless individuals through supported socialization: The buddies project. *Psychiatric Rehabilitation Journal, 26*(2), 191–196.

Fitzsimons, S., & Fuller, R. (2002). Empowerment and its implications for clinical practice in mental health: A review. *Journal of Mental Health, 11*(5), 481–499.

Flannery, R. B., Jr., Penk, W. E., & Addo, L. (1996). Resolving learned helplessness in the seriously and persistently mentally ill. In S. M. Soreff (Ed.), *Handbook for the treatment of the seriously mentally ill* (pp. 239–256). Seattle: Hogrefe and Huber.

Fleming, J., & Ward, D. (1999). Research as empowerment: The social action approach. In W. Shera & L. M. Wells (Eds.), *Empowerment practice in social work: Developing richer conceptual foundations* (pp. 370–389). Toronto: Canadian Scholars' Press.

Flower, S. L. (1999). Resolving voluntary mental health treatment disputes in the community setting: Benefits of and barriers to effective mediation. *Ohio State Journal of Dispute Resolution, 14,* 881–905.

Forbes, J., & Sashidharan, S. P. (1997). User involvement in services-Incorporation or challenge? *British Journal of Social Work, 27,* 481–498.

Ford, L. H. (1995). *Providing employment support for people with long-term mental illness: Choices, resources, and practical strategies.* Baltimore: Paul H. Brookes.

Fossey, E., Epstein, M., Findlay, R., Plant, G., & Harvey, C. (2002). Creating a positive experience of research for people with psychiatric disabilities by sharing feedback. *Psychiatric Rehabilitation Journal, 25*(4), 369–378.

Foulks, E. F. (2000). Advocating for persons who are mentally ill: A history of mutual empowerment of patients and profession. *Administration and Policy in Mental Health, 27*(5), 353–367.

Fox, R. (2000). Involving consumers in the review of organizational performance: Lessons learned. In G. V. Sluyter (Ed.), *Total quality management in mental health and mental retardation* (pp. 47–55). Washington, DC: American Association on Mental Retardation.

Frank, R. G., Goldman, H. H., & Hogan, M. (2003). Medicaid and mental health: Be careful what you ask for. *Health Affairs, 22*(1), 101–113

Frese, F. J., III. (1997). The mental health service consumer's perspective on mandatory treatment. In M. R. Munetz (Ed.), *Can mandatory treatment be therapeutic?* (pp. 17–26). San Francisco: Jossey-Bass.

Frese, F. J., III. (1998). Advocacy, recovery, and the challenges of consumerism for schizophrenia. *Psychiatric Clinics of North America, 21*(1), 233–249.

Gammonley, D., & Luken, K. (2001). Peer education and advocacy through recreation and leadership. *Psychiatric Rehabilitation Journal, 25*(2), 170–178.

Gardner, W. Lidz, C. W., Hoge, S. K., Monahan, J., Eisenberg, M. M., Bennett, N. S., Mulvey, E. P., & Roth, L. H. (1999). Patients' revisions of their beliefs about the need for hospitalization. *American Journal of Psychiatry, 156*(9), 1385–1391.

Geller, J. L. (1989). Deinstitutionalization in 19th-century America. *Hospital and Community Psychiatry, 40*(1), 85–86.

Geller, J. L. (2000). The last half-century of psychiatric services as reflected in *Psychiatric Services. Psychiatric Services, 51*(1), 41–67.

Geller, J. L., Brown, J., Fisher, W. H., Grudzinskas, A. J., & Manning, T. D. (1998). A national survey of "consumer empowerment" at the state level. *Psychiatric Services, 49*(4), 498–503.

Geller, J. L, & Harris, M. (1994). *Women of the asylum: Voices from behind the walls, 1840– 1945.* New York: Anchor Books/Doubleday.

Geller, J. L., McDermeit, M., Grudzinskas, A. J., Jr., Lawlor, T., & Fisher, W. H. (1997). A competency-based approach to court-ordered outpatient treatment. In M. R. Munetz (Ed.), *Can mandatory treatment be therapeutic?* (pp. 81–95). San Francisco: Jossey-Bass.

Gerbasi, J. B., Bonnie, R. J., & Binder, R. L. (2000). Resource document on mandatory outpatient treatment. *Journal of the American Academy of Psychiatry and the Law, 28*(2), 127–144.

Gerhart, U. C. (1990). *Caring for the chronic mentally ill.* Itasca, IL: F. E. Peacock.

Gilbride, D., Stensrud, R., Vandergoot, D., & Golden, K. (2003). Identification of the characteristics of work environments and employers open to hiring and accommodating people with disabilities. *Rehabilitation Counseling Bulletin, 46*(3), 130–137.

Gilson, S. F. (1998). Choice and self-advocacy: A consumer's perspective. In P. Wehman & J. Kregel (Eds.), *More than a job: Securing satisfying careers for people with disabilities* (pp. 3–23). Baltimore: Paul H. Brookes.

Gingerich, S. (2002). Guidelines for social skills training for persons with mental illness. In A. R. Roberts & G. J. Greene (Eds.), *Social workers' desk reference* (pp. 392–396). New York: Oxford University Press.

Glasman, D. (1991, September 5). The challenge of patient power. *Health Service Journal, 101,* 16–17.

Glisson, C. (2000). Organizational climate and culture. In R. J. Patti (Ed.), *The handbook of social welfare management* (pp. 195–218). Thousand Oaks, CA: Sage.

Goffman, E. (1961). *Asylums: Essays on the social situation of mental patients and other inmates.* Garden City, NY: Anchor Books/Doubleday.

Goldkamp, J. S., & Irons-Guynn, C. (2000). *Emerging judicial strategies for the mentally ill in the criminal caseload: Mental health courts in Fort Lauderdale, Seattle, San Bernardino, and Anchorage.* Washington, DC: U.S. Department of Justice, Office of Justice Programs, Bureau of Justice Assistance.

Gollaher, D. (1995). *Voice for the mad: The life of Dorothea Dix*. New York: The Free Press.

Gowdy, E. L., Carlson, L. S., & Rapp, C. A. (2003). Practices differentiating high-performing from low-performing supported employment programs. *Psychiatric Rehabilitation Journal, 26*(3), 232–239.

Graeber, D. A., Moyers, T. B., Griffith, G., Guajardo, E., & Tonigan, S. (2003). A pilot study comparing motivational interviewing and an educational intervention in patients with schizophrenia and alcohol use disorders. *Community Mental Health Journal, 39*(3), 189–202.

Griffin, P. A., Steadman, H. J., & Heilbrun, K. (1991). Designing conditional release systems for insanity acquittees. *Journal of Mental Health Administration, 18*(3), 231–241.

Griffin, P. A., Steadman, H. J., & Petrila, J. (2002). The use of criminal charges and sanctions in mental health courts. *Psychiatric Services, 53*(10), 1285–1289.

Grisso, T., & Appelbaum, P. S. (1995). The MacArthur Treatment Competence Study. III: Abilities of patients to consent to psychiatric and medical treatments. *Law and Human Behavior, 19*(2), 149–174.

Grisso, T., & Appelbaum, P. S. (1998). *Assessing competence to consent to treatment: A guide for physicians and other health professionals*. New York: Oxford University Press.

Grob, G. N. (1973). *Mental institutions in American: Social policy to 1875*. New York: The Free Press.

Grob, G. N. (1983). *Mental illness and American society, 1875–1940*. Princeton, NJ: Princeton University Press.

Grob, G. N. (1991). *From asylum to community: Mental health policy in modern America*. Princeton, NJ: Princeton University Press.

Group for the Advancement of Psychiatry, Committee on Government Policy. (1994). *Forced into treatment: The role of coercion in clinical practice* (Report No. 137). Washington, DC: American Psychiatric Press.

Guadagnoli, E., & Ward, P. (1998). Patient participation in decision-making. *Social Science and Medicine, 47*(3), 329–339.

Gulcur, L., Stefancic, A., Shinn, M., Tsemberis, S., & Fischer, S. N. (2003). Housing, hospitalization, and cost outcomes for homeless individuals with psychiatric disabilities participating in continuum of care and housing first programs. *Journal of Community and Applied Social Psychology, 13*(2), 171–186.

Gutiérrez, L., GlenMaye, L., & DeLois, K. (1995). The organizational context of empowerment practice: Implications for social work administration. *Social Work, 40*(2), 249–258.

Gutiérrez, L. M., DeLois, K. A., & GlenMaye, L. (1995). Understanding empowerment practice: Building on practitioner-based knowledge. *Families in Society, 76*(9), 534–542.

Gutiérrez, L. M., Parsons, R. J., & Cox, E. O. (1998). *Empowerment in social work practice: A sourcebook*. Pacific Grove, CA: Brooks/Cole.

Hagner, D., & Marrone, J. (1995). Empowerment issues in services to individuals with disabilities. *Journal of Disability Policy Studies, 6*(2), 17–36.

Handler, J. F. (1973). *The coercive social worker: British lessons for American social services*. Chicago: Rand McNally College Publishing Company.

Handler, J. F. (1986). *The conditions of discretion: Autonomy, community, bureaucracy*. New York: Russell Sage Foundation.

Handler, J. F. (1990). *Law and the search for community.* Philadelphia: University of Pennsylvania Press.

Handler, J. F. (1992). Dependency and discretion. In Y. Hasenfeld (Ed.), *Human services as complex organizations* (pp. 276–297). Newbury Park, CA: Sage.

Handler, J. F. (1996). *Down from bureaucracy: The ambiguity of privatization and empowerment.* Princeton, NJ: Princeton University Press.

Hanrahan, M., Matorin, S., & Borland, D. (1986). Promoting competence through voter registration. *Social Work, 31*(2), 141–143.

Hardiman, E. R., & Segal, S. P. (2003). Community membership and social networks in mental health self-help agencies. *Psychiatric Rehabilitation Journal, 27*(1), 25–33.

Harp, H. T. (1987). Oppression within the group. In S. Budd, H. T. Harp, & S. Zinman (Eds.), *Reaching across: Mental health clients helping each other* (pp. 188–193). Sacramento, CA: California Network of Mental Health Clients.

Harp, H. T. (1994). Empowerment of mental health consumers in vocational rehabilitation. *Psychosocial Rehabilitation Journal, 17*(3), 83–89.

Harp, H. T., & Zinman, S. (Eds.). (1994). *Reaching across II: Maintaining our roots: The challenge of growth.* Sacramento, CA: California Network of Mental Health Clients.

Hasenfeld, Y. (1987). Power in social work practice. *Social Service Review, 63*(1), 469–483.

Havel, J. T. (1992). Associations and public interest groups as advocates. *Administration and Policy in Mental Health, 20*(1), 27–44.

Haynes, K. S., & Mickelson, J. S. (2002). *Affecting change: Social workers in the political arena* (5th ed.). Boston: Allyn and Bacon.

Hemmens, C., Miller, M., Burton, V. S., Jr., & Milner, S. (2002). The consequences of official labels: An examination of the rights lost by the mentally ill and mentally incompetent ten years later. *Community Mental Health Journal, 38*(2), 129–140.

Hendrickson-Gracie, K., Staley, D., & Neufeld-Morton, I. (1996). When worlds collide: Resolving value differences in psychosocial rehabilitation. *Psychiatric Rehabilitation Journal, 20*(1), 25–31.

Henry, A. D., Barreira, P., Banks, S., Brown, J., & McKay, C. (2001). A retrospective study of clubhouse-based transitional employment. *Psychiatric Rehabilitation Journal, 24*(4), 344–354.

Henry, A. D., Nicholson, J., Clayfield, J., Phillips, S., & Stier, L. (2002). Creating job opportunities for people with psychiatric disabilities at a university-based research center. *Psychiatric Rehabilitation Journal, 26*(2), 181–190.

Hess, R. E., Clapper, C. R., Hoekstra, K., & Gibison, F. P., Jr. (2001). Empowerment effects of teaching leadership skills to adults with a severe mental illness and their families. *Psychiatric Rehabilitation Journal, 24*(3), 257–265.

Hiday, V. A. (2003). Outpatient commitment: The state of empirical research on its outcomes. *Psychology, Public Policy, and Law, 9*, 8–32.

Hoge, M. A., & Grottole, E. (2000). The case against outpatient commitment. *Journal of the American Academy of Psychiatry and the Law, 28*(2), 165–170.

Hoge, S. K., & Feucht-Haviar, T. C. (1995). Long-term, assenting psychiatric patients: Decisional capacity and the quality of care. *Bulletin of the American Academy of Psychiatry and the Law, 23*(3), 343–352.

Holland, T. P, Knoick, A., Buffum, W., Smith, M. K., & Petchers, M. (1981). Institutional structure and resident outcomes. *Journal of Health and Social Behavior, 22*(4), 433–444.

Holmes, G. E., & Saleebey, D. (1993). Empowerment, the medical model, and the politics of clienthood. *Journal of Progressive Human Services, 4*(1), 61–78.

Holstein, J. A. (1993). *Court-ordered insanity: Interpretive practice and involuntary confinement.* New York: Aldine de Gruyter.

Holter, M. C., Mowbray, C. T., Bellamy, C. D., MacFarlane, P. & Dukarski, J. (2004). Critical ingredients of consumer run services: Results of a national survey. *Community Mental Health Journal, 40*(1), 47–63.

Hughes, R., & Weinstein, D. (Eds.). (2000). *Best practices in psychosocial rehabilitation.* Columbia, MD: International Association of Psychosocial Rehabilitation Services.

Hunter, R. H. (1999). Public policy and state psychiatric hospitals. In W. D. Spaulding (Ed.), *The role of the state hospital in the twenty-first century* (pp. 25–34). San Francisco: Jossey-Bass.

Husted, J. R. (1999). Insight in severe mental illness: Implications for treatment decisions. *Journal of the American Academy of Psychiatry and the Law, 27*(1), 33–49.

Hutchinson, S. A., Wilson, M. E., & Wilson, H. S. (1994). Benefits of participating in research interviews. *IMAGE: Journal of Nursing Scholarship, 26*(2), 161–164.

Isaac, R. J., & Armat, V. C. (1990). *Madness in the streets: How psychiatry and the law abandoned the mentally ill.* New York: The Free Press.

Ishiyama, T. (1970). The mental hospital patient-consumer as a determinant of services. *Mental Hygiene, 54*(2), 221–229.

Jackson, R. L. (2001). *The clubhouse model: Empowering applications of theory to generalist practice.* Belmont, CA: Brooks/Cole.

Jacobson, N. (2001). Experiencing recovery: A dimensional analysis of recovery narratives. *Psychiatric Rehabilitation Journal, 24*(3), 248–256.

Jacobson, N., & Curtis, L. (2000). Recovery as policy in mental health services: Strategies emerging from the states. *Psychiatric Rehabilitation Journal, 24*(4), 333–341.

Jacobson, N., & Greenley, D. (2001). What is recovery? A conceptual model and explication. *Psychiatric Services, 52*(4), 482–485.

Jansson, B. S. (2003). *Becoming an effective policy advocate: From policy practice to social justice* (4th ed.). Pacific Grove, CA: Brooks/Cole.

Järbrink, K., Hallam, A., & Knapp, M. (2001). Costs and outcomes management in supported housing. *Journal of Mental Health, 10*(1), 99–108.

Jasper, C. A. (1997). Moving forward: Consumer initiatives through leadership. In C. T. Mowbray, D. P. Moxley, C. A. Jasper, & L. L. Howell (Eds.), *Consumers as providers in psychiatric rehabilitation* (pp. 209–218). Columbia, MD: International Association of Psychosocial Rehabilitation Services.

Joint Commission on Mental Illness and Health. (1961). *Action for mental health: Final report of the Joint Commission on Mental Illness and Health.* New York: Basic Books.

Joint Commission on the Accreditation of Healthcare Organizations (n.d.). Official Web site. Retrieved on September 12, 2003 from http://www.jcaho.org.

Joint Commission revises standards for behavioral health care. (2000, May 25). *Report on Medical Guidelines and Outcomes Research, 11*(11), 8–10.

Jorgensen, J., & Schmook, A. (2000). *Offices of consumer affairs: A pathway to effective public mental health services.* Alexandria, VA: National Technical Assistance Center for State Mental Health Planning.

Kapp, M. B. (1996). Treatment and refusal rights in mental health: Therapeutic justice and clinical accommodation. In B. D. Sales & D. W. Shuman (Eds.), *Law, mental health, and mental disorder* (pp. 279–293). New York: Brooks/Cole.

Kasinsky, J. (1987). Cooptation. In S. Budd, H. T. Harp, & S. Zinman (Eds.), *Reaching across: Mental health clients helping each other* (pp. 177–181). Sacramento, CA: California Network of Mental Health Clients.

Katan, J., & Prager, E. (1986). Consumer and worker participation in agency-level decision-making: Some considerations of their linkage. *Administration in Social Work, 10*(1), 79–88.

Kaufmann, C. L. (1996). The lions' den: Social identifies and self help groups. *The Community Psychologist, 29*(3), 11–13.

Kemp, R., David, A., & Hayward, P. (1996). Compliance therapy: An intervention targeting insight and treatment adherence in psychotic patients. *Behavioural and Cognitive Psychotherapy, 24,* 331–350.

Kennedy, J. A. (1992). *Fundamentals of psychiatric treatment planning.* Washington, DC: American Psychiatric Press.

Kennedy, M. J. (1994). Customers come first. In C. J. Sundram (Ed.), *Choice and responsibility: Legal and ethical dilemmas in services for persons with mental disabilities* (pp. 25–28). Albany, NY: New York State Commission on Quality Care for the Mentally Disabled.

Kent, H., & Read, J. (1998). Measuring consumer participation in mental health services: Are attitudes related to professional orientation? *International Journal of Social Psychiatry, 44*(4), 295–310.

Kessler, R. C., Mickelson, K. D., & Zhao, S. (1997). Patterns and correlates of self-help group membership in the United States. *Social Policy, 27*(3), 27–46.

Kieffer, C. H. (1984). Citizen empowerment: A developmental perspective. In J. Rappaport, C. Swift, & R. Hess (Eds.), *Studies in empowerment: Steps toward understanding and action* (pp. 9–36). New York: Haworth Press.

Kilian, R., Lindenbach, I., Löbig, U., Uhle, M., Petscheleit, & Angermeyer, M. C. (2003). Indicators of empowerment and disempowerment in the subjective evaluation of the psychiatric treatment process by persons with severe and persistent mental illness: A qualitative and quantitative analysis. *Social Science and Medicine, 57*(6), 1127–1142.

Kirsh, B. (2000). Factors associated with employment for mental health consumers. *Psychiatric Rehabilitation Journal, 24*(1), 13–21.

Kloos, B., Zimmerman, S. O., Schrimenti, K., & Crusto, C. (2002). Landlords as partners for promoting success in supported housing: "It takes more than a lease and a key." *Psychiatric Rehabilitation Journal, 25*(3), 235–244.

Knisley, M. B., Hyde, P. S., & Jackson, E. (2003). Involvement of state and local mental health authorities in addressing the employment needs of people with serious mental illness. In D. P. Moxley & J. R. Finch (Eds.), *Sourcebook of rehabilitation and mental health practice* (pp. 127–142). New York: Kluwer Academic/Plenum Publishers.

Koch, J. R., Lewis, A., & McCall, D. (1998). A multistakeholder-driven model for developing an outcome management system. *Journal of Behavioral Health Services and Research, 25*(2), 151–162.

Kopelowicz, A., Wallace, C. J., & Zarate, R. (1998). Teaching psychiatric inpatients to re-enter the community: A brief method of improving the continuity of care. *Psychiatric Services, 49*(10), 1313–1316.

Korman, H., Engster, D., & Milstein, B. M. (1996). Housing as a tool of coercion. In D. L. Dennis & J. Monahan (Eds.), *Coercion and aggressive community treatment: A new frontier in mental health law* (pp. 95–113). New York: Plenum.

Koyanagi, C., & Belivacqua, J. J. (2001). Managed care in public mental health systems. In R. B. Hackey & D. A. Rochefort (Eds.), *The new politics of state health policy* (pp. 186–206). Lawrence, KS: University Press of Kansas.

Kruger, A. (2000). Schizophrenia: Recovery and hope. *Psychiatric Rehabilitation Journal, 24*(1), 29–37.

Kryah, R., Linhorst, D. M., & Anderson, J. (2003, April). *An evaluation of client empowerment at BJC Behavioral Health.* St. Louis, MO: Saint Louis University, School of Social Service, Center for Social Justice Education and Research.

Kumar, S. (2000). Client empowerment in psychiatry and the professional abuse of clients: Where do we stand? *International Journal of Psychiatry in Medicine, 30*(1), 61–70.

Kurtz, S., Stone, J. L., & Holbrook, T. (2002). Clinically sensitive peer-assisted mediation in mental health settings. *Health and Social Work, 27*(2), 155–159.

La Fond, J. Q., & Durham, M. L. (1992). *Back to the asylum: The future of mental health law and policy in the United States.* New York: Oxford University Press.

Lake v. Cameron, 364 F. 2nd 657 (D.C. Cir. 1966).

Lamb, H. R. (1984). Deinstitutionalization and the homeless mentally ill. *Hospital and Community Psychiatry, 35*(9), 899–907.

Lamb, H. R. (1998). Deinstitutionalization at the beginning of the new millennium. *Harvard Review of Psychiatry, 6*, 1–10.

Lamb, H. R. (2001). A century and a half of psychiatric rehabilitation in the United States. In H. R. Lamb & L. E. Weinberger (Eds.), *Deinstitutionalization: Promise and practice* (pp. 99–110). San Francisco: Jossey-Bass.

Lamb, H. R., & Weinberger, L. E. (1993). Therapeutic use of conservatorship in the treatment of gravely disabled psychiatric patients. *Hospital and Community Psychiatry, 44*(2), 147–150.

Lamb, H. R., & Weinberger, L. E. (1998). Persons with severe mental illness in jails and prisons: A review. *Psychiatric Services, 49*(4), 483–492.

Lamb, H. R., Weinberger, L. E., & Gross, B. H. (1999). Community treatment of severely mentally ill offenders under the jurisdiction of the criminal justice system: A review. *Psychiatric Services, 50*(7), 907–913.

Lamb, H. R., Weinberger, L. E., & Reston-Parham, C. (1996). Court intervention to address the mental health needs of mentally ill offenders. *Psychiatric Services, 47*(3), 275–281.

Langan, P. A., & Levin, D. J. (2002, June). *Recidivism of prisoners released in 1994: Bureau of Justice Statistics special report* (NCJ 193427). Washington, DC: U.S. Department of Justice, Office of Justice Programs, Bureau of Justice Statistics.

Lefley, H. P. (1996). *Family caregiving in mental illness.* Thousand Oaks, CA: Sage.

Lefley, H. P. (1997). Mandatory treatment from the family's perspective. In M. R. Munetz (Ed.), *Can mandatory treatment be therapeutic?* (pp. 7–16). San Francisco: Jossey-Bass.

Lehman, A. F. (1995). Vocational rehabilitation in schizophrenia. *Schizophrenia Bulletin, 21*(4), 645–656.

Lessard v. Schmidt, 349 F. Supp. 1078 (E.D. Wis. 1972).

Levine, M. (1981). *The history and politics of community mental health.* New York: Oxford University Press.

Liberman, R. P., Hilty, D. M., Drake, R. E., & Tsang, H. W. H. (2001). Requirements for multidisciplinary teamwork in psychiatric rehabilitation. *Psychiatric Services, 52*(10), 1331–1342.

Lidz, C. W., Hoge, S. K., Gardner, W., Bennett, N. S., Monahan, J., Mulvey, E. P., & Roth, L. H. (1995). Perceived coercion in mental health admission. *Archives of General Psychiatry, 52*(12), 1034–1039.

Linhorst, D. M. (1991). The use of single room occupancy (SRO) housing as a residential alternative for persons with a chronic mental illness. *Community Mental Health Journal, 27*(2), 135–144.

Linhorst, D. M. (1999). The unconditional release of mentally ill offenders from indefinite commitment: A study of Missouri insanity acquittees. *Journal of the American Academy of Psychiatry and the Law, 27*(4), 563–579.

Linhorst, D. M. (2002a). A review of the use and potential of focus groups in social work research. *Qualitative Social Work: Research and Practice, 1*(2), 208–228.

Linhorst, D. M. (2002b). Federalism and social justice: Implications for social work. *Social Work, 47*(3), 201–208.

Linhorst, D. M., & Eckert, A. (2002). Involving people with mental illness in evaluation and performance improvement. *Evaluation and the Health Professions, 25*(3), 284–301.

Linhorst, D. M., & Eckert, A. (2003). Conditions for empowering people with severe mental illness. *Social Service Review, 77*(2), 279–305.

Linhorst, D. M., Eckert, A., & Hamilton, G. (2005). Promoting participation in organizational decision making by clients with severe mental illness. *Social Work, 50*(1), 21–30.

Linhorst, D. M., Eckert, A., Hamilton, G., & Young, E. (2001). The involvement of a consumer council in organizational decision making in a public psychiatric hospital. *Journal of Behavioral Health Services and Research, 28*(4), 427–438.

Linhorst, D. M., Hamilton, G., Young, E., & Eckert, A. (2002). Opportunities and limitations to empowering persons with severe mental illness through treatment planning. *Social Work, 47*(4), 425–434.

Linhorst, D. M., & Turner, M. A. (1999). Treatment of forensic patients: An emerging role for public psychiatric hospitals. *Health and Social Work, 24*(1), 18–26.

Linhorst, D. M., Young, E., Eckert, A., & Hamilton, G. (1999, July). *An evaluation of client empowerment at St. Louis Psychiatric Rehabilitation Center.* St. Louis, MO: Saint Louis University, School of Social Service, Center for Social Justice Education and Research.

Link, B. G., & Phelan, J. C. (1999). Labeling and stigma. In C. S. Aneshensel & J. C. Phelan (Eds.), *Handbook of the sociology of mental health* (pp. 481–494). New York: Kluwer Academic/Plenum Publishers.

Link, B. G., Phelan, J. C., Bresnahan, M., Stueve, A., & Pescosolido, B. A. (1999). Public conceptions of mental illness: Labels, causes, dangerousness, and social distance. *American Journal of Public Health, 89*(9), 1328–1333.

Livermore, G., Nowak, M., Stapleton, D., Kregel, J., Bouchery, E., & Glosser, A. (2003, March 11). *Evaluation design for the Ticket to Work Program: Preliminary process evaluation.* Falls Church, VA: The Lewin Group.

Longo, D. A., Marsh-Williams, K., & Tate, F. (2002). Psychosocial rehabilitation in a public psychiatric hospital. *Psychiatric Quarterly, 73*(3), 205–215.

Lord, J., Ochocka, J., Czarny, W., & MacGillivary, H. (1998). Analysis of change within a mental health organization: A participatory process. *Psychiatric Rehabilitation Journal, 21*(4), 327–339.

Lucksted, A., & Coursey, R. D. (1995). Consumer perceptions of pressure and force in psychiatric treatments. *Psychiatric Services, 46*(2), 146–152.

Lyons, J. S., Cook, J. A., Ruth, A. R., Karver, M., & Slagg, N. B. (1996). Service delivery using consumer staff in a mobile crisis assessment program. *Community Mental Health Journal, 32*(1), 33–40.

Manderscheid, R. W., & Henderson, M. J. (2001). Where is mental health likely to be a century hence? An editorial perspective. In R. W. Manderscheid & M. J. Henderson (Eds.), *Mental health, United States, 2000* (pp. 1–2). Rockville, MD: U.S. Department of Health and Human Services, Substance Abuse and Mental Health Services Administration, Center for Mental Health Services.

Manning, S. S. (1999). Building an empowerment model of practice through the voices of people with serious psychiatric disability. In W. Shera & L. M. Wells (Eds.), *Empowerment practice in social work: Developing richer conceptual foundations* (pp. 102–118). Toronto: Canadian Scholars' Press.

Manning, S. S., & Gaul, C. E. (1997). The ethics of informed consent: A critical variable in the self-determination of health and mental health clients. *Social Work in Health Care, 25*(3), 103–117.

Manning, S. S., & Suire, B. (1996). Consumers as employees in mental health: Bridges and roadblocks. *Psychiatric Services, 47*(9), 939–943.

Margolin, L. (1997). *Under the cover of kindness: The invention of social work.* Charlottesville: University Press of Virginia.

Marshall, T. B., & Solomon, P. (2000). Releasing information to families of persons with severe mental illness: A survey of NAMI members. *Psychiatric Services, 51*(8), 1006–1011.

Mason, G., & Soreff, S. (1996). Quality improvement and serious mental illness. In S. M. Soreff (Ed.), *Handbook for the treatment of the seriously mentally ill* (pp. 517–530). Seattle: Hogrefe and Huber.

Mason, R., & Boutilier, M. (1996). The challenge of genuine power-sharing in participatory research: The gap between theory and practice. *Canadian Journal of Community Mental Health, 15*(2), 145–152.

Mazade, N. A., Glover, R. W., & Hutchings, G. P. (2000). Environmental scan 2000: Issues facing state mental health agencies. *Administration and Policy in Mental Health, 27*(4), 167–181.

McCabe, S., & Unzicker, R. E. (1995). Changing roles of consumer/survivors in mature mental health systems. In L. I. Stein & E. J. Hollingsworth (Eds.), *Maturing mental health systems: New challenges and opportunities* (pp. 61–73). San Francisco: Jossey-Bass.

McCarthy, J., & Nelson, G. (1991). An evaluation of supportive housing for current and former psychiatric patients. *Hospital and Community Psychiatry, 42*(12), 1254–1256.

McGee, S. A. (2002, November). Empowering the people. *Essence, 33*(7), 116.

McKenna, B. G., Simpson, A. I. F., & Coverdale, J. H. (2003). Patients' perception of coercion on admission to forensic psychiatric hospital: A comparison study. *International Journal of Law and Psychiatry, 26*, 355–372.

McLean, A. (1995). Empowerment and the psychiatric consumer/ex-patient movement in the United States: Contradictions, crisis, and change. *Social Science and Medicine, 40*(8), 1053–1071.

Mead, S., Hilton, D., & Curtis, L. (2001). Peer support: A theoretical perspective. *Psychiatric Rehabilitation Journal, 25*(2), 134–141.

Meagher, J. (1996). *Partnership or pretence: A handbook of empowerment and self-advocacy for consumers of psychiatric services and those who provide or plan those services* (2nd ed.). Strawberry Hill, Australia: Psychiatric Rehabilitation Association.

Means, R., & Smith, R. (1994). *Community care: Policy and practice.* London: MacMillan.

Mechanic, D. (1999). *Mental health and social policy: The emergence of managed care* (4th ed.). Boston: Allyn and Bacon.

Mechanic, D. (2001). Mental health policy at the millennium: Challenges and opportunities. In R. W. Manderscheid & M. J. Henderson (Eds.), *Mental health, United States, 2000* (pp. 53–63). Rockville, MD: U.S. Department of Health and Human Services, Substance Abuse and Mental Health Services Administration, Center for Mental Health Services.

Megivern, D., Pellerito, S., & Mowbray C. (2003). Barriers to higher education for individuals with psychiatric disabilities. *Psychiatric Rehabilitation Journal, 26*(3), 217–231.

Meinert, R., & de Loyola, S. (2002). The national Protection and Advocacy system: What social workers need to know. *Journal of Social Work in Disability and Rehabilitation, 1*(1), 15–26.

Mental Health Association of Greater St. Louis. (n.d.). Official Web site. Retrieved on December 17, 2003 from http://www.mhagstl.org.

Mental Health Association of Southeastern Pennsylvania. (n.d.). Official Web site. Retrieved on December 17, 2003 from http://www.mhasp.org.

Miller, P. S. (2000). The evolving ADA. In P. D. Blanck (Ed.), *Employment, disability, and the Americans with Disabilities Act: Issues in law, public policy, and research* (pp. 3–15). Evanston, IL: Northwestern University Press.

Miller, R. D. (1999). Coerced treatment in the community. *Psychiatric Clinics of North America, 22*(1), 183–196.

Miller, W. R., & Rollnick, S. (2002). *Motivational interviewing: Preparing people for change* (2nd ed.). New York: Guilford Press.

Mok, B., & Mui, A. (1996). Empowerment in residential care for the elders: The case of an aged home in Hong Kong. *Journal of Gerontological Social Work, 27*(1/2), 23–35.

Monahan, J., Hoge, S. K., Lidz, C. W., Eisenberg, M. M., Bennett, N. S., Gardner, W. P., Mulvey, E. P., & Roth, L. H. (1996). Coercion to inpatient treatment: Initial results and implications for assertive treatment in the community. In D. L. Dennis & J. Monahan (Eds.), *Coercion and aggressive community treatment: A new frontier in mental health law* (pp. 13–28). New York: Plenum Press.

Monahan, J., Lidz, C. W., Hoge, S. K., Mulvey, E. P., Eisenberg, M. M., Roth, L.H., et al. (1999). Coercion in the provision of mental health services: The MacArthur studies. In J. P. Morrissey & J. Monahan (Eds.), *Research in community mental health: Vol. 10. Coercion in mental health services—international perspectives* (pp. 13–30). Stamford, CT: JAI Press.

Morrell-Bellai, T. L., & Boydell, K. M. (1994). The experience of mental health consumers as researchers. *Canadian Journal of Community Mental Health, 13*(1), 97–110.

Morris, G. H. (1997). Placed in purgatory: Conditional release of insanity acquittees. *Arizona Law Review, 39,* 1061–1114.

Morrissey, J. P., & Monahan, J. (1999). Coercion in mental health services: Introduction and overview. In J. P. Morrissey & J. Monahan (Eds.), *Research in community mental health: Vol. 10. Coercion in mental health services—international perspectives* (pp. 1–9). Stamford, CT: JAI Press.

Moses, L. (2003, August 25). Selling "empowerment." *Editor and Publisher, 136*(30), 6.

Moss, K., Ullman, M., Starrett, B. E., Burris, S., & Johnsen, M. C. (1999). Outcomes of employment discrimination charges filed under the Americans with Disabilities Act. *Psychiatric Services, 50*(8), 1028–1035.

Mowbray, C. T. (1997). Benefits and issues created by consumer role innovation in psychiatric rehabilitation. In C. T. Mowbray, D. P. Moxley, C. A. Jasper, & L. L. Howell (Eds.), *Consumers as providers in psychiatric rehabilitation* (pp. 45–63). Columbia, MD: International Association of Psychosocial Rehabilitation Services.

Mowbray, C. T., Brown, K. S., Furlong-Norman, K., & Soydan, A. S. (2000). *Supported education and psychiatric rehabilitation: Models and methods.* Columbia, MD: International Association of Psychosocial Rehabilitation Services.

Mowbray, C. T., Leff, S., Warren, R., Jr., McCrohan, N. M., & Bybee, D. (1997). Enhancing vocational outcomes for persons with psychiatric disabilities: A new paradigm. In S. W. Henggeler & A. B. Santos (Eds.), *Innovative approaches to difficult to treat populations* (pp. 311–348). Washington, DC: American Psychiatric Press.

Mowbray, C. T., & Moxley, D. P. (1997). Consumers as providers: Themes and success factors. In C. T. Mowbray, D. P. Moxley, C. A. Jasper, & L. L. Howell (Eds.), *Consumers as providers in psychiatric rehabilitation* (pp. 504–517). Columbia, MD: International Association of Psychosocial Rehabilitation Services.

Mowbray, C. T., Moxley, D. P., Jasper, C. A., & Howell, L. L. (Eds.). (1997). *Consumers as providers in psychiatric rehabilitation.* Columbia, MD: International Association of Psychosocial Rehabilitation Services.

Mowbray, C. T., Moxley, D. P., Thrasher, S., Bybee, D., McCrohan, N., Harris, S., et al. (1996). Consumers as community support providers: Issues created by role innovation. *Community Mental Health Journal, 32*(1), 47–67.

Mowbray, C. T., Robinson, E. A. R., & Holter, M. C. (2002). Consumer drop-in centers: Operations, services, and consumer involvement. *Health and Social Work, 27*(4), 248–261.

Moxley, D. P., Jacobs, D. R., & Wilson, L. W. (1992). Building a clubhouse from the ground up: A strategic perspective. *Psychosocial Rehabilitation Journal, 16*(2), 125–139.

Moxley, D. P., & Mowbray, C. T. (1997). Consumers as providers: Forces and factors legitimizing role innovation in psychiatric rehabilitation. In C. T. Mowbray, D. P. Moxley, C. A. Jasper, & L. L. Howell (Eds.), *Consumers as providers in psychiatric rehabilitation* (pp. 2–34). Columbia, MD: International Association of Psychosocial Rehabilitation Services.

Mueser, K. T., Becker, D. R., & Wolfe, R. (2001). Supported employment, job preferences, job tenure, and satisfaction. *Journal of Mental Health, 10*(4), 411–417.

Mueser, K. T., Noordsy, D. L., Drake, R. E., & Fox, L. (2003). *Integrated treatment for dual disorders: A guide to effective practice.* New York: The Guilford Press.

Munetz, M. R., Galon, P. A., & Frese, F. J., III. (2003). The ethics of mandatory community treatment. *Journal of the American Academy of Psychiatry and the Law, 31*(2), 173–183.

Nash, M. (2002). Voting as a means for social inclusion for people with a mental illness. *Journal of Psychiatric and Mental Health Nursing, 9*(6), 697–703.

National Alliance for the Mentally Ill. (n.d.-a). About NAMI. Retrieved on September 2, 2003 from http://www.nami.org.

National Alliance for the Mentally Ill. (n.d.-b). Official Web site. Retrieved on December 17, 2003 from http://www.nami.org.

National Alliance for the Mentally Ill. (n.d.-c). NAMI Consumer Council. Retrieved on December 17, 2003 from http://www.nami.org/template .cfm?section=Consumer_Council.

National Alliance for the Mentally Ill. (1995). Involuntary commitment and court-ordered treatment. Retrieved on September 19, 2003 from http:// www.nami.org.

National Association of Consumer/Survivor Mental Health Administrators. (n.d.). Mission, publications, membership list. Retrieved on November 20, 2003 from http://www.nasmhpd.org/consurdiv.htm.

National Association of Protection and Advocacy Systems. (n.d). The origins of P&A and CAP systems. Retrieved on April 30, 2003 from http://www .protectionandadvocacy.com.

National Association of Social Workers. (1999). *Code of ethics of the National Association of Social Workers.* Washington, DC: Author.

National Association of State Mental Health Program Directors. (n.d.-a). Core elements of a successful office of consumer affairs. Retrieved on November 20, 2003 from http://www.nasmhpd.org/core.htm.

National Association of State Mental Health Program Directors. (n.d.-b). Official Web site. Retrieved on November 12, 2003 from http://www.nasmhpd.org.

National Association of State Mental Health Program Directors. (1989, December). Position statement on consumer contributions to mental health service delivery systems. Retrieved on May 23, 2004 from http://www.nasmhpd .org/general_files/position_statement/contribps.htm.

National Association of State Mental Health Program Directors. (1996, July). Position statement on housing and supports for people with psychiatric disabilities. Retrieved on October 15, 2003 from http://www.nasmhpd.org/ housingps.htm.

National Committee for Quality Assurance. (n.d). Official Web site. Retrieved on September 14, 2003 from http://www.ncqa.org.

National Consumer Council and State Presidents' Council Joint task force report on consumer inclusion and integration in NAMI. (2002). Retrieved on December 17, 2003 from http://www.nami.org/template.cfm?section= Consumer_Council.

National Consumer Supporter Technical Assistance Center. (2001). *How to develop and maintain a consumer advisory board.* Alexandria, VA: National Mental Health Association.

National Consumer Supporter Technical Assistance Center. (n.d.). The national mental health voter empowerment project. Retrieved on November 12, 2003 from http://www.ncstac.org/contents/projects/voter_emp.htm.

National Consumer Supporter Technical Assistance Center. (2002, September). *Launching a successful voter empowerment campaign.* Alexandria, VA: National Consumer Supporter Technical Assistance Center and the National Mental Health Association. Retrieved on November 12, 2003 from http://www.ncstac .org/contents/projects/voter_emp.htm.

National Empowerment Center. (n.d.). Official Web site. Retrieved on June 10, 2004 http://www.power2u.org.

National Mental Health Association. (n.d.-a). More about NMHA. Retrieved on December 17, 2003 from http://www.nmha.org/about/index.cfm.

National Mental Health Association. (n.d.-b). NMHA and the history of the mental health movement. Retrieved on December 17, 2003 from http://www.nmha.org/about/history.cfm.

National Mental Health Association. (n.d.-c). Official Web site. Retrieved on December 17, 2003 from http://www.nmha.org.

National Mental Health Consumers' Self-Help Clearinghouse. (n.d.). Official Web site. Retrieved on June 10, 2004 from http://www.mhselfhelp.org.

Neese-Todd, S., & Pavick, F. (2000). Person-centered practices in psychosocial rehabilitation. In R. Hughes & D. Weinstein (Eds.), *Best practices in psychosocial rehabilitation* (pp. 95–111). Columbia, MD: International Association of Psychosocial Rehabilitation Services.

Nelson, G., Hall, G. B., & Walsh-Bowers, R. (1999). Predictors of the adaptation of people with psychiatric disabilities in group homes, supportive apartments, and board-and-care homes. *Psychiatric Rehabilitation Journal, 22*(4), 381–389.

Nelson, G., Lord, J., & Ochocka, J. (2001). Empowerment and mental health in community: Narratives of psychiatric consumer/survivors. *Journal of Community and Applied Social Psychology, 11*(2), 125–142.

Nelson, G., Ochocka, J., Griffin, K., & Lord, J. (1998). "Nothing about me, without me": Participatory action research with self-help/mutual aid organizations for psychiatric consumer/survivors. *American Journal of Community Psychology, 26*(6), 881–912.

Nelson, G., & Walsh-Bowers, R. (1994). Psychology and psychiatric survivors. *American Psychologist, 49*(10), 895–896.

Newman, S., Harkness, J., Gaister, G., & Reschovsky, J. (2001). Bricks and behavior. The repair and maintenance costs of housing for persons with mental illness. *Real Estate Economics, 29*(2), 277–304.

Nicholson, R. A. (1999). The effects of coerced psychiatric hospitalization and treatment. In J. P. Morrissey & J. Monahan (Eds.), *Research in community mental health: Vol. 10. Coercion in mental health services—international perspectives* (pp. 141–174). Stamford, CT: JAI Press.

Noble, J. H., Jr. (1998). Policy reform dilemmas in promoting employment of persons with severe mental illnesses. *Psychiatric Services, 49*(6), 775–781.

Noble, J. H., Jr., Honberg, R. S., Hall, L. L., & Flynn, L. M. (1997, January). *A legacy of failure: The inability of the federal-state vocational rehabilitation system to serve people with severe mental illnesses.* Arlington, VA: National Alliance for the Mentally Ill.

Noordsy, D. L., Schwab, B., Fox, L., & Drake, R. E. (1996). The role of self-help programs in the rehabilitation of persons with severe mental illness and substance use disorders. *Community Mental Health Journal, 32*(1), 71–81.

North, C. A. (1987). *Welcome, silence: My triumph over schizophrenia.* New York: Simon and Schuster.

Ochocka, J., Janzen, R., & Nelson, G. (2002). Sharing power and knowledge: Professional and mental health consumer/survivor researchers working together in a participatory action research project. *Psychiatric Rehabilitation Journal, 25*(4), 379–387.

O'Connor v. Donaldson, 422 U.S. 563 (1975).

O'Day, B., & Killeen, M. (2002). Does U.S. federal policy support employment and recovery for people with psychiatric disabilities? *Behavioral Sciences and the Law, 20,* 559–583.

O'Flynn, D., & Craig, T. (2001). Which way to work? Occupations, vocations and opportunities for mental health service users. *Journal of Mental Health, 10*(1), 1–4.

Ogilvie, R. J. (1997). The state of supported housing for mental health consumers: A literature review. *Psychiatric Rehabilitation Journal, 21*(2), 122–131.

O'Hara, A., & Cooper, E. (2003, May). *Priced out in 2002.* Boston: Technical Assistance Collaborative, Washington, DC: Consortium for Citizens with Disabilities Housing Task Force.

O'Hara, C. C., & Harrell, M. (1991). *Rehabilitation with brain injury survivors: An empowerment approach.* Gaithersburg, MD: Aspen Publishers.

Olley, M. C., & Ogloff, J. R. P. (1995). Patients' rights advocacy: Implications for program design and implementation. *Journal of Mental Health Administration, 22*(4), 368–376.

Olmstead v. L.C., by Zimring, 527 U.S. 581 (1999).

Orrin, D. (1997). Consumer involvement in policy making. *Psychiatric Rehabilitation Journal, 21*(1), 75–79.

Owen, C., Rutherford, V., Jones, M., Wright, C., Tennant, C., & Smallman, A. (1996). Housing accommodation preferences of people with psychiatric disabilities. *Psychiatric Services, 47*(6), 628–632.

Paris, D. C., & Reynolds, J. F. (1983). *The logic of policy inquiry.* New York: Longman.

Parkinson, S., Nelson, G., & Horgan, S. (1999). From housing to homes: A review of the literature on housing approaches for psychiatric consumers/survivors. *Canadian Journal of Community Mental Health, 18*(1), 145–164.

Parry, J., & Gilliam, F. P. (2002). *Handbook on mental disability law.* Washington, DC: American Bar Association.

Parsons, R. J. (2002). Guidelines for empowerment-based social work practice. In A. R. Roberts & G. J. Greene (Eds.), *Social workers' desk reference* (pp. 396–401). New York: Oxford University Press.

Patton, M. Q. (1997). *Utilization-focused evaluation: The next century text* (3rd ed.). Thousand Oaks, CA: Sage.

Paulson, R. I. (1991). Professional training for consumers and family members: One road to empowerment. *Psychosocial Rehabilitation Journal, 14*(3), 69–80.

Peck, E., Gulliver, P., & Towel, D. (2002). Information, consultation or control: User involvement in mental health services in England at the turn of the century. *Journal of Mental Health, 11*(4), 441–451.

Peled, E., & Leichtentritt, R. (2002). The ethics of qualitative social work research. *Qualitative Social Work: Research and Practice, 1*(2), 145–169.

Penney, D. J. (1994). Choice, common sense, and responsibility: The system's obligations to recipients. In C. J. Sundram (Ed.), *Choice and responsibility: Legal and ethical dilemmas in services for persons with mental disabilities* (pp. 29–32). Albany, NY: New York State Commission on Quality Care for the Mentally Disabled.

Perlin, M. L. (1992). On "sanism." *SMU Law Review, 46*(2), 373–407.

Pescosolido, B. A., Monahan, J., Link, B. G., Stueve, A., & Kikuzawa, S. (1999). The public's view of the competence, dangerousness, and need for legal coercion of persons with mental health problems. *American Journal of Public Health, 89*(9), 1339–1345.

Petrila, J., & Brink, T. (2001). Mental illness and changing definitions of disability under the Americans with Disabilities Act. *Psychiatric Services, 52*(5), 626–630.

Petrila, J., & Levin, B. L. (1996). Impact of mental disability law on mental health policies and services. In B. L. Levin & J. Petrila (Eds.), *Mental health services: A public health perspective* (pp. 38–62). New York: Oxford University Press.

Petrila, J., Ridgely, M. S., & Borum, R. (2003). Debating outpatient commitment: Controversy, trends, and empirical data. *Crime and Delinquency, 49*(1), 157–172.

Pilgrim, D., & Waldron, L. (1998). User involvement in mental health service development: How far can it go? *Journal of Mental Health, 7*(1), 95–104.

Poythress, N. G., Petrila, J., McGaha, A., & Boothroyd, R. (2002). Perceived coercion and procedural justice in the Broward County mental health court. *International Journal of Law and Psychiatry, 25,* 517–533.

Pratt, C. W., & Gill, K. J. (1990). Sharing research knowledge to empower people who are chronically mentally ill. *Psychosocial Rehabilitation Journal, 13*(3), 75–79.

Pratt, C. W., Gill, K. J., Barrett, N. M., & Roberts, M. M. (1999). *Psychiatric rehabilitation.* New York: Academic Press.

President's New Freedom Commission on Mental Health. (2003). *Achieving the promise: Transforming mental health care in America: Final report.* Rockville, MD: U.S. Department of Health and Human Services.

Provencher, H. L., Gregg, R., Mead, S., & Mueser, K. T. (2002). The role of work in the recovery of persons with psychiatric disabilities. *Psychiatric Rehabilitation Journal, 26*(2), 132–144.

Pulier, M. L., & Hubbard, W. T. (2001). Psychiatric rehabilitation principles for re-engineering board and care facilities. *Psychiatric Rehabilitation Journal, 24*(3), 266–274.

Pyke, J., & Lowe, J. (1996). Supporting people, not structures: Changes in the provision of housing support. *Psychiatric Rehabilitation Journal, 19*(3), 5–12.

Race, K. E. H., Hotch, D. F., & Packer, T. (1994). Rehabilitation program evaluation: Use of focus groups to empower clients. *Evaluation Review, 18*(6), 730–740.

Rapp, C. A. (1998). *The strengths model: Case management with people suffering from severe and persistent mental illness.* New York: Oxford University Press.

Rapp, C. A. (2002). A strengths approach to case management with clients with severe mental disabilities. In A. R. Roberts & G. J. Greene (Eds.), *Social workers' desk reference* (pp. 486–491). New York: Oxford University Press.

Rapp, C. A., Shera, W., & Kisthardt, W. (1993). Research strategies for consumer empowerment of people with severe mental illness. *Social Work, 38*(6), 727–735.

Rappaport, J. (1985). The power of empowerment language. *Social Policy, 16*(2), 15–21.

Rappaport, J. (1987). Terms of empowerment/exemplars of prevention: Toward a theory for community psychology. *American Journal of Community Psychology, 15*(2), 121–148.

Recovery, Inc. (n.d.). Official Web site. Retrieved on June 8, 2004 from http://www.recovery-inc.com.

Reeve, P., Cornell, S., D'Costa, B., Janzen, R., & Ochocka, J. (2002). From our perspective: Consumer researchers speak about their experience in a community mental health research project. *Psychiatric Rehabilitation Journal, 25*(4), 403–408.

Reisch, M. (2002). Legislative advocacy to empower oppressed and vulnerable groups. In A. R. Roberts & G. J. Greene (Eds.), *Social workers' desk reference* (pp. 545–551). New York: Oxford University Press.

Reisner, R., & Slobogin, C. (1990). *Law and the mental health system: Civil and criminal aspects* (2nd). St. Paul, MN: West Publishing.

Repper, J., Ford, R., & Cooke, A. (1994). How can nurses building trusting relationships with people with severe and long-term mental health problems? Experiences of case managers and their clients. *Journal of Advanced Nursing, 19,* 1096–1104.

Richan, W. C. (1996). *Lobbying for social change* (2nd ed.). New York: Haworth.

Ridgway, P., Simpson, A., Wittman, F. D., & Wheeler, G. (1998). Home making and community building: Notes on empowerment and place. In B. L. Levin, A. K. Blanch, & A. Jennigs (Eds.), *Women's mental health services* (pp. 155–174). Thousand Oaks, CA: Sage.

Ridgway, P., & Zipple, A. M. (1990). The paradigm shift in residential services: From the linear continuum to supported housing approaches. *Psychosocial Rehabilitation Journal, 13*(4), 11–31.

Riger, S. (1993). What's wrong with empowerment. *American Journal of Community Psychology, 21*(3), 279–292.

Robbins, K. I., & Van Rybroek, G. J. (1995). The state psychiatric hospital in a mature system. In L. I. Stein & E. J. Hollingsworth (Eds.), *Maturing mental health systems: New challenges and opportunities* (pp. 87–101). San Francisco: Jossey-Bass.

Robbins, S. P., Chatterjee, P., & Canda, E. R. (1998). *Contemporary human behavior theory: A critical perspective for social work.* Boston: Allyn and Bacon.

Rochefort, D. A. (1997). *From poorhouses to homelessness: Policy analysis and mental health care* (2nd ed.). Westport, CT: Auburn House.

Rogers, E. S., Chamberlin, J., Ellison, M. L., & Crean, T. (1997). A consumer-constructed scale to measure empowerment among users of mental health services. *Psychiatric Services, 48*(8), 1042–1047.

Rogers, E. S., & Palmer-Erbs, V. (1994). Participatory action research: Implications for research and evaluation in psychiatric rehabilitation. *Psychiatric Rehabilitation Journal, 18*(2), 3–12.

Rogers, S. (1993a, Fall-Winter). How to make a consumer affairs office work. *The Key: National Mental Health Consumers' Self-Help Clearinghouse Newsletter, 2*(1), 6–12.

Rogers, S. (1993b, Fall-Winter). Nationwide, mixed review of offices of consumer affairs. *The Key: National Mental Health Consumers' Self-Help Clearinghouse Newsletter, 2*(1), 1–12.

Rollins, A. L., Mueser, K. T., Bond, G. R., & Becker, D. R. (2002). Social relationships at work: Does the employment model make a difference. *Psychiatric Rehabilitation Journal, 26*(1), 51–61.

Rooney, R. (2002). Working with involuntary clients. In A. R. Roberts & G. J. Greene (Eds.), *Social workers' desk reference* (pp. 709–713). New York: Oxford University Press.

Rooney, R. H. (1992). *Strategies for work in involuntary clients.* New York: Columbia University Press.

Rosenbaum, S., & Teitelbaum, J. (2004, June). *Olmstead at five: Assessing the impact.* Washington, DC: Kaiser Commission on Medicaid and the Uninsured.

Rosenfeld, B. D., & Turkheimer, E. N. (1995). Modeling psychiatric patients' treatment decision making. *Law and Human Behavior, 19*(4), 389–405.

Rosenfield, S. (1992). Factors contributing to the subjective quality of life of the mentally ill. *Journal of Health and Social Behavior, 33,* 299–315.

Rosenman, S., Korten, A., & Newman, L. (2000). Efficacy of continuing advocacy in involuntary treatment. *Psychiatric Services, 51*(8), 1029–1033.

Roth, D., & Crane-Ross, D. (2002). Impact of services, met needs, and service empowerment on consumer outcomes. *Mental Health Services Research, 4*(1), 43–56.

Rothman, D. J. (2002a). *Conscience and convenience: The asylum and its alternatives in Progressive America* (Rev. ed.). New York: Aldine de Gruyter.

Rothman, D. J. (2002b). *The discovery of the asylum: Social order and disorder in the New Republic* (Rev. ed.). New York: Aldine de Gruyter.

Rothman, J. C. (2003). *Social work practice across disability.* New York: Allyn and Bacon.

Rouse v. Cameron, 373 F.2nd 451 (D.C. Cir. 1966).

Rowe, M., Benedict, P., & Falzer, P. (2003). Representation of the governed: Leadership building for people with behavioral health disorders who are homeless or were formerly homeless. *Psychiatric Rehabilitation Journal, 26*(3), 240–248.

Rubin, W. V., Snapp, M. B., Panzano, P. C., & Taynor, J. (1996). Variation in civil commitment processes across jurisdictions: An approach for monitoring and managing change in mental health systems. *Journal of Mental Health Administration, 23*(4), 375–388.

Ryan, T., & Bamber, C. (2002). A survey of policy and practice on expenses and other payments to mental health service users and carers participating in service development. *Journal of Mental Health, 11*(6), 635–644.

Sabin, J. E., & Daniels, N. (1999). Public-sector managed behavioral health care: III. Meaningful consumer and family participation. *Psychiatric Services, 50*(7), 883–885.

Saleebey, D. (2002). *The strengths perspective in social work practice* (3rd ed.). Boston: Allyn and Bacon.

Salyers, M. P., Becker, D. R., Drake, R. E., Torrey, W. C., & Wyzik, P. F. (2004). A 10-year follow-up of a supported employment program. *Psychiatric Services, 55*(3), 302–308.

Salzer, M. S. (1997). Consumer empowerment in mental health organizations: Concept, benefits, and impediments. *Administration and Policy in Mental Health, 24*(5), 425–434.

Salzer, M. S., & Mental Health Association of Southeastern Pennsylvania Best Practices Team. (2002). Consumer-delivered services as best practice in mental health care delivery and the development of practice guidelines. *Psychiatric Rehabilitation Skills, 6*(3), 355–382.

Salzer, M. S., Rappaport, J., & Segre, L. (2001). Mental health professionals' support of self-help groups. *Journal of Community and Applied Social Psychology, 11*(1), 1–10.

Salzer, M. S., & Shear, S. L. (2002). Identifying consumer-provider benefits in evaluations of consumer-delivered services. *Psychiatric Rehabilitation Journal, 25*(3), 281–288.

Sapinsley, B. (1991). *The private war of Mrs. Packard.* New York: Paragon House.

Scalora, M. J. (1999). No place else to go: The changing role of state hospitals and forensic mental health services. In W. D. Spaulding (Ed.), *The role of the state hospital in the twenty-first century* (pp. 59–69). San Francisco: Jossey-Bass.

Schizophrenics Anonymous. (n.d.) Schizophrenics Anonymous—Contact information. Retrieved on June 8, 2004 from http://www.schizophrenia.com/help/Schizanon.html.

Schneider, R. L., & Lester, L. (2001). *Social work advocacy: A new framework for action.* Belmont, CA: Brooks/Cole.

Schopp, R. F. (2003). Outpatient civil commitment: A dangerous charade or a component of a comprehensive institution of civil commitment? *Psychology, Public Policy, and Law, 9,* 33–69.

Schriner, K., Ochs, L. A., & Shields, T. G. (1997). The last suffrage movement: Voting rights for persons with cognitive and emotional disabilities. *Publius, 27*(3), 75–96.

Schur, L. A. (2002). Dead end jobs or a path to economic well being? The consequences of non-standard work among people with disabilities. *Behavioral Sciences and the Law, 20,* 601–620.

Schwartz, C., & Gidron, R. (2002). Parents of mentally ill adult children living at home: Rewards of caregiving. *Health and Social Work, 27*(2), 145–154.

Scott, R. (1998). *Professional ethics: A guide for rehabilitation professionals.* New York: Mosby.

Scull, A. (1985). Deinstitutionalization and public policy. *Social Science and Medicine, 20*(5), 545–552.

Scull, A. (1989). *Social order/mental disorder: Anglo-American psychiatry in historical context.* London: Routledge.

Secker, J., Grove, B., & Seebohm, P. (2001). Challenging barriers to employment, training and education for mental health service users: The service user's perspective. *Journal of Mental Health, 10*(4), 395–404.

Segal, S. P., Hardiman, E. R., & Hodges, J. Q. (2002). Characteristics of new clients at self-help and community mental health agencies in geographic proximity. *Psychiatric Services, 53*(9), 1145–1152.

Segal, S. P., Hodges, J. Q., & Hardiman, E. R. (2002). Factors in decisions to seek help from self-help and co-located community mental health agencies. *American Journal of Orthopsychiatry, 72*(2), 241–249.

Segal, S. P., Silverman, C., & Temkin, T. (1993). Empowerment and self-help agency practice for people with mental disabilities. *Social Work, 38*(6), 705–712.

Segal, S. P., Silverman, C., & Temkin, T. (1995). Measuring empowerment in client-run self-help agencies. *Community Mental Health Journal, 31*(3), 215–227.

Sharfstein, S. S., Clemens, N. A., Everett, A. S., Fassler, D., Padrino, S. L., Peele, R., Regier, D. A., & Riba, M. B. (2003, April 3). *A vision for the mental health system.* Arlington, VA: American Psychiatric Association.

Shepard, M. (1997). Site-based services for residents of single-room occupancy hotels. *Social Work, 42*(6), 585–592.

Shera, W. (2001). Managed care and the severely mentally ill: Current issues and future challenges. In N. W. Veeder & W. Peebles-Wilkins (Eds), *Managed care services: Policy, programs, and research* (pp. 230–242). New York: Oxford University Press.

Sherman, P. S., & Porter, R. (1991). Mental health consumers as case management aides. *Hospital and Community Psychiatry, 42*(5), 494–498.

Silberberg, J. M., Vital, T. L., & Brakel, S. J. (2001). Breaking down barriers to mandated outpatient treatment for mentally ill offenders. *Psychiatric Annals, 31*(7), 433–440.

Silver, E. (1995). Punishment or treatment? Comparing the lengths of confinement of successful and unsuccessful insanity defendants. *Law and Human Behavior, 19*(4), 375–388.

Silver, E., Cirincione, C. & Steadman, H. J. (1994). Demythologizing inaccurate perceptions of the insanity defense. *Law and Human Behavior, 18*(1), 63–70.

Simon, B. L. (1990). Rethinking empowerment. *Journal of Progressive Human Services, 1*(1), 27–39.

Simon, B. L. (1994). *The empowerment tradition in American social work: A history.* New York: Columbia University Press.

Simpson, E. L., & House, A. O. (2002). Involving users in the delivery and evaluation of mental health services: Systematic review. *British Medical Journal, 325*, 1265–1268.

Sines, D. (1994). The arrogance of power: A reflection on contemporary mental health nursing. *Journal of Advanced Nursing, 20*, 894–903.

Slade, E., & Salkever, D. (2001). Symptom effects on employment in a structural model of mental illness and treatment: Analysis of patients with schizophrenia. *Journal of Mental Health Policy and Economics, 4*, 25–34.

Slobogin, C. (1995). Therapeutic jurisprudence: Five dilemmas to ponder. *Psychology, Public Policy, and Law, 1*(1), 193–219.

Smith, M. K., & Ford, J. (1986). Client involvement: Practical advice for professionals. *Psychosocial Rehabilitation Journal, 9*(3), 25–34.

Social Security Administration. (2004). *2004 red book: A summary guide to employment support for individuals with disabilities under the Social Security Disability Insurance (SSDI) and Supplemental Security Income (SSI) programs.* Retrieved on April 9, 2004 from http://www.socialsecurity.gov/work/ResourcesToolkit/redbook.html.

Solomon, P. (1996). Research on the coercion of persons with severe mental illness. In D. L. Dennis & J. Monahan (Eds.), *Coercion and aggressive community treatment: A new frontier in mental health law* (pp. 129–145). New York: Plenum Press.

Solomon, P., & Draine, J. (1998). Consumers as providers in psychiatric rehabilitation. In P. W. Corrigan & D. F. Giffort (Eds.), *Building teams and programs for
effective psychiatric rehabilitation* (pp. 65–77). San Francisco: Jossey-Bass.

Solomon, P., & Draine, J. (2001). The state of knowledge of the effectiveness of
consumer provided services. *Psychiatric Rehabilitation Journal, 25*(1), 20–27.

Solomon, P., Draine, J., & Marcus, S. C. (2002). Predicting incarceration of clients
of a psychiatric probation and parole service. *Psychiatric Services, 53*(1), 50–56.

Souder v. Brennan, 367 F. Supp. 808 (D.D.C. 1973).

Spaulding, W. D., Sullivan, M. E., & Poland, J. S. (2003). *Treatment and
rehabilitation of severe mental illness.* New York: Guilford Press.

Specht, H., & Courtney, M. E. (1994). *Unfaithful angels: How social work has
abandoned its mission.* New York: The Free Press.

Staples, L. H. (1990). Powerful ideas about empowerment. *Administration in
Social Work, 14*(2), 29–42.

Staples, L. H. (1999). Consumer empowerment in a mental health system:
Stakeholder roles and responsibilities. In W. Shera & L. M. Wells (Eds.),
Empowerment practice in social work: Developing richer conceptual foundations
(pp. 119–141). Toronto: Canadian Scholars' Press.

Starkey, D., & Leadholm, B. A. (1997). PRISM: The psychiatric rehabilitation
integrated service model—a public psychiatric hospital model for the 1990s.
Administration and Policy in Mental Health, 24(6), 497–508.

Stavis, P. F. (1994). Paternalism and autonomy in the ownership and control
over money and property by persons with mental disability. In C. J. Sundram
(Ed.), *Choice and responsibility: Legal and ethical dilemmas in services for persons
with mental disabilities* (pp. 199–218). Albany, NY: New York State Commission on Quality Care for the Mentally Disabled.

Stavis, P. F. (1999). The Nexum: A modest proposal for self-guardianship by
contract, a system of advance directives and surrogate committees-at-large
for the intermittently mentally ill. *Journal of Contemporary Health Law and
Policy, 16*, 1–95.

Steadman, H. J. (1992). Boundary spanners: A key component for the effective
interactions of the justice and mental health systems. *Law and Human
Behavior, 16*(1), 75–87.

Steadman, H. J., Davidson, S., & Brown, C. (2001). Mental health courts: Their
promise and unanswered questions. *Psychiatric Services, 52*(4), 457–458.

Steadman, H. J., McGreevy, M. A., Morrissey, J. P., Callahan, L. A., Robbins,
P. C., & Cirincione, C. (1993). *Before and after Hinckley: Evaluating insanity
defense reform.* New York: Guilford Press.

Steadman, H. J., Morris, S. M., & Dennis, D. L. (1995). The diversion of mental
ill persons from jails to community-based services: A profile of programs.
American Journal of Public Health, 85(12), 1630–1635.

Stefan, S. (2002). *Hollow promises: Employment discrimination against people with
mental disabilities.* Washington, DC: American Psychological Association.

Stein, M. A. (2000). Employing people with disabilities: Some cautionary thoughts
on a second-generation civil rights statute. In P. D. Blanck (Ed.), *Employment,
disability, and the Americans with Disabilities Act: Issues in law, public policy, and
research* (pp. 51–67). Evanston, IL: Northwestern University Press.

Stolle, D. P., Wexler, D. B., & Winick, B. J. (2000). *Practicing therapeutic jurisprudence:
Law as a helping profession.* Durham, NC: Durham Academic Press.

Sullins, C. D. (2003). Adapting the empowerment evaluation model: A mental health drop-in center case example. *American Journal of Evaluation, 24*(3), 387–398.

Sundram, C. J. (1994). A framework for thinking about choice and responsibility. In C. J. Sundram (Ed.), *Choice and responsibility: Legal and ethical dilemmas in services for persons with mental disabilities* (pp. 3–16). Albany, NY: New York State Commission on Quality Care for the Mentally Disabled.

Swanson, J. W., Tepper, M. C., Backlar, P., & Swartz, M. S. (2000). Psychiatric advance directives: An alternative to coercive treatment? *Psychiatry, 63*(2), 160–172.

Swartz, M. S., Hiday, V. A., Swanson, J. W., Wagner, H. R., Borum, R., & Burns, B. J. (1999). Measuring coercion under involuntary outpatient commitment: Initial findings from a randomized controlled trial. In J. P. Morrissey & J. Monahan (Eds.), *Research in community mental health: Vol. 10. Coercion in mental health services—international perspectives* (pp. 57–77). Stamford, CT: JAI Press.

Swartz, M. S., Swanson, J. W., & Monahan, J. (2003). Endorsement of personal benefit of outpatient commitment among persons with severe mental illness. *Psychology, Public Policy, and Law, 9,* 70–93.

Swift, C., & Levin, G. (1987). Empowerment: An emerging mental health technology. *Journal of Primary Prevention, 8*(1–2), 71–94.

Szasz, T. S. (1974). *The myth of mental illness* (Rev. ed.). New York: Harper and Row.

Tanzman, B. (1993). An overview of surveys of mental health consumers' preferences for housing and support services. *Hospital and Community Psychiatry, 44*(5), 450–455.

Thornicroft, G., Rose, D., Huxley, P., Dale, G., & Wykes, T. (2002). What are the research priorities of mental health service users? *Journal of Mental Health, 11*(1), 1–5.

Torrey, E. F. (1994). Protecting the rights, the person, and the public: A biological basis for responsible action. In C. J. Sundram (Ed.), *Choice and responsibility: Legal and ethical dilemmas in services for persons with mental disabilities* (pp. 37–44). Albany, NY: New York State Commission on Quality Care for the Mentally Disabled.

Torrey, E. F., & Kaplan, R. J. (1995). A national survey of the use of outpatient commitment. *Psychiatric Services, 46*(8), 778–784.

Torrey, E. F., & Zdanowicz, M. (2001). Outpatient commitment: What, why, and for whom. *Psychiatric Services, 52*(3), 337–341.

Townend, M., & Braithwaite, T. (2002). Mental health research-the value of user involvement. *Journal of Mental Health, 11*(2), 117–119.

Townsend, E. (1998). *Good intentions overruled: A critique of empowerment in the routine organization of mental health services.* Toronto: University of Toronto Press.

Townsend, E., Birch, D. E., Langley, J., & Langille, L. (2000). Participatory research in a mental health clubhouse. *Occupational Therapy Journal of Research, 20*(1), 18–44.

Trupin, E., & Richards, H. (2003). Seattle's mental health courts: Early indicators of effectiveness. *International Journal of Law and Psychiatry, 26,* 33–53.

Turkheimer, E., & Parry, C. D. H. (1992). Why the gap? Practice and policy in civil commitment hearings. *American Psychologist, 47*(5), 646–655.

Turner, M., Korman, M., Lumpkin, M., & Hughes, C. (1998). Mental health consumers as transitional aides: A bridge from the hospital to the community. *Journal of Rehabilitation, 64*(4), 35–39.

Turton, N. (2001). Welfare benefits and work disincentives. *Journal of Mental Health, 10*(3), 285–300.

Unger, K. V. (1998). *Handbook for supported education: Providing services for students with psychiatric disabilities.* Baltimore: Paul H. Brookes.

U.S. Department of Health and Human Services. (1999). *Mental health: A report of the Surgeon General.* Rockville, MD: U.S. Department of Health and Human Services, Substance Abuse and Mental Health Services Administration, Center for Mental Health Services, National Institutes of Health, National Institute of Mental Health.

U.S. Department of Health and Human Services. (2001). *Mental health: Culture, race, and Ethnicity—A supplement to Mental health: A report of the Surgeon General.* Rockville, MD: U.S. Department of Health and Human Services, Public Health Service, Office of the Surgeon General.

U.S. Department of Health and Human Services. (2003). *Strategies for developing treatment programs for people with co-occurring substance abuse and mental disorders.* Rockville, MD: U.S. Department of Health and Human Services, Substance Abuse and Mental Health Services Administration.

U.S. Department of Labor. (n.d.). *Work Opportunity Tax Credit.* Retrieved on April 2, 2004 from http://www.uses.doleta.gov/wotcdata.asp.

U.S. Department of Veterans Affairs. (2000, July). *Mental health consumer council guide.* Washington, DC: U.S. Department of Veterans Affairs, VA Mental Health Consumer Liaison Council of the Committee on Care of Severely Chronically Mentally Ill Veterans.

Valentine, M., & Capponi, P. (1989). Mental health consumer participation on boards and committees: Barriers and strategies. *Canada's Mental Health, 37*(2), 8–12.

Vandergang, A. J. (1996). Consumer/survivor participation in the operation of community mental health agencies and programs in metro Toronto: Input or impact? *Canadian Journal of Community Mental Health, 15*(2), 153–170.

Vander Henst, J. A. (1997). Client empowerment: A nursing challenge. *Clinical Nurse Specialist, 11*(3), 96–99.

Vandiver, V. L., & Corcoran, K. (2002). Guidelines for establishing effective treatment goals and treatment plans with Axis I disorders. In A. R. Roberts & G. J. Greene (Eds.), *Social workers' desk reference* (pp. 297–304). New York: Oxford University Press.

Vess, J. (2001). Implementation of a computer assisted treatment planning and outcome evaluation system in a forensic psychiatric hospital. *Psychiatric Rehabilitation Journal, 25*(2), 124–132.

Walters, B. (2003, September 4). Camp: Music from the motion picture. *Rolling Stone, 930,* 140.

Wang, Q., Macias, C., & Jackson, R. (1999). First step in the development of a clubhouse fidelity instrument: Content analysis of clubhouse certification reports. *Psychiatric Rehabilitation Journal, 22*(4), 294–301.

Ware, N. (1999). Evolving Consumer Households: An experiment in community living for people with severe psychiatric disorders. *Psychiatric Rehabilitation Journal, 23*(1), 3–10.

Ware, N. C., & Goldfinger, S. M. (1997). Poverty and rehabilitation in severe psychiatric disorders. *Psychiatric Rehabilitation Journal, 21*(1), 3–9.

Warner, R. (2000). *The environment of schizophrenia: Innovations in practice, policy and communications.* Philadelphia: Brunner-Routledge.

Watson, A., Luchins, D., Hanrahan, P., Heyrman, M. J., & Lurigio, A. (2000). Mental health courts: Promises and limitations. *Journal of the American Academy of Psychiatry and the Law, 28*(4), 476–482.

Weiner, B. A., & Wettstein, R. M. (1993). *Legal issues in mental health care.* New York: Plenum Press.

Weinstein, D. (2000). Housing. In R. Hughes & D. Weinstein (Eds.), *Best practices in psychosocial rehabilitation* (pp. 275–293). Columbia, MD: International Association of Psychosocial Rehabilitation Services.

Weinstein, D., & Hughes, R. (2000). What is psychosocial rehabilitation? In R. Hughes & D. Weinstein (Eds.), *Best practices in psychosocial rehabilitation* (pp. 35–62). Columbia, MD: International Association of Psychosocial Rehabilitation Services.

Wells, S. M. (2001). Overview of barriers and strategies. In C. Bianco & S. M. Wells (Eds.). (2001). *Overcoming barriers to community integration of people with mental illnesses* (pp. 3–16). Delmar, NY: Advocates for Human Potential.

Wells-Moran, J., & Gilmur, D. (2002). *Supported education for people with psychiatric disabilities: A practical manual.* New York: University Press of America.

Wernet, S. P. (1999). An introduction to managed care in human services. In S. P. Wernet (Ed.), *Managed care in human services* (pp. 1–22). Chicago: Lyceum Books.

Wexler, D. B. (1990). *Therapeutic jurisprudence: The law as a therapeutic agency.* Durham, NC: Carolina Academic Press.

Wexler, D. B. (1992). Putting mental health into mental health law. *Law and Human Behavior, 16*(1), 27–38.

Wexler, D. B. (1996). Therapeutic jurisprudence in clinical practice. *American Journal of Psychiatry, 153*(4), 453–455.

White House Domestic Policy Council. (2004, March). *The President's New Freedom Initiative for People with Disabilities: The 2004 progress report.* Washington, DC: Author.

Whyte, W. F. (Ed.). (1991). *Participatory action research.* Newbury Park, CA: Sage.

Wiederanders, M. R., Bromley, D. L., & Choate, P. A. (1997). Forensic conditional release programs and outcomes in three states. *International Journal of Law and Psychiatry, 20*(2), 249–257.

Wilk, R. J. (1994). Are the rights of people with mental illness still important? *Social Work, 39*(2), 167–175.

Wilkinson, W., & Frieden, L. (2000). Class-ceiling issues in employment of people with disabilities. In P. D. Blanck (Ed.), *Employment, disability, and the Americans with Disabilities Act: Issues in law, public policy, and research* (pp. 68–100). Evanston, IL: Northwestern University Press.

Willer, B. S., Guastaferro, J. R., Zankiw, I., & Duran, R. (1992). Applying a rehabilitation model to residential programs for people with severe and persistent mental disorders. In J. W. Jacobson, S. N. Burchard, & P. J. Carling (Eds.), *Community living for people with developmental and psychiatric disabilities* (pp. 37–52). Baltimore: Johns Hopkins University Press.

Williams, J., & Lindley, P. (1996). Working with mental health service users to change mental health services. *Journal of Community and Applied Social Psychology, 6,* 1–14.

Wilson, S. (1996). Consumer empowerment in the mental health field. *Canadian Journal of Community Mental Health, 15*(2), 69–85.

Winick, B. J. (1997). The jurisprudence of therapeutic jurisprudence. *Psychology, Public Policy, and Law, 3*(1), 184–206.

Winick, B. J. (2001). The civil commitment hearing: Applying the law therapeutically. In L. E. Frost & R. J. Bonnie (Eds.), *The evolution of mental health law* (pp. 291–308). Washington, DC: American Psychological Association.

Winick, B. J. (2003). Outpatient commitment: A therapeutic jurisprudence analysis. *Psychology, Public Policy, and Law, 9,* 107–144.

Woodside, H., & Luis, F. (1997). Supported volunteering. *Psychiatric Rehabilitation Journal, 21*(1), 70–74.

Wyatt v. Stickney, 325 F. Supp. 781 (1971).

Wyatt v. Stickney, 344 F. Supp. 373 (Ala. 1972a).

Wyatt v. Stickney, 344 F. Supp. 387 (Ala. 1972b).

Young, K. (2001). Working toward recovery in New Hampshire: A study of modernized vocational rehabilitation from the viewpoint of the consumer. *Psychiatric Rehabilitation Journal, 24*(4), 355–367.

Young, S. L., & Ensing, D. (1999). Exploring recovery from the perspective of people with psychiatric disabilities. *Psychiatric Rehabilitation Journal, 22*(3), 219–231.

Zimmerman, M. A. (1990). Taking aim on empowerment research: On the distinction between individual and psychological conceptions. *American Journal of Community Psychology, 18*(1), 169–177.

Zimmerman, M. A. (1995). Psychological empowerment: Issues and illustrations. *American Journal of Community Psychology, 23*(5), 581–599.

Zimmerman, M. A. (2000). Empowerment theory: Psychological, organizational and community levels of analysis. In J. Rappaport & E. Seidman (Eds.), *Handbook of community psychology* (pp. 43–63). New York: Kluwer Academic/Plenum Publishers.

Zimmerman, M. A., & Warschausky, S. (1998). Empowerment theory for rehabilitation research: Conceptual and methodological issues. *Rehabilitation Psychology, 43*(1), 3–16.

Zinman, S. (1987). Issues of power. In S. Budd, H. T. Harp, & S. Zinman (Eds.), *Reaching across: Mental health clients helping each other* (pp. 182–187). Sacramento, CA: California Network of Mental Health Clients.

Zipple, A. M., Drouin, M., Armstrong, M., Brooks, M., Flynn, J., & Buckley, W. (1997). Consumers as colleagues: Moving beyond ADA compliance. In C. T. Mowbray, D. P. Moxley, C. A. Jasper, & L. L. Howell (Eds.), *Consumers as providers in psychiatric rehabilitation* (pp. 406–418). Columbia, MD: International Association of Psychosocial Rehabilitation Services.

Index

National Mental Health Consumers
    Association, 184–185
National Mental Health Consumers'
    Self-Help Clearinghouse, 185,
    291, 292
National Voter Empowerment
    Project, 188
National Voter Registration Act of
    1993, 187
New Freedom Commission on
    Mental Health, 36, 95, 111, 168,
    181–182, 218, 227, 230, 270
nursing, 3, 62, 84–85, 98

O'Connor v. Donaldson, 42
Offices of Consumer Affairs,
    182–184, 201, 302, 308
Olmstead v. L. C. by Zimring, 44, 47
organizational decision making
    choices in, 149–150
    defined, 141
    empowerment potential of, 142
    explicit agreements on
        participation in, 151–152
    financial compensation for
        participation in, 154–155
    guidelines for empowerment
        through, 164–166
    mutual trust and respect within,
        146–147
    participation skills for, 144–145
    participation structures and
        processes for, 150–153
    and psychiatric symptoms,
        143–144
    psychological readiness for,
        145–146
    reciprocal concrete incentives in,
        147–149
    resources for, 153–156
    supportive culture for, 156–157
    sustaining involvement in, 153

Packard, Elizabeth, 22, 167
parens patriae legal model, 41, 44, 45,
    52, 56
participatory action research, 244,
    249–250, 258, 260, 267, 306.
    See also research

performance improvement, 243–244.
    See also research
planning boards, state and regional,
    176–177
planning and policy making
    choices in, 174–175
    by consumer groups, 184–186
    defined, 167
    empowerment potential of, 168
    guidelines for empowerment
        through, 200–202
    mutual trust and respect for,
        171–172
    participation skills for, 170
    participation structures and
        processes for, 174–188
    and psychiatric symptoms,
        169–170
    psychological readiness for,
        170–171
    reciprocal concrete incentives in,
        172–173
    resources for, 188–190
    supportive culture for, 190–191
police power legal model, 41, 45, 56
policy making. *See* planning and
    policy making
poorhouses. *See* almshouses
poverty, 39, 65, 205, 212, 218, 228,
    241
powerlessness, definition of, 12
President's New Freedom
    Commission on Mental Health.
    See New Freedom Commission
    on Mental Health
probation and parole, 53, 179
procedural justice. *See* justice,
    procedural
Protection and Advocacy agencies,
    47, 76–77, 99, 100
psychiatric rehabilitation, 3, 81–82,
    91, 95, 97, 101, 109, 133, 139,
    140, 142, 157, 166, 208, 228,
    240, 306
psychiatric symptoms.
    See symptoms, psychiatric
psychiatry, 3, 21, 60, 62, 83–84, 98,
    156, 228, 284
psychology, 3, 26, 84, 98

Learning Resources
Centre